W9-BSU-507

The *Annual Review of Adult Learning and Literacy* is an important part of the Dissemination Initiative of the National Center for the Study of Adult Learning and Literacy (NCSALL). NCSALL is a collaborative effort between the Harvard Graduate School of Education and World Education, a nonprofit organization based in Boston. NCSALL's partners include The Center for Literacy Studies at the University of Tennessee, Rutgers University in New Jersey, and Portland State University in Oregon. NCSALL is funded by the Educational Research and Development Centers Program, award number R309B60002, as administered by the U.S. Department of Education's Office of Educational Research and Innovation through its National Institute for Postsecondary Education, Libraries, and Lifelong Learning.

NCSALL is pursuing a program of basic and applied research that is meant to improve programs that provide educational services to adults who have low literacy skills, who do not speak English, or who do not have a high school diploma. Ongoing studies include research on learner motivation, teaching and learning, staff development, and accountability.

The contents of the *Annual Review* do not necessarily represent the positions or policies of the U.S. Department of Education, nor are they endorsed by the federal government.

Annual Review of Adult Learning and Literacy

Volume 1

John Comings, Barbara Garner,
Cristine Smith, Editors

Annual Review of Adult Learning and Literacy

Volume 1

A Project of

The National Center for the Study of
Adult Learning and Literacy

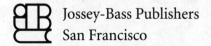

Jossey-Bass Publishers
San Francisco

The material in this publication is based on work sponsored wholly or in part by the Office of Educational Research and Improvement, U.S. Department of Education, under contract number R309B60002. Its contents do not necessarily reflect the views of the department or any other agency of the U.S. Government.

Jossey-Bass books and products are available through most bookstores. To con-tact Jossey-Bass directly, call (888) 378-2537, fax to (800) 605-2665, or visit our website at www.josseybass.com.

Substantial discounts on bulk quantities of Jossey-Bass books are available to corporations, professional associations, and other organizations. For details and discount information, contact the special sales department at Jossey-Bass.

ISBN 0-7879-4741-5

ISSN has been applied for.

Manufactured in the United States of America on Lyons Falls Turin Book. TCF This paper is acid-free and 100 percent totally chlorine-free.

FIRST EDITION
HB Printing   10 9 8 7 6 5 4 3 2 1

The Jossey-Bass

Higher and Adult Education Series

⁓ Contents

~~~ List of Tables, Figures, and Exhibits

Tables

Figures

Exhibits

~~~ Foreword

For many people, learning to read is neither natural nor easy. In my case, I attended school in the 1930s and 1940s, and my learning disability, dyslexia, was not recognized or understood. Even today many learning disabilities go undiagnosed. Some undiagnosed youngsters get involved with alcohol or drugs. Others lack the encouragement at home even to attend school. There are many different reasons why some of us do not learn to read. That is why we need continual research about how people learn, and why some of us do not learn. Literacy should be looked at from many perspectives, especially that of the individual learner, so everyone who has a learning problem can be helped to work through his or her unique circumstances.

Because of my struggle to learn to read as a child, becoming a reader as an adult was something I never thought I would experience. I was ashamed to let others know that I could not read, so I became adept at hiding it. I had a good memory, a good vocabulary, and good comprehension of what was going on around me. My job in a meat-packing plant afforded me a good living and did not require reading skills. My wife noticed my problem when I was trying to read a children's book to our young daughter, but we did not discuss it because she recognized that I was sensitive about it.

Some years later, she read an article about Olympic gold medal winner Bruce Jenner, who had dyslexia. She suggested to me that I might have the same learning disability. I decided to be tested and was found to have dyslexia. I was elated to learn that there was a reason that I had not been able to learn to read—that I was not just dumb. At that point, I decided to seek reading help and, at age fifty-four, enrolled in an adult reading program at Iowa Central Community College.

It takes a lot of courage to walk into a literacy program to ask for reading help. Before my first reading lesson, I was so nervous that I drove around the campus three times before going inside to be tutored one-on-one. When I walked out of my first lesson, I was drenched with perspiration. Many adult learners have similar experiences. Staying in a literacy program takes support from a lot of people. During the first year of lessons, I wanted to quit many times, but my tutor kept me going by pointing out how much I had progressed. She was a wonderful, caring, determined lady who knew how to make me want to go on. My wife and my daughter, then a teenager, were also encouraging and supportive. I stayed in this reading program for two and a half years, and I learned to read.

Since learning to read, I have traveled many miles, both figuratively and literally. As an adult student I did public speaking, telling my life story. I was on the advisory board for a reading program, and I helped set up a support group for adult students. I helped plan the Iowa Adult Literacy Congresses. I have become a literacy coordinator at Iowa Central Community College. As a coordinator, I speak to church groups and civic organizations about our adult literacy program. I encourage people to become tutors and help match tutors with adult students. I set up classes in English for speakers of other languages (ESOL), and I work with and encourage adults to get reading help and to attend General Education Development (GED) classes. As a literacy advocate, I have attended Individual Education Plan (IEP) meetings at the request of parents of children with learning differences. School representatives, the parents of the child, and others invited to attend IEP meetings work together to formulate the child's individual plan. Because I want to learn more about my dyslexia, I have attended many learning disability conferences. In 1993 and 1995, I traveled with delegations to Eastern Europe to look at various special education systems. I was also privileged to do a fellowship with the National Institute for Literacy in 1996. I am one of the founders of and chairman of the board for the new national adult learner organization, Voice for Adult Literacy United for Education (VALUE).

Like my learning to read and like my career in adult literacy, awareness of problems connected with literacy in the United States did not blossom overnight. It takes a great deal of time and thought not only to conduct research but to spread awareness of it to others, both inside and outside the field. It is very important that people who make policy and pass legislation be well informed about the latest trends in adult literacy research and practice. Their decisions have a big impact on the lives of adult learners. That is why I am thankful that the National Center for the Study of Adult Learning and Literacy (NCSALL) is dedicated to spreading the word about research. In bringing new and important reports from the field to its readers, NCSALL's *Annual Review of Adult Learning and Literacy* will also help bring about the development of more effective services for people who are now in or thinking of joining literacy programs, just as I did several years ago.

ARCHIE WILLARD

—〰— Preface

The National Center for the Study of Adult Learning and Literacy (NCSALL) and Jossey-Bass, Inc., Publishers, are establishing the *Annual Review of Adult Learning and Literacy* to serve as the journal of record for the field of adult learning and literacy. Each year the authors whose work is published in this series will present and analyze the research literature and best practices concerning issues of importance to the field. The contributors will concern themselves with educational programs serving adults who have limited literacy and math skills, have limited English skills, or have not obtained a high school diploma. The *Review* is geared toward an audience of policymakers, scholars, and practitioners who are dedicated to improving the quality of adult basic education (ABE), adult English for speakers of other languages (ESOL), and adult secondary education (ASE) programs.

The author of the foreword to this first volume of the *Review* is an adult new reader who has taken on a leadership role in the national adult learner movement. Archie Willard is one of the founders of Voice for Adult Literacy United for Education (VALUE), a national organization of adult new readers who are leaders in their communities and states. In asking him to write this foreword, we—the editors of the *Review*—are expressing our view that the adults who study in ABE, ESOL, and ASE programs are to be the focus of this publication not as subjects but as equal participants. In later volumes, the foreword will be written by representatives from other stakeholder groups in the field—policymakers, practitioners, researchers, and the like—giving them the opportunity to present their points of view. Willard draws from his personal history to provide the human context for the chapters that follow. He makes the vital point that while adult learning and literacy programs can transform lives, transformation is built on a foundation made of the courage and hard work of each adult learner.

In Chapter One, "The Year 1998 in Review," Fran Tracy-Mumford summarizes the important events of the year in the field of adult learning and literacy, many of which will lead to significant future developments. As state director of adult education in Delaware, Tracy-Mumford has been involved in many of these events. Her chronicle of the year is a contribution to what will be an ongoing record of the history of the field in subsequent volumes of the *Review*.

One event occurring in 1998 that will have repercussions for the field of adult literacy was the publication of the National Research Council (NRC) report *Preventing Reading Difficulties in Young Children for Adult Learning and Literacy*. The report, funded by the U.S. Department of Education through a grant to the NRC, represents an effort to synthesize all the research on literacy learning for young children and to recommend an approach to the problem that is grounded in research and draws on the best practices from all the different theories of reading. In Chapter Two, Catherine E. Snow, the principal author of the NRC report, and John Strucker, a NCSALL researcher and expert in adult reading, examine the implications of the report for the field of adult literacy. In bringing these two scholars together, we have been able to make the findings of valuable research on the K–12 system relevant to the practice of adult literacy.

One issue that came up at almost every adult learning and literacy forum we attended in 1998 concerned the influx of sixteen and seventeen year olds into adult education programs. Sensing a growing trend, we asked University of Wisconsin professor Elisabeth Hayes to look into the phenomenon. She found that little exists on young adult learners in adult education programs in the way of formal research or even practical guidelines. Conducting a telephone survey, she produced a foundation piece, Chapter Three in this book, on which further research can be built.

There was a time when helping students pass the GED (General Educational Development) test was a sufficient goal. Now higher levels of education and training are essential to secure a good job with benefits, and students must be prepared to be successful in community college or vocational training. In Chapter Four Stephen Reder explores the overlap between ABE programs and community colleges by looking at the literacy skills of postsecondary education students, the remedial programs that serve them, the effectiveness of these programs and ABE in helping students succeed, and the issue of coordination between these two systems.

A growing awareness of the links between health and literacy surfaced in both the popular press and scholarly work in 1998. Public health scholars Rima E. Rudd, Barbara A. Moeykens, and Tayla C. Colton, colleagues at the Harvard School of Public Health, examined the medical and public health research literature on the links between health and literacy, identifying trends in research and in practice. Chapter Five provides support for those who argue that adult literacy programs have an impact on the lives of learners. It also makes a strong case that public health practitioners should consider the adult learning class as a powerful venue for health education.

As issues of accountability come to the forefront of public policy, so does the question of assessment. How is the ESOL field handling assessment? This question is addressed in Chapter Six by Carol H. Van Duzer, a research associate at the Center for Applied Linguistics, and Robert Berdan, a professor at California State University at Long Beach, who trace the evolution of assessment practices in adult ESOL and suggest areas for research and improved practice.

Adult literacy research, policy, and practice cross national borders, and many lessons learned can and should be shared internationally. With this goal in mind, we plan to include in each volume of the *Review* an investigation of the adult learning and literacy system of a country dealing with issues similar to those we face in the United States. In this first volume, Mary Hamilton and Juliet Merrifield describe in Chapter Seven the evolution of the adult literacy system in the United Kingdom, highlighting its similarities to and differences with the U.S. system and proposing areas of strength in the U.K. system for possible adaptation or adoption.

In Chapter Eight, David J. Rosen, director of the Adult Literacy Resource Institute in Boston, explores four challenges to the integration of electronic technology into adult literacy programs. The first is how to provide teachers and adult learners with access to hardware, software, and Internet connections. The second is how to plan effectively for the introduction and use of electronic technology at the state, local, and school levels. The third challenge involves how to provide the proper staff development so that practitioners will be able to use the technology—hardware, software, and Internet connections—as an effective tool for teaching and learning. The fourth challenge concerns the direction of public policy, especially federal technology policy, which now excludes some kinds of adult education programs from funding.

In a practical follow-up to this chapter, technology experts Jeff Carter and Lou Wollrab present a technology bibliography—an annotated list of paper and electronic sources of information on the selection and use of various forms of technology in adult learning and literacy programs.

As the *Review* goes to press, all those involved in adult literacy and learning are working to ensure passage of President Clinton's year 2000 budget initiatives for adult literacy. The presidential initiatives include $468 million (an increase of $95 million from 1997) for the expansion of adult education state grants to challenge state and local governments to make dramatic improvements in program quality; $70 million for an English literacy and civics initiative to provide states and local communities with competitive grants that link expanded access to high-quality English-language instruction with practical instruction in civics and life skills; $23 million for America Learns Technology to subsidize the development of technology for adult learners; $2 million for a High Skills Communities campaign to mobilize states and local communities to implement strategies to promote ABE; and a Workplace Education Tax Credit for employers that provide certain workplace literacy, English literacy, and basic education programs for their eligible employees.

Should the initiatives pass, this *Review* will be a valuable resource for those seeking information on best practices grounded in sound research and theory. Even if it does not pass, and we continue our work with the more modest resources we had in 1998, we hope the *Review* will be a place for people in the field to turn for information that will help them use their resources more effectively.

JOHN COMINGS
BARBARA GARNER
CRISTINE SMITH
EDITORS

~~ The Editors

John Comings is director of the National Center for the Study of Adult Learning and Literacy (NCSALL) at the Harvard Graduate School of Education. Before coming to Harvard, he spent twelve years as vice president of World Education. Comings worked on adult education programs in Nepal for six years and in Indonesia for two years and has helped design and evaluate adult education programs in several countries in Asia, Africa, and the Caribbean. In the United States, he has served as the director of the State Literacy Resource Center in Massachusetts, assisted in the design of instructor training programs, and directed projects that focused on improving the teaching of math and health in adult education programs.

Barbara Garner is director of publications for NCSALL and a senior program officer at World Education. Having held many different positions in the field of adult basic education, including teacher, staff developer, program administrator, and curriculum writer, she currently edits the NCSALL publication *Focus on Basics*.

Cristine Smith is NCSALL coordinator and a senior program officer at World Education. Smith coordinates NCSALL's dissemination initiative, is directing a four-year study on adult basic education staff development under NCSALL, and is national coordinator of the Practitioner Dissemination and Research Network operated by NCSALL. She has worked on staff development issues in the field of adult literacy for twelve years.

〰 The Contributors

Robert Berdan is joint professor of linguistics and educational psychology at California State University, Long Beach. He formerly coordinated linguistic research at the Southwest Regional Laboratory for Education Research and Development and at the National Center for Bilingual Research. His publications include his work on the development of theoretical models of language variation in adult second language development.

Jeff Carter works for World Education as the project director of Eastern LINCS, one of four regional LINCS (Literacy Information and Communication System) sites supported by the National Institute for Literacy. Eastern LINCS publishes teacher materials on the World Wide Web and provides Internet training in partnership with state literacy resource centers in fourteen states. His writing on education and educational technology has appeared in several national publications.

Tayla C. Colton is a research assistant in health and literacy studies at the Harvard School of Public Health. She is coauthor of *Annotated Bibliography of Medical and Public Health Literature Addressing Literacy Issues* and has worked on a number of other NCSALL studies.

Mary Hamilton is senior research fellow in the Department of Educational Research at Lancaster University in the United Kingdom. She has worked for a number of years as a researcher and teacher in the field of adult basic education and literacy. She is especially interested in the development of collaborative research methodologies, informal adult learning, policy issues, and comparative perspectives on adult basic education, especially across industrialized societies. She is coeditor of *Worlds of Literacy: Multilingual Matters* (1994) and coauthor with David Barton of *Local Literacies: A Study of Reading and Writing in One Community* (1988).

Elisabeth Hayes is associate professor at the University of Wisconsin–Madison, where she is affiliated with the Department of Curriculum and Instruction and the graduate program in continuing and vocational education. She has provided staff development programs for adult literacy teachers throughout Wisconsin and conducted research on topics such as the outcomes of receiving the General Educational Development credential and the use of portfolio assessment in adult basic education. On the national level, she has been actively involved in the Commission on Adult Basic Education, the American Association for Adult and Continuing Education, the American Educational Research Association, and the Commission of Professors of Adult Education. She has published numerous journal articles, book chapters, and research reports and is coeditor of the *Handbook of Adult and Continuing Education—Year 2000,* under the sponsorship of the AAACE.

Juliet Merrifield is director of the Learning from Experience Trust, London, England. She was the founding director of the Center for Literacy Studies at the University of Tennessee and earlier was codirector of research at the Highlander Research and Education Center in Tennessee. Her publications include *Contested Ground: Performance Accountability in Adult Basic Education* (a NCSALL research report, 1998) and *Life at the Margins: Literacy, Language, and Technology in Everyday Life* (1997), coauthored with Mary Beth Bingman, Kathleen deMarrais, and David Hemphill.

Barbara A. Moeykens is a research specialist in the Department of Health and Social Behavior at the Harvard School of Public Health, where she is a member of the department's Health and Literacy Studies Team and is involved in both qualitative and quantitative research in behalf of NCSALL. Her work is informed by more than twelve years of public health research experience (including in health communication and social marketing) and formal training in focus group research and clinical diagnostic interviews.

Stephen Reder is University Professor at Portland State University. He has conducted studies of the influence of literacy on speaking among the Vai in West Africa and of literacy development and communication practices in a variety of ethnic communities and contextual settings. He has also conducted research on the mutual effects of literacy and schooling on social and economic outcomes in adult life. He is currently directing a large-scale longitudinal study of adult literacy and learning for NCSALL, and he serves on numerous local, state, and national advisory groups and task forces to improve adult education and literacy.

David J. Rosen is director of the Adult Literacy Resource Institute in Boston. He has published widely on the use of technology in adult education and has served as a consultant to Literacy Partners of New York City to establish the national What Works Literacy Partnership funded by the Lila Wallace Readers' Digest Fund. He is founder and past chair of the Boston Literacy Telecommunications Collaborative and current chair of the Massachusetts Adult Literacy and Technology Team. He is also the moderator of National Literacy Advocacy, an electronic list.

Rima E. Rudd teaches graduate courses in public health program design and evaluation, health education strategies, and health and literacy at the Harvard School of Public Health. She is director of educational programs for the school's Department of Health and Social Behavior and is principal investigator for several community-based public health studies. Most of her work concerns the health effects of racial, ethnic, and economic disparities and the links between health and literacy.

Catherine E. Snow is the Henry Lee Shattuck Professor of Education and chair, Human Development and Psychology, at the Harvard Graduate School of Education. Her extensive publications on the topics of language development and literacy development include coauthorship of the books *Pragmatic Development* (1996) and *Unfulfilled Expectations: Home and School Influences on Literacy* (1991). She has served as codirector of the Child Language Data Exchange System, editor of *Applied Psycholinguistics,* a board member at the Center for Applied Linguistics, and a member of the National Research Council Committee on Establishing a Research Agenda on Schooling for Language Minority Children. She is a member of the National Academy of Education.

John Strucker is a research associate at NCSALL and a lecturer in education at the Harvard Graduate School of Education. Before coming to NCSALL he was an adult basic education (ABE) teacher at the Community Learning Center in Cambridge, Massachusetts, where he specialized in teaching beginning and intermediate reading and in diagnostic reading assessment. He also designed the course Theory and Practice of Adult Reading, a laboratory practicum for teachers of ABE and English for speakers of other languages (ESOL) that was sponsored by the Massachusetts Department of Education.

Fran Tracy-Mumford is state director of adult education at the Delaware Department of Education. She is chair of the Policy Committee of the National Council of State Directors and a past chair of the National Council of State Directors of Adult Education. Her publications include the monographs *Student Retention: Creating Student Success* and *Examining the Impact of Programs Funded by the Adult Education Act.* She is also the author of the study *Impact of Adult Education and Family Literacy on the Family.*

Carol H. Van Duzer is a research associate at the National Clearinghouse for ESL Literacy Education (NCLE), Center for Applied Linguistics, in Washington, D.C. She has taught English for speakers of other languages (ESOL), trained teachers, and directed special projects. Most recently, at NCLE, she directed the development of the research agenda for adult ESOL. She is the author of *A Day in the Life of the Gonzalez Family* (1999) and has coauthored materials for adult English-language learners. She serves on the TESOL Task Force on Adult Education Program Standards.

Archie Willard is a literacy coordinator at Iowa Central Community College. He was the recipient of a fellowship from the National Institute for Literacy to study best practices in adult learner leadership in 1996, and he participated in two exchange programs to Eastern Europe to study its educational approaches to people with learning disabilities. He is one of the founders of and chair of the board for the national adult learner organization Voice for Adult Literacy United for Education (VALUE). He regularly speaks to community organizations as an advocate for adult literacy programs and counsels adults who are in or are planning to enter such programs.

Lou Wollrab is information coordinator for the Massachusetts System for Adult Basic Education Support (SABES), with overall responsibility for the organization and dissemination of materials held in the SABES resource collections and on the SABES Web site.

Annual Review of Adult Learning and Literacy

Volume 1

CHAPTER ONE

The Year 1998 in Review

Fran Tracy-Mumford

T he year 1998 was one of immense change for adult learning and literacy, as significant new legislation was passed and the field headed more deeply into the mainstream. Along with these developments came greater demands for program accountability, expanded strategic alliances and partnerships, new instructional methodologies, changes in public policy, and advancements in technology that change the nature of the teaching-learning experience for both teachers and learners.

ADULT LEARNER DEMOGRAPHICS

The number of adult learners enrolled in programs funded by the Adult Education Act (AEA, as amended by the National Literacy Act of 1991) reached more than 4 million in 1997. (Comparable data for 1998 was not available when this chapter was prepared.) Since 1994 there has been a steady increase in the number of adults attending classes in English for speakers of other languages (ESOL), signifying a significant demographic shift in service delivery: the number of ESOL students served (39 percent of the total) is now almost equal to that of adult basic education (ABE) students served (38 percent of total; the balance consists of enrollees in adult secondary education; see Exhibit 1.1). The "big five" ESOL states of California, Florida, Illinois, New York, and Texas enroll 82 percent of the ESOL population (Elliott, 1998). Although these five states account for most of the numerical increase in ESOL students, every state has made percentage gains in services to this population group, marking a migration in service toward the ESOL target population.

Of all students served, most were under the age of forty-five. More than one-third (37 percent) of all enrollees were between the ages of sixteen and twenty-four (see Exhibit 1.1). A majority of enrollees (54 percent) were female. As of 1997, about 11 percent of all adult education students lived at or below the poverty level, and 1 percent of enrollees were in correctional facilities. Approximately 50 percent of all students were employed (Elliott, 1998).

The primary motivation for enrollment expressed by new students in adult education and literacy programs was to improve their basic skills. Adult learners sought basic skills to get a job, get a better job, prepare for college admission, get a high school diploma or the Gen-

Total served 4,042,172	
Program Service	
Adult basic education	38%
English for speakers of other languages	39%
Adult secondary education	23%
Age of Participants	
16–24	37%
25–44	47%
45–59	11%
60+	5%
Race of Participants	
White	32%
Black	17%
Hispanic	38%
Asian	12%
Other	1%

Exhibit 1.1.   Demographics of Adult Education Participants, 1997.

Source: U.S. Department of Education statistical performance report tables.

eral Educational Development (GED) credential, or help their children achieve success in school. More than 300,000 (35 percent) did receive a high school diploma or GED, another 300,000 obtained a job or advanced in a job, and 175,000 (4 percent) entered other educational training programs (Elliott, 1998).

The annual expenditure for educating these adults is low in comparison with the costs of educating a child. In 1997, the average amount spent on an adult student was $300, with half of the states spending between $150 and $299 per student (Elliott, 1998). The national average spent on a child was $3,982, with a range from $2,974 to $10,053 (U.S. Department of Education, 1997).

While more than 4 million adults enrolled in classes in 1997, at least another 1 million were on waiting lists. And because every state does not maintain waiting lists, the number of individuals waiting for services was likely greater than the 1 million reported (Tracy-Mumford, 1998). The average wait for a seat to become available in a program ranged from four months to one year. Maintenance of waiting lists generally pays off. The lists tend to garner attention and mobilize support from state policymakers, who sometimes respond with state funds to decrease the number of adult learners waiting for services.

LANDMARK AND OTHER SIGNIFICANT LEGISLATION

After a lengthy four-year process, federal legislation for adult education and employment and training was signed into law, consolidating more than fifty employment, training, and literacy programs, including the Adult Education Act, the National Literacy Act, and the Job Training Partnership Act. Taking into account the relationship between literacy skills and success in the workplace, Congress placed the adult education and employment-training systems in one piece of legislation, although under separate title and governance by Congress (Brustein & Mahler, 1998). The Adult Education and Family Literacy Act (AEFLA) is Title II of the Workforce Investment Act (WIA).

This new legislation calls for the federal government, states, and local jurisdictions to join in a partnership to carry out its mandates. Title II goals continue to address the broad purposes of adult education, which are to "(1) assist adults in becoming literate and obtain the knowledge and skills necessary for employment and self-sufficiency; (2) assist parents in obtaining the educational skills necessary to become full partners in their children's education; and (3) assist adults in completing high school or the equivalent" (section 202). The AEFLA continues many of the provisions of the AEA and maintains adult education as a state grant–operated program, and it considers adult education, family literacy, and English literacy programs to share the same purpose. Most of the AEFLA investment continues to be placed in the state grant program, which now totals $345 million (Murphy & Johnson, 1998).

Under the WIA, each state is to develop a five-year plan that lays out a leadership strategy to improve its adult education and literacy services. Federal funding will be tied to improvements in services state by state, and both federal and state governments will evaluate a state's progress by monitoring the degree to which it achieves the goals stated in its plan. During the plan development process, state agencies are to consult with adult literacy providers in their states.

States may submit their plans as a comprehensive education plan or as part of a unified workforce development plan. Regardless of the process chosen, Congress wants states to coordinate adult education and family literacy services with employment and training, and it wants the states to be able to track the progress of programs over time.

The WIA in its entirety gives adult education a voice and a vote on newly formed State Workforce Investment Boards. This is the first time that adult education and family literacy are guaranteed a seat at the table where decisions are made about policies and services that affect clients of adult education and job training employment. The WIA also mandates adult education representation on local boards (Murphy, 1998).

Under the AEFLA, the criteria for states to consider in awarding grants to local programs (section 231) place heavy emphasis on capacity to deliver services to adults. The twelve criteria that states must take into consideration in awarding grants or contracts to local providers (see Exhibit 1.2) define a new role for local providers, the state, and the clients served. First, the state and local providers share responsibility in setting and meeting state accountability measures. Second, the local provider establishes a partnership with the learner to achieve results related to skill gains that prepare adults for employment, family responsibilities, and citizenship. Because of these new roles, local program results must be linked directly to state goals and performance measures.

1. *Measurable Goals*
   The degree to which the eligible provider will establish measurable goals for participant outcomes

2. *Past Effectiveness*
   The past effectiveness of an eligible provider in improving the literacy skills of adults and families. After the adoption of a state's performance measures, the state must also take into account whether the provider met or exceeded such performance measures, especially with respect to those adults with the lowest levels of literacy

3. *Serving Those Most in Need*
   The commitment of the eligible provider to serve individuals in the community most in need of literacy services, including individuals with low income or minimal literacy skills

4. *Intensity of Services*
   Whether the program is of sufficient intensity and duration for participants to achieve substantial learning gains and uses instructional practices—such as phonemic awareness, systemic phonics, fluency, and reading comprehension—that research has proven to be effective in teaching individuals to read

5. *Effective Practices*
   Whether the activities are built on a strong foundation of research and effective educational practice

6. *Use of Technology*
   Whether the activities effectively employ advances in technology, including the use of computers

7. *Real-Life Context*
   Whether the activities provide learning in a real-life context to ensure that an individual has the skills necessary to compete in the workplace and exercise the rights and responsibilities of citizenship

8. *Staffing*
   Whether well-trained instructors, counselors, and administrators staff the activities

9. *Coordination*
   Whether the activities are coordinated with other resources in the community

10. *Flexible Schedules*
    Whether the activities offer flexible schedules and support services, such as child care and transportation

11. *Information Management*
    Whether the activities maintain a high-quality information management system that has the capacity to report participant outcomes and to monitor performance

12. *English Literacy*
    Whether the local communities have a demonstrated need for additional English literacy programs

**Exhibit 1.2. Criteria for Awarding Grants
Under the Adult Education and Family Literacy Act.**
Source: Adult Education and Family Literacy Act of 1998.

Highlights of the AEFLA

DIRECT AND EQUITABLE ACCESS. States must ensure that all eligible providers have direct and equitable access to apply for local grants (section 231[c][1]). Steps that states take to ensure that potential providers have the right to apply for federal funds and be treated fairly in consideration of their application for funding (Spieghts, 1998) are to be described in each state plan. Eligible to receive funding are "local education agencies, community-based organizations, volunteer literacy programs, institutions of higher education, public and private non-profits, libraries, public housing authorities, consortia of the organizations listed above, and other non-profits" (section 231). All applicants will be placed "on equal footing . . . to compete for funds to provide services that the state has identified that it wants to support," wrote Bill Raleigh, director of government affairs at Laubach Literacy Action, on the National Literacy Advocacy (NLA) listserv.

SET-ASIDES. With the exception of support for corrections education and service to other institutionalized individuals, the AEFLA has no provisions for set-asides (section 225). States may not allocate more than 10 percent of state grant funds for programs in this category, and priority is given to serve individuals who are likely to leave the institution within five years of program participation. No other subpopulation is named to receive specific allocations, and the funding cap for adult secondary education participation was removed.

STATE LEADERSHIP ACTIVITIES. A new category of funding included in the AEFLA is state leadership. Although the category is new, the allowable activities are not. Not more than 12.5 percent of the state grant allocation may be used for any or all of the allowable activities, which include professional development, technical assistance, maintenance of literacy resource centers, activities of statewide significance, curriculum development, support services, promotion of linkages with workforce development, and/or development of linkages with postsecondary education institutions (section 223).

As states make the transition from the AEA to the AEFLA, they are confronted with the problem of maintaining current levels of service for professional development and state literacy resource centers with a smaller percentage of funds allowed in this category. Increased funding for federal program year 1999 does not offset the percentage loss of allowable funds that could be used for these services under the AEA. Previously states were required to spend a minimum of 15 percent of the state grant on special projects and training, and many states exceeded that percentage.

ACCOUNTABILITY. The AEFLA obligates states to establish a comprehensive accountability system that will assess continuous program improvement. Three specific indicators of performance are outlined in the law. Core indicators relate to:

1. Demonstrated improvements in literacy skills levels in reading, writing, and speaking the English language, in numeracy, in problem solving, in English language acquisition, and in other literacy skills

2. Placement, retention, or completion of postsecondary education, training, unsubsidized employment, or career advancement

3. Receipt of high-school diploma or equivalent (section 212)

Other indicators that a state adds must be negotiated with the secretary of the U.S. Department of Education (ED).

States are developing indicators and setting levels of performance for each indicator that will be used to measure state progress with guidance from the ED Division of Adult Education and Literacy. Performance indicators are written for three years only. Performance measures for years 4 and 5 will be written later and will be based on agreed-on levels of performance with the ED.

INCENTIVES. The WIA provides for incentive grants to states that exceed adjusted performance levels in Titles I and II and in Perkins Vocational Education. It also gives states the flexibility to expend incentive funds on innovative programs consistent with the requirements of any or all of these three programs. The process a state should use to prepare its application for proposed uses of incentive monies has not yet been determined (Murphy, 1998).

NATIONAL EMPHASIS. Two entities are charged with responsibilities at the national level: the National Institute for Literacy (NIFL) and the ED. Allowable funding for each is 1.5 percent of the total appropriation, not to exceed $8 million.

The NIFL (section 242) was created to provide national leadership regarding literacy, coordinate literacy services and policy, and serve as a national resource for adult education and literacy programs by providing current information to the field related to literacy and supporting the creation of new ways to offer services of proven effectiveness. To meet the purposes of the AEFLA, the NIFL is authorized to do the following:

- Establish a national electronic database
- Coordinate support for the programs and services across federal agencies
- Collect and disseminate information on methods of advancing literacy that show great progress
- Advise Congress and federal departments and agencies regarding development of policy
- Provide policy and technical assistance to federal, state, and local entities for the improvement of policy and programs relating to literacy, including national organizations and associations
- Encourage federal agencies to support literacy efforts
- Help establish a reliable and replicable literacy research agenda

New legislation continues the NIFL's current work with a refinement of its responsibilities.

The greatest change at the national level is in the leadership provided by the Department of Education. National Leadership Activities replace National Programs. The department is charged with:

- Providing technical assistance to states in developing and using performance measures
- Providing technical assistance for professional development and with developing, improving, identifying, and disseminating the most successful methods and technology for providing adult education and literacy
- Carrying out research, such as establishing the number of adults functioning at the lowest levels
- Developing and replicating model programs, particularly those for the learning disabled, ESOL learners, and workplace populations

A stronger role for the ED is outlined through leadership activities to support states in achieving continuous program improvement. President Clinton's request to increase 1999 funding for National Leadership Activities to $93 million puts teeth into this stronger supportive role.

Other Legislation Affecting Adult Education and Literacy

Several pieces of legislation directly or indirectly affect adult learners.

THE NATIONAL SCHOOL-TO-WORK ACT. All states receive school-to-work grants as of 1999. Each state grant must have an out-of-school or adult education component. School-to-work connections and alliances are to be made to connect learners with preparation for work. Activities within states include development of career portfolios, career planning, identification of programs of study leading to career paths, employability skills certifications, and work-based learning.

READING EXCELLENCE ACT OF 1998. The America Reads Initiative held a National Reading Summit to highlight the findings of the Committee on the Prevention of Reading Difficulties in Young Children chaired by Catherine Snow of the Harvard Graduate School of Education. The committee, charged with translating research findings into practical application for parents, educators, and publishers of reading texts, found that for children to become effective readers, they need a solid literacy foundation provided in a language-rich home environment. Children in families with an "impoverished language and literacy environment have high incidence of reading difficulties" as they enter school. Access to an early childhood environment that promotes language growth is essential to reading success (Snow, Burns, & Griffin, 1998). Family literacy was highlighted at the summit as an effective approach that has a positive influence on children and parents. (In Chapter Two Catherine Snow and John Strucker apply the findings of the committee's report to the experience of people who learn to read as adults.)

The Reading Excellence Act will provide grants to state education agencies. In these grants, states must describe how they will promote coordination between literacy programs, including the AEFLA, to increase the effectiveness of services designed to improve the reading skills of adults and children. The act also directs the NIFL, in coordination with the National Center for Family Literacy, to disseminate information on research related to family literacy (Peyton, 1998).

THE PERSONAL RESPONSIBILITY AND WORK OPPORTUNITIES RECONCILIATION ACT OF 1996. Since the passage of this act, the adult education and literacy community has been attempting to make sense of the work-first policy that has discouraged and in some cases abandoned adult education in an effort to reform the welfare system. Providers across the nation scrambled to find a way to provide service and put new programs in place. The work-first approach led to decreased participation in adult education classes, and when clients of Temporary Assistance to Needy Families (TANF) did attend, they attended for shorter periods of time and on a part-time basis.

Successful providers adapted to the work-first goal of the welfare reform law, focusing on employment-related goals, hands-on work experience, performance-based outcomes, involvement of private sector employers, early intervention in addressing potential problems in the workplace, job coaches and developers, and extensive support services (Murphy & Johnson, 1998).

AMENDMENTS TO THE HEAD START ACT. The Head Start Act amendments passed in 1998 introduced a formal role for family literacy, including adult education. To comply with the amendments, local adult education programs must incorporate family literacy services as part of their design. The amendments encourage collaboration and partnership between providers of Head Start and providers of adult education services, and they allow for technical assistance to ensure that additional linkages are made for child development and parent education (Peyton, 1998).

BASIC SKILLS CERTIFICATION SYSTEMS

The mandate in the Adult Education and Family Literacy Act for performance measures has generated new interest in basic skills certification systems. Merrifield (1998) speaks to the importance of building capacity to perform and be accountable. Certification systems are emerging as a vehicle to certify skill gains at levels prior to graduation from high school or the attainment of the GED. In the development process, commonalities and differences have appeared from state to state. Commonalities are found in the purpose for creating certificates, responses from students, alignment with national reporting, and acceptance by the general public and business communities. System differences have emerged in skill areas identified for certification, measures used for skill verification, and methodology used in issuing certificates.

Seven states currently offer basic skills certificates at the state, regional, or local program level. Another thirty states and territories are at various stages of development in creating a basic skills certification system. At the implementation stage, basic skill certificates document the knowledge and skills of adults in any or all of the skill areas of reading, writing, mathematics, employability, and computer literacy (see Table 1.1 for the areas covered by the seven states offering certificates). States and programs using basic skills certification systems have found the system helpful in reporting individual learning gains to students, celebrating learner achievements, documenting program results in basic skills areas, and reporting aggregate program achievement of students to policy makers. Basic skills certificates reward students (and programs) in their quest for excellence and will be helpful to states in documenting attainment of state goals.

For fiscal year 2000, the ED will be recommending new national reporting levels that will articulate learner gains in smaller intervals. Basic skills certificates can be used to verify and document these gains. The two processes of reporting and certifying can work in tandem.

State	Reading	Writing	Math	ESOL	Employability
California				√	
Colorado	√		√		
Delaware	√	√	√		
Iowa	√		√		
Oregon	√		√		
Tennessee	√		√		
West Virginia	√		√		√

Table 1.1.   Content of Basic Skills Certification Systems.

TEACHING AND LEARNING: STANDARDS AND INSTRUCTIONAL PRACTICES

The production of content standards at the national and state levels is fueling program and curricular changes. While national development of standards for ABE continues, several states have aligned or adopted their state's K–12 standards for adult learners.

National Standards

To ensure a solid foundation for the improvement of adult learning and literacy nationwide, a set of national standards, Equipped for the Future (EFF), has been developed through the National Institute for Literacy. These standards establish the skills that learners must demonstrate across the three adult roles of family member, citizen, and worker and specify the knowledge and skills adults need to be competitive in the global economy. Practitioners from several states are working with the NIFL to gather data and establish specific levels of performance for each standard (Stein, 1997). Many states have embraced EFF as their state's content framework and have written EFF into their state plans for the AEFLA.

The call for ESOL standards is crisscrossing the nation. The group Teachers of English to Speakers of Other Languages (TESOL) has a standards task force that will roll out new adult ESOL standards at its 1999 national conference. States continue searching for curriculum and appropriate assessments for ESOL.

Literacy Volunteers of America added a new dimension to standards when its board approved program standards to certify volunteer literacy programs. Standards are based on effective program operation and designed to ensure more effective literacy instruction. By June 1999 local affiliates are to have signed an agreement committing themselves to certification. To become certified, programs must meet eighteen qualifying standards in the areas of development, organization, and finance and personnel and must also meet ten of fourteen additional standards in the same three topic areas.

The Correctional Education Association developed standards for quality correctional education programs that have been adopted by the National Corrections Association. Standards certify quality correctional education programs within institutions. Training of certified monitors is taking place to gear up for the anticipated demand for certification by adult and juvenile facilities.

State Standards

The alignment of content standards between adult education and K–12 continues at a state level in California, Delaware, Massachusetts, Texas, and Wisconsin. Alignment of literacy skills with occupational standards has enormous instructional implications in the new legislation. States are placing a heavy emphasis on SCANS (Secretary's Commission on Achieving Necessary Skills) workplace competencies and employability skills. Most southern states have promoted workplace and employment skills as a means of improving the foundation skills of workers as well as the economy itself. These programs have focused on identifying literacy standards that connect learners with the skills they need to become high-performing employees. North Carolina, California, and Massachusetts have begun development of standards or certifications for ESOL, or both.

Curriculum Changes

Under the AEFLA, an expanded list of basic skills has moved the field beyond the Three R's to include spoken English, problem solving, and other literacy skills, such as computer skills and employability skills. States are required to develop core indicators of performance around these skills. Several states are including computer literacy as a basic skill, and many are developing or linking curriculum to employability skills (for instance, reporting to work on time, solving problems, working effectively in groups, finding and keeping a job). Use of the Internet to obtain reliable and accurate information is another new skill to be taught in many adult education programs.

Developing curriculum to match content standards becomes a challenge at the state level. Networks or consortia such as the Adult Numeracy Network and Literacy South are helping to develop curriculum to support skill development.

Methodologies

Legislation speaks to providing classes of sufficient duration and intensity to obtain learning gains and performance outcomes with the expectation that service will vary by type of student served. Customizing instruction for intensity of service is one of the criteria that states must use in awarding local grants. More experiential, contextual, and student performance–based approaches are being introduced into adult education programs. Instructional programs are using a variety of technologies, such as video, the Internet, CD-ROMs, and e-mail, to augment in-class experiences.

Virginia, partnering with Great Britain, has taken off in a unique direction to promote an adult learner project model. This methodology enables the adult learner to identify and document short-term learning needs and gains as opposed to documentation of learning through standardized tests. In the project model, adults identify a specific short-term goal tied to personal need. Instruction is then targeted to the learner's goal and documented when achieved. This model is adaptable to workplace settings where learners have a very targeted, short-term learning goal linked to success on the job. Extensive work has been devoted to this instructional practice, and exchange visits to and from England are moving the project forward. (For an overview of the adult basic education system in the United Kingdom, see Chapter Seven.)

Use of Technology in Instruction

New paradigms for when and where adults can learn have broadened perspectives on access to previously unserved populations and new instructional delivery models. For years postsecondary education has capitalized on distance delivery. No longer is a fixed time, place, or single location the norm for adult learning. The new reality is that learning takes place anytime, anyplace, anywhere. Several states, companies, and organizations have invested in distance-learning programming for adult literacy learners. KET, PBS, and Intelecom are offering or developing programs for distance delivery in GED (KET), ESOL (Intelecom), employability skills (KET/PBS), and family literacy (Intelecom). Cyber high schools for adults are operating in Colorado, Delaware, Florida, Minnesota, and Nebraska.

Providers of distance learning offer learners access both synchronously and asynchronously. Learning environments are customized to accommodate the diversity of learners, learning styles, and learning needs. Some models are self-contained, and others extend classroom learning time. Live programming for workplace skills and basic skills is used in New York, California, and Washington, which have special funding allocations for technology innovation. Star Schools projects funded by the ED have jump-started other distance delivery models, such as Project Class in Nebraska and the PBS LiteracyLink project. Project Class received funding to develop distance-learning high school courses on the World Wide Web, and PBS LiteracyLink has received funding to design an on-line instruction site for adult learners.

As distance learning and on-line learning methodologies capture the attention of more adult educators, it will be important to address critical questions about the infrastructure needed to sustain the system, the skills that instructors need, the instructor-learner interaction, and the matching of content with the most appropriate technology (software and other materials) (Neeley, Niemi, & Ehrhard, 1998). As one writer on distance learning said, "We must not forget that education is a social process, not purely a technological one, as we continue to utilize the increasing array of electronic devices for asynchronous and synchronous learning" (Charp, 1998). (For related information and resources, see Chapter Eight and the Resources section.)

PROFESSIONAL DEVELOPMENT

New legislation, content standards, technology, and contextual approaches to learning are driving instructional change, and instructional change is driving professional development. Knowledge of new approaches and flexibility in delivery is essential to implementing new methodologies. Changes in the delivery system point to a massive recommitment from adult educators to become and remain current.

The hallmark of adult education instructional staff is their dedication to and support of students, a vital quality that must not be lost as the delivery system evolves. Professional development on the scale outlined by the changes described for adult education will take time, effort, and financial commitment. Financial commitment and teacher certification may put more full-time instructors in adult education programs, one of the recommendations for 1999 made by the president and the National Coalition for Literacy to Congress.

Communication with the field through the NIFL's Literacy Information and Communications System (LINCS) project is bringing adult literacy–related resources, expertise, and knowledge on-line to the field. Regional hubs offer training in the planning and use of technology. PBS LiteracyLink also offers professional development resources and training for literacy educators through LitTeacher. On-line courses allow instructors to learn in a flexible manner and to communicate with experts in the field on a variety of topics.

Through efforts of the National Adult Literacy and Learning Disabilities (ALLD) Center, the learning disabilities resource guidebook, *Bridges to Practice,* was released at train-the-trainer sessions conducted across the nation. The *Bridges* tool kit is designed for instructors to take research to practice and align assessment with teaching and learning. ALLD's ultimate goal is to help providers better meet the needs of adults with learning disabilities.

The Practitioner Dissemination and Research Network (PDRN) of the National Center for the Study of Adult Learning and Literacy (NCSALL) began operation as a strategic alliance between practitioners and researchers to disseminate research results to the field and provide feedback to researchers. Practitioner inquiry is included as part of the PDRN.

ADULT LEARNER MOVEMENT

Birth of a full-scale adult learner movement was launched as a result of several key events. The movement got its momentum from the national adult learner congresses sponsored by Laubach Literacy Action and partners of the National Coalition for Literacy, a national adult learner forum sponsored by the Department of Education (and facilitated by the National Adult Education Professional Development Consortium) and grassroots leadership conferences at the state level.

The National Adult Literacy Congresses forged a network of adult learners. From the congresses, a cadre of adult learners pressed for statewide efforts that evolved into student organizations (see Table 1.2). At least five states have a student organization, and seven hold annual student conferences.

In late 1997, the Department of Education held a national student leadership forum in Washington, D.C., where adult learners from each state gathered to discuss issues affecting them as learners. From there, several adult learners launched a national student leadership forum in 1998 at the Highlander Center in Tennessee, where forty-one adult learners attended.

At the Highlander meeting, student literacy leaders mapped out a national student organization, Voice for Adult Literacy United for Education (VALUE), and elected an eleven-member board. VALUE

State	Organization	Conference	Activities
California		Regional adult learner conferences	
Delaware	OAASIS (Organization of Alumni and Adult Students in Service) board meets quarterly; student workers meet monthly Member of the Interagency Council on Adult Literacy	Conference and recognition event annually since 1995	Annual student legislative dinner; publication on family support; voter registration; health screening; student support for retention; book drives; student 100-hour pins (for 100 hours of instruction); family appreciation certificates; scholarships; GED financial assistance; emergency student fund; fundraising
Georgia		Annual student conference	Student survey
Illinois	Board meets quarterly	Conferences since 1993	
Iowa	Newly formed five-member board	Conference since 1990	
Massachusetts	Newly formed	Student conference	
Minnesota		Annual conference	
Mississippi	Run entirely by students	Annual conference	
New Hampshire		Annual student congress since 1990	
Ohio	Adult Learners for the Future	Conference since 1994	Student support; public awareness; voting campaign; publications on citizen participation; newsletter
Rhode Island	Student network	Adult Education Day since 1994	Journal of Learners writings published semimonthly; Adult Education Day
Vermont		Annual student conference	

Table 1.2. Adult Learner Leadership Opportunities, by State.
Source: National Literacy Advocacy Listserv, 1998.

activities will include conferences, newsletters, and advocacy. VALUE wants to expand the role of adult learners as leaders in the effort to promote literacy throughout the nation. It promises to be a resource for adult learners, literacy practitioners, and policymakers.

Finally, the National Council of State Directors of Adult Education adopted a focus on student leadership as a goal. It will emphasize provision of technical assistance to states to help organize adult learners for leadership and advocacy.

NATIONAL INITIATIVES IN ADULT EDUCATION

A number of initiatives sponsored by national groups and organizations either got under way in 1998 or continued on their previous course to support or provide leadership for the field of adult education and literacy. These initiatives aim to support a wide variety of interests, from research to public awareness.

Awareness Campaigns

Significant national programs have funding levels of $1 billion or more. The National Coalition for Literacy, piloted by its policy committee, is preparing a national effort to secure a state grant program allocation of $1 billion over five years for adult education. This effort reflects the belief of many who work in the field of adult education and literacy that there will be no real impact on literacy until programs of longer duration and greater intensity receive more funding support.

The public awareness campaign supported by the NIFL, Literacy: It's a Whole New World, made the business community the focus of its efforts in 1998. The NIFL released a new packet of information targeting the business community with the message that literacy amounts to more than reading and writing and that it is vital to personal success in the workplace. The material in the packet emphasizes the multiple purposes of literacy: educating children, getting people off welfare, and getting people into jobs. Media kits were developed and distributed nationally.

The third effort to boost public awareness of the value of adult literacy is the campaign by an adult education program to petition the U.S. Postal Service to create a commemorative stamp dedicated to adult literacy. Petitions for signature are being circulated across the country.

Health and Literacy

An increasing number of research studies are documenting the connection between literacy and health, especially low literacy and poor health (see Chapter Five). A major event of the year has been the mass media's increasing coverage of such studies (Hohn, 1998).

The GED

The GED Testing Service (GEDTS) has made progress on several fronts.

It has clarified its policy on providing accommodations for adults with learning disabilities. Policy is now aligned with that specified in the Americans with Disabilities Act and the Individuals with Disabilities Education Act. GEDTS changed its approval process to authorize accommodations for individuals with learning disabilities by shifting the approval of accommodations to the state level. GED administrator training and certification, which took place toward the end of the year, served to ensure a uniform implementation of national policy and procedures. This change will result in more efficient handling of applications and a reduction in the time it takes to obtain approvals for accommodations.

The GEDTS increased the minimum passing score required for each state to issue a GED credential. The minimum score is to be not less than 40, with an average of 45 for each of the five tests in the GED battery. This change affected states that had not previously adopted the minimum 40/average 45 criteria and resulted in a slight decrease in the number of examinees passing the GED where the new minimum pass score requirements were instituted.

The GEDTS continues preparation for GED2000, the new test intended to take learners into the twenty-first century. The questions asked on this new test will be more pertinent to real-life applications and will reflect the content standards now being implemented by all states. Five major changes are being made in the GED2000:

• There will be one English/language arts test.

• The test will offer multiple-choice responses as well as alternative formats, such as graphing responses on the math test or gridding answers without any choices.

• Students will be able to use a calculator for a major portion of the mathematics test.

- There will be an interdisciplinary test that will use authentic materials from real-life situations.
- Examinees will receive reports on their performance in terms of both content and skills instead of a single standard score on each test.

Examinees will be asked to use information processing skills, interpret a broad range of texts across core academic disciplines, and use and analyze information provided in authentic, or real-world, contexts. When the new test is introduced in 2001, any examinee who did not pass all sections of the test version being administered until then will have to take the entire new test; the old and the new tests will not equate.

National Center for the Study of Adult Learning and Literacy

NCSALL completed its second year. Several studies have emerged and others are under way that will provide the field with information on teaching-learning models, learner persistence, best practices and effective models in professional development, assessment, health and literacy, and the impact of the GED on the lives of examinees. Working in conjunction with other groups, NCSALL has produced a research agenda for adult education and literacy and adult ESOL.

National Assessment of Adult Literacy

In preparation for the next generation of the national adult literacy assessment, the National Assessment of Adult Literacy (NAAL) held focus groups to discuss data elements for the ensuing adult literacy assessment. The NAAL will assess adult literacy in the areas of prose, document, and quantitative skills. The next assessment is to be conducted in 2002. States will again have the option to draw larger samples to produce data on skill levels in their state. Background papers are being prepared to guide the direction of the next national assessment.

ERIC Clearinghouse

The U.S. Department of Education renewed its contract with the ERIC (Educational Resources Information Center) Clearinghouse on Adult, Career, and Vocational Education to provide for research on topics of interest to adult education and family literacy. ERIC's mission was approved without change of provider or interruption of service.

New National Center for Community Literacy

A new national center for adult literacy, the Lindy Boggs National Center for Community Literacy, was established at Loyola University in New Orleans. The center's mission is to link the university to the community by focusing on the literacy needs of public housing residents. The center will develop a library collection specializing in the linkage of literacy and public housing, conduct research on the literacy needs of public housing neighborhoods, and develop demonstration projects designed in collaboration with public housing residents.

CONCLUSION

Following are a few final words on the gains made in 1998 and the needs that must be met in the years ahead.

Gains in 1998

The Adult Education and Family Literacy Act offers the field of adult education and family literacy the promise of entering the mainstream of public policy and instructional delivery. New legislation nudged each state to reassess its current direction and identify state policy and program delivery changes that will promote more effective alliances with federal, state, and local entities. A new role for the ED is outlined in legislation for national leadership activities and promises a stronger connection with states. Instructional delivery is changing as new standards for program quality and instructional content are applied. Innovative instructional models are being developed by means of distance learning and the use of technology as both a tool for learning and a basic skill. A number of research studies are being implemented to inform practice, and adult learners created a vehicle through which they can voice their concerns about the policy and practice of adult education and literacy.

Future Needs

Now that legislation has been created outlining what the field must do, the field must determine how to change practice. Adequate tools will be needed to implement the necessary changes to the system. Programs are faced with preparing a new adult learner, who learns in different ways, is younger, and needs more assistance with English literacy. The field must bring every instructional program into the new century with the technology needed for both instruction and management of data, and instruction must be provided by a highly proficient teaching staff. The current part-time delivery system must be transformed into a full-time delivery system, with educators who are prepared to teach the new adult learner. States must develop information management systems that collect information for informing the public and policymakers of the successes and weaknesses in the system.

Reporting performance on a local, state, national, and international basis will be critical in determining the impact the field is having on the target population as a whole. Unless the undereducated population raises its skills to a globally competitive level, the field will not have been successful. NAAL is gearing up to report national progress. The International Adult Literacy Survey (IALS) could be used to make international comparisons of success. IALS allows the United States to compare its progress with that of other countries on the basis of economic indicators such as productivity and earnings, effect of years of education on productivity and earnings, and the "wage premium" of high literacy skills and the "wage penalty" associated with low performance (Organization for Economic Cooperation and Development, 1997).

To fulfill the intentions of the AEFLA, Congress must provide serious funding for the state grant program for adult education and literacy systems, funding that will allow the field to retool for learner success. Achievement of a $1 billion program funding level by the year 2004 is imperative.

—◁∿▷—

The year 1998 was "unbelievable" (Darling, 1998). The long-overdue passage of adult education and literacy legislation has become a reality, presenting the field with opportunities for growth and redirection to lead adult learners into the new millennium. The events of the year confirm the slogan of the NIFL's public awareness campaign: literacy is "a whole new world"—for the nation, for the states, and for providers and learners.

References

Brustein, M., & Mahler, M. (1998). *The administrator's guide to the Adult Education and Family Literacy Act of 1998.* Washington, DC: National Adult Education and Professional Development Consortium.

Charp, S. (1998, November). Distance learning. *T.H.E. Journal, 26*(4), 4.

Darling, S. (1998, December). The family literacy Congress. *Momentum, 1,* 2.

Elliott, B. (1998, October). *Digest of adult education statistics—1998.* Washington, DC: Department of Education, Office of Vocational and Adult Education.

Hohn, M. (1998). *Empowerment health education in adult literacy: A guide for public health and adult literacy practitioners, policymakers, and funders.* Literacy leader fellowship program report. Washington, DC: National Institute for Literacy.

Johnson, A. (1998, September 21). *Policy update: Workforce Investment Act offers opportunities for adult and family literacy.* Washington, DC: National Institute for Literacy.

Merrifield, J. (1998). *Contested ground: Performance accountability in adult basic education.* Cambridge, MA: National Center for the Study of Adult Learning and Literacy.

Murphy, G. (1998). *Points of emphasis in the Adult Education and Family Literacy Act.* Washington, DC: National Council of State Directors of Adult Education.

Murphy, G., & Johnson, A. (1998, September). *What works: Integrating basic skills into welfare-to-work.* Washington, DC: National Institute for Literacy.

Neeley, L., Niemi, J., & Ehrhard, B. (1998, November). Classes going the distance so people don't have to: Instructional opportunities for adult learners. *T.H.E. Journal, 26*(4), 72–74.

Organization for Economic Cooperation and Development, Human Resources Development. (1997). *Literacy skills for the knowledge society.* Canada.

Peyton, T. (1998, December). Family literacy and the 105th Congress. *Momentum, 1,* 3.

Raleigh, B. (1998). *Direct and equitable access.* National Literacy Advocacy Listserv.

Snow, C., Burns, S., & Griffin, P. (1998). *Preventing reading difficulties in young children for adult learning and literacy.* Washington, DC: Committee on the Prevention of Reading Difficulties in Young Children, National Research Council, National Academy Press.

Snyder, T., Hoffman, C., & Geddes, C. (1997). *Digest of educational statistics, 1997* (NCES 98–015). Washington, DC: U.S. Department of Education, National Center for Education Statistics.

Spieghts, D. (1998, October 29). Would a $1 billion appropriation buy direct and equitable access? *Report on Literacy Programs,* 164.

Stein, S. (1997, February). *Equipped for the future: A reform agenda for adult literacy and lifelong learning.* Washington, DC: National Institute for Literacy.

Sticht, T. (1998, September). *Beyond 2000: Future directions for adult education.* Unpublished report, U.S. Department of Education.

Tracy-Mumford, F. (1998). *AEA students on waiting lists.* Unpublished report, National Council of State Directors of Adult Education.

U.S. Congress. (1998, July). Workforce Investment Act of 1998. *Congressional Record.*

U.S. Department of Education. (1997). Statistical performance tables.

CHAPTER TWO

Lessons from *Preventing Reading Difficulties in Young Children for Adult Learning and Literacy*

Catherine E. Snow
John Strucker

~~~

In the spring of 1998 the National Research Council released a report, *Preventing Reading Difficulties in Young Children for Adult Learning and Literacy (PRD)*. This report, produced by a committee that included members identified with quite diverse perspectives on reading instruction, was widely heralded as having the potential to "end the reading wars." *PRD* was written with the goal of contributing to the prevention of reading difficulties by documenting the contributions of research to an understanding of reading development and the conditions under which reading develops with the greatest ease. The report started by presenting the best current, research-based model of skilled reading as a basis for reviewing the literature to determine which groups and individuals are at greatest risk of failure and what factors are associated with the reduction of risk. The perhaps somewhat utopian vision offered by *PRD* was that if the long list of recommendations within the report were implemented, the incidence of reading difficulties among American school children would be reduced from 15 percent to 40 percent down to 3 percent to 5 percent—eventually.

The most frequent question encountered by members of the *PRD* committee as they talk about the report to groups of educators is, "But what do we do about the middle and secondary school students who haven't learned to read? Will the recommendations in the report help them?" A similar question could be formulated about the many adults in the United States with poor literacy skills. This chapter discusses the implications of the report for adult literacy and family literacy programs, including programs teaching English for speakers of other languages (ESOL). The questions we address include the following: What is the relevance of the research base reviewed in the report to understanding adult literacy performance and instructional practice for adults? Are the risk factors identified in the report as justifying secondary prevention efforts equally applicable to adult learners? What is the future of adult basic education (ABE) in a world where reading difficulties have truly been well prevented?

We begin with a brief summary of the findings of PRD that we consider most relevant to ABE and ESOL. We then present six case studies of adult literacy learners to illustrate how the issues brought up in PRD are and are not directly relevant to adult literacy difficulties. We conclude by suggesting areas of adult literacy in need of further research and ways that teacher preparation for adult literacy practitioners might be improved.

PRD limited its purview to research relevant to early reading, through third grade. The report identifies six opportunities that, if accessible to every child, would greatly decrease the risk of reading difficulties:

1. Support for the acquisition of language and of sufficient metalinguistic awareness to approach the segmentation of speech into smaller units that could be related to alphabetic writing

2. Exposure to print and to literacy uses and functions

3. Development of enthusiasm for reading

4. Opportunities to grasp and master the alphabetic principle[1]

5. Access to preventive services if needed

6. Access to intervention as soon as reading difficulties emerge

With reference to the early years of school, the six opportunities define domains to which excellent reading instruction must attend; in other words, early adequate reading instruction provides children with the opportunity to acquire knowledge of and facility with the alphabetic principle and with sufficient practice to achieve fluency in the application of the alphabetic principle so that the construction of meaning is not disrupted.

The issues that emerge in higher stages of reading development (reading to learn, acquisition of literate vocabulary, education in content areas, and reading for critical purposes) are not covered by the report (although the report's discussion of the importance of decontextualized language skills even in the preschool years prefigures the important topic of the obstacles that at-risk learners face in some of these areas). A large proportion of ABE students—both those who are reading disabled and those who are not but still have all of the other risk factors—are stuck precisely at these later stages of literacy development.

RISK FACTORS

Preventing Reading Difficulties in Young Children for Adult Learning and Literacy devotes considerable attention to the task of defining risk factors and using the research literature as a basis for deciding which children are at an elevated risk of reading difficulties. We use this section of the report as a basis for comparison with factors associated with the risk of low literacy in the adult population.

Which Children Are at Risk for Literacy Problems?

The report distinguishes group and individual risk factors—not because the difference has any theoretical significance but because the strategies for identifying and providing secondary prevention efforts differ for the two types of risk. The most important group risk factors are listed here, but it is important to note that these factors are likely to be correlated with one another and, thus, that it has been impossible to determine the contribution of each individually:

• *Attending a chronically low-achieving school.* If a school consistently scores well below average on norm-referenced reading tests, any child attending that school (even children who do not bring other risk factors with them) is at elevated risk of reading difficulty. It has been widely documented that even middle-class children attending generally low-ranked schools do poorly. The consistently poor performance of such schools suggests the absence of a coherent strategy for teaching reading, a paucity of attentive teachers with high expectations for student success, and/or the adoption of unsuccessful approaches to teaching reading.

• *Having low proficiency in English.* Latino children are about twice as likely as Anglo children to read below average for their age. Although it is difficult to sort out precisely what percentage of the elevated risk of Latino children can be attributed to low proficiency in English (since many Latinos are native English speakers), clearly poor English skills at the time that reading instruction commences constitutes one source of risk. This risk cannot be attributed primarily to the child; it represents a failure of the educational system to develop adequate methods for introducing such children to literacy and ambivalence about the role of Spanish in their literacy instruction.

• *Speaking a nonstandard dialect of English.* Children who speak dialects of English identified with poverty, ethnic minorities, or immigrant groups (such as Caribbean or Indian English) are at elevated risk of literacy difficulties. It is not entirely clear whether these difficulties can be attributed directly to the children's unfamiliarity with standard English, the poverty and limited education of the families from which they come, the reactions school personnel have to nonstandard speakers, or problems of mapping their own phonological system onto the phoneme-grapheme correspondences being taught. Thus, although we know that nonstandard speakers, like non-English speakers, need special attention and better-than-average instruction, we cannot use the fact of elevated risk as a basis for deciding the cause of the difficulties.

• *Living in a community of poverty.* Coming from a home with limited financial and educational resources is, in and of itself, not a major risk factor. However, living in such a home when it is located in a community composed of similarly situated families, and with the high likelihood that the neighborhood school will show generally poor achievement levels, does constitute a major risk.

Individual risk factors, which may and often do coincide with the group risks, include the following:

• *Delayed or disordered language development.* Children with a history of language problems are very likely to encounter difficulties in learning to read. Reading builds on the child's analysis of his or her own phonological, lexical, and grammatical knowledge. Children for whom such knowledge is shaky, still developing, and poorly consolidated are on much shakier ground when asked to engage in metalinguistic tasks such as performing phoneme segmentation, learning sound-symbol correspondences, or writing.

• *Hearing impairments.* The deaf population in general shows poor reading achievement. In fact, deaf children must learn English as a second language, just as native speakers of Spanish or Chinese do, and they are additionally challenged by the difference in mode between their native language (a gesture-based system) and the aural-oral mode of English. Although deaf children can learn enough about the alphabetic system to read at a third- or fourth-grade level, evidently the inaccessibility of a phonological representation of English makes further progress extremely difficult for many.

• *Developmental delays or disorders.* Children with any of a wide variety of developmental challenges—mental retardation, emotional problems, attention deficits—will find learning to read more difficult than children without such risks. It is worthy of note that there is very high comorbidity for emotional problems and communication disorders and that approximately 50 percent of children with attention deficit disorder also have diagnosed language problems. The documented comorbidity rates may reflect a deeper reality that early in childhood, any developmental problem is likely to be reflected in a variety of domains. Reading, as a challenging problem area, is likely to be one of the affected domains.

Who Is at Risk in the Adult Population?

To discuss those parts of *PRD* that might relate to practice and research in the fields of adult basic education and adult education in English for speakers of other languages, we first need to summarize what is known about the demographic characteristics of adult literacy students and then what is known about the reading accomplishments of this population.

Not surprisingly, many adult literacy students embody some of the demographic risk factors associated with early reading difficulties in *PRD* and in previous national reports on reading (National Assessment of Educational Progress, 1995; Anderson, Hiebert, Scott, & Wilkinson, 1985)—factors such as poverty and membership in ethnic or linguistic minority groups. As noted in *PRD*, poverty is not by itself necessarily a risk factor for reading, but economic disadvantages are strongly associated with other risk factors, such as having fewer literacy-building experiences in early childhood and receiving poor-quality schooling.

Since the mid-1970s researchers have consistently described the U.S. adult literacy population in similar socioeconomic terms: most students are poor or low income, minority groups are disproportionately represented, and increasing numbers are not native speakers of English (Cook, 1977; Hunter & Harman, 1985; Kirsch, Jungeblut, Jenkins, & Kolstad, 1993; Sticht, 1988, 1998). Despite occasional reports of financially successful people who have reading difficulties (Johnston, 1985), adult literacy classes are overwhelmingly composed of the poor, the underemployed, and the unemployed.

Why are we bothering to restate the obvious: that adult literacy students come from poor, educationally disadvantaged backgrounds? As we turn to describing the kinds of reading difficulties ABE/ESOL students face, we want to keep in mind the interaction of their academic difficulties with their life histories and current socioeconomic circumstances. Like other human activities, reading ability develops in various social contexts over time. So, for example, when we discuss the vocabulary knowledge of adult students, we will also discuss how their childhood and adult exposure to words may have influenced its development.

SKILLED READING

PRD is focused on the period from birth through third grade, a crucial time in language and literacy acquisition. Through school-based instruction and independent reading, children learn to decode words independently, become automatic and fluent at word recognition, and begin to develop the skills in reading to learn that will allow them to use reading as a lifelong tool for education and enjoyment.

How Does Literacy Develop Through Grade 3?

PRD identifies several domains of development that are crucial to the emergence of solid literacy skills during the early school years.

COGNITIVE, EMOTIONAL, AND SOCIAL DEVELOPMENT. It should be clear that reading, a complex achievement, is more likely to develop in a risk-free way in children who are healthy and physiologically intact and show normal developments in the domains of cognition (in particular, understanding symbolization), emotionality and attention, and sociability.

LANGUAGE DEVELOPMENT. Children start to produce language sometime around their first birthday, but if they have been exposed to sufficient spoken language, they have already organized their speech discrimination systems to match the language they will learn. Children also typically understand several words or phrases before they start to speak. Children's language development is a prerequisite to reading in some indirect and direct ways.

First, the texts children use when they first learn to read are composed of words and grammatical structures. Children who know those words and structures orally will have easier access to meaning through reading. Second, as children acquire more vocabulary words, they become increasingly sensitive to the internal differences in the sounds and sequences of sounds of those words—awareness that is crucial to mastering the alphabetic principle. Third, children who have the opportunity to use language in a wide variety of communicative tasks learn about the different forms of communication appropriate to different situations—that talking on the telephone requires giving more explicit information than chatting face to face, that telling stories requires sequencing events, that talking about fantasy worlds and hypotheses requires forms like *pretend, suppose,* and *if.* In every respect, the progress of language development during the preschool and early school years must be seen as one aspect of literacy development.

PHONOLOGICAL AWARENESS. For children learning to read an alphabetic language such as English, phonological awareness constitutes a precursor to reading in its own right. Phonological awareness refers to the ability to focus on the sounds of language rather than the meaning. Early evidence of children's phonological awareness often comes from their language play (*willy, wally, wooly*), their enjoyment or production of rhymes (*cat, sat, fat, pat*), or their ability to question language forms (*Is his name Rory because he makes so much noise?*).

Language segmentation abilities also reveal phonological awareness; typically young children can segment a sentence into meaningful units (*The little girl/ate/lots of ice cream.*), but only at about age four will children reliably isolate meaningless, grammatical words such as *the* and *of* as separate units. Four year olds can typically be shown how to separate syllables as well; syllables are relatively accessible, pronounceable units. Much more challenging is the ability to segment a word or syllable into its component sounds (phonemes): recognizing, for example, that *cat* has three parts, /c/, /a/, and /t/. Children who understand this are said to have achieved phonemic awareness, important because it is crucial in learning to read English to understand that letters stand for phonemes, not syllables or words.

Phonemic awareness develops gradually. A relatively easy phonemic awareness task involves removing the first "little bit" from a word (*say the name Fred without the fff*) or thinking of words that start with the same sound. Segmenting or matching on final sounds is more difficult. Removing medial sounds (*say Fred without the rrrr*) is extremely hard. While research makes clear that phonemic awareness continues to develop during the early stages of conventional reading, it is clear that children with no capacity to recognize, segment, or attend to individual phonemes will have a very hard time understanding phonics-based instruction, which presupposes such understanding.

LITERACY DEVELOPMENT. By literacy development, we mean development of understandings about the functions and uses of print, an understanding that language used in books may differ in certain ways from that used orally, an appreciation for literacy activities, as well as the development of the skills of reading and writing in conventional ways. Children arrive at school with vastly different amounts and kinds of experience in using literacy or seeing literacy used in their homes. Those who have had lots of chances to be read to, practice writing or scribbling, use magnetic letters (of the sort that attach to the refrigerator door), recognize letters and words in print they see in their daily environments, and so on will be much better prepared for reading instruction.

Is There Development in Reading After Grade 3?

Of course, considerable development in language and literacy occurs beyond third grade, even for learners who are progressing as expected in literacy. A comparison of the books read by children at the end of third grade and those read by children even just a few years older makes clear how much is left to learn after the basic reading skills are established. Older readers can handle a wider variety of text types, a much higher incidence of rare or unknown vocabulary items, and more complex sentences and rhetorical structures; they can understand literary devices signaling irony, sarcasm, humor, multiple perspectives, violations of the time line, hypothetical and counterfactual reasoning, and much more.

ADVANCED LANGUAGE SKILLS. These developments in literacy skills parallel enormous developments after grade 3 in children's oral language skills. The new language skills typical of this developmental period have been variously referred to as *decontextualized* (Snow, 1983) or *focused* (Scollon & Scollon, 1982), as *oral literacy* (Tannen, 1982), and as *extended discourse skills* (Ninio & Snow, 1996). All of these terms refer to the characteristic that language can be used in a more autonomous way—to create realities rather than just referring to reality and to represent relatively complex states of affairs. Often these uses of language are also reflexive and analytic. Giving definitions, for example, requires that children analyze their own knowledge of word meanings and figure out which aspects of what they know about a word are likely to be shared. This decontextualized, or extended, use of language is relevant to literacy precisely because the texts that older children come to read use this sort of language. They are likely to be introducing novel, often complex information in ways that presuppose little shared background information and with the pragmatic features typical of distanced communication. Such texts create demands that are quite different from those of primary grade readings; early texts are mostly narratives, using only the few thousand most common words of English, telling about relatively familiar sorts of individuals and events, appearing together with contextualizing pictures, and benefiting from support for comprehension through instructional activities.

The presentation of more decontextualized texts to slightly older children may indeed generate new cases of reading difficulties even among children who have developed as expected through grade 3. More likely, though, the children who found the texts of the later elementary grades impossible to comprehend were showing some difficulties at earlier stages of reading as well, but perhaps slight enough that they were masked by strengths in some components of the reading process.

MATTHEW EFFECTS. The organizing metaphor of "Matthew effects" was introduced to the field of reading by Keith Stanovich (1986) to explain the development of individual differences in both reading and more general cognitive functioning in verbal areas. It takes its name from the "rich get richer and the poor get poorer" discussion in the Gospel according to Matthew. Interweaving inherited and environmental factors, Stanovich argued that relatively small cognitive differences (especially in phonological processing) among young children can lead to wide and socially significant differences in adult outcomes, not just in reading but in verbal intelligence.

Here is a schematic version of how Matthew effects might play out. If a child has a *phonological processing difficulty* at the outset of reading instruction, then the acquisition of *word analysis skills* in kindergarten and first grade may be imperiled. If *word analysis skills* are not developed, then the child's *decoding* (the ability to figure out the pronunciations of unknown words independently) is compromised. In addition, her ability to progress from analyzing letter sounds to orthographic processing (recognizing letter and syllable patterns as units) may not develop adequately. If the child cannot *decode* independently, then it is more difficult and frustrating for her to practice *reading independently.* If the child cannot practice *reading independently,* then *fluent reading* may fail to develop by the end of third grade. If *fluent reading* is not in place by the end of third grade, there are at least two results.

First, reading is less enjoyable, leading the child to read less (thus adversely affecting fluency itself). Second, if fluent reading fails to develop, then reading to learn in the later grades is imperiled for two related reasons: first, because the child must devote too much effort to word recognition, leaving insufficient resources to devote to comprehension (Perfetti, 1985), and, second, because when reading is disfluent and slow, the longer clauses and sentences that increasingly occur in content passages in the middle grades cannot be processed as effectively. If the ability to read to learn does not develop sufficiently, the child's ability to use reading to acquire vocabulary and concepts is affected, and schoolwork becomes increasingly difficult. Since knowledge in school subjects is cumulative, incomplete acquisition of basic vocabulary and background concepts in middle school can imperil high school learning.

Notice that even in this brief schematic representation of what Stanovich called a "cascade" of reading difficulties, cognitive-neurological factors are reciprocally related to behavioral-environmental factors. For example, the early phonological difficulty (of presumed neurological-cognitive origin) ultimately leads to the behavioral consequence of reading less, which impedes the acquisition of the cognitive skills in automatic word recognition. Stanovich also raised the issue that reading ability and verbal IQ are reciprocally related, especially as readers move into adulthood. (See also Stanovich, 1991, and Siegel, 1989.) In practice this means that a forty-five-year-old adult who has been a lifelong nonreader is likely to score lower on verbal IQ tests than a forty-five-year-old who has been a lifelong reader; this is because the nonreader could not use reading to acquire some of the skills and knowledge needed for such tests.

With respect to the ABE/ESOL population, Stanovich's (1986) discussion of social environmental factors is especially relevant. The development of phonological awareness seems to have a strong inherited component, but it is probably also strongly influenced by the child's exposure to oral language in infancy and early childhood. If a child's exposure to oral language is substantially limited, comprising substantially fewer words and phoneme distinctions, then he may have fewer sounds on which to practice and develop his phonological awareness.

In a study of preschool children's vocabulary learning, Hart and Risley (1995) found that children of welfare families had far fewer language interactions with adults and were exposed to far fewer different words than were children from working-class and middle-class families. As a consequence, the children from welfare families not only knew the meanings of fewer words than the other children, but they were acquiring new vocabulary at a much slower rate, falling increasingly behind the other children in vocabulary knowledge with the passage of time. Thus, it is possible that the vocabulary difficulties of some ABE students began long before school, in early childhood, with the establishment of slower rates of vocabulary learning and less developed schema for learning new words.

WHERE ARE ADULT LITERACY STUDENTS ON THIS DEVELOPMENTAL CONTINUUM? ABE and some ESOL students can be found at every point along this schematic representation of reading difficulties. Some students appear stalled at early stages of reading by severe unremediated phonological difficulties. However, it is much more common for ABE/ESOL students to enroll with partial or incomplete development of the various reading skills: partial acquisition of phonological awareness (reflected in decoding problems and poor spelling), fluency lagging the equivalent of several grade levels (often called grade equivalents, or GEs)[2] behind untimed silent comprehension, vocabulary levels lagging behind their years of school completion, and background knowledge in the content areas stalled below 5 GE.

Until recently, many ABE programs were unaware of difficulties in decoding and fluency, particularly among students reading above 5 GE in silent reading (Strucker, 1997). Indeed, in programs where teachers were advised not to ask adults to do oral reading because it was not an "authentic" literacy act, decoding and fluency problems could go undetected for months or years. But if current models of the reading process are accurate (Chall, 1983; Perfetti, 1985; Stanovich, 1986; Adams, 1994; Snow, Burns, & Griffin, 1998), poor decoding and lack of fluency will greatly impede the acquisition of levels of vocabulary and content knowledge that students need to pass the General Educational Development (GED) tests. Even modest gains in those processing areas can lead to substantial gains in comprehension for ABE learners.

What Does It Take to Be a Skilled Reader?

Although there has been considerable controversy about the nature of skilled reading and the degree to which all skilled readers are similar to one another, in recent years a consensus has developed among researchers, who agree that skilled readers can do the following:

- Read all or most of the words on the page
- Notice most of the letters in each word and use the letters to access a phonological representation of the word
- Read words quickly because they have automatized the processes of letter recognition and phonological access through practice
- Rely heavily on context cues for comprehension
- Use context cues only minimally for word recognition, which is primarily driven by using letters to access sounds
- Almost always read with a purpose, focus on meaning, and self-monitor their comprehension

Research comparing skilled and less skilled readers at any age or grade level typically finds differences in a wide variety of dimensions. Skilled readers are better than age-matched poorer readers in vocabulary, world knowledge, literal as well as inferential comprehension, and comprehension monitoring and repair strategies. Skilled readers are also typically better than poorer readers in various skills relevant to word identification (getting to the right pronunciation) and lexical access (getting to the right word), knowledge of how spelling patterns relate to pronunciation, sensitivity to relative frequency of letter strings, speed of word reading, and use of context to select the right meaning for homographs (different words spelled the same way).

The development of these reading skills rests on an appreciation of the alphabetic principle—knowledge that letters represent phonemes—and mastery of that principle through large amounts of practice reading. Practice in reading produces fluency, or the ability to read relatively quickly and without conscious attention to the process of word identification. Without some level of fluency, comprehension of longer texts is very difficult, because the construction of meaning is disrupted by the difficulty and slowness of word recognition.

Among the six opportunities to learn, three relate specifically to this model of skilled reading: children need opportunities to learn and master the alphabetic principle, focus on reading for meaning at every stage of instruction, and have enough opportunities to practice reading to achieve fluency. The fourth opportunity—to develop enthusiasm about literacy—is crucial. Most children encounter obstacles somewhere along the road to literacy, and without a clear understanding of how important and potentially pleasurable literacy achievement is, they are unlikely to persist.

Conclusions Concerning Skilled Reading

It should be clear that in discussing either children or adults, we start from three assumptions about reading.

First, skilled reading is the product of a developmental process that starts early in life and changes both qualitatively and quantitatively as readers grow older and experience literacy more widely.

Second, although advanced readers experience reading as a seamless process, it is helpful to view reading as the product of several different lines of development and to view skilled reading as the integration of several components (visual word identification, phonological access, lexical access, monitoring for comprehension, and so on).

Third, the relationships between the components change as the reader develops (Stanovich, 1986; Chall, 1983; Curtis, 1980). For example, when beginning readers are learning letter-sound correspondences (word analysis or phonics), they usually perfect that skill on text that contains highly familiar words. This allows them to map the letter combinations onto words whose phonological representations are well known and easily accessible. They are not expected to learn new words at the same time they are learning the alphabetic principle. However, within a few years after learning to read, successful readers are reading to learn and using reading itself to expand and deepen their vocabulary knowledge. At this stage of reading development, it is crucial that they read text with new and sufficiently challenging vocabulary and concepts. The word analysis skills that were an important focus of instruction for the beginning reader have become automatized, making fluent word recognition possible. At this stage word analysis skills are consciously employed only when decoding and spelling unfamiliar words.

THE ADULT BASIC
EDUCATION POPULATION

In reviewing *PRD*, some adult educators may argue that not many of their students currently fall within this 0 to 3 GE beginning level of reading achievement. But as the estimates that follow suggest, a surprisingly large percentage of adults attending literacy programs fall directly within this category in reading. Of course, it is rare to find adults (except for ESOL beginners in English) who have not developed sufficient oral language skills to support initial reading instruction.

To What Members of the
ABE Population Is *PRD* Relevant?

It is impossible to say with precision what percentage of the students in the ABE/ESOL system read at 3 GE or below. Not all ABE students (especially those below 4 GE) are given norm-referenced tests in reading, and when they are tested, they are usually not assessed with the same instruments nationwide or even from one center to another within most states. To complicate matters further, in some areas of the United States many beginning adult readers are served by volunteer tutoring programs that may not use norm-referenced tests or keep centralized records. A preliminary analysis of data from the forthcoming Adult Reading Components Study (ARCS) by Strucker and Davidson indicates that about 9 percent of the students enrolled in ABE classes scored below 4 GE on a silent reading comprehension test.[3]

Reder (1997) analyzed four databases, including the National Adult Literacy Survey (NALS) (Kirsch, Jungeblut, Jenkins, & Kolstad, 1993),[4] to define the characteristics and participation of "first-level learners," the target population for basic literacy services. Of the 15 million adult, native speakers of English, ages sixteen and above, estimated to function at NALS Level 1, approximately 6 million function at the lowest levels of Level 1 (Reder, 1997). Although the NALS was not designed to map directly onto grade-equivalent scores, it seems likely that many of these 6 million adults read approximately at 3 GE or below.

ESOL enrollments of students below 3 GE present a different picture. By definition, nearly all adults enrolling in beginning ESOL classes would be likely to have limited English reading skills until they have learned how to decode English and have learned enough English vocabulary to read at above 3 GE in English. How many of these students are there? In 1996, the U.S. Department of Education's Office of Vocational and Adult Education (OVAE) reported that about 40 percent of all U.S. adult basic education students were enrolled in ESOL classes. Estimating that one-third of these 40 percent were enrolled in beginning ESOL classes (a conservative estimate because in many areas beginning ESOL is more heavily enrolled than intermediate or advanced), this means that at least 13 percent of the total U.S. enrollment in ESOL classes is made up of students reading English at 3 GE or below.

Taken together with Strucker and Davidson's preliminary estimate of 9 percent of native speakers reading at 3 GE or below, this means that more than 20 percent of the ABE/ESOL population may actually be reading at or below the level directly addressed by the *PRD*.

The relevance of the report is not restricted to adult students who are currently reading at 3 GE or below. In addition to those adults reading at 3 GE or below, many more ABE students and some ESOL students may have experienced significant difficulties in language and reading at these early stages of development when they were children. Some of these students may have completely overcome the early reading problems, but for others their early difficulties continue to affect their subsequent progress. Thus, we will be discussing not only what is known from the research about adult readers at 3 GE and below but also what is known about the range of adult readers—from beginners all the way through GED candidates.

What Is Known About ABE and ESOL Students as Readers?

At the outset we must admit that we have to restrict much of our discussion to ABE readers because little research has been done on adult ESOL reading in populations other than students at universities. The

National Adult Literacy Survey (NALS) (Kirsch, Jungeblut, Jenkins, & Kolstad, 1993) provided a rich and rigorously developed picture of the functional literacy skills of U.S. residents aged sixteen to sixty-five by showing what proportion of adults were able to perform simulated real-world literacy tasks at various levels. However, its assessments were not designed to shed light on why a given reader or groups of readers might have had difficulty with various NALS literacy tasks. Although it is likely that most adults enrolled in ABE/ESOL programs would end up in the two lowest levels of the NALS, the precise reading difficulties that led to these results cannot be inferred from the NALS data.

Our best sources of information on the reading difficulties of adults come from reading clinics (Johnson & Blalock, 1987; Chall, 1994). Based on adult readers' profiles from the Harvard Adult Literacy Initiative, Chall (1994) made the following observations:

> When we had assessed and taught about 100 adults, we began to be aware of two patterns of scores—one that was common among adults for whom English was a second language; the other resembled the patterns of strengths and weaknesses found among children and adults who tend to be diagnosed as having learning disabilities.
>
> We found the ESL group . . . to be relatively stronger in the . . . word recognition or print aspects of reading, as distinguished from the meaning or comprehension aspects. The "learning disability" pattern . . . [includes] . . . adults . . . who are relatively stronger in word meaning and relatively weaker in the print aspects of reading—word recognition and analysis, spelling, and oral reading.

Other researchers have documented the presence of learning disabilities and reading disabilities in the adult literacy population. Read and Ruyter (1985) and Read (1988a, 1988b), in studies of prison inmates, found that a majority of those who were reading below high school levels showed signs of moderate to severe decoding and word recognition problems, which the researchers believed were rooted in phonological processing deficits. In a reading/age-matched study, Pratt and Brady (1988) found that the low-literacy adults they tested resembled reading-disabled children rather than normally progressing elementary school readers, based on decoding and phonological processing difficulties among those adults.

A number of investigators have documented the persistence of childhood reading disabilities into adulthood (Bruck, 1990, 1992;

Johnson & Blalock, 1987; Fink, 1998; Strucker, 1995, 1997; Spreen & Haaf, 1986). Bruck's research focused on people who had been reading disabled as children but had managed to become relatively successful adult readers. She found that even those successful adult readers still had difficulty with phoneme deletion tasks that most children have mastered by the end of third grade. Fink's research (1998) with highly successful adult dyslexics indicated that despite attaining high levels of silent reading comprehension, many of her subjects continued to exhibit spelling difficulties and slow rates of reading.

In a cluster analysis study of 120 adult literacy students in Massachusetts, Strucker (1995, 1997) found strong evidence to confirm Chall's observation that adult literacy students tend to fall into either the reading-disabled or ESOL categories. Of a total of nine clusters of adult learners, from beginners through GED levels, five clusters strongly conformed to Chall's twofold characterization (see Figures 2.1 and 2.2). Two apparently "learning-disabled" clusters emerged in which the learners were much stronger in the meaning-based aspects of reading (vocabulary and comprehension) than in the print aspects (phonological awareness, word analysis, word recognition, spelling, and oral reading). These two clusters were made up exclusively of native speakers of English, with more than 95 percent of the cluster members reporting that they had received "extra help" in reading when they were children, ranging from one-on-one tutoring and Chapter 1 or Title 1 placement (66 percent) to formal classification as

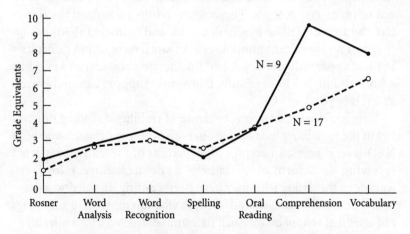

Figure 2.1.   Grade-Equivalent Scores on the Test Battery Components of Two Groups of Reading-Disabled Native Speakers.

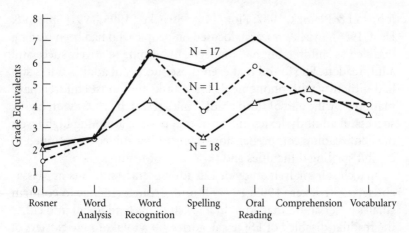

Figure 2.2.   Grade-Equivalent Scores on the Test Battery Components of Three Groups of ESOL and Inner-City Young Adults.

learning disabled by school authorities (29 percent). Three other clusters were made up of 75 percent ESOL learners who were much stronger in the print aspects (phonological awareness,[5] word analysis, word recognition, spelling, and oral reading) and much weaker in the meaning-based aspects of reading (vocabulary and comprehension).

Interestingly, the remaining 25 percent of the learners in those three "ESOL" clusters were actually native speakers of English; they were young adults of various ethnic backgrounds who had dropped out of inner-city schools. These young adults resembled the inner-city children described by Chall, Jacobs, and Baldwin (1990) in that they had no significant phonological or word recognition difficulties but had apparently not developed the literate vocabularies in middle school and high school reading that would support comprehension at levels beyond 4–5 GE.

Strucker also found strong evidence of childhood reading difficulties in the remaining four clusters. In both beginners' clusters and both GED-level clusters, an average of 58 percent of the learners reported receiving some form of "extra help" as defined above. (Not every learner in this study who may have been reading disabled was diagnosed in childhood. Generally people who are more than fifty years old attended school before such determinations were formalized.)

The NALS touched briefly on the incidence of learning disabilities in the population as a whole by asking a single yes/no question: "Do you currently have a learning disability?" Reder (1995) analyzed responses to that question with respect to years of school completion, economic attainment, and NALS level attainment. Among native speakers of English in the sample as a whole, 2.8 percent answered this question in the affirmative, but among the Level 1 participants, this figure was 9.5 percent, dropping to 0.24 percent among Level 5 participants. Reder concluded, "Learning disabilities are concentrated primarily among adults at the lowest literacy level."

CASE HISTORIES OF SIX ADULT LEARNERS

To make our discussion of adult learners more concrete, we present six brief case histories of typical adult learners from Boston-area adult literacy centers and the Harvard Adult Reading Laboratory (Strucker, 1995, 1997). Strucker (1995) tested 120 adults using six components of reading (word analysis or phonics, word recognition, spelling, oral reading, silent reading comprehension, and oral vocabulary) and also conducted a brief test of phonemic awareness. (See the chapter appendix for an explanation of the assessments used.) Each student's score on these measures made up his or her reading profile. The 120 individual profiles were then subjected to cluster analysis, with the result that nine clusters of adult readers emerged, ranging from beginning levels of reading all the way up through GED. The individuals whose stories are presented here had reading test scores and educational backgrounds typical of students in their respective clusters. Their real names are not used here.

Joseph, a Beginning Reader

At the time of testing in 1994, Joseph, an African American living in Boston, was fifty-nine years old. He had grown up on the outskirts of a small town in South Carolina, where his family were sharecroppers raising cotton and tobacco. He reported that his father could read "a little" but that his mother was completely illiterate. His test scores as an adult indicated that he could recognize words at an early first-grade level and had not mastered the most basic levels of word analysis skills. Joseph was unable to read the 3 GE reading comprehension passage, the lowest GE available in the battery used. His oral vocabulary at 5 GE was actually slightly higher than that of many adult nonreaders from working-class backgrounds. Following is his reading profile:

Rosner	1 GE[6]
Word analysis	1 GE
Word recognition	1 GE
Spelling	1.5 GE
Oral reading	1 GE
Comprehension	Not attempted
Oral vocabulary	5 GE

Joseph is a living compendium of the risk factors, both social and personal, identified in *PRD*. He attended a segregated, rural school that was a two-mile walk from his home and where, based on his reports, he received poor-quality reading instruction. Classes were large, and what few books there were could not be taken home. His only memories of reading instruction were of the teacher's writing words on the blackboard and the children being asked to spell them letter by letter, and then being asked to read them.[7] After his father died, when Joseph was eight years old, he had to work in the fields for most of the year to contribute to the family income, and he attended school only sporadically from that point on, eventually dropping out permanently at age sixteen. Poor-quality schools coupled with poor attendance was a common experience among low-literacy adults of Joseph's generation, especially if they grew up in rural areas.

Based on current phonemic awareness testing and subsequent attempts to teach the alphabetic principle to Joseph using a variety of methods, we feel it is likely that Joseph has a phonologically based reading disability. A subsequent evaluation at the Massachusetts General Hospital Speech and Communications Disorders Program confirmed these observations. This basic phonological processing difficulty was discussed at length in *PRD* as the most prevalent personal risk factor for early reading problems.

We cannot tell with certainty how severe Joseph's phonological disability was when he was a child. Results of intervention studies cited in *PRD* suggest that if children with moderate disabilities in this area receive early instruction in phonological awareness, their rates of reading failure can be greatly reduced. (See summaries of this research by Blachman, 1994, 1997.) These kinds of early interventions did not exist when Joseph started school in the late 1930s. We can only speculate on what might have been the results if he had been given such help. Phonological development in children not only contributes to reading success; reading and spelling themselves probably contribute reciprocally to phonological development (Blachman, 1997). In Joseph's case, fifty years of *not* reading or spelling may have caused whatever limited phoneme awareness skills he possessed as a child to deteriorate. As is often the case with ABE students, Joseph's personal risk factors for reading difficulties, such as his inherited phonological difficulties, were undoubtedly exacerbated by social risk factors: his lack of exposure to reading and books as a young child and the particularly inadequate reading instruction he reported receiving in school.

Despite this formidable array of risk factors, Joseph has enjoyed considerable success in life. He worked in a number of factories from the 1950s to 1980s, rising to low-level supervisory positions in some of them through his hard work and excellent interpersonal skills. Joseph married a woman who was a high school graduate, and once their children were grown he worked overtime so that she could attend college and eventually earn a master's degree in business administration. They own a triple-decker home in Boston and have raised three children, and his wife now uses her computer and accounting skills to manage their small trucking company, which also employs their sons. She and the sons draw special maps for Joseph to follow when he has to make a delivery to an unfamiliar location, and she helps him study for truck driving licensing tests. Joseph is the treasurer of his church, but he would like to be able to read from the Bible at services and teach Sunday school.

In many ways Joseph resembles the low-literacy adults described by Fingeret (1983) who are able to rely on family members and networks of friends to help them successfully negotiate the world of print. Still, Joseph's accomplishments are remarkable even in the context of the 1950s, 1960s, and 1970s, when workers with minimal reading skills could find steady employment at good wages in factories. In today's job market Joseph's success would be much harder to replicate without basic literacy skills.

Richard, a More Advanced Beginner

Richard was born in a city near Boston; he is the son of West Indian immigrants. He was twenty-four years old and unmarried when he was tested in 1994. He had enrolled in ABE classes because he wanted to earn a high school diploma in order to enlist in the military. Richard's mother worked as a secretary most of his life, and he and his siblings were read to as children; they were expected to do well in school. His older sister graduated from college. Richard's K–12 schooling, however, featured many interruptions because his mother moved frequently up and down the East Coast during his childhood:

> I was never in kindergarten at all, and during first, second, and third grade we moved all the time. [Teachers] didn't really deal with my reading problems because by the time they noticed them, we had moved. . . . I'm still very hurt to this day. . . . If I'd had an education, I could have done anything.

Eventually, when he was in fifth grade, Richard's teachers did more than notice his reading problems; he was placed in special education classes from middle school on, and he received remedial reading instruction. In high school he was a popular, outgoing student and earned varsity letters in football and basketball. Because he was bright, well spoken, and a good athlete, his friends assumed he would go on to college with a scholarship. In reality, however, Richard's reading had remained stalled at primary school levels.

In the middle of his junior year in high school, his mother moved the family to Florida. Richard reenrolled in school there but dropped out to take on a full-time job in a fast food restaurant. A year later he returned to Boston, where he has since worked in a number of jobs, including security guard, dishwasher, and clothing salesman.

Here is Richard's reading profile:

Rosner	1.5 GE
Word analysis	1.5 GE[8]
Word recognition	2 GE
Spelling	1.5 GE
Oral reading	4 GE
Comprehension	4 GE
Oral vocabulary	6 GE

Richard's print skills (word analysis, word recognition, and spelling) were much weaker than his meaning-related skills (oral reading, comprehension, and oral vocabulary). His grade-equivalent adult scores should not automatically be interpreted to mean that he is identical to a first grader in word analysis or identical to a sixth grader in oral vocabulary. The miscue patterns of adults and children can be very different. In vocabulary, for example, Richard probably knows many words he has learned through his work experience and adult life that a sixth grader might not know, while a sixth grader might have learned the meanings of social studies and science words in school that Richard's reading difficulties prevented him from learning when he was that age.

Richard's basic word analysis skills were incomplete, and he seemed to lack confidence in the skills he possessed. His phonemic awareness was comparable with what would be expected at the end of first grade. His word recognition and oral reading miscues involved guesses based on the first few letters of a word and its overall shape, again with much uncertainty about vowels: *witch* for *watch, courage* for *carriage,* and *nicest* for *notice,* for example. However, in the oral reading of passages, he was able to use the context to monitor and self-correct some of his decoding mistakes. Although Richard scored at 4 GE in oral reading, his reading was not fluent; it contained several self-corrections, hesitations, and repetitions.

Silent reading comprehension was an area of relative strength for Richard, but he took more than ten minutes to read and answer four questions on the 100-word 4 GE passage, suggesting much rereading and self-correcting as he laboriously constructed the meaning of the passage. At 6 GE, Richard's oral vocabulary was his strongest skill overall. However, some responses reflected his word analysis and phonological difficulties: he described the word *console* as, "When you put something where you can't see it," confusing it with *conceal.* Other responses were vague and imprecise: the *environment,* he said, is "a place you like."

Richard's severe difficulties with decoding and spelling led to his placement in an adult reading class that focused on developing reading fluency and accuracy. Even though silent reading comprehension skills were not explicitly emphasized in this class (although lots of fiction, poetry, and plays were read), after five months Richard began to score at or above 6 GE in silent reading tests, as long as they were administered untimed. It appeared that his modest progress in the print aspects of reading had begun to help him unlock his strengths in the meaning aspects of reading.

Based on his adult testing, it is very clear that he is burdened by the kinds of phonological difficulties identified in *PRD*, so it is not surprising that Richard was eventually identified by the public schools as in need of extra help in basic reading. Unfortunately he did not get this help until he was in the fifth grade and already several years behind in reading. Moreover, we have no information about the nature of the help he received. If the recommendations in *PRD* had been followed when Richard was a young child, his potential reading difficulties would have been identified much earlier.

Moving from one school district to another, as Richard's family did, is bound to constitute a risk factor for any child, and this is especially true for children with reading disabilities. We can hope that *PRD* will help to make classroom teachers more aware of the need to evaluate a new student's reading immediately, perhaps simply by using an informal reading inventory, so that even children who must change schools frequently can receive extra help in reading as early as possible.

After a year of adult reading classes, Richard had to drop out to work two jobs to help support his mother when she became ill. As in childhood, Richard's education had once again been interrupted.

Comparing Richard with the previous student, Joseph, is instructive, because both appear to have roughly similar risk factors in the area of phonological processing. However, the social and historical milieus in which their reading developed were quite dissimilar. Joseph's parents were not literate, few books were available in his childhood, and he attended poor, rural schools. Richard's mother was highly literate, and Richard attended urban schools some forty years later, when it was routine to diagnose and attempt to treat children with reading disabilities. The practical difference between Richard's word recognition score at 2 GE and Joseph's at 1 GE is much greater than a one-grade difference might mean at higher levels—for example, between 7 GE and 8 GE. As a result of his eleven years of schooling, including some direct help in reading, Richard can recognize enough words to be able to perform somewhat laboriously in oral reading at 4 GE and equally laboriously in silent reading at 4 GE as well, relying heavily in both areas on his context analytical skills. Joseph, on the other hand, recognizes too few words to be able to do any meaningful independent reading at all—too few words to be able to create a context to analyze. Because Richard's sister and many of his high school friends graduated from college, Richard locates himself very much in the literate world. He knows that he would need to read independently to reach his career goal of joining the military. Joseph has organized his life so that he can function with external networks of support in literacy. Joseph views himself as generally successful in life; Richard, as yet, does not.

Rose, a Reading-Disabled Intermediate Reader

Rose is a divorced mother of two who grew up in a white blue-collar family in a series of small towns in eastern Massachusetts. She was age twenty-eight at the time this case history was compiled in 1993 and enrolled in a welfare-to-work program near Boston. Her pattern of reading scores fits that of the reading-disabled adults whom Chall (1994) described. Her print skills (including phoneme awareness) were much weaker than her comprehension and vocabulary skills. Her strong word analysis score suggested that she had, however, mastered basic phonics (consonant sounds and long and short vowels). Reflecting this, her reading of short words was accurate, but she had difficulty on longer, polysyllabic words.

She remembered having a formal evaluation for learning disabilities in kindergarten: "From the beginning I was in special needs [classes]." When asked what extra help she had received in reading, Rose remembered very little attention to her reading. She attributed this to the fact that her schooling occurred during a period of cutbacks in special education and that she and others her age were part of "a lost generation that was just passed on from one year to the next." In fact, she has very few memories of her primary grades at all, except that she got into trouble at school "for always hiding in the closet and refusing to come out." Rose's life outside school was traumatic in the extreme. She was abused sexually during four separate periods in her childhood, from age four through fourteen, by several different male relatives and neighbors. In addition, her mother was an alcoholic who abused her and her siblings verbally and physically.

Rose graduated from high school in a suburb of Boston and went to work as a housekeeper at a hospital. During this time she sometimes experienced cocaine and alcohol problems. She eventually ended up in an abusive marriage to a man with a history of mental illness and violent brushes with the law. Although she tried to leave her husband several times, his threats against her and their children prevented her from doing so. Finally, after he was arrested and imprisoned for the rape of a woman in a shopping center, Rose was able to divorce him. While on welfare, she began to receive counseling and psycho-therapy for the first time in her life.

Rose explained that her psychiatrist had not been sure how to char-acterize her condition. As in some forms of schizophrenia, Rose heard voices, but the voices had names and defined personalities: "Sally," who was passive and accommodating, and "Kevin," who was mean and domineering. Her psychiatrist told Rose that she may have been on the verge of developing "multiple personality disorder" just when her therapy and antipsychotic medication intervened. Rose reported that her therapy had been unusually successful. After eighteen months of treatment, her medication was reduced and eventually discontinued, and her twice-weekly talk therapy sessions were reduced to monthly telephone check-ins with her therapist. After discontinuing the med-ication, Rose reported that she still heard the voices occasionally (Sally more than Kevin) but was able to minimize their effects by telling her-self "they're both coming from me."

Here is Rose's reading profile:

Rosner	1 GE
Word analysis	3 GE
Word recognition	3 GE
Spelling	3 GE
Oral reading	5 GE
Comprehension	7 GE
Oral vocabulary	6 GE

The profile dates from the period just before her antipsychotic medication was reduced, so it is possible that the medication may have temporarily depressed her functioning in reading. After ten months of twenty-hours-per-week instruction in reading, writing, math, and computer skills, Rose boosted her score on a timed silent reading test to 9.5 GE. She and her teachers felt that this improvement was due partly to the instruction she had received and partly to the fact that she was no longer taking the psychoactive medication. The following fall semester, Rose planned to enroll in a community college wood-working class to develop a portfolio that she could use to apply for a cabinet-making program at a private art school.

Rose's childhood, for all its horror and abuse, did include the presence of books and literacy-related activities in her home. Her teachers seemed to realize that she was in need of special education services, but Rose was unable to remember much about the nature of the help she received in school, so we cannot judge the content or effectiveness of her schooling. Was she placed in special education classes because of poor reading skills or because of troubling behavior stemming from sexual abuse? Was her behavior so troubling that it masked reading problems? In any case, somewhere along the way she acquired basic phonics skills. Building on this firm foundation, her adult education teachers were able to give Rose systematic practice with polysyllabic words and plenty of oral reading. In a relatively short time, her ability to decode longer words improved dramatically, and her silent reading rate also improved from about 100 words per minute to about 160.

Rose's reading disability may have hurt her reading development and educational success less than the extreme psychological trauma of her childhood, teenage, and young adult years. Compared with adults like Joseph or Richard, Rose's reading disability seems quite moderate to mild. Despite her difficulties with phoneme awareness, word recognition, and spelling, Rose's ability as an adult to improve in decoding at the syllable level with coaching and practice suggests that she is able to use orthographic patterns to read more difficult words. (See Bruck, 1992, Adams, 1994, & Blachman, 1997, on this point concerning how much phoneme awareness is necessary to read.) Like the adults in Bruck's study, Rose has great difficulty with phoneme awareness at the level of manipulating individual sounds, but she is able to perform tasks involving onset and rime, or word families, and use that awareness to read. Typical of readers with word recognition difficulties, Rose's oral reading (where she can use context support) at 5 GE is considerably stronger than her isolated word recognition (where there is no context) at 3 GE.

Rose's story serves as a reminder that when analyzing adult readers, we need to bear in mind more than the social risk factors that may have contributed to their reading development; we also need to consider other aspects of their life histories that have shaped that development. But this is not easy or always possible when it comes to trauma and mental illness. Rose's ABE teachers made what proved to be effective decisions about her reading instruction based solely on her initial reading assessment and ongoing evaluations of her classroom progress, months before she had disclosed to them any of her psychiatric history. But without the success of her psychotherapy, it is unlikely that she would have made the progress in reading that she did. In any case, teachers and researchers need to know more about the effects (both long term and current) of psychiatric and emotional disorders and the medications used to treat them on the reading of adult learners.

Jissette, an Advanced ESOL Student in ABE

Jissette, a native speaker of Spanish who was born in Puerto Rico, was thirty-two years old at the time she was assessed in 1993. Like Rose, she was a divorced mother enrolled in a welfare-to-work program near Boston. At the time of assessment, Jissette spoke fluent, grammatically correct English.

Jissette spent her early years in a small agricultural and marketing town in the mountains of Puerto Rico. There was no kindergarten, so she entered school in first grade at age six. She recalled that learning to read was easy for her: "I read like machine—sometimes too fast. . . . The teacher used to say I read so fast I 'ate the punctuation.'" When she was age eleven, her family moved to Boston, where she was enrolled in a regular (that is, not bilingual, transitional, or ESOL) fifth-grade class. "At first I couldn't understand a word the teacher or other kids said . . . but twice a week they took me to this man who spoke Spanish, and that was the only part I liked. He started teaching me English." The ESOL tutoring continued through sixth grade, when Jissette's family moved to a neighborhood where a bilingual Spanish-English seventh-grade class was available. "I loved this class, and I got my first good grades since leaving Puerto Rico."

But then her family moved back to Puerto Rico, to a small city on the southwest coast of the island. "I had trouble again. The only class I got an 'A' in was English." Her family returned to the Boston area the next year, and Jissette enrolled in high school, where she enjoyed the ninth and tenth grades and developed an interest in modern dance. Then, at age sixteen, halfway through eleventh grade, "I quit like a stupid!"—and she moved in with her boyfriend. At age seventeen she gave birth to her first child. Several years later she met and married another man, and they had four children together. When her husband was jailed for a drug offense, Jissette applied for welfare to support her children. After a period of what she called "deep depression," Jissette joined a Pentecostal church. She credits the church members with giving her the support she needed to divorce her husband and return to school. Her educational goals were to earn a GED and then enter a training program to become a bilingual medical secretary.

Here is Jissette's reading profile:

Rosner	3 GE
Word analysis	3 GE
Word recognition	7 GE
Spelling	3 GE
Oral reading	7 GE
Comprehension	6 GE
Oral vocabulary	4 GE

Jissette's profile closely matches the "ESOL" pattern that Chall (1994) described: her print skills are much stronger than her meaning-based skills. Her miscues in word recognition and oral reading occurred primarily on high-level unfamiliar words, and they reflected confusion between Spanish and English, especially on cognates (*eemahgeenahteeve* for *imaginative*) and Spanish/English close cognates (*tronkeel* for *tranquil*).

The only factor that might have placed Jissette at risk for early reading failure in English was that she grew up in a Spanish-speaking rather than English-speaking family. The quality of her schooling, from elementary school in Puerto Rico through high school in the United States, seems to have been adequate, but the emotionally disruptive and linguistically confusing effects of her family's moves back and forth between Puerto Rico and the United States during her middle school years could have placed her at risk. Indeed, these linguistic and cultural switches may have contributed to Jissette's current occasional phonics confusions between the two languages. (Not reading much in either language after leaving high school probably contributed as much to the appearance of these difficulties when she was tested as an adult.) Despite the fact that her first school encounter with English could have been better than a twice-weekly pullout for ESOL tutoring, that tutoring and her bilingual class the following year were ultimately sufficient to help Jissette transfer her Spanish decoding skills to English.

The key to Jissette's success that offset these risk factors and allowed her to become fluent and automatic at English word recognition is probably the fact that she had already become a fluent reader—"like a machine"—in Spanish. A rule of thumb among many experienced teachers of adult ESOL is that if a student has fifth-grade or better reading skills in another alphabetic language, acquiring the alphabetic principle in English is usually not difficult.[9] This coincides with findings from Collier and Thomas (1988) showing that immigrant children have little long-term difficulty acquiring literacy in English if they arrive after third grade. They often show persistent lags if taught to read first in English. The reverse implications of this rule are important as well. If a student does *not* have 5 GE skills in NALS Level 1, ESOL teachers will need to teach English phonics more deliberately, following the general recommendations of *PRD* for children: direct, systematic, sequential teaching of the sound-symbol correspondences coupled with generous amounts of reading in interesting text at the appropriate level of challenge.

Although Jissette's strong decoding skills transferred from Spanish to English, her English vocabulary lagged. Nevertheless, Jissette's initial 4 GE score in oral vocabulary may not have been a true reflection of her long-dormant English vocabulary knowledge. Since leaving high school at age sixteen, Jissette had been living almost entirely among Spanish speakers, and what little reading she had done during this time was also primarily in Spanish. As Sticht (1988) and others have cautioned, when adults have been away from reading, test taking, and school for many years, their initial assessment scores may be unduly low simply because they are a bit rusty. They tend to return to higher, more accurate basal levels of achievement after a few weeks back in school have helped to eliminate this rustiness. In addition, Jissette's 6 GE score in silent reading comprehension suggests that when given context, she is good at figuring out the meanings of unfamiliar words; this strongly suggests that her expressive oral vocabulary test score of 4 GE is lower than the receptive vocabulary knowledge available to her for reading connected text.

Indeed, once in adult education classes, Jissette showed herself to be an exemplary vocabulary learner. She manifested a strong interest in words, took careful notes on word meanings, and asked clarifying questions about the nuances and multiple uses of words she encountered in reading. With a minimal amount of direct instruction, Jissette was able to apply her strong Spanish print skills to make vocabulary associations between Spanish-English cognates. Again, her Spanish reading ability was the key, because Spanish-English cognates are much more apparent in print than in oral language.

Although her attendance was spotty because of her children's frequent bouts with asthma, Jissette, like Rose, made excellent progress in her ten months of classes. By the end of the school year, when she took a timed, norm-referenced test, she had raised her vocabulary to 6.4 GE and her reading comprehension to 8.7 GE. The following year Jissette enrolled in a GED program, after which she planned to exploit her Spanish-English skills by studying to become a bilingual medical secretary.

Terry, a Pre-GED Reader

Terry is an African American, born and raised in Boston. She was twenty-eight years old, the mother of two, and attending a welfare-to-work program when she was assessed in 1993. Terry's parents were both literate: her father was a retired Coast Guard officer and worked for a car dealership, and her mother was a licensed practical nurse.

Terry did not recall having any problems with early reading in kindergarten or first grade. However, her teachers must have detected some difficulties, because she was referred for Title 1 help halfway through first grade.[10] She went to the school's resource room four times a week to work with the reading specialist. At first she was not happy about being pulled from class, "but I liked it once I got to know the teacher and realized I wasn't different from the other kids. The reading teacher was really nice." The Title 1 instruction must have been regarded as successful by her teachers, because it was discontinued after Terry's first-grade year.

Terry's father died when she was in third grade, but the family's economic situation remained sound because their house was paid for and her mother continued to work. Terry reports that she was successful and happy in school through fifth grade:

Then the racial problems [the Boston school busing crisis of 1974] were starting. They were going to send me to . . . [school] in South Boston, which my mother did not want, because they were stoning the buses down there. So she sent me to live with my aunt in the suburbs. It was nice there, but too "country" for me. There were like five black kids in the whole school. But I liked it. I got interested in volleyball and gymnastics and won some trophies.

Two years later, Terry returned to the Boston schools for seventh grade. In May of her eighth-grade year, her mother died of cancer. "I missed my eighth-grade graduation, but one teacher was very nice and took me and my sister out to dinner to make up for it."

Terry and her younger siblings moved in with a friend of their mother, and the following fall Terry entered high school. From the beginning, she recalls, "I got hooked up with the wrong people," and it was during this time that Terry began to have trouble with alcohol.

In the summer following her freshman year, at age fifteen, Terry discovered she was five months pregnant. She did not return to high school but moved in with her older brother, who was living in the family house. However, he was dealing drugs and treated her abusively, so after her son was born, Terry moved out, rented an apartment, and tried to survive on her parents' social security benefits and Aid for Families with Dependent Children (welfare).

In the intervening years, Terry lost and regained custody of her son and enrolled four separate times in ABE programs to try to get her GED. Eventually she moved to a city near Boston, where she now resides with her first child and a second son born in 1992. She was no longer in contact with this child's father and supported both children with grants from welfare. Terry believed that her problems with alcohol kept her from earning her GED or acquiring job training: "Last year when my brother died of AIDS I got scared. Where has my life been going? When I'm not in school and [when I'm] doing nothing, my drinking gets worse and I get depressed."

In 1993 she and her younger son (who was diagnosed with lead poisoning) enrolled in an Even Start Family Literacy Program. Through that program Terry completed her GED in 1995. She planned to enroll in a culinary arts school to become a chef, an interest she acquired as a little girl from her father, who had been a chef in the Coast Guard.

Here is her reading profile:

Rosner	1 GE
Word analysis	3 GE
Word recognition	10 GE
Spelling	5 GE
Oral reading	12 GE
Comprehension	6 GE
Oral vocabulary	7 GE

Despite difficulties with reading in first grade, Terry's print skills were very strong in word analysis and word recognition and relatively strong in oral reading. Terry's surprisingly low phonological awareness and spelling scores may represent the persistence into adulthood of the phonological difficulties (see Bruck, 1992) that perhaps led her teachers to place her in Title 1 when she was a first grader.[11] Like Rose, Terry has an excellent grasp of basic phonics at the letter-sound level, possibly as a result of the Title 1 instruction. Terry's spelling miscues were usually phonetically correct, involving the omission of virtually silent letters (*goverment*) or reproducing what she heard in her own Boston accent, in which the letter *r* is often vestigial (*excesize* for *exercise*). Terry mastered the 12 GE oral reading passage, but closer scrutiny of her self-corrections, hesitations, and repetitions reveals her level of fluent, effortless reading to be somewhat lower, at about 7–8 GE.

Terry's 6 GE score in silent reading comprehension may be lower than her actual level of functioning. She narrowly missed answering a sufficient number of multiple-choice questions correctly to pass the 7 and 8 GE passages, but she gave excellent oral summaries of both passages, and one month later she scored 8.9 GE on a timed test of silent reading comprehension. Terry's expressive vocabulary at 7 GE is typical of pre-GED learners, almost to the point of defining readers in this cluster. The vocabulary development of these students probably slowed after they left high school and did not grow much in literate, academic areas during the intervening years.

In summary, Terry appears to have begun first grade with a personal risk factor in the area of phonological processing (as revealed by her phonological awareness and spelling), but early intervention may have served to minimize its effects on her word recognition and fluency. Her adult reading development seems to be more the product of risk factors that caused her to leave school after ninth grade. This in turn was probably related to family tragedies and dislocations stemming from the deaths of her parents and the historical factor of the Boston school busing crisis of the mid–1970s. Students like Terry remind us that eliminating or minimizing early reading risk factors is not sufficient. Those with multiple risk factors will remain at risk throughout their school years.

In Strucker's 1995 study, the cluster of which Terry was a member had the highest percentage of high school dropouts—higher even than clusters of less skilled readers. Having become relatively strong decoders and fairly fluent readers coming out of third grade, readers like

Terry fell behind in the vocabulary and content areas in middle school and high school, and eventually they dropped out. In these respects they closely resemble the young readers whom Chall, Jacobs, and Baldwin described in *The Reading Crisis* (1990).

Generally the ABE system is quite successful at helping students with a profile like Terry's to earn their GED. In a year or less of work on content-area reading comprehension, math, and essay writing, these students usually gain the mixture of knowledge and test-taking skills they need to pass the GED. One area of concern, however, is that such students often just squeak through with low passing scores; the correspondingly low levels of skills they have attained may make it difficult for them to succeed in postsecondary education and thereby increase their earning power. In a finding that may relate the importance of adequate skills for minority students, Tyler, Murnane, and Willett (in press) concluded that "basic skills matter more in determining the earnings of nonwhites than they do in determining the earnings of young white dropouts."

Brian, an Advanced Adult Reader

Brian is white, and at the time of testing in 1994 he was forty-three years old and unmarried. Although he had graduated from high school in 1970, he was referred to a literacy program for reading assessment by a teacher running a computer accounting course for a local veterans' organization. She was concerned that his 10 GE score in word recognition on a screening test might indicate that he would have trouble understanding the course material. Further assessment revealed that although Brian had substantial spelling and phonics difficulties, he was nevertheless able to comprehend expository text at slightly above 12 GE. With minimal tutoring in writing, Brian completed the accounting course successfully.

Brian came from a literate family: both parents had graduated from high school, and his father was an electrician and his mother was a medical transcriptionist. Brian reported that he and his siblings were read to as children and that books were plentiful in his home when he was growing up. He did not attend kindergarten and began his first-grade year in parochial school, but he reported that he was kicked out for behavior problems and completed first grade in public school. Brian remembered that "reading was a little slow in the beginning. . . I had a lot of help from my mother, but I did learn to read OK."

Spelling was especially difficult for him throughout school, he recalled, and it has remained a problem area for Brian in adult life.

When he was about to enter high school, his parents sent him to live with a childless uncle and aunt in Norfolk, Virginia. "My parents decided there was too much going on here," Brian explained. "It was the '60s and there were a lot of drugs around." He enjoyed living with his uncle and aunt, and he felt that he became a better reader in high school because of the challenging material he was given to read. He especially remembered how much he enjoyed reading Shakespeare's plays in eleventh grade. "When I turned 18 in 1970," he recalled, "the Vietnam War was on. I had a low number [in the draft lottery], so I enlisted. I spent five years in the Army, two tours in Vietnam. I first started reading on my own in the service because there was nothing to do a lot of the time. I found a series of action-adventure books that I really liked, and I read all of them."

After leaving the army, Brian tried his hand at a number of careers:

> My MOS [military occupational specialty] was just infantry, so when I got out I wasn't qualified for anything. I started doing construction and a little carpentry. I went to community college for hotel management, but I didn't finish because the reading was too much. I went back to construction, tried roofing for a while, made storm doors and windows, and even tried starting my own small construction business.

Brian had always made a good living in construction, but he began to worry that once he got into his forties, he would begin to have serious health problems if he stayed in the building trades. It was then that he enrolled in and successfully completed his computer accounting course. He has since found a job in that field.

Although Brian is not an ABE student (he graduated from high school, and the job training program he was enrolled in was not part of the ABE system), he is typical of many adult readers who want to succeed in the postsecondary system. We have included his case study because his adult reading profile suggests that he had some early reading difficulties in first grade that were at least partly overcome with timely help from his mother. But notice Brian's report that in community college: "The reading was too much." This was a fairly common complaint of advanced post-GED level readers in Brian's cluster. Many had tried community college or four-year colleges but dropped out because they had trouble keeping up with the volume of reading and had trouble writing papers.

Here is his reading profile:

Rosner	2 GE
Word analysis	2 GE
Word recognition	10 GE
Spelling	4 GE
Oral reading	12 GE
Comprehension	12 GE
Oral vocabulary	12 GE

Brian's profile is marked by strong meaning-based skills and significantly weaker print-based skills: 12 GE or higher[12] in silent reading comprehension, oral vocabulary, and oral reading, but much weaker scores in phoneme awareness, word analysis, and spelling, and a slightly weaker score in word recognition. Brian's word analysis performance was very weak, especially at the level of individual letter sounds: he was able to supply correctly only thirteen of twenty-one consonant sounds in isolation. Although his oral reading was at least 12 GE, he barely met the minimum error criteria for the 10 GE and 12 GE passages. Moreover, his reading was not fluent; it included numerous repetitions and self-corrections, and by 12 GE had become very slow and labored. Spelling mastery at GE 4 means that Brian was unable to spell correctly 5 GE words such as *island, improve, listen, special,* and *neighbor.*

Although Brian reported no formal diagnosis of reading disability in childhood, he resembles the "partially compensated dyslexics" described in a study of successful adult dyslexics (Fink, 1998). The partially compensated dyslexics in Fink's study averaged 16.9 GE (slightly above the fourth year of college) in silent reading comprehension. But on the Diagnostic Assessments in Reading (DAR, the same battery Brian received), 30 percent of this group were below 12 GE in word recognition, 56 percent were below 12 GE in oral reading accuracy, and 79 percent were below 12 GE in spelling. In an oral reading task of real-word passages that included occasional pseudowords, the compensated dyslexic group read at less than one-fourth the rate of normal controls in words per minute (Fink, 1998).

So if a reader like Brian is able to comprehend at or near college level, what is the problem? We need to take into account the actual demands of postsecondary education. Depending on the particular course of study, college programs can require hundreds of pages per week of "reading to learn the new," term papers, and written exams. Although Brian mastered 12 GE in oral reading, his many repetitions and self-corrections at levels 8 through 12 suggest that his level of fluent and effortless reading might be considerably below this, perhaps closer to 6–7 GE. This level may explain why Brian found the reading in his college courses to be "too much." With regard to Brian's 4 GE spelling, computer spell checkers (which were not available when he first tried college in the mid–1970s) could be of great assistance to him. But the function of spell checkers is to flag spelling errors *after* they have been made. At adult GE levels 4 and below, spellers such as Brian report that their spelling problems sometimes inhibit their expression; too often the content of what they write is influenced by what they can spell (Strucker, 1995).

In recent years colleges and community colleges have instituted programs in reading, writing, and study skills specifically designed to help adults (including former ABE students) make the transition to postsecondary education. (See Chapter Four for a full discussion of the issues involved in this transition.) These programs also try to help adults choose a field of study matched to their strengths. In this regard, the computer accounting training program was a good choice for Brian. Although it required some precise reading, the volume of that reading was relatively light. And in addition to accounting training, the program allowed Brian to acquire touch-typing and word processing skills, including use of the spell checker, that may help him to write more fluently.

SUGGESTIONS FOR IMPROVING ADULT LITERACY PRACTICE AND RESEARCH

The case studies reflect the wide variety of pathways that can lead to inadequate literacy levels in adulthood. Most of these adult poor readers suffered the risk factors identified in *PRD* as contributing to poor literacy outcomes, but their difficulties were also likely exacerbated by life circumstances not directly relevant to literacy (Rose, Terry, and Jissette) or by the cumulative effects of poor reading referred to as Matthew effects (Joseph and Richard). Now we turn to suggestions for improving adult literacy practice and research, based on the *PRD* findings.

Children's Reading Difficulties
Illuminate Adult Literacy Learning

The case studies illustrate the fact that many of today's adult literacy students were yesterday's at-risk children. Moreover, for people like these adults, significant risk factors were present in the early stages of learning to read. Two recommendations for practitioners and researchers flow from this understanding:

- We should attempt to find out as much as possible about the childhood literacy experiences of adult literacy students, including parents' level of education, access to literacy activities, and history, if any, of reading problems.

- Because early reading difficulties can affect later reading ability (even for relatively successful readers at the pre-GED level), adult literacy practitioners need to be aware of the entire continuum of reading development, including the period of kindergarten to third grade covered in *PRD*. Practitioners need to be able to determine the effect a processing problem that originated in early reading may be having on the progress of an intermediate or GED-level adult reader. Components testing can help with this (Chall & Curtis, 1990; Roswell & Chall, 1994; Strucker, 1997). We need more research on what instructional approaches might work for these intermediate adult readers. Is it necessary for such students to review and master all of basic phonics, or are there shortcuts that would get better results?

Even if the field of adult literacy were to adapt the *PRD* recommendations in early reading instruction to the needs of adult learners and address their processing difficulties, the field would still be faced with some of the Matthew effects of early reading difficulties in the ABE and ESOL population. Specifically, if early processing problems adversely affected the middle school stages of reading to learn when these adults were children (Chall, 1983; Stanovich, 1986), then they tend to have difficulties in three related areas:

- Vocabulary knowledge and vocabulary acquisition skills
- Different genres of decontextualized written language
- Background knowledge acquired from school subjects

Although the ESOL population generally does not include a high percentage of people with phonologically based processing problems, because many of them were not able to complete high school (or even middle school), they also have difficulties in the above three areas, compounded by having to take on these problems in English.

Few research and intervention studies have been done on the degree to which this gap in skills and knowledge from middle school or high school must be addressed to allow for self-sustaining reading development in adult life and to allow these adults to read to learn at the postsecondary level. Do we have to fill in all or most of the missing skills and knowledge, or, as Sticht (1975, 1987) argued, can we help adults build their reading outward from a narrower, perhaps job-related foundation of skills and knowledge? These questions are not only important to adult educators; they are also central for middle and high school educators who teach at-risk adolescents.

Reading disabilities of presumed neurological origin played a dominant role in the severe reading difficulties of Joseph and Richard and appear to have contributed to a lesser extent to the more moderate-to-mild reading difficulties of Rose, Terry, and Jissette. What does the presence of such reading difficulties imply for instructional methods for ABE students? This question was addressed in a comprehensive and thoughtful review by Fowler and Scarborough (1993), who concluded that whether an adult reader meets various K–12 legal definitions of reading disabilities or learning disabilities may be of more theoretical than practical significance for instructional purposes. The authors reviewed the research on successful instructional approaches for children who were classified as reading disabled and children who are simply poor readers, and they also surveyed the more limited research on adult literacy students. The research on both children and adults indicated that poor readers who had been formally classified as reading disabled and poor readers who had not been so classified shared persistent difficulties with word recognition, fluency, and reading rate—so-called print skills.

Moreover, the authors reported that the approaches that were successful in remediating these word recognition difficulties among reading-disabled adults were also successful with other poor readers. Fowler and Scarborough also emphasized the need to assess the various components of reading so that adults with severe word recognition and fluency problems could be identified and receive instruction specifically designed to address those needs.[13]

Although we agree with Fowler and Scarborough's conclusions, we are concerned that some policymakers or practitioners who may not have read their report in its entirety may misinterpret the authors' observation that "it matters *little* [emphasis ours] whether a reading problem stemmed originally from a localized intrinsic limitation, from a general learning problem, or from inadequate educational opportunity" (1993, p. 77).

There are important instances in which we believe it matters more than "little." For example, in the case of adult beginning readers, it is true that the best-practice instructional methods may not differ; generally structured language approaches such as the Wilson Reading System and Orton-Gillingham are effective with students who are known to be reading disabled as well as with students for whom that determination has not been made. However, speaking practically, *the pace of instruction and amount of repetition needed* can vary quite a bit, depending on whether a student is severely phonologically disabled (like Joseph), somewhat less so (like Richard), or not phonologically disabled at all. If teachers are unaware of the issue of pace, they can give up too soon on an adult beginner who is making slow initial progress.[14]

With intermediate readers such as Rose or Terry, the issue of the pace of instruction is also important. Students at 6–8 GE who have word recognition difficulties may not progress as fast as those who do not have such difficulties. For example, such students may need more practice than others with polysyllabic words encountered in high school–level reading. The level at which they read fluently and effortlessly may be well below their tested level of silent reading comprehension. How are teachers to know this? As Fowler and Scarborough point out, ABE teachers need to understand the nature of reading disability, even though a formal diagnosis may not be possible or necessary for most of their students, if they are to teach the right stuff in the right way. The place to start is with assessments that go beyond the traditional group-administered silent reading tests. Such tests do not indicate whether someone who scores above 6 GE may still require instruction to improve word recognition, fluency, and rate. ABE programs often assume that all students who enter scoring at 8 GE or above in silent reading are immediately ready to make rapid progress toward the GED in the traditional classes that address the five GED content areas. But for students who are reading disabled (such as those whose scores are depicted in Figure 2.1), the 8 GE score may represent peak functioning that may not improve until they are able to improve their reading accuracy and rate.

From the perspective of ABE students themselves, the question of whether they are reading disabled can be significant, quite apart from the issue of what instructional methods should be used with them. Adults older than age fifty may have grown up before K–12 systems formally diagnosed reading disabilities; unfortunately, in many cases they were assumed by the schools and their families to be mentally retarded, and they were treated as such. In addition, in some states learning-disabled adults are eligible for vocational rehabilitation services if their learning disabilities can be documented. Students in welfare-to-work programs who are learning disabled can petition for more time to complete their education and job training. Similarly, reading-disabled students taking the GED may be eligible for accommodations in the administration of the tests. If ABE teachers are trained to recognize such reading difficulties, they may be able to advise students on whether they should seek a formal evaluation.

We are not suggesting that a formal learning disabilities apparatus similar to the K–12 special education bureaucracy be imported into ABE and adult ESOL. For the reasons we have discussed having to do with the difficulty of—to use Fowler and Scarborough's term—"disentangling" reading disabilities from other factors, the legalistic criteria of K–12 learning disabilities would be impossible to implement. This in itself is an important difference between K–12 reading and adult literacy. Moreover, many thoughtful researchers and practitioners have come to question the usefulness of these criteria and the expense and time needed to employ them in K–12 education. (See Spear-Swerling & Sternberg, 1996, and Foorman, Francis, Shaywitz, Shaywitz, & Fletcher, 1997, for reviews of this issue.)

In ABE and ESOL teachers are free to be what Mel Levine calls "phenomenologists"; that is, they can observe and diagnose a difficulty without having to name it or label the person who has the difficulty. They are then free to work with their student to address that difficulty using best instructional practice, without having to go through cumbersome and expensive classification procedures, some of which may be based on outdated understandings of brain functioning (Levine, 1994; Spear-Swerling & Sternberg, 1996).

We Need More Information About Middle School

PRD was limited to reviewing research about beginning readers and young children. There is a lot to learn about reading after grade 3, and it is possible that an entirely new set of reading challenges will emerge

in the middle school years for some children who are helped to negotiate the difficulties of the early grades with better prevention and better instruction. Thus, it is clear that we need to continue to investigate
the instructional strategies that work to promote comprehension,
analysis, word learning, inference, and critical thinking for children in
later elementary and secondary schools, and that such investigations
will benefit adult literacy instruction.

Adult Literacy Populations Are Changing

One of the reasons we have attempted to articulate the relevance of
*Preventing Reading Difficulties in Young Children for Adult Learning
and Literacy* to adult literacy is because of the dramatic shifts we are
now seeing in adult literacy learners. The increased proportion of
ESOL learners was noted above, but it should be pointed out as well
that a very large proportion of this ESOL group will probably be non-
or semiliterate in their first language. With the shifts in policies concerning welfare and work requirements for women, even those with
young children, it is almost inevitable that adult literacy programs will
be serving an increased proportion of women seeking job-related literacy skills. Many of these women will have well-developed but rusty
literacy skills, while others may have left school after having achieved
only rudimentary control over English literacy.

More Attention to Reading
in Professional Development

A major recommendation of *PRD* is that preservice teacher education
include both more and more thoughtful attention to reading; it is argued that to teach reading effectively, a teacher would need to understand something about language acquisition, linguistics, rhetoric,
bilingualism, and orthographic systems as well as pedagogical methods. It is further recommended that professional development in this
area be delivered in such a way that this full variety of topics can be
addressed, thereby giving the various adults (classroom teacher, reading specialist, tutor, ESOL teacher, and so forth) who deal with any
child learner a coherent view of literacy development and of the child's
needs. The call for elevated standards, strengthened professional development, and more coherent systems of instruction could also be
extended to those working with the adult learner. In fact, credentialing of adult literacy instructors is typically not required, nor are there

widely recognized programs of professional preparation for adult literacy teachers. Some adult literacy practitioners are, of course, credentialed K–12 teachers, but they may still have had rather little direct instruction in how people learn to read and none in how to address the learning needs of adults.

Social as Well as Academic Factors Play a Role

One of the lessons of the case studies we have presented, and one understood as well by every adult literacy teacher, is the degree to which progress toward high-level literacy for adults is threatened by their life circumstances: the difficulties they have attending class regularly and finding time to study outside class and the worries induced by familial disruption, illness, unemployment, residential uncertainty, and other such factors. These inevitably interfere with an optimal focus on learning to read. We cannot expect to solve the problems of adult literacy achievement by focusing exclusively on better methods for teaching reading. Improving the quality of adult learners' lives more broadly is not only socially responsible but necessary.

WHAT NEXT?

We hope that this summary of a report focused on child literacy learners will be of interest to adult literacy practitioners because the descriptions of literacy development, risk factors, and opportunities to learn have direct relevance to their work. It would be very useful to have a second report, analogous to *PRD*, focusing on the questions of risk, development, and instruction for learners in the middle grades and beyond. Such a report would raise new issues related to the older learners' special needs for support of vocabulary development, comprehension strategies, and ways of using literacy in seeking and transmitting knowledge. Even if such a study is not completed, though, we believe that certain extrapolations can be made from the information already gathered and reviewed and that this information should form a central core of content in the professional development of adult literacy teachers.

Appendix: The Tests Used

The Rosner in the score profiles refers to the Test of Auditory Awareness Skills (Rosner, 1975), a brief assessment of phonological awareness that begins by asking the respondent to perform a series of increasingly difficult tasks. First, he or she is asked to delete one word from two-word compound words, then syllables, then initial consonant sounds, then final consonant sounds, and finally to delete a single sound from a consonant blend. The GE scores reported for this test are based on Rosner's published norms for the various levels of task difficulty.

The cluster analysis of the 120 students for both the Rosner and various Diagnostic Assessments of Reading (DAR) components was based not on GE scores but on standardized scores. The DAR (Roswell & Chall, 1992) was developed for use with adults or children based on assessment practices used in the Harvard Reading Laboratory and the Harvard Adult Literacy Initiative.

The DAR Word Analysis Test assesses basic phonics up to about the third-grade level, using ninety-two items, including a respondent's ability to produce the consonant sounds and his or her skill at reading consonant blends, short vowels in isolation and in short words, the rule of silent *e*, and vowel digraphs. The GE scores were extrapolated from the similar Rowell-Chall Test of Word Analysis Skills, which gives estimates of the grades at which students normally acquire the various skills assessed on both tests.

DAR word recognition measures word reading on graded word lists, from the beginning of first grade (1–1) through 12 GE. The DAR spelling, oral reading (graded short passages), and silent reading comprehension (short graded passages followed by questions and an oral summary) measures are criterion-referenced assessments of increasing difficulty. DAR word meaning is an expressive vocabulary test (similar to the WAIS-R) in which the respondent is asked to define groups of increasingly more difficult words.

Notes

1. To master the alphabetic principle is to understand that letters and combinations of letters correspond in a systematic way to the words and syllables of spoken language.

2. We will use the term *grade equivalent* (GE) when discussing adults. However, to say that an adult "reads at 5 GE" does not necessarily imply that he "reads like an average fifth-grade child." In vocabulary, for example, the adult may know the meanings of more words in areas pertaining to adult work life and psychological development than a fifth grader would, but the adult may not have learned or may not remember the meanings of some words associated with fifth-grade social studies or science. In the area of reading rate, average fifth graders can read about 150 words per minute with comprehension (Harris & Sipay, 1990), but many adult readers at 5 GE read more slowly. See also Pratt

and Brady (1988) on the differences between the reading of adult literacy students and of age-matched children.

3. The ARCS randomly sampled approximately six hundred students enrolled in ABE classes and four hundred students enrolled in ESOL classes in twenty-seven learning centers in Texas, Tennessee, and six states in the Northeast. The students were tested with a battery of reading tests, and those who spoke Spanish also were tested in Spanish reading. For logistical reasons, no students from corrections were included, nor were students participating in programs taught by volunteers.

4. The NALS assessed prose, document, and quantitative literacy using simulated real-world tasks of increasing difficulty and complexity in a sample of approximately twenty-six thousand adults, ages sixteen to sixty-five. NALS levels progressed from the most basic, Level 1, through the most difficult, Level 5. By way of illustration, prose literacy tasks at Level 1 "require the reader to read relatively short text to locate a single piece of information." Level 2 prose literacy tasks require in part "low-level inferences" and the ability to "integrate two or more pieces of information" (Kirsch, Jungeblut, Jenkins, & Kolstad, 1993).

5. Scholes (1991) also found that on this assessment, ESOL learners outperformed reading-disabled native speakers.

6. The Rosner is a test of phonological awareness including items that require phoneme deletion.

7. The method of teaching reading that Joseph described is one that Horace Mann railed against in the 1830s (Adams, 1994). It is particularly disastrous because it can lead children to think that there is a direct correspondence between the letter *names* in English and their sounds. To this day some adults from rural areas of the English-speaking Caribbean countries report having been taught with this method.

8. The highest extrapolated score possible for both phonemic awareness and word analysis is 3 GE.

9. Why this rule holds and under what circumstances and for which alphabetic languages would be important questions to explore through further research on adults.

10. Title 1, also called Chapter 1 at times, refers to special federal funding available to schools with a high proportion of children living in poverty.

11. Ten other adults in Strucker's 1995 study showed a similar pattern of very weak phonological awareness with very strong word recognition and oral reading fluency. Nine reported they had received early intervention in reading. This pattern is now being studied in larger samples of adult learners to estimate its prevalence and to learn what factors may contribute to it.

12. We describe his score as 12 GE or higher because the Diagnostic Assessments of Reading have a ceiling of 12 GE.

13. Strucker (1997) made a similar point.

14. Beginners who are not phonologically disabled are admittedly rare among learners who attended school in the United States. But ABE teachers occasionally meet students from some West African nations or parts of the English-speaking Caribbean who are not literate in any language but experience few difficulties learning to decode.

References

Adams, M. (1994). *Beginning to read.* Cambridge, MA: MIT Press.

Anderson, R. C., Hiebert, E. H., Scott, J. A., & Wilkinson, I. A. G. (1985). *Becoming a nation of readers: The report of the Commission on Reading.* Washington, DC: National Academy of Education, Commission on Education and Public Policy.

Blachman, B. A. (1994). What we have learned from longitudinal studies of phonological processing and reading, and some unanswered questions: A response to Torgesen, Wagner, and Rashotte. *Journal of Learning Disabilities, 27,* 287–291.

Blachman, B. A. (1997). Early intervention and phonological awareness: A cautionary tale. In B. A. Blachman (Ed.), *Foundations of reading acquisition and dyslexia.* Hillsdale, NJ: Erlbaum.

Bruck, M. (1990). Word recognition skills of adults with childhood diagnoses of dyslexia. *Developmental Psychology, 26,* 439–454.

Bruck, M. (1992). Persistence of adults' phonological awareness deficits. *Developmental Psychology, 28,* 874–886.

Chall, J. S. (1983). *Stages of reading development.* New York: McGraw-Hill.

Chall, J. S. (1994). Patterns of adult reading. *Learning Disabilities: A Multidisciplinary Journal, 5,* 29–33.

Chall, J. S., & Curtis, M. E. (1990). Diagnostic achievement testing in reading. In C. R. Reynolds & R. W. Kamphaus (Eds.), *Handbook of psychological and educational assessment of children* (Vol. 1). New York: Guilford Press.

Chall, J. S., Jacobs, V., & Baldwin, L. (1990). *The reading crisis.* Cambridge, MA: Harvard University Press.

Collier, V. P., & Thomas, W. P. (1988, April 7). *Acquisition of cognitive-academic language proficiency: A six-year study.* Paper presented at the annual meeting of the American Educational Research Association, New Orleans.

Cook, W. (1977). *Adult literacy education in the United States.* Newark, DE: International Reading Association.

Curtis, M. E. (1980). Development of the components of reading. *Journal of Educational Psychology, 72,* 656–669.

Fingeret, H. A. (1983). Social networks: A new perspective on independence and illiterate adults. *Adult Education Quarterly, 33,* 133–146.

Fink, R. (1998). Literacy development in successful men and women with dyslexia. *Annals of Dyslexia, 48,* 311–346.

Foorman, B., Francis, D. J., Shaywitz, S., Shaywitz, B., & Fletcher, J. (1997). The case for early intervention. In B. A. Blachman (Ed.), *Foundations of reading acquisition and dyslexia.* Hillsdale, NJ: Erlbaum.

Fowler, A. E., & Scarborough, H. S. (1993). *Should reading disabled adults be distinguished from other adults seeking literacy instruction? A review of theory and research.* Philadelphia: National Center for Adult Literacy.

Harris, A. J., & Sipay, E. R. (1990). *How to increase reading ability.* New York: Longman.

Hart, B., & Risley, T. R. (1995). *Meaningful differences in the everyday experience of young American children.* Baltimore: Paul H. Brookes Publishing Co.

Hunter, C., & Harman, D. (1985). *Adult illiteracy in the United States.* New York: McGraw-Hill.

Johnson, D., & Blalock, J. (Eds.). (1987). *Adults with learning disabilities.* New York: Grune and Stratton.

Johnston, P. H. (1985). Understanding reading disability: A case study approach. *Harvard Educational Review, 55,* 153–177.

Kirsch, I., Jungeblut, A., Jenkins, L., & Kolstad, A. (1993). *Adult illiteracy in America: A first look at the results of the National Adult Literacy Survey.* Washington, DC: National Center for Education Statistics, U.S. Department of Education.

Levine, M. (1994). *Educational care: A system for understanding and helping children with learning problems at home and in school.* Cambridge, MA: Educators Publishing Service.

National Assessment of Educational Progress. (1995). *NAEP 1994 reading: A first look—Findings from the National Assessment of Educational Progress* (rev. ed.). Washington, DC: U.S. Government Printing Office.

Ninio, A., & Snow, C. E. (1996). *Pragmatic development.* Boulder, CO: Westview.

Office of Vocational and Adult Education. (1996). *1996 enrollment of participants by instructional programs.* Washington, DC: OVAE, U.S. Department of Education.

Perfetti, C. A. (1985). *Reading ability.* New York: Oxford University Press.

Pratt, A., & Brady, S. (1988). Relation of phonological awareness to reading disabilities in children and adults. *Journal of Educational Psychology, 90.*

Read, C. (1988a). *Adults who read like children: The psycholinguistic bases. Report to the U.S. Department of Education.* Madison: Wisconsin Center for Education Research, University of Wisconsin–Madison.

Read, C. (1988b). *Phonological awareness and adult readers. Report to the U.S. Department of Education.* Madison: Wisconsin Center for Education Research, University of Wisconsin–Madison.

Read, C., & Ruyter, L. (1985). Reading and spelling skills in adults of low literacy. *Remedial and Special Education, 6,* 43–51.

Reder, S. (1995). *Literacy, education, and learning disabilities.* Philadelphia: National Center on Adult Literacy, University of Pennsylvania.

Reder, S. (1997). *First level learners: Characteristics and participation of adult basic literacy learners.* Bethesda, MD: Abt Associates.

Rosner, J. (1975). *Helping children overcome learning difficulties: A step-by-step guide for parents and teachers.* New York: Walker.

Roswell, F. G., & Chall, J. S. (1992). *Diagnostic assessments in reading.* Chicago: Riverside Press.

Roswell, F. G., & Chall, J. S. (1994). *Creating successful readers.* Chicago: Riverside Press.

Scholes, R. J. (1991). Phoneme deletion and literacy in native and non-native speakers of English. *Journal of Research in Reading, 14,* 130–140.

Scollon, R., & Scollon, S. (1982). *Narrative, literacy, and face in interethnic communication.* Norwood, NJ: Ablex.

Siegel, L. S. (1989). IQ is irrelevant to the definition of learning disabilities. *Journal of Learning Disabilities, 22,* 469–479.

Snow, C. E. (1983). Literacy and language: Relationships during the preschool years. *Harvard Educational Review, 53,* 165–189.

Snow, C. E., Burns, S., & Griffin, P. (1998). *Preventing reading difficulties in young children.* A report of the National Research Council. Washington, DC: Academy Press.

Spear-Swerling, L., & Sternberg, R. J. (1996). *Off track: When poor readers become "learning disabled."* Boulder, CO: Westview Press.

Spreen, O., & Haaf, R. G. (1986). Empirically derived learning disabilities subtypes: A replication attempt and longitudinal patterns over 15 years. *Journal of Learning Disabilities, 19,* 360–406.

Stanovich, K. (1986). Matthew effects in reading: Some consequences of individual differences in the acquisition of literacy. *Reading Research Quarterly, 21,* 360–406.

Stanovich, K. (1991). Discrepancy definitions of reading disability: Has intelligence led us astray? *Reading Research Quarterly, 26,* 360–497.

Sticht, T. (1975). *A program of army functional job reading training: Development, implementation, and delivery systems* (HumRRO-FR-WD(CA)–75–7). Alexandria, VA: Human Resources Organization.

Sticht, T. (1987). *Functional context education: Workshop resource notebook.* San Diego, CA: Applied Behavioral and Cognitive Sciences.

Sticht, T. (1988). Adult literacy education. In E. Rothkopf (Ed.), *Review of research in education.* Washington, DC: American Educational Research Association.

Sticht, T. (1998). *Beyond 2000: Future directions for adult education.* El Cajon, CA: Applied Behavioral and Cognitive Sciences.

Strucker, J. (1995). *Patterns of reading in adult basic education.* Unpublished doctoral dissertation, Harvard University Graduate School of Education, Cambridge, MA.

Strucker, J. (1997). What silent reading tests alone can't tell you. *Focus on Basics, 1,* 13–17.

Tannen, D. (Ed.). (1982). *Spoken and written language: Exploring orality and literacy.* Norwood, NJ: Ablex.

Tyler, J. H., Murnane, R. J., & Willett, J. B. (forthcoming). *Estimating the impact of the GED on the earnings of young dropouts using a series of natural experiments.* Cambridge, MA: National Center for the Study of Adult Learning and Literacy.

CHAPTER THREE

Youth in Adult Literacy Education Programs

Elisabeth Hayes

~~~

The growing number of youth enrolling in adult literacy education is a little-documented trend across the nation that is having a major impact on programs in some areas but appears to be unnoticed by educational policymakers and researchers. Relatively steady high school completion rates conceal the fact that a growing proportion of young adults is earning an alternative high school credential rather than completing a traditional high school program (National Center for Education Statistics, 1997b). Although not all of these youth enroll in adult literacy education, adult programs are serving increasing numbers of this population.

A central question is whether youth enrollments provide an opportunity for adult literacy education to serve dropouts as soon as possible after they leave school (thereby improving their ability to obtain better jobs, pursue further education, and contribute to their communities), or whether problems associated with serving these youth outweigh any benefits. The information I gathered for this chapter does not suggest a definitive answer to this question, but it does lay the groundwork for a more informed response. There is clearly a need for more research to determine, for example, whether adult literacy education is successful in helping these youth earn high school credentials. In addition, there are important policy issues, such as whether adult literacy programs should receive additional funding to serve such youth.[1]

DEFINITION OF TERMS

I use *adult literacy education* as an umbrella term to refer to several kinds of educational programs described here: adult basic education (ABE), consisting of basic skills instruction at a pre–high school level, and adult secondary programs (also referred to as high school completion programs) that provide instruction at a high school level and are typically oriented toward helping students earn one of several alternative high school credentials. Most frequently they prepare students to earn a certificate of General Educational Development (GED) by taking a five-part examination that assesses test takers' knowledge of content areas representative of high school curricula (accordingly, ABE classes are sometimes referred to as "pre-GED"). Another option, adult high school programs, allows students to obtain a school district diploma by earning high school credits through independent study or adult education classes. A third option for people in adult secondary programs is the External Diploma Program (EDP), which awards a diploma based on students' demonstration of proficiency in a number of academic and life skill areas, such as consumer knowledge and health and safety skills. The EDP is usually considered most appropriate for adults who have gained skills through life experiences, such as holding a job or managing a household. Presumably for that reason, it was not mentioned by respondents in the interviews I conducted for this chapter as an option for youth.

To understand youth enrollment in adult literacy education, it is also helpful to understand what other educational options are available to young dropouts. Typically the emphasis in most states has been on dropout prevention programs rather than programs for students who have already dropped out (Varner, n.d.). The most obvious option for dropouts is to return to traditional high school, unless they were expelled for disciplinary reasons. Some school districts offer at-risk students special programs, such as alternative high schools, teenage parent programs, and programs for substance abusers. In some cases, adult education programs have received funds from school districts and become formally designated as alternative high schools.

The federal Job Training Partnership Act (JTPA) of 1983 provides support for programs that combine job training and high school completion for dropouts. The 1994 School-to-Work Opportunities Act has promoted the development of school-to-work programs for out-of-school youth as well as those in school. However, despite this seemingly wide array of alternatives, most states do not have comprehensive policies or systems for serving dropouts. Accordingly, the availability of educational programs for dropouts can vary considerably from one state or school district to another.

For the purpose of this chapter, I use the terms youth or teens to refer to sixteen and seventeen year olds. I focused primarily on young people of these ages because they seemed to present the most distinctive issues and challenges while also representing the group with the most significant increase in number. These young people are likely to be enrolling in adult literacy education with little or no break after leaving high school. There are societal and familial expectations that they should be in school. State GED testing policies often place certain restrictions on their pursuit of an alternative credential. In addition, this group tends to be considered the responsibility of the public schools, while the more traditional target population for adult literacy education is people over the age of eighteen. However, I could not always exclude people outside this age group when collecting information. In some cases, the only statistics available are for a population defined as sixteen to eighteen or sixteen to twenty-one years old. Similarly, professionals in the field sometimes included people eighteen, nineteen, or twenty years old in discussions of issues related to youth enrollment. Thus I have tried to indicate when these older students were discussed. No magic age determines adulthood in terms of maturity levels, but specific ages do play a role in terms of issues such as the effects of legislation and responsibility for funding.

DOCUMENTING THE TREND

Obtaining concrete data on the number of youth enrolling in adult literacy education is a difficult task. In fact, data on youth are not compiled at the national level, and few states and programs could provide data on only sixteen and seventeen year olds alone. In this section, I report what data I could obtain about youth enrollments in adult literacy education. I also discuss two more indirect indicators of youth enrollment: data on school dropouts and GED testing statistics. In reporting these data, I do not make a distinction between youth enrolled in adult basic education versus those in GED or other high school completion programs. In general, this distinction was not made by the practitioners who gave me information. For the most part, practitioners described their work with youth in the context of high school completion classes. The primary exception to this tendency concerned programs in a few states with mandatory school attendance policies that prohibited youth from enrolling in GED preparation programs. In these cases, youth were sometimes enrolled in adult basic education until they reached the legal age for moving into GED classes. This emphasis on high school equivalency studies may not reflect teens' skill levels as much as the extent to which earning a credential is a driving force behind their participation in adult literacy education.

Adult Literacy Education Program Data

On the national level, the youngest age category for data reporting until 1997 was students sixteen to twenty-four years old. (The youngest age category was changed to sixteen to eighteen years for fiscal year [FY] 1997, but at the time I was collecting information, these data were not available on a national level.) Since the mid-1990s, the numbers in this category have not grown noticeably (P. Dorsey, U.S. Department of Education, personal communication, July 1, 1998).[2] Obviously, though, this category is too broad to indicate trends specifically in enrollment of younger teens. Yet it is worth noting that this age category represents a significant proportion of the total adult literacy education enrollments—approximately 37 percent in 1996. Some states have considerably higher proportions of enrollments in this age group. For example, in Louisiana, Kansas, and North Carolina, where I spoke to practitioners experiencing large youth enrollments, the proportion of sixteen to twenty-four year olds was 62 percent, 52 percent, and 47 percent, respectively. Conversely, there were also states with much lower proportions in this age group. For example, students ages sixteen to twenty-four make up only 19 percent of the 1996 enrollment in Massachusetts. These figures suggest that youth enrollments vary considerably in scope and, presumably, in impact among states. There does not seem to be an obvious relationship between youth enrollments in adult literacy education and state dropout rates. For example, in 1994–1995 Louisiana and Massachusetts had comparable dropout rates of 3.5 percent (National Center for Education Statistics, 1997b).

On the state level, most of the nineteen state directors who responded to my inquiries indicated that state-level data were limited to the national reporting category of ages sixteen to twenty-four up to FY 1997. Accordingly, most of them could not provide actual data on trends in youth enrollment statewide. However, the proportion of sixteen to eighteen year olds in programs for adults in 1997 is an indication of the significant presence of this group. Seven states providing information in this category reported that students sixteen to eighteen years old made up between 13 percent and 21 percent of the total adult literacy education population served. In Wisconsin, separate statistics have been compiled on sixteen to eighteen year olds who are served in adult literacy education through contracts with local high schools. The number of students in these programs grew from 673 in FY 1991 to 4,571 in FY 1997. Four state directors (North Carolina, South Dakota, Arkansas, Arizona) were able to provide separate statistics for sixteen to seventeen year olds over a period of several years. Data from each of these states indicated growth in the proportion of teenagers. For example, in South Dakota the proportion of this age group grew from 11.9 percent in FY 1995 to 20.6 percent in FY 1997. In Arizona, teenagers composed 14.5 percent of adult literacy education students in FY 1997, up from 5.1 percent in FY 1993. Other states described informal reports of growing numbers of teen enrollments. The state director in Kansas estimated that almost 60 percent of non-ESOL (English for speakers of other languages) students in many programs in her state were now youth.

Only three state directors who responded did not report data or observations of noticeable increases. In Michigan, new state legislation prohibits enrollment of students under the age of twenty in state-funded adult education programs, and there has been a decrease in number. I talked to program directors in the other two states (Iowa and Tennessee) that did not report a large increase in youth enrollment. Both programs, although not observing an increase in youth, were serving significant numbers of teenagers in school district–funded programs. I talked with a number of practitioners in other states who served youth in separately funded programs. This suggests that adult literacy education enrollment data will not provide a complete picture of how many youth are served by adult literacy education programs, since these figures are likely to include only students in federally funded programs, not those who are in classes funded through other sources.

I gathered program-level information from twenty-three practitioners in twenty states. Obviously one or two programs cannot be representative of trends in an entire state, but they did provide a varied picture of programs across the country. Most practitioners reported informal observations of increased youth enrollment. Among those who could provide statistics, there was considerable variability in the proportion of youth served by their programs. Several gave statistics on the enrollment of sixteen to eighteen year olds in 1997, which ranged from 16 percent to 50 percent. Five had data on 1997 enrollments of sixteen to seventeen year olds, which ranged from 14 percent to 30 percent. Even the programs with lower proportions of youth indicated that they were having significant effects on the program.

National Even Start data provide another indication of trends in youth enrollment in adult literacy education. According to Tracey Rimdzius of the U.S. Department of Education (Planning and Evaluation Services, personal communication, Aug. 17, 1998), the proportion of teen parents (those under age twenty) in Even Start programs grew from 9 percent in 1994–1995 to 13 percent in 1996–1997. Among new enrollees only, 17 percent were teen parents in 1996–1997, a trend partly attributed to welfare reform policies.

School Dropout Data

School dropout data are relevant in suggesting whether there has been an increase in the number of teenage dropouts that might increase the number of youth potentially seeking adult literacy education. Nationally, the percentage of students who dropped out of school in 1996 was 5 percent, a rate that has not changed considerably since the late 1980s (National Center for Education Statistics, 1997b). Some of these dropouts eventually return to traditional high school or some alternative program. Recent NCES data show an increase in the proportion of eighteen to twenty-four year olds who ultimately earn an alternative credential versus a traditional high school diploma. In 1988, the NCES began to collect data that distinguished regular graduation from alternative routes to earning a high school diploma. From 1988 to 1993, about 80 percent of eighteen to twenty-four year olds completed high school through regular graduation, and about 4.5 percent completed through an alternative route (the remaining 15 percent had not earned a credential). Since 1993, the percentage completing through regular graduation decreased nearly 5 percentage points to

76.4 percent in 1996, while that completing through an alternative route increased to 9.8 percent. This trend would be concealed if only the overall high school completion statistics for this age group were examined, since these have not changed substantially over the past decade; the overall rate was 84.5 percent in 1988 and 86.3 percent in 1996 (National Center for Education Statistics, 1997b).

The NCES does not report the ages at which the population completed an alternative credential, nor does it specify how the alternative was earned. Of course, not all youth who earn an alternative credential participate in an adult literacy education program. They may take the GED without attending classes, and a few states have permission to administer the GED for special cases in the context of traditional high schools. These youth may also earn another type of alternative credential developed by states or local districts. However, the rise in alternative credentialing does provide an indirect indication that more youth may be leaving school and entering alternative programs such as adult literacy education.

Other national data indicate that more dropouts are returning to complete their high school credential at relatively young ages. According to *The Condition of Education 1996* (National Center for Education Statistics, 1996, p. 50), dropouts from the 1990 high school sophomore class were more likely to return to school within two years than dropouts from the 1980 sophomore class. Although 66.4 percent of 1980 dropouts had not returned to school or earned a diploma two years after leaving school, only 42.5 percent of 1990 dropouts were still dropouts after two years of leaving school. By 1992, approximately 31.0 percent of 1990 dropouts were enrolled in some kind of educational program: 1.9 percent returned to a traditional high school, and 29.5 percent had entered an alternative program, which could include adult literacy education. Although these figures do not provide direct evidence of a growth in youth enrollment in ABE, they do indicate that dropouts who return to school are likely to be younger than in previous decades.

GED Testing Data

GED testing data offer some additional evidence that growing numbers of youth are seeking to earn alternative high school credentials. There have been variable trends since 1990, but overall the proportion of younger test takers has increased. The proportion of GED test takers ages sixteen to seventeen dropped somewhat from 10.2 percent in 1988 to 8.3 percent in 1991. Since 1991, however, the proportion has grown steadily to 14.6 percent of GED test takers in 1997 (GED Testing Service, 1988–1997). The proportion of test takers ages eighteen to nineteen in 1997 was 26.8 percent, contributing to a total of 41.4 percent of GED test takers who were under the age of twenty (GED Testing Service, 1988–1997). In serving such a high proportion of youth, the GED Testing Program is clearly serving a population much different from the one it was originally intended to serve. In terms of trends, it is notable that over two decades, the proportion of test takers under the age of twenty has not shown dramatic changes, varying between about 31 percent and 40 percent of the total test-taking population (National Center for Education Statistics, 1997a). The recent fluctuations may seem particularly dramatic since they have occurred in a relatively short time frame. Most recently, the proportion of sixteen to nineteen year olds taking the test grew from a low of 32.5 percent in 1992 to the current high of 41.4 percent. Notably, the proportion of sixteen to seventeen year olds grew more substantially in this five-year period (increasing from 8.7 percent to 14.6 percent of test takers) than that of eighteen to nineteen year olds (increasing from 23.8 percent to 26.8 percent of test takers) (GED Testing Service, 1988–1997).

Trends

This brief assessment provides indications of an overall trend toward greater youth enrollment in adult literacy education, although the extent of this trend is quite variable across states and programs. The exact number of students sixteen to seventeen years old has not been compiled by all programs, but among those that could provide statistics, there were often dramatic increases in youth enrollments. Over the past few years, the proportion of youth doubled and even tripled in some programs, with youth now accounting for up to a third or more of their total student enrollments. Annual high school dropout rates have remained fairly consistent over recent years. However, the number of dropouts who eventually earn an alternative high school credential has increased, and they are earning these credentials at younger ages. This trend may be linked to the recent growth in the proportion of GED test takers who are below the age of twenty.

EXPLAINING THE TRENDS

These trends are affected by broader national issues as well as by a diversity of state and local policies and populations. Some of these figures, particularly the GED testing data, raise the question of whether the currently climbing number of youth is really a novel and potentially lasting trend or part of a pattern of increasing and decreasing youth enrollment. This question was also raised by some of the long-term practitioners I interviewed, who described past periods of greater emphasis on serving youth in adult literacy education.

Increase in the Youth Population

More rapid growth in the number of youth in the overall population, relative to older age cohorts, may be one factor contributing to their increasing number in adult literacy education. According to the U.S. Bureau of the Census (1996), from 1990 to 1994 the number of youth of high school age (fourteen to seventeen years old) grew by 8.4 percent—higher than for any other age groups except adults ages thirty-five to forty-four and adults age seventy-five and older. In contrast, the number of adults ages eighteen to twenty-four actually declined by 5.8 percent. The growing youth cohort is particularly notable given that the number of fourteen to seventeen year olds overall declined by 17.5 percent between 1980 and 1990.

These figures suggest that while the overall high school dropout rate may have remained fairly constant in the early 1990s, the *actual number* of dropouts may have increased, reflecting the overall increase in the high school age population. In fact, from 1992 to 1996, the number of dropouts ages sixteen to twenty-four grew, with some fluctuations, from 3.4 million to 3.6 million (National Center for Education Statistics, 1997b). Furthermore, these figures suggest that the variations in proportions of young GED test takers, as well as youth participation in adult literacy education, may be attributable at least in part to the changing number of youth in the overall population.

Employment-Related Factors

Two additional factors that may be affecting youth enrollment in adult literacy education are the higher skill levels required for many jobs and the correspondingly higher educational levels expected of potential employees. Young dropouts are less employable than in the past and thus may recognize the importance of a high school credential at a younger age. There is mixed evidence of an increase in the skills required for all jobs, with some analysts pointing to a growing number of low-skill, but also low-wage, jobs (Bernhardt, Morris, Hancock, & Scott, 1998). It is evident that higher-level skills and more credentials are needed for employment that offers a living wage. In addition, it is taking longer for young workers to find full-time employment than it has in the past. A recent study found that high school dropouts in particular are more likely to experience intermittent unemployment and to rely on part-time jobs for more years than in the past (Bernhardt, Morris, Hancock, & Scott, 1998). One state director commented that up to the past decade or so, it was quite possible for youth who dropped out of school to find a job that paid a living wage—and often a higher salary than their well-credentialed teachers were earning! Now, however, such jobs are harder to find.

This situation may account for the increasingly higher educational aspirations of high school students in general. According to Forgione (1998), in 1992, 69 percent of high school seniors said that they hoped to graduate from college, compared with 39 percent of 1982 seniors. The proportion going directly on to college rose from 51 percent in 1982 to 65 percent in 1996. Some practitioners reported that the desire to go on to college was mentioned by some teen dropouts who enrolled in their adult literacy education programs.

Parents may now have higher educational expectations for their children and may put more pressure on their children to stay in school or earn an alternative credential. A number of practitioners mentioned parental expectations as one reason that youth enrolled in their programs. As one practitioner put it, parents are giving their children an ultimatum: stay in school or get out of the house. Those young people who have left school are not ready to work, so they enroll in adult literacy education. Perhaps the strong economy and low unemployment may mean that parents are more likely to have jobs and an income to support dropouts if they enroll in adult literacy education. In less fortunate times, they might instead be encouraging their children to find jobs and contribute to the family income or become self-supporting.

Educational Reform Efforts

School reform, a perennial issue, has surfaced as a particularly prominent national concern. The reform efforts are linked to concerns that schools are not adequately preparing youth for the increasingly so-phisticated demands of the workplace. The National Education Goals, the Improving America's Schools Act of 1994, and the 1994 School-to-Work Opportunities Act are several of the more prominent exam-ples of national efforts to spur school reform on state and local levels. Among other directives, states are being asked to develop standards for educational achievement, develop new means of assessing achieve-ment, prepare students for the workforce better, and develop more rigorous curricula. The National Education Goals established by the U.S. Department of Education include increasing high school com-pletion rates while instituting higher expectations for student perfor-mance, goals that may seem contradictory. In general, schools are expected to find alternative means of educating youth who in the past might have dropped out: "The pressures placed on the educational system to turn out increasingly larger numbers of qualified lifelong learners have led to an increased interest in the role that alternative methods of high school completion may play in helping some stu-dents meet these goals" (National Center for Education Statistics, 1997b, p. 1). These alternative methods may include adult literacy ed-ucation programs.

The national reform efforts provide a context and impetus for state legislation that directly or indirectly encourages young dropouts to en-roll in adult literacy education. States and local districts have great lee-way in deciding how to operate their educational systems, which makes it difficult to generalize on a national level. Many states were imple-menting their own legislative changes and reform efforts prior to the national legislation, and examples of how these have affected adult lit-eracy education are available from several states. In the mid–1980s, Wisconsin raised its compulsory school attendance age from sixteen to eighteen years to encourage more youth to complete high school. However, it soon became apparent that an alternative was needed for youth who were not able to succeed in traditional high schools. Ac-cordingly, the state passed legislation that allowed high schools to con-tract with adult literacy education programs to provide basic education and high school completion courses for youth ages sixteen to eighteen. The number of youth in these programs has grown dramatically since the early 1990s.

In 1992 the North Carolina Department of Public Instruction im-plemented a policy allowing local schools to count students who en-rolled in community colleges as transfers instead of dropouts. As a result, adult basic education programs (which operate primarily through the community colleges in North Carolina) saw a jump in the enrollment of sixteen to seventeen year olds from 4,205 in 1992–1993 to 12,229 in 1993–1994, with a slow increase to 15,514 in 1996–1997.

Up to 1993, Arkansas had a compulsory school law requiring students to remain in school until they graduated or reached the age of eighteen. In 1993, an additional law was passed that allowed a waiver for sixteen and seventeen year olds to leave school and enroll in adult literacy education with certain provisions. This led to an influx of youth into adult literacy education programs that reached a statewide high of 7,343 participants who were sixteen and seventeen years old in 1994. According to the state director, one year the enrollment of sixteen and seventeen year olds in adult literacy education represented 12 percent of all sixteen and seventeen year olds in the state.

In Kansas, already experiencing a considerable increase in youth enrollments, the legislature recently passed a new law that may increase these enrollments still further. The law raises the age of compulsory school attendance from sixteen to eighteen and strengthens penalties for truancy. However, parents can withdraw sixteen and seventeen year olds from school through a waiver process. According to the Kansas state director, parents whose children are sanctioned under the new, stricter truancy laws have essentially two choices: go to court and face potential penalties or withdraw their child from school. Apparently many parents are choosing the latter course and then enrolling their child in adult literacy education. Further, some courts are trying to mandate enrollment of fourteen and fifteen year olds suspended for truancy in adult literacy education because there is no other place to refer them.

In the early 1980s, reports such as *A Nation at Risk* (National Commission on Excellence in Education, 1983) severely criticized the quality of school curricula and levels of student achievement. In response, many states increased graduation requirements, insisting that students earn a larger number of credits and take more advanced academic courses. According to a U.S. Department of Education report (1994), there have been virtually no studies of the effects of these reforms on school dropout rates, which could lead to a greater enrollment in adult literacy education.

Anecdotal evidence from Louisiana suggests how such reforms could contribute to increased youth participation in adult literacy education. In a telephone interview, one adult literacy education program director explained that in the mid–1980s, the state board of elementary and secondary education began to raise the standards for high school graduation, implementing new requirements for completion of more academically rigorous course work. As a result, many youth who had difficulty meeting these requirements began to leave high school and enroll in adult literacy education. Their numbers became so significant that in 1991, federal grant monies intended for research, pilot efforts, and staff development were instead used to create a staff development conference on youth that was offered several times.

The unexpected effects of such policies have led some states to make policy revisions that may reduce the number of youth enrolling in adult literacy education, or at least limit the increase. The North Carolina policy of counting dropouts as transfers was reevaluated, and according to the state director, schools are now required to count such students as dropouts. It is too early to determine the impact of this change. Because of the huge number of youth enrolling in adult literacy education, Arkansas in 1995 instituted more requirements for students to meet before being free to drop out, leading to some reduction in adult literacy education enrollments of youth, although numbers still remain high. In contrast, Michigan is an example of a state in which legislation has effectively restricted the number of youth in adult literacy education. In 1995 the state legislature eliminated the eligibility of most youth under the age of twenty for enrollment in adult literacy education programs. According to the state director, the prevailing feeling among policymakers was that youth under the age of twenty could return to K–12 schools or to alternative programs operated by the schools. They did not want to provide state funding for such youth in adult literacy education programs. Unfortunately, this had the negative effect of forcing some smaller programs to close because of lower enrollments. This suggests just how significant younger students are as a clientele for adult literacy education.

GED Testing Policies and Compulsory School Attendance

States' GED testing policies have a significant impact on youth's eligibility for taking the test and, accordingly, on their enrollment in adult literacy education programs intended to prepare learners for GED testing. The GED Testing Service set national guidelines in 1992 requiring test takers to be age sixteen or older and not enrolled in high school (a small number of states have received approval to administer the GED to in-school youth). States have the option of setting their own age requirements as long as sixteen remains the minimum age of eligibility. Consequently, age policies vary tremendously across states. Some states make a distinction between the age required for testing and that required for issuance of the credential. More than 20 percent of states permit a sixteen year old to take the test under special conditions but withhold the credential until the individual reaches age eighteen or his or her high school class graduates (L. R. Hone, special projects manager, GED Testing Service, personal communication, July 6, 1998).

The more stringent state policies set minimum age requirements for testing and issuance of the credential at eighteen or nineteen years old, often linking the policies to compulsory school attendance ages. Typically such policies include a few exceptions for younger individuals in special circumstances, such as those in correctional institutions. For example, in Wisconsin, test takers must be eighteen years and six months of age or their high school class must have graduated. Special permission may be granted for seventeen year olds to take the test if they are incarcerated, enrolled in a federal Job Corps program, or in school and determined to be at risk in accordance with a waiver program granted by the GED Testing Service. In contrast, other states set a minimum age of sixteen with a few additional restrictions. For example, in Arkansas test takers must be sixteen years of age and meet provisions specified in the state's adult literacy education attendance and enrollment policies.

South Dakota offers a recent example of the potential impact of GED testing policies. According to the state director, the minimum age for GED testing in South Dakota was lowered in 1997 from eighteen to sixteen years. The change was made to make the policy consistent with the compulsory school attendance law allowing individuals to leave high school at sixteen years of age. The percentage enrollment of sixteen to seventeen year olds in South Dakota adult literacy education programs grew from 11.9 percent in 1995 to 20.6 percent in 1997.

More stringent age policies for GED test taking have the effect of restricting enrollment of youth in some states. The need for waivers and other approval can make it more difficult for youth to enroll, and in some cases age restrictions prohibit their enrollment altogether. A Tennessee program director explained, for example, that she was not allowed to enroll youth under the age of eighteen in any state-funded adult literacy education classes. An outreach specialist in California noted that it was not legal to serve anyone under eighteen, with few exceptions, in GED preparation classes. However, in these programs and in others, youth may be enrolled in different kinds of high school completion programs. Wisconsin serves underage youth through a special contract system with the public schools. The Tennessee program director reported that she developed separate classes for seventeen year olds funded by the local school district. Similarly, in the California program, the outreach coordinator described a variety of separate programs designed specifically to serve youth, in some cases allowing them to earn credits that their referring high school will count toward their regular high school diploma. Maine's state GED test administrator notes that the age restrictions for GED testing have led most youth to enroll in adult high school programs, where the age restrictions are determined by local school districts. Thus, the impact of GED age restrictions varies greatly, and even in situations with more stringent restrictions, programs may be serving a considerable number of youth in alternative programs.

Welfare Reform

Recent welfare reform efforts have been another factor affecting youth enrollment in some adult literacy education programs. Welfare reform seems to have affected youth enrollment in two ways. First, the emphasis on work first and greater restrictions placed on educational participation for welfare recipients have reduced the number of adults participating in adult literacy education programs, according to reports from several program staff members. Some programs have begun to recruit more youth to offset dropping enrollments of adult students. A director of a family literacy program in Indiana explained that the threat of a dwindling number of adult students, who now had to work rather than attend adult literacy education, led her staff to seek out teen mothers to maintain enrollment levels in their program. In this case, the majority of teens were recruited through a residential program for young mothers. In other cases, the stipulation that teen mothers receiving welfare must stay in school and can count high school or equivalency programs as approved work activities has increased the number of these young mothers who participate in adult literacy education programs. Quite a few practitioners described classes initiated specifically for this population.

Availability and Effectiveness
of School-Based Alternatives

The availability of alternative educational programs can affect both the number and the type of youth served by adult literacy education. In some regions, adult literacy education appears to offer virtually the only alternative form of high school completion for youth who drop out of school. For example, a Louisiana program director observed that at the time the state high school reform efforts were put into effect, adult literacy education was one of the few alternative programs available to dropouts. Not surprisingly, the program was inundated by youth unsuccessful in meeting the new graduation requirements. In other cases, adult literacy education is a last resort for students who have been unsuccessful in various school-based alternative programs. A program director in Idaho noted the existence of several alternative programs in her area, adding, "We get those who've been through the whole system." Typically these are students who have been incapable of meeting attendance or behavior requirements, which means that adult literacy education is being left with the most difficult of all dropouts to serve.

The relationship between the adult literacy education program and the school system serving such students varies. At a minimal level, most high schools have to provide some kind of consent form or waiver allowing the student to study for an alternative high school credential. On the other end of the spectrum are adult literacy education programs that have contracted with school districts to become providers of district-funded alternative high school programs. Some of these arrangements are recent, and others are long-standing. For example, a director of a program operating through a community college in Iowa reported having had a cooperative agreement with local school districts to provide alternative high school classes for more than thirty years. In between are programs like one in West Virginia that has cultivated referrals from schools without formal designation or transfer of funds. In addition to increased referrals from high schools, some programs are seeing growing numbers of young offenders referred by the courts to adult literacy education to complete a high school credential rather than returning them to the schools.

It was beyond the scope of my efforts here to determine if increased youth participation in adult literacy education can be attributed to the general ineffectiveness of other alternative programs or to problems in the high schools themselves. Some adult literacy education program staff mentioned that schools in their areas were making considerable efforts to retain at-risk students and were meeting with some success. These reports tended to come from staff who were serving youth in their programs, including some who had well-developed alternative programs specifically for youth but had not seen noticeable increases in recent youth enrollments. On the other hand, some staff suggested that increased use of drugs and violence in the schools was contributing to more student dropouts and more referrals. Yet national figures do not indicate an increase in high school dropout rates, though it does appear that more students are being served by alternative programs. There have been few rigorous evaluations of dropout prevention programs, and therefore little documented evidence of their effectiveness is available. Some well-publicized program models seem to have promise for increasing the achievement and completion rate of these students, but existing studies suggest that many programs often fail to have significant impact (U.S. Department of Education, 1994).

I located only one study that provides insight into the reasons that high school dropouts give for why they might choose adult literacy education over the option of returning to their high school. Metzer (1997) surveyed 158 high school dropouts in one Illinois county. Of these dropouts, 75 (47 percent) returned to school within one year of dropping out. The reasons these youth gave for returning to school do not seem to differ tremendously from reasons commonly reported by older adults. The most commonly reported reason was "wanting a better job and a better life." More notable, 45 of these returnees entered a GED program, while only 26 returned to high school. Reasons given by students for choosing the GED program included its flexibility, its "personal approach," and the perception that it was the shortest option leading to a credential. The drawbacks of reenrollment in high school included the time it would take to make up missed credits and the more rigid daily schedule. The dropouts also described the stigma of having dropped out as a barrier to returning to high school. They anticipated that teachers might question their seriousness and peers might be critical and ridicule them for having dropped out. In fact, dropouts who did reenroll in their high school reported such reactions from teachers and peers. Metzer observes that for some dropouts, reentering high school was an admission that leaving school was a mistake, implying that they had failed both in school and out of school. The fear of failing again in the same environment could prompt them to seek out adult literacy education—a fresh start in a new situation.

Of course, many dropouts who enroll in adult literacy education do not have the option of returning to high school, because they have been expelled or otherwise prohibited from returning. Even for those who do not have a choice, peer groups may be an important influence on their decision to enroll in adult literacy education rather than stay out of school altogether. Metzer (1997) found that feelings of social isolation were commonly described by the dropouts he interviewed, particularly those who could not find decently paid employment. Returning to school was a way to reconnect with a peer group. Other dropouts in an adult literacy education program might be perceived as a more compatible group than potentially condescending peers still in high school. The North Carolina program director suggested that growth in teen enrollments has made it more acceptable for others to enroll in adult literacy education, where they could socialize with friends from high school who had also dropped out.

Trends

A variety of factors appear to contribute to the growing number of teenagers in adult literacy education. The recent increase in the overall number of youth has created a larger high school population as well as a larger number of potential dropouts. The overall national concern with improving the skills of the workforce and reducing the number of welfare recipients has led to new policies that require schools to raise academic standards and at the same time find new ways to educate the least successful students. These young people themselves may seek out educational alternatives in an effort to increase their chances of securing employment that pays a living wage. They may choose adult literacy education because they want to avoid the stigma associated with returning to traditional high school and because they prefer a more flexible schedule.

YOUTH'S IMPACT ON
ADULT LITERACY EDUCATION

Currently educators and policymakers appear to be in a state of flux regarding how best to serve youth at risk. Overall, there seems to be little concrete evidence of what type of education would best help these youth succeed academically and in the workplace.

Characteristics of Young Dropouts

Most of the adult educators I interviewed described changes made in their programs to accommodate the needs of youth better. In general, teens were described as less mature, less motivated, and less responsible than typical adult students. One coordinator rather fondly described them as still being "fun-loving children." They were often characterized as directionless, with poorly defined educational and career goals. Behavior problems were often mentioned, ranging from students' hanging out in halls and wasting time to using drugs and engaging in fights. Some practitioners made distinctions between certain "types" of youth when describing their needs and concerns. One group of young teens mentioned by several practitioners were home-schooled youth who were seeking a high school credential. The number of such students apparently has not grown significantly, and they typically were described as well behaved and having no significant impact on the program. Teen mothers receiving public assistance were described as less problematic than the youth population overall by one teacher, because they seemed to be more motivated and had the support of case workers. Several practitioners said that an increasing number of youth had learning disabilities (LD) and attention deficit disorder (ADD), factors contributing to their lack of success in traditional high school. The most difficult group to handle appeared to be youth who were mandated by court to attend the adult literacy education program.

Accordingly, the type of youth served was significant in determining the program changes deemed necessary to meet their needs. For example, the Tennessee program serves only teens referred out of public schools for truancy; students removed for discipline problems were sent to another alternative school. Not surprisingly, the director of this program reported few discipline issues in her classes. As another example, one program in Maine was designed to serve primarily youth with ADD or LD, and its instructional approach was oriented specifically to address these students' learning differences, which minimized behavior problems. These examples suggest that one useful strategy for adult literacy education programs may be to designate particular groups of teens to be served and to turn down other youth unless the program is equipped to meet all of their special needs.

Frequently program staff felt that the characteristics of youth were not suited to the adult-oriented education that they were used to providing. Much adult literacy education stresses self-paced, individualized instruction, assuming that most adult learners are self-motivated, goal directed, and willing to take responsibility for their own learning. These assumptions are clearly at odds with how the youth were perceived. In a few rare cases, program staff reported that they were refusing to serve youth, but most often they were trying to find ways of handling youth, with different levels of enthusiasm and success.

Integration Versus Separation

One point of debate in serving youth is whether to integrate them into classes with adults or set up separate classes. In some programs, adult students have been so disturbed by the influx of youth and their behavior that many have dropped out.

In programs that integrate youth with adults, a key strategy reported by a number of staff is to keep the proportion of youth low, at most less than half, while others suggested less than one-third or even less. Some programs assign youth to different classes to separate them from peers who create disruptions when together. Other practitioners reported that even a few youth could create enough problems to disrupt the class and alienate the adults. But many felt that youth responded to the more serious atmosphere of a largely adult class and improved their behavior, rising to the adults' level of maturity. A benefit of mixing adults and youth was that the adults could be positive role models in terms of the value they placed on education and their diligent study habits. Teens could also become more motivated to earn their credential by being exposed to some of the hardships that these adults had experienced as a result of their lack of education. One staff member reported that her program deliberately pairs adults and youth so that they can serve as peer tutors and learn from each other. She cited an example of a sixty-six-year-old man paired with a sixteen-year-old boy. The young man helped his older partner with math, and the senior assisted the teenager with English. A further benefit, she reported, was that the teenager became much less of a problem in class.

The few studies on research that have examined the effects of age-integrated classes on adult and adolescent students suggest that age integration has benefits similar to those reported by the practitioners I interviewed. Elder (1967) and Carter (1988) found that age integration in adult literacy and vocational education courses had positive effects on youth, including encouraging appropriate, adultlike behavior and increasing the young students' desire to do well. Outcomes for adult students were not reported, except for one benefit that Elder (1967) noted: adults felt that their interpersonal relationships with youth improved, in the class as well as in other contexts. A more recent study by Darkenwald and Novak (1997) of adults and traditional-age students in college classes suggests that higher proportions of adult students might have a positive impact on academic performance for both youth and adults. However, as noted in this study, the outcomes of age integration may be affected by a wide variety of other factors, including the students' academic ability, topic of study, and mode of instruction. Mixing youth and adults may not be beneficial in all situations.

In a few extreme situations, adult literacy education programs have become almost entirely focused on serving youth. A Louisiana program director reported that the great increase in young dropouts resulting from curriculum reforms in that state, combined with adults' resistance to enrolling in classes with youth, led to a situation in which many programs were serving only teens. He resisted this trend in his program by deliberately designing classes to attract older students, thus keeping the proportion of youth to a less disruptive level. In particular, his program serves a high proportion of adults with high school diplomas who are preparing for employment testing. He believed that the adults provided a stabilizing influence and positive role modeling for the teens.

Other programs have established separate classes for youth to avoid disrupting adult students and to provide alternative methods of instruction. In some cases programs have been required to create separate classes because they receive special funds from school districts to serve as alternative schools. In a few instances, the segregation seemed to occur on its own. A program director in North Carolina explained that most youth were counseled into the adult high school program, since it was more structured and more suited to their needs. As a result, most adult students had begun to enroll in the GED preparation classes to avoid the youth's disruptive influence.

One strategy used in some programs employs an initial interview or trial period of instruction, and sometimes both, to determine a teen's maturity level. Based on the teen's maturity, he or she is either assigned to a class for youth or allowed to attend a class with adult students. A New Hampshire program uses this approach to assign youth to an alternative high school program or to the adult GED class. The alternative school has highly structured classes, with twelve to fifteen teams of students in a class, taught by pairs of teachers. The GED classes are less structured, but youth are expected to stay drug free, focus on their studies, and attend class regularly. A student-created and -enforced attendance policy requires students with more than three absences to defend their absences before a committee. Approximately 25 to 30 percent of students in the adult program are teens.

Other youth-specific classes are worth noting as examples of how programs are handling this population. The most extensive and well-developed system for serving teens I found through my interviews operates in the Los Angeles school district and reflects extensive collaboration between high schools, vocational training programs, and adult literacy education. Overall, the system is intended to prevent youth from dropping out of high school rather than serving them once they have left. Students at risk of dropping out are given a wide range of educational alternatives to enable them to meet school requirements and complete their degrees. Alternative Work Education Centers (AWECs), operated in connection with adult literacy education programs, provide counseling, courses, and referrals to other programs. Students still enrolled in school can take vocational courses in the evenings and receive elective high school credit. They can also take alternative high school classes offered by AWECs to make up missed or failed classes. The AWEC classes are designed exclusively for teens, while the vocational courses serve primarily adults, with small numbers of teens allowed to attend any course. According to the outreach specialist, state law bars enrollment of anyone under the age of eighteen in GED preparation classes (unless certain conditions are met), and young people must be seventeen years, ten months old to take the GED; AWECs thus provide an initial stop-gap for younger students. The outreach specialist suggested that one reason for the apparent success of the AWEC program is that the classes are small; no more than 100 to 150 students are enrolled at a site, in contrast to the 1,000 or more students who are often served in a Los Angeles school.

Another program with several youth options, part of Mechanic Falls–Poland Adult and Community Education in Maine, was described by its alternative education coordinator. This woman appears to be the driving force behind the development of these options, and her passion for working with youth is obvious even over the telephone. She has extensive experience working with youth in other settings, particularly those with special needs. Many adult literacy education program directors in Maine have been resistant to accepting youth, partly because school districts have been reluctant to provide district funds for their instruction. However, this program coordinator was able to negotiate with the local school board to become designated as an alternative school and receive district funding. This effort was prompted by a large influx of youth a few years ago, which the coordinator speculated was due to an increase in the length of high school classes to eighty minutes each. Eighty-minute classes appeared to be too long for students with LD or ADD, who could not sustain their concentration for the entire class period. In the adult literacy education alternative program, students prepare learning contracts, specifying objectives they will complete to earn adult high school credits. The program offers a couple of different classes for at-risk youth still enrolled in high school. The Graduate Support Program provides summer school courses for teens who need to make up failed or missed courses. A Graduate Homework Support Program provides after-school tutoring for high school students during the school year. Finally, the Young Adult Education Program allows teens who are living independently to attend classes with adults if they demonstrate appropriate maturity levels.

The California and Maine examples are very different in some ways. The Los Angeles program is a large-scale collaborative effort supported by state legislation, which provided some funding for staff to develop and manage the program. In contrast, the Maine program was initiated by individual effort in the context of one smaller program. Particularly notable in both, however, is the emphasis on dropout prevention as well as recovery. In other words, program staff are actively working with school districts to provide means of keeping youth in school, not just serving as a dumping ground for dropouts. Both states provide a variety of options for youth, recognizing the differing needs within this population. Each program built on strengths of adult education as an alternative to what the traditional high school offered. The Los Angeles outreach specialist noted that adult education was selected as the site for the AWECs because of its open entry–open exit format and its competency-based curriculum, both perceived as important ways to keep at-risk students engaged in education. In Maine, the program was able to provide classes that supported the regular high school curriculum, but at different times and with more individualized attention. It also offered more flexible class formats and teaching styles that could accommodate special needs. Additional funding was important for establishing and sustaining the separate youth programs, although the Maine coordinator noted that staff pay was not proportional to the actual effort they devoted to the teen program.

Changes in Instruction

Some of the program staff I contacted for this report stated that few changes were made in their instructional approaches and that the youth responded well to the existing format. Indeed, many felt that adult education could be more responsive to the needs of youth than the regular high school because it allowed for individualized, self-paced instruction. However, those who thought no instructional modifications were necessary were definitely in the minority. These tended to be staff who were dealing with smaller proportions of youth integrated into adult classes.

Most programs have at a minimum established new rules for attendance and classroom behavior for youth in both integrated and separate classes. Some programs present these rules to students in the form of a written code of conduct that students must sign and agree to follow. For example, an Arizona learning center's code of conduct consists of nine guidelines, several of which were mentioned frequently by staff in other programs. One rule, "Students should not disturb others in the classroom," is intended to minimize disruptions for adult students in particular. Another common problem was addressed by this rule: "Lingering or remaining idle about the hallways, classrooms, etc. without any useful reason for being here is prohibited." Other rules addressed issues such as attending class, using drugs and alcohol, dressing properly, and tampering with computer equipment. West Virginia has developed a set of procedures for dealing with sixteen to eighteen year olds who are attending adult education because they have withdrawn or been expelled from school, who are meeting requirements for obtaining or maintaining a driver's license, or who have been ordered by a court to attend. Students are given a sheet listing "Rights and Responsibilities of Adult Students" and must sign a contract agreeing to maintain regular attendance, appropriate behavior, and educational progress. How strictly rules such as those in Arizona or West Virginia are enforced seems to vary across states and programs, but most staff agreed that it was better to be strict than lenient. One staff person said that by refusing to compromise the rules, staff let the teens know that they are serious about supporting their learning. When students do leave the program, staff hope they will return later, when they are more motivated to learn. In fact, several practitioners gave examples of youth who did leave their adult education programs only to return years later with more motivation to learn.

In terms of teaching methods, many staff in a variety of states described the need to provide youth with more structure by giving more specific assignments with due dates and doing more goal setting and generally more monitoring of youth progress. Many staff described the benefits of smaller classes for teens, contrasting the size of adult education classes with high school classes. Some staff indicated that they deliberately kept classes small, some to as few as twelve students per class. The importance of good rapport and a close student-teacher relationship was mentioned as a means of counteracting the experience of the many teens who felt they had been ignored in school or that previous teachers had not cared about them. A few staff noted that hands-on learning strategies were more suited to the learning styles of most teens. Others found that computer-based instruction was particularly appealing to teens. Some relied primarily on individualized instruction, and others used combinations of individualized, small group, and structured classes.

Except for the provision of rules and more teacher direction, none of the instructional methods described for use with teens seemed to be radical departures from methods used with adult students. Several staff described instructional innovations that seemed effective with adults as well as teens. One program coordinator commented that it was inaccurate to claim that one instructional approach works for adults and another for teens. Rather, some adults and teens could benefit from a more structured, teacher-directed approach, while other adults and teens benefited from a more self-directed, independent approach.

The extent to which appropriate instructional methods for adults differ from those for children and youth has been the object of a long-standing debate in the field of adult education. Similar conclusions have been drawn by other adult education practitioners and scholars: instructional methods for both adults and youth should vary according to the learner's individual characteristics, the subject matter, the goals of the educational program, and so on. Self-directed, independent instruction may pose particular problems for youth because it contrasts so greatly with the instructional format they have learned to expect in school. They may need to be introduced to a less structured environment more gradually.

Curriculum Changes

Curriculum changes were less frequently mentioned by practitioners, and many indicated that they used the same curriculum with youth as with adults or that curriculum changes were being made to benefit both groups. High school credit programs offering courses to be counted toward the referring school's high school diploma were perhaps the most distinctive developments. A few practitioners mentioned that the curriculum had to be relevant to hold the youth's attention, and so they tried to incorporate instruction in life skills with hands-on activities, such as cooking a meal in a unit on nutrition.

A number of interviewees mentioned teens' need for career guidance and job skills. In particular, they expressed the belief that teens needed more sophisticated skills, such as more advanced math skills, the ability to think critically, and computer skills, to find jobs that paid a living wage. Welfare reform has had effects on most adult education programs, and many are moving toward a more work-related curriculum for adults as well as teens. A program director in West Virginia described Workscans, a school-to-work type curriculum that seemed to appeal to both youth and adults. The Iowa program coordinator described a major effort to provide teens with more career development activities. This adult education program is associated with a community college that has been contracting with local public schools to provide alternative education classes for several decades. The teens can study for the GED, work toward an adult high school diploma, or earn credits toward a local high school diploma from their referring school. In the past few years school districts have requested that additional career development activities be provided for the teens they refer. Among other reasons, eastern Iowa has seen a growth in technology-based jobs that require higher skills. Since the school districts provide funding, the program has been able to hire career development specialists who are putting together activities such as job shadowing, internships, and other types of work-based learning. Most programs, however, lack the funding to support such activities. No one, for example, mentioned receiving funds through the federal or state school-to-work program. At this point, adult education programs seem to be primarily trying to integrate more work-related material into their existing curriculum for teens.

Staff Development

A number of interviewees emphasized the importance of preparing teachers to handle young students. Louisiana developed a statewide training workshop using federal funds and offered it several times in the early 1990s, when there was a major influx of youth to adult literacy programs. Others mentioned that working with young students had been the topic for sessions at their state adult education conference. The Tennessee program coordinator who oversees the classes for seventeen year olds stressed the provision of staff training and explained that it is always available to teachers of these classes. This training covers a wide variety of topics, including workshops led by local police on how to identify and address drug-related problems. Because the teachers' salaries were paid by district funds, she noted, the teachers could attend in-service programs offered to all teachers in the local schools. A Nebraska program director explained that all staff have attended mediation and conflict resolution training and that "effective staff communication has proven to be the most effective tool in preventing problems. Staff realize that what they say and how they say it can either promote a confrontation or diffuse a potentially difficult situation."

Trends

The impact of youth varies across programs and locales. In many cases, the growing number of young students has led programs to adopt new rules, impose more structure, adapt instruction and curriculum, and even create new classes. In some situations, serving youth has interfered with programs' ability to attract and retain adult students. Although some practitioners feel successful in their efforts to work with this younger population, others are less sanguine. Educating youth in adult education programs raises not only practical questions but also philosophical ones about the purpose and role of adult education.

ISSUES FOR RESEARCH, POLICY, AND PRACTICE

This review suggests a number of issues for further research, policy, and practice: determining the reasons youth are enrolling in adult literacy education and their degree of success in earning an alternative credential or in pursuing other outcomes, such as employment; determining whether adult literacy education should serve youth at all, and, if so, what funds should be used to support programs that serve youth; and determining the best ways to meet the educational needs of youth while continuing to serve the older adult population effectively.

Research

One starting point for research is to document trends in youth enrollment in adult education more systematically. Separate documentation of youth enrollment up to this point has been limited or nonexistent in many programs; most have included sixteen-to-seventeen-year-old students in the larger age category of sixteen to twenty-four year olds. Now that states are required to report separate data on sixteen to eighteen year olds in federally funded programs, national and state data on trends will be more accessible in a few years. However, all youth served in adult education programs may not be included in these data, which may have to be collected on a local program level. Such information is important as a basis for policymaking and funding decisions.

We need more information about why young dropouts are enrolling in adult education programs, what the characteristics of such youth are, and what alternative programs exist. Are youth enrolling in adult education because they recognize the benefits of completing a high school education, or are the majority enrolling because of mandates from courts or social service agencies or pressure from parents? How many of these youth have learning disabilities or emotional and behavioral problems that affect their ability to learn in any setting?

A further question is how these enrollments are affected by school reform initiatives. There is little research to date on how school reform affects dropout rates. If school systems are successful in their efforts to meet the directive of the National Education Goals to reduce dropout rates and improve the achievement of all students, these efforts might reduce the number of dropouts enrolling in adult education. Based on my interviews, it does appear that more alternative high school programs are being developed, at least in some regions. In addition, policies that initially increased youth enrollment in adult education have been revised in some states. Monitoring more closely the relationship between adult education participation and school reform efforts could lead to more informed policymaking as well as greater understanding of the factors affecting young people's educational paths.

A particularly important question for further study concerns the outcomes for young dropouts who enroll in adult education. How many are successful in earning a GED or other high school credential? Some practitioners I interviewed thought they had a high success rate with youth, while others were far more pessimistic, suggesting that most youth repeated their previous pattern of dropping out of school. A number of practitioners believed that youth who dropped out of adult education often returned to the program a few years later, when they had more real-world experience that increased their maturity and motivation to complete their education. Thus their early introduction to adult education should not be considered a failure but rather an opportunity to make them aware of adult education options and give them a positive impression of the program. Charting the patterns of young dropouts' participation in adult education would provide a greater understanding of how adult education affects youth's attitudes toward education, as well as their attainment of the more concrete goal of earning a credential.

Aside from earning a credential, what are other outcomes of adult education participation for young dropouts, such as employment and further education? A recent report on high school dropouts (U.S. Department of Education, 1994) identified concerns about youth enrollment in GED preparation programs based on the findings of a study by Cameron and Heckman (1991). Cameron and Heckman concluded that GED graduates are comparable with high school dropouts in terms of employment variables such as wages and job tenure and that they are substantially worse off than regular high school graduates. However, their study had several weaknesses, including the fact that the comparisons were made in young adulthood, when the GED graduates had an average of six years of work experience as graduates—less than what high school graduates would have had. This inexperience may have limited the opportunities GED graduates had for comparable career advancements.

In a more recent, carefully controlled study, Tyler (1998) found that earning a GED had a "substantial" impact on the earnings of white dropouts sixteen to twenty-one years old five years after they obtained the credential. However, he points out that the increase in annual earnings was only $1,500, not enough to move the recipients out of poverty. In addition, earning the GED appeared to have no significant impact on the earnings of nonwhite GED holders.

As suggested in the Department of Education report, to determine adequately the benefits of GED completion for youth (and older adults), there is a need for more controlled, longitudinal studies of GED recipients, high school dropouts, and traditional high school graduates. Do relative outcomes vary according to the age at which the GED credential is earned? For example, we might expect that earning a credential at a younger age would enable young dropouts to advance more quickly in a career path. But perhaps older GED recipients have more concrete goals and have developed other skills through experience that enable them to make more immediate and substantial employment gains. Findings from such research could have implications for the kind of alternative education provided for high school dropouts of all ages.

Finally, researchers might take note of the criticism in the same report that research on school dropouts has been largely atheoretical. Most studies have been descriptive, focusing on the characteristics of dropouts rather than providing explanations of their behavior. Accordingly, many dropout prevention and recovery programs have been based on unexamined assumptions about at-risk categories of youth. The Department of Education report describes several theoretical perspectives, including social capital, achievement motivation, social bonding, and authentic education, that could provide frameworks for research and more explicit rationales for the design of education for young dropouts. Critical educational perspectives offer a framework for exploring the significance of race, class, and gender in the experiences of young dropouts within the contexts of traditional high schools, adult education, and the workplace. Fine's (1991) work provides an excellent example of a critical ethnographic study of these factors in the high school experiences of dropouts. Horowitz's (1995) participant observation study of teen mothers in a GED preparation program offers another example of research exploring these factors.

Perspectives such as these might be fruitfully applied and developed in future investigations of young dropouts in adult education.

Policy

While further research can provide more information about youth in adult education, a significant policy issue is whether youth should be served by adult education. Most of the practitioners interviewed agreed that the best place for youth is in a traditional high school program. However, opinions were mixed about whether adult education should serve youth who were not successful in the traditional high school environment. Should young dropouts be allowed, even encouraged, to attend adult education classes if regular school is available to them as an option? One approach to policy, reflected in Michigan's legislation, is to prohibit youth from participating in adult education as a means of discouraging them from dropping out.

From another perspective, some young people need a different learning environment from the traditional high school. To address their needs, policies should ensure that adult education, along with other options, is available to provide a more flexible and perhaps more feasible instruction for this group. In addition, from a policy perspective it might seem advantageous to provide additional support for adult education programs that serve youth successfully. If adult education can help dropouts improve their skills and earn a credential at younger ages, these young people's lifelong earnings and their roles as parents and citizens may be considerably enhanced, benefiting not only themselves but society as a whole.

The allocation of funds—for example, Adult Education Act (AEA) grant funds, school district dollars, special grants for alternative programming—to serve youth is an integral part of this issue. Currently local and state policies vary considerably about the use of funds to serve youth. Policies are partially dependent on mandatory school attendance requirements. In Wisconsin, for example, with mandatory school attendance up to age eighteen, it is not legal to serve youth under age eighteen in AEA-funded high school completion programs. In states with lower age requirements, funding arrangements vary. While some school districts provide full financial support for youth programs offered through adult education, a more common complaint was that adult education receives no school district dollars for these students. Some practitioners argued that if funds are provided to school districts for these youth, the school districts should either serve them or transfer the funds to adult literacy education. From this perspective, serving youth in adult literacy education takes away from the limited funds available to serve older adult students.

On the other hand, AEA funds are currently mandated to support programs that serve out-of-school individuals age sixteen and older. Adult literacy education programs do not provide the wider range of courses or as many hours of instruction as high schools typically offer. Is it therefore justifiable to use only adult literacy education funds to support these programs? Further, if adult literacy education is successful with young dropouts, the number of older adults who need basic education and high school completion programs will gradually decline, reducing the likelihood that such adults will be displaced by younger students.

Another issue that emerged from this review concerns the process of establishing educational policy in general. It seems evident that many educational policies are established with little or no consideration of their potential impact on adult literacy education (such as raising standards, lowering the dropout age, and mandating education for juvenile offenders). In general, adult literacy education needs to be considered as part of the entire educational system when policies are being developed. While adult educators have been increasingly active in influencing public policies that directly relate to adult literacy education, we must also make more concerted efforts to identify and contribute to policies that will have less direct but no less significant impact on which students programs are expected to serve and how they serve them.

Practice

If we assume that the trend toward more youth seeking alternative credentials continues and that policies support the continued enrollment of youth in adult literacy education, how should practitioners respond? How can programs best serve the needs of youth while continuing to serve the older adult population?

One primary issue concerns the role that adult literacy education should take in providing education for youth. Ideally, adult literacy education should not be a dumping ground for any student that high schools cannot serve. Programs already take on a variety of roles, ranging from serving selective groups of students (such as habitual truants or those with learning disabilities) to supporting dropout prevention programs for in-school youth. Finding ways to collaborate more closely with school systems, social service agencies, and the criminal justice system seems to have been important for programs that gave the most positive reports about their work with young dropouts. In defining their role, practitioners may need to decide that they are not equipped to serve the needs of all young dropouts. This can be a tough decision for practitioners with a tradition of serving anyone who walks through their door, but in the long run it may be in the best interests of students and programs.

It is not clear whether one kind of instructional approach is more appropriate and helpful than others in serving all youth. Like adult students, youth have diverse needs and abilities, and a variety of instructional options may be successful. I can tentatively suggest that young dropouts served in adult literacy education seem to have certain characteristics that distinguish them from many adult students. Some prominent examples are a greater tendency for inappropriate behavior, difficulty staying on task, and more desire for socialization with peers.

To some extent, these tendencies may be explained by the life situations of these youth. Youth are less likely to have experiences that develop a sense of responsibility and maturity, such as raising a family or holding a long-term job. Youth may have a greater need for social bonding than older adults. For many young people, their peers at school form their primary social group, while adults may have more well-developed social networks outside classes and be more focused on family and work relationships. Quigley's (1992) research indicates that dropouts may generally value education but resist schooling because of negative previous school experiences. Resistance to any form of schooling may be more acute for youth since they have been so recently alienated from school. Some are mandated to attend, and their behavior may reflect resistance to this externally imposed requirement. Their disruptive behaviors could in part reflect an acting out against the culture of schooling rather than immaturity per se.

How to respond to these and other concerns remains a key issue for practice. One approach is to maintain a low proportion of youth in relation to adult students, which seems to moderate problematic behavior. However, this approach may be possible only in programs serving smaller numbers of youth, and it raises again the issue of whether adult literacy education programs should restrict the number of youth they are willing to serve. In programs serving large numbers of youth, separate classes are one strategy. In this case, a key issue is to what extent instruction should be designed to replicate the structure of traditional high school in terms of attendance rules, closely monitored instruction, and so forth. If adult literacy education becomes more like a traditional school, will it simply recreate the conditions that led these youth to drop out in the first place?

Closely related to instruction are issues of appropriate curriculum. One practitioner felt that youth should be provided with a bare bones curriculum—just enough to help them earn a credential and prepare them to enter the workforce. Others suggested that to make the transition to the workplace, youth need more extensive support, such as career exploration opportunities. In addition, adult literacy education might provide preparation for other life roles, such as parenting or community involvement. Or should youth be provided with a broader academic curriculum, more or less equivalent to high school, that will prepare them for further education? Clearly these issues apply to curriculum for adult students as well, but they may be more acute for youth if adult literacy education is expected to take on more of the role of traditional high schools and as standards for school achievement are scrutinized.

Responding to these issues involves practical as well as philosophical considerations. Most programs have limited time and funding, so curriculum decisions need to be made within the context of these constraints. Another practical issue is that of staff development. There seems to be widespread agreement that staff development is essential to prepare adult literacy education teachers to work with youth. But what teachers need to know is not completely clear, since evidence of what works in educating young dropouts is limited. One key focus for staff development seems to be what might be described as human relations training. Teachers may need to learn conflict resolution strategies, develop different communication skills, and otherwise gain more ability to build positive relationships with youth (as well as to help youth develop positive relationships with other students). In addition, teachers may need more insight into the life situations of these youth and the problems that affect their learning, such as drug abuse and gang violence.

CONCLUSION

As one administrator commented in his reply to my survey, we commonly talk of a future vision of lifelong education and the benefits of intergenerational classrooms. Youth involvement in adult literacy education might be seen as a step toward realizing an ideal of seamless connections across educational contexts and age groups.

The realities of youth involvement in adult literacy education, however, suggest in a very concrete way how this ideal may pose some challenges to our current educational structures and philosophies. In particular, the issue is not simply one of combining age groups. The youth enrolling in adult literacy education have not succeeded in school systems that have far greater resources than most adult literacy programs. Is it realistic to expect adult programs to be more effective with even less support, while at the same time serving adult students who also have significant barriers to learning? By even enrolling such youth, are adult educators guilty of relieving the public schools of their responsibility to find more effective ways of educating these young people? As one program director stated, these youth deserve a chance—but who will provide it?

Serving such youth may be an opportunity for adult literacy educators to assume an enhanced and more integrated role within a higher-quality educational system that serves all students more effectively. Or young dropouts could overburden already understaffed and underfunded adult literacy programs, resulting in inadequate education for the traditional adult clientele as well as for youth. Whether young dropouts become an opportunity or a problem for adult literacy education may depend on how we respond.

Notes

1. Since the growth in youth enrollments appears to be a recent trend, there are few published resources that provide relevant information. The Internet allowed me to collect information that otherwise would have been difficult and much more time-consuming to locate. I made use of government documents available on-line from the Web sites of agencies such as the National Center for Education Statistics (NCES). I used listservs to make initial inquiries and contacts with practitioners across the country. E-mail was helpful in allowing me to contact state directors of adult education and local coordinators of adult literacy programs. I used telephone interviews to get additional information from practitioners who were identified by state directors as potentially helpful contact persons. Some practitioners gathered comments from youth themselves for use in this chapter. I obtained responses from state

directors in nineteen states and twenty-three practitioners in twenty states: Alaska, Arizona, Arkansas, California, Idaho, Iowa, Kansas, Louisiana, Maine, Michigan, Montana, Nebraska, North Carolina, North Dakota, South Dakota, Tennessee, Vermont, Washington, West Virginia, and Wisconsin. Other states or programs may not be experiencing similar trends, but this small, nonrandom sample is sufficient to suggest that youth enrollments are having enough impact across the country to merit greater attention.

2. When citing information provided by the respondents to my survey, I refer to them by title only to avoid a distracting number of personal citations. The only informants I cite by name are three people who were not part of the survey of administrators and program staff. They work in federal offices and provided me with national statistics.

References

Bernhardt, A., Morris, M., Hancock, M., & Scott, M. (1998, February). *Work and opportunity in the post-industrial labor market* (IEE Brief No. 19). New York: Institute on Education and the Economy, Columbia University.

Cameron, S. V., & Heckman, J. J. (1991). *The non-equivalence of high school equivalents* (Working Paper No. 3804). Cambridge, MA: National Bureau of Economic Research.

Carter, J. L. (1988). *Age-integration and interpersonal relationships in a vocational shop setting.* Unpublished doctoral dissertation, Rutgers University.

Darkenwald, G., & Novak, R. (1997). Classroom age composition and academic achievement in college. *Adult Education Quarterly, 47*(2), 108–116.

Elder, G. H. (1967). Age integration and socialization in an educational setting. *Harvard Educational Review, 37,* 594–619.

Fine, M. (1991). *Framing dropouts.* Albany: State University of New York Press.

Forgione, P. D. (1998, April). *Achievement in the United States: Progress since a nation at risk?* Washington, DC: National Center for Education Statistics. Available at [http://nces.ed.gov/Pressrelease/reform/].

GED Testing Service. (1988–1997). *Who took the GED? GED statistical reports 1988–1997.* Washington, DC: American Council on Education.

Horowitz, R. (1995). *Teen mothers: Citizens or dependents?* Chicago: University of Chicago Press.

Metzer, D. (1997, March). *When do high school dropouts return to education and why?* Paper presented at the Annual Meeting of the American Educational Research Association, Chicago. (ERIC Document Reproduction Service No. ED 411 125).

National Center for Education Statistics. (1996, June). *The condition of education 1996* (NCES 96–304). Washington, DC: U.S. Government Printing Office.

National Center for Education Statistics. (1997a). *Digest of education statistics 1997.* Washington, DC: U.S. Government Printing Office.

National Center for Education Statistics. (1997b, December). *Dropout rates in the United States: 1996.* Washington, DC: National Center for Education Statistics. Available at [http://nces.ed.gov/pubs98/dropout/].

National Commission on Excellence in Education. (1983). *A nation at risk.* Washington, DC: U.S. Department of Education.

Quigley, A. (1992). Looking back in anger: The influences of schooling on illiterate adults. *Journal of Education, 174*(1), 104–121.

Tyler, J. H. (1998). The GED: Whom does it help? *Focus on Basics, 2*(B), 1, 3–6.

U.S. Bureau of the Census. (1996). *Population profile of the United States: 1995* (Appendix A). Washington, DC: U.S. Government Printing Office.

U.S. Department of Education. (1994). *Reaching the national education goals: Goal 2.* Washington, DC: U.S. Department of Education. Available at [http://www.ed.gov/pubs/ReachingGoals/Goal_2/].

Varner, W. (n.d.) *A legislative tour of the states.* Baltimore: National Dropout Prevention Network. Available at [http://www.dropoutprevention.org/edpol/edpolicy.htm].

CHAPTER FOUR

Adult Literacy and Postsecondary Education Students
Overlapping Populations and Learning Trajectories

Stephen Reder

————

Concerns about improving the literacy proficiencies of the nation's adults are increasingly evident in public discourse about education and workforce policy in the United States. Improved adult literacy has become a national education goal. Recent proposals to upgrade the skills of America's workforce and promote lifelong learning (among them the President's 1999 State of the Union address, the 1999 White House Lifelong Learning Summit, and the administration's fiscal year 2000 budget request) have highlighted the need to raise levels of adult literacy. This discussion has focused on expanding and strengthening the country's adult education system, which historically

Thanks to John Comings, Barbara Garner, Barbara Holland, Cecil Smith, and Cristine Smith for their careful reading of an early draft of this chapter and useful suggestions for improving it. Thanks also to Tucki Folkers, John Hartwig, and Ron Pugsley for interesting conversations about these topics. I also learned much from the lively Internet discussion on the NLA list moderated by David Rosen.

has served adults needing better basic skills and high school equivalency. The focus of adult literacy education programs in the United
States has traditionally been to prepare adults who have not completed
high school to gain the skills and knowledge needed to pass the GED
(General Educational Development) tests or otherwise obtain high
school equivalency certification.

The high school diploma or equivalent at one time did provide individuals in the United States with reasonable access to well-paying
jobs and other resources and opportunities. Changes in technology,
labor markets, and globalization, however, have increasingly demanded that individuals now obtain not only the skills and knowledge traditionally learned in high school (and certified by the GED)
but also postsecondary education and credentials. As a result, demand
for and access to postsecondary education has dramatically expanded
in the United States since World War II. Increasing numbers of adults
who in earlier eras might not have participated in postsecondary education are now attempting to obtain a college education and degree.
Many of these students, whether enrolled in four-year, two-year, or
proprietary training institutions,[1] have high school diplomas but have
not developed the reading, writing, and math skills needed to succeed
in postsecondary programs. Helping these students, as well as adults
without high school credentials, to improve their basic skills is required if we are to meet the goal for adult literacy set by the National
Education Goals Panel (1997).

THE CHANGING FACE OF THE NATION, ITS EDUCATIONAL INSTITUTIONS, AND ITS ADULT STUDENTS

For many adults, there is much more at stake here than just meeting
educational goals that someone else has set. Education is critical for
labor market success, and it is now clear that in the United States, economic gaps between the education haves and have-nots are widening,
reflecting increasing economic returns to higher education (see, for
example, Grubb, 1997). Recent data released by the U.S. Bureau of the
Census, for example, indicate the continuing relative erosion of earnings for those with little formal education. According to March 1998
census data, the mean annual earnings of U.S. adults age eighteen and
over rise dramatically with education:[2]

No high school diploma/equivalent: $16,124

High school diploma/equivalent: $22,895

Associate's degree: $29,877

Bachelor's degree: $40,478

Advanced degree: $64,229

Literacy skills are also important determinants of individuals' labor market outcomes. At given levels of education, increasing levels of literacy are associated with, for example, higher expected earnings (Finn & Gerber, 1998; Harrington & Sum, forthcoming). As Figure 4.1 shows, individuals need both educational credentials and high levels of literacy. Data in the figure are from the National Adult Literacy Survey of 1992,

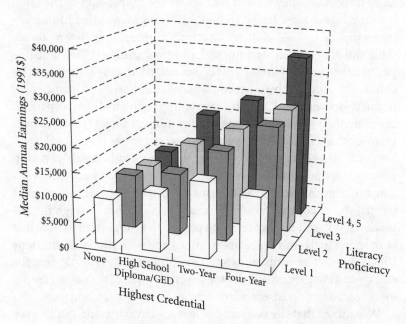

Figure 4.1.   Income by Education and Literacy.
Note: The height of each bar is the median of individuals' earnings during the year preceding the interview, plotted as a joint function of their highest degree attained and assessed level of literacy proficiency.
Source: National Adult Literacy Survey, 1992. Author calculations.

which assessed the prose, document, and quantitative literacy abilities of a random sample of the nation's adults age sixteen and above (Kirsch, Jungeblut, Jenkins, & Kolstad, 1993).

The data in the figure show median earnings as a function of highest degree obtained and assessed literacy proficiency.[3] To obtain livable incomes, most individuals need to "climb the hill" contoured in the figure—that is, obtain both postsecondary credentials and relatively high levels of literacy proficiency. Elsewhere I have shown that both literacy skills and postsecondary educational credentials enhance adults' economic outcomes as well as their access to lifelong learning opportunities (Reder, forthcoming).

Literacy Development and Literacy Selection

Although both educational credentials and literacy skills are economically important, they are not necessarily the by-product of the same learning experiences. In the United States and many other industrialized societies, of course, there is a strong association between literacy skills and educational attainment. In a recent study (1998a), I distinguished two kinds of literacy processes underlying the strong positive correlation observed between educational attainment and literacy proficiency. On one hand, the more schooling individuals participate in, the more their literacy develops and the more proficient they become. I termed this a literacy development process. On the other hand, literacy proficiency is often a gatekeeper that limits individuals' access to educational opportunities; successively higher levels of education become increasingly selective in terms of their literacy requirements. I termed this selective filtering of literacy proficiencies through the educational system a literacy selection process. It is important to note that both individuals (through self-selection) and educational institutions (through selective admissions and retention practices) implement literacy selection processes. Literacy selection often acts as a gatekeeper for access to both postsecondary education and career ladders.

We will see that the concepts of literacy development and literacy selection are central to understanding the overlapping relationships between the student populations in adult education and postsecondary programs. There are tensions between policies and programs designed to promote effective literacy development and those designed to promote effective literacy selection. Understanding the difference between literacy development and literacy selection may prove particularly helpful in designing new policies and programs to coordinate basic skills education better across the adult education and postsecondary education arenas.

Expanding Contexts for Adult Literacy Development

There have been two broad categories of societal response in the United States to these increasing demands for more literacy and more education: the expansion of adult literacy training and the expansion of postsecondary education.

Sticht (1998) documents the ongoing historical expansion of adult literacy training within federally funded adult education programs. Besides growth in the overall number of adults being served, Sticht describes the changing composition of the adult learners who participate, particularly the increasing percentage of English for speakers of other languages (ESOL) students.

Another important change in the composition of adult education students can be found in the data collected in the recent National Evaluation of Adult Education Programs (NEAEP). Reporting on program clientele characteristics surveyed by the NEAEP, Development Associates (1993) estimated that 33 percent of the participants in federally funded adult education programs in 1991–1992 had a high school diploma, equivalency, or above. A significant fraction of these high school graduates were individuals born and educated outside the United States who may need English-language skills or U.S. educational credentials, or both. A clearer picture emerges from disaggregating these results by nativity using the NEAEP public use data set. Among U.S.-born adult education participants, 14 percent had a high school diploma, equivalency, or a higher degree.[4] Thus, a substantial fraction of individuals who did not need to participate in federally funded ABE (adult basic education), ASE (adult secondary education), or ESOL programs to obtain a secondary credential nevertheless chose to participate in these basic skills training programs.

Since some individuals receiving public assistance or unemployment benefits may have been referred or even mandated to participate in basic skills programs, it is possible that high school graduates participated because of their welfare or employment status. If this were the case, we might want to think about their participation as related less to their goals and more to the goals of some public agency. To examine this possibility, I compared the welfare and labor force status of program participants who did or did not have a high school diploma or above. There were no significant differences in the labor force or welfare status of these two groups of adult education students. The NEAEP also asked students about their reasons for participating. I compared the reasons given by students with and without the high school diploma or equivalent. A diverse set of reasons was provided by both groups, with no obvious differences between the reasons or goals given by the two groups for participating in these basic skill programs.

It thus seems reasonable to conclude that many individuals, regardless of whether they have a secondary credential, seek to improve their basic skills through participation in adult education programs. Federally funded programs, traditionally designed to serve adults lacking such credentials, are now serving a broader population, including adults who already have the credentials to participate in postsecondary education and training. Many of these high school graduates participating in basic skills training may be actively preparing for or even already enrolled in postsecondary education or training.[5]

In addition to such growth in the size and capacity of the adult education system, strong indications emerge that adult literacy training is increasingly taking place in other contexts as well. A recent review of research on adults' participation patterns in basic skills training examined a number of national surveys conducted during the 1990s (Reder, 1997b). Analysis of these nationally representative data sets indicates that basic skills training is broadly distributed among the adult population at diverse levels of education and literacy proficiency. The poor correspondence between the participation patterns revealed by these surveys and those evident in the administrative databases of adult education programs suggests that many adults are probably receiving basic skills training outside federally funded adult education programs—including programs in postsecondary education institutions and in the workplace.

Further evidence about the increasing role of the workplace in providing basic skills training comes from a study conducted by the American Management Association based on an annual survey of businesses that asked whether companies were providing remedial training. The survey results indicate rapid increases in the provision of basic skills training by the private sector. Here is the estimated percentage of all companies providing remedial basic skills training by year (National Alliance of Business, 1996, p. 6):

1989	3.8 percent
1990	13.5 percent
1991	14.8 percent
1992	17.6 percent
1993	20.2 percent
1994	20.0 percent

Adult Literacy and the Expansion of Postsecondary Education

Another important response to the increasing economic demands for postsecondary credentials and higher levels of literacy has been the expansion of access to postsecondary education for students who in earlier times were unlikely to go to college. The earliest federal access policies sought to overcome financial barriers to postsecondary education. Beginning with the GI Bill after World War II, these policies focused on helping returning veterans. With the passage of the Higher Education Act of 1965, the initial focus of access policies on ameliorating financial barriers broadened. Lack of either academic preparation or essential basic skills was no longer seen as a legitimate barrier to postsecondary education. Some institutions lowered admissions standards, and others opened their doors to nearly anyone seeking a college education. During this period, community colleges grew considerably, as did four-year schools that provided easier or even open admissions to high school graduates (Ruppert et al., 1998).

This increased access to postsecondary institutions resulted in the enrollment of large numbers of adults with relatively poor basic skills, in turn driving the expansion of developmental or remedial education programs within vocational schools and two-year and four-year colleges. When we examine data on the extent of remedial basic skills education, we will find that a large percentage—perhaps between one in four and one in three—of undergraduate students enroll in such remedial courses. Many of these students might not have gone to college without the support of such access policies.

Many of these nontraditional students are women or members of minority groups, and they tend to differ in other important ways from the college students typical of earlier eras. Often juggling program enrollment and class attendance with demanding employment and family responsibilities, many students are able to attend only part time and may take many years to complete programs and earn their degrees (Bach et al., forthcoming; Horn, 1996). Many of these students exhibit complex patterns of enrollment and attendance involving multiple institutions. Some students may begin their postsecondary education in a community college and later transfer to a four-year institution to complete a bachelor's degree. Other students, particularly those in urban areas, enroll concurrently in multiple institutions, accumulating credits across institutions and programs to attain degrees and achieve personal goals (Bach et al., forthcoming).

Researchers have considered traditional college students to be those who enter postsecondary education directly after high school and attend full time until graduating two or four years later. In contrast, nontraditional students have been identified in terms of seven characteristics:

- Delayed enrollment (that is, older age at the start of post-secondary education)
- Part-time attendance
- Financial independence
- Full-time employment while enrolled
- Having dependents other than a spouse
- Being a single parent
- Not having obtained a standard high school diploma (see, for example, Horn, 1996)

Using composite indexes of nontraditionality constructed from these factors, researchers have found steady increases in the overall nontraditionality of college students in recent years. They have also found less persistence and degree completion to be associated with increasing amounts of nontraditionality (Berkner, Cuccaro-Alamin, & McCormick, 1996; Horn, 1996; Horn & Berktold, 1998; Kojaku & Nunez, 1998).

Enduring Controversies
Surrounding Remedial Education

Some enduring controversies likely must be addressed before better coordination can be established between basic skills education in postsecondary programs and adult education programs. Questions and tensions arise around issues of turf, budget, program design and control, and the appropriateness of offering basic skills programs in postsecondary settings. The lowering of basic skills standards for admissions and the concomitant provision of remedial courses have been particularly controversial, often pitting higher educators against each other (Ballard & Clanchy, 1988; Hull, 1998; Mickler & Chapel, 1989). Critics of expanded academic access to and remedial support for postsecondary education argue that students without the literacy skills needed to succeed academically should not be admitted (that is, a literacy selection position). Proponents of broader access, on the other hand, argue for equity of opportunity: rather than being penalized for their poor academic preparation, they believe that these students should be provided with additional opportunities and support for strengthening their basic skills (that is, a literacy development position). Levin, Koski, and Bersola (1998), responding to the chronically marginalized and stigmatized status of students in remedial courses, suggest that these students might be more effectively served by innovative programs designed to "accelerate" rather than "remediate" their skill development.

This debate has become political and highly charged. In many states that once supported the broadening of access to higher education, policymakers and legislatures have scaled back financial support, often targeting students with poor basic skills. Admissions requirements have been tightened and budgets reduced for remedial programs. The City University of New York, for example, has reversed its historical course by ending its open admissions policy and decimating its remedial programs (Cooper, 1998). In Atlanta, Georgia State University decided to forgo more than $1.5 million in credit-hour revenues by not admitting any developmental students during 1998–1999 in order to "improve its image" (S. Gowen, personal communication, 1998). And the California State University system adopted a policy in January 1996 that substantially scaled back remedial courses on its twenty-two campuses. Other examples abound.

The Need for a Comparative Picture of Adult Literacy and Postsecondary Students

Postsecondary education—like the workplace—has become an important but controversial venue for basic skills training. New legislation, such as the Workforce Investment Act (WIA) of 1998, and recent proposals of the Clinton administration for broadening adult literacy education seek to coordinate basic skills training with workforce upgrading and lifelong learning. Surprisingly, little effort has been made to develop improved policy and programs for coordinating basic skills education either within postsecondary education or between postsecondary institutions and other types of adult basic skills programs.

Perhaps this is understandable in part because there is little research to inform these issues. In particular, little information has been available about the literacy abilities of the nation's postsecondary students or the way in which their abilities compare with those of adult literacy students, other prospective college students, and the general population.

LITERACY PROFICIENCY AND POSTSECONDARY EDUCATION

Previous large-scale research on the educational characteristics and outcomes of postsecondary students has generally relied on college admission tests such as the SAT and ACT, grades, and persistence and attainment measures. Comparable information is typically not available for adult literacy learners outside postsecondary institutions and may even be incompletely compiled for students inside postsecondary institutions. It has thus been difficult to compare systematically the literacy proficiencies of adults inside and outside of postsecondary institutions. Using data from the 1992 National Adult Literacy Survey (NALS), I present a new comparative analysis of the postsecondary students' literacy proficiencies.

National Adult Literacy Survey

Because I make considerable use of secondary analyses of the NALS data, it will be helpful to review briefly the major features of this survey. The NALS survey, conducted by the Educational Testing Service under contract with the National Center for Education Statistics, used an adult literacy profiling approach developed by Irwin Kirsch and his colleagues. This approach combines individual assessment methods based on item-response theory with large-scale population survey methods to profile the literacy proficiencies of adults on three defined literacy scales: prose, document, and quantitative literacy. NALS participants responded to a series of open-ended literacy tasks, such as completing a form, locating requested information on a map, extracting information from newspaper articles, and processing numerical information from charts and diagrams. Literacy proficiency scores on 0 to 500 point scales were estimated for respondents based on their responses to these functional literacy tasks. (Technical details of the survey and assessment techniques are described in Campbell, Kirsch, & Kolstad, 1992; Kirsch, Jungeblut, Jenkins, & Kolstad, 1993; Mosenthal & Kirsch, 1994.)

The NALS data analyzed here are from the household sample of 24,944 individuals randomly selected from the U.S. noninstitutionalized population age sixteen and above. These individuals were contacted and interviewed in their homes between January and August 1992. In addition to performing the simulated functional literacy tasks, survey respondents answered questions from an orally administered background questionnaire. Questionnaire responses provided information about participants' demographic characteristics, educational status and experiences, employment and training experiences, economic status, perceptions of and uses of literacy and various languages spoken in the home, and other background information.

Literacy Proficiencies of Postsecondary Students

Previous research with the NALS has compared the literacy proficiencies of adults at different levels of educational attainment (Baldwin, 1995; Barton & Lapointe, 1995; Kirsch, Jungeblut, Jenkins, & Kolstad, 1993; Howard & Obetz, 1998; Reder, 1998a). These studies all report monotonically increasing levels of adult literacy with each year of additional education. Such comparisons are very helpful, of course, but are somewhat indirect indicators of the literacy skills of the population of enrolled postsecondary students at any given level. Displays of literacy proficiency as a function of highest degree attained reflect the skills of adults who have completed given levels of postsecondary education but exclude individuals who completed the preceding level and are working toward completion of the given level, as well as individuals who completed the given level and are working toward completing the subsequent level. A further complication in interpreting displays of the adult population's literacy in terms of educational attainment is that many adults completed their postsecondary education years prior to the assessment, so that their assessed skills may not be representative of the population of postsecondary students at any given time.

IDENTIFYING CURRENTLY ENROLLED POSTSECONDARY STUDENTS WITHIN THE NALS. Fortunately, it is possible to identify and examine the characteristics of a representative subsample of currently enrolled postsecondary students within the NALS database. Two background questions asked about whether individuals were currently enrolled as students and, if so, working toward what degree. By identifying correspondents who are no longer in high school, are currently students, and are working toward a postsecondary credential, we can operationally define a subpopulation of currently enrolled postsecondary students within the NALS database. Within this group of currently enrolled postsecondary students, we can distinguish the following subgroups in terms of the degree they expect to receive: vocational/trade/business certificate, associate's degree, bachelor's degree, or advanced or professional degree.

Before describing the literacy proficiencies of the population of postsecondary students, it is important to validate that the population identified within NALS in this manner corresponds reasonably to and is representative of the population enrolled in postsecondary institutions at the time the NALS data were collected.[6] This cross-validation can be accomplished by comparing several sources of information about the size and characteristics of the U.S. postsecondary population at similar points in time:

- NALS: Winter-Spring-Summer 1992
- Integrated Postsecondary Education Data System: Fall 1991
- Integrated Postsecondary Education Data System: Fall 1992
- U.S. Census Bureau, Current Population Survey: Fall 1991
- U.S. Census Bureau, Current Population Survey: Fall 1992

The Integrated Postsecondary Education Data System (IPEDS) is an annual compilation of information about postsecondary institutions and their students carried out each fall by the U.S. Department of Education. The Current Population Survey (CPS) is a monthly general population survey conducted by the U.S. Census Bureau, with a supplement devoted to education each October. In order to bracket the NALS data, collected during the winter and spring of 1992, we compare both the fall 1991 and fall 1992 data from IPEDS and from CPS.

Table 4.1 displays the estimated size of the currently enrolled postsecondary student population from these disparate sources. The table shows the estimated numbers of undergraduate and graduate and total postsecondary students according to each source. Two columns are listed for the NALS; the left NALS column includes students pursuing vocational/trade/business certificates as well as those pursuing academic degrees, whereas the right NALS column includes only those pursuing academic (two-year, four-year, or graduate) degrees. Many of the analyses exclude nonacademic enrollees to maintain a higher level of comparability with other sources and classification systems.[7]

In general, a reasonable overall match exists between the population sizes estimated by NALS, IPEDS, and CPS for this time period. NALS seems to underestimate undergraduate and overestimate graduate enrollment, but considering the differences in information sources and survey methodology involved, the correspondence seems fairly reasonable. Further evidence of the comparability of these postsecondary student populations is provided in Table 4.2, which compares the demographic characteristics of the academic enrollees estimated by NALS and IPEDS.[8]

	NALS 1992 All Postsecondary Enrollees	NALS 1992 Academic Enrollees	IPEDS Fall 1991	IPEDS Fall 1992	CPS[a] Fall 1991	CPS[a] Fall 1992
Total	15,201	13,310	14,359	14,487	14,447	14,390
Undergraduate	11,552	9,661	12,439	12,538	12,160	11,855
Graduate	3,649	3,649	1,920	1,949	2,287	2,535

Table 4.1. Comparison of Currently Enrolled Postsecondary Students, 1991–1992 (in thousands).
[a]Author-adjusted estimates to include students thirty-five years of age and older.

Percentage	NALS 1992 Postsecondary Academic Enrollees	IPEDS Fall 1991
Men	48.5	45.3
Minority	25.4	21.2
Under age twenty-five	52.9	55.0
Ages twenty-six to thirty-four	26.6	25.1
Age thirty-five and up	20.4	20.0

Table 4.2. Comparison of Demographic Characteristics, NALS and IPEDS.

Table 4.2 displays very similar demographic characteristics for the currently enrolled postsecondary student population as identified through two quite different sampling frames. These results should increase confidence in the validity of the NALS subpopulation identified as postsecondary students. We next turn to profiling some of their important literacy characteristics.

LITERACY PROFICIENCIES OF POSTSECONDARY STUDENTS. Figure 4.2 displays the mean NALS literacy proficiencies for enrolled postsecondary students expecting degrees at the vocational, associate's, bachelor's, and postgraduate levels. Each cluster of bars in the figure shows the mean proficiency of a given literacy scale (prose, document, quantitative, or combined).[9] Proficiency scores are each scaled 0 to 500 and are broken down into five proficiency ranges, termed Level 1 (lowest) through Level 5 (Kirsch, Jungeblut, Jenkins, & Kolstad, 1993). Horizontal lines in the figure denote performance thresholds between adjacent proficiency levels. For example, the horizontal line at the scale value of 225 is the threshold between Level 1 and Level 2, and the horizontal line above it at the scale score of 275 marks the threshold between Levels 2 and 3.

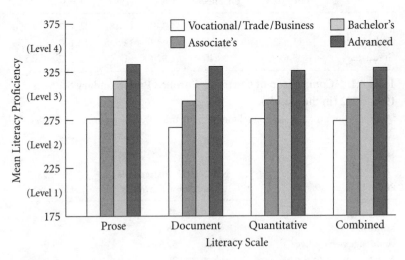

Figure 4.2.   Literacy Proficiency of
Currently Enrolled Postsecondary Students.
Source: National Adult Literacy Survey, 1992. Author calculations.

The same pattern is seen in the cluster of bars for each literacy scale. Currently enrolled postsecondary students have progressively higher mean literacy proficiencies at progressively higher levels of postsecondary education. Notice that these mean proficiency levels are at or above the threshold of Level 3 identified by the National Educational Goals Panel (1997) as the standard benchmark for adult literacy. The mean proficiencies of postsecondary students seeking vocational, trade, or business certificates are just at this threshold level, whereas the mean proficiencies of students in higher levels of postsecondary education are progressively higher, eventually surpassing the Level 4 threshold among postgraduate students. The fact that mean proficiency scores reach such levels does not, of course, imply that the proficiencies of all students are at that high a level. Figure 4.3 shows the corresponding percentages of students at each postsecondary stage who score below the Level 3 benchmark on the various literacy scales.

At progressively higher levels of postsecondary education, fewer of the enrolled students have proficiencies below Level 3. In the certificate programs, roughly half (46–54 percent) of the students have subbenchmark proficiencies across the prose, document, and quantitative scales, with most low scores occurring on the quantitative scale. Among associate's degree candidates, 23 to 30 percent have subbenchmark

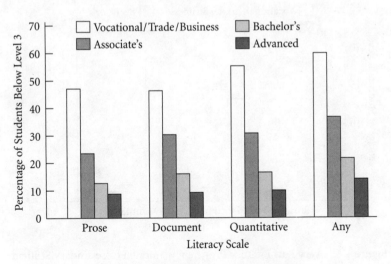

Figure 4.3. Low Literacy Proficiency Among Postsecondary Students.
Source: National Adult Literary Survey, 1992. Author calculations.

proficiencies. The corresponding percentages for bachelor's candidates are 12 to 16 percent, whereas only 8 to 10 percent of graduate students have a given proficiency below Level 3.

Substantial numbers of postsecondary students have proficiencies below Level 3. How many of these students have proficiencies at the lowest proficiency range (that is, Level 1)? Figure 4.4 displays the corresponding percentages of postsecondary students scoring in Level 1. Very small percentages of postsecondary students appear to be functioning at the lowest literacy level on any of the scales (proficiency score less than 225). Only 2 to 3 percent of students in baccalaureate or advanced degree programs have one or more proficiencies in Level 1, whereas more than 20 percent of students in certificate programs score at Level 1 on one or more proficiencies (most often on quantitative literacy). On all but the quantitative scale, less than 5 percent of two-year candidates score at the lowest proficiency level.

Analyses in the remainder of this section will be limited to students in academic degree programs (that is, the associate's, bachelor's, and advanced degree levels). This encompasses approximately 13.3 million currently enrolled students.[10] The literacy proficiencies of these academic postsecondary students are displayed in Table 4.3. The pro-

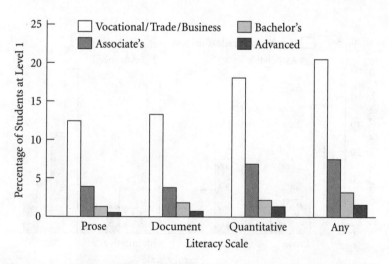

Figure 4.4.   Very Low Literacy Proficiency Among Postsecondary Students.
Source: National Adult Literacy Survey, 1992. Author calculations.

ficiencies on the various literacy scales exhibit nearly identical means and distributions over the five proficiency levels. From 15 percent to 17 percent of these students have literacy proficiencies below Level 3, with the preponderance of these students' sub-benchmark scores in Level 2.

More than one in five (22 percent) postsecondary students perform below Level 3 on one or more of the three NALS literacy scales. This represents a population of 2.9 million students performing at Level 1 or 2, of whom 30 percent are enrolled in two-year degree programs, 53 percent in bachelor's degree programs, and 17 percent in advanced degree programs. These low-scoring students have the following characteristics:

43 percent men, 57 percent women

55 percent minorities

15 percent limited English proficient (LEP)

24 percent not born in the United States (9 percent immigrated within the past five years)

Average age 26.6

88 percent live in a metropolitan area

25 percent live in households at or near the poverty level

If we focus on just postsecondary students scoring at Level 1 on one or more of the literacy scales, we find even higher concentrations of minority, immigrant, poor, and LEP students. The approximately

Type	Mean Proficiency	Percentage Level 1	Percentage Level 2	Percentage Level 3	Percentage Level 4	Percentage Level 5
Prose	315	2	13	44	37	4
Document	317	2	12	43	38	5
Quantitative	313	2	15	43	38	3
Combined	314	3	14	42	36	6

Table 4.3.   Literacy Proficiencies of Degree-Seeking Postsecondary Students.
Source: National Adult Literacy Survey (1992). Author calculations.

474,000 academic postsecondary students scoring at Level 1 on one or more of the proficiency scales have the following characteristics:

59 percent men, 41 percent women

81 percent minorities

42 percent LEP

42 percent not born in the United States (23 percent immigrated within the past five years)

Average age 27.7

90 percent live in a metropolitan area

29 percent live in households at or near the poverty level

To impart some idea of how the literacy skills of postsecondary students influence their progress through the postsecondary system, I will compare the proficiencies of three groups of adults having a slightly different relationship to given levels of postsecondary education. Figure 4.5 displays, for each level of postsecondary education, the mean NALS literacy proficiencies of three groups of adults: currently enrolled students working toward the given degree (group A), adults

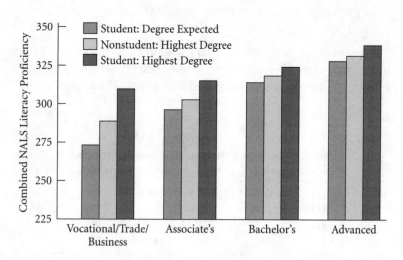

Figure 4.5.   Literacy Selection and
Literacy Development in Postsecondary Education.
Source: National Adult Literacy Survey, 1992. Author calculations.

who are not currently students who have attained the given degree (group B), and currently enrolled students who have attained the given degree and are continuing their studies (group C). These three groups are arranged from left to right within each cluster of bars in the figure. The figure shows a clear pattern among these groups across the various levels of postsecondary education. Overall literacy scores increase in each group as we move across progressively higher levels of postsecondary education.[11]

The effects of literacy development and literacy selection can be seen in the consistent patterning of the three groups' scores at each educational level in the figure. Postsecondary students working toward a given degree (group A) have lower scores than adults who are no longer students but previously attained that degree (group B). Group A is lower than group B because group A includes some postsecondary students whose skills may preclude them from attaining the degree that group B has already attained (literacy selection) and because some additional skill growth may take place as they complete their target degree (literacy development). The literacy scores of group B are in turn lower than those of group C, whose members are postsecondary students who have already attained the given degree and are currently working toward a higher level (group C). Again, this pattern is expected because of the effects of both literacy development (students in group C have taken additional education beyond the given degree level) and literacy selection (some group C students have been self-selected or institutionally selected for a higher-level degree program).

These clear-cut patterns offer further evidence that the literacy skills and knowledge assessed by the NALS are relevant to student success within the postsecondary system. Of course, the other factors described in the introduction also influence postsecondary outcomes (Berkner, Cuccaro-Alamin, & McCormick, 1996; Horn, 1996), and basic skills besides those assessed by NALS are needed for success in college (Baldwin, Kirsch, Rock, & Yamamoto, 1995; Barton & Lapointe, 1995; Pascarella & Terenzini, 1991).

LITERACY PROFICIENCIES OF GED RECIPIENTS IN POSTSECONDARY EDU-CATION. Because most adult literacy students who enroll in postsecondary education qualify for admission by passing the GED tests, the literacy skills of GED recipients who later become postsecondary students are of particular interest. According to Baldwin (1995), the NALS literacy proficiencies of these recipients appear equivalent to those of adults who attained a high school diploma (but went no further). This may not imply, however, that GED recipients' basic skills are on a par with those who finished high school and chose to continue with their education. Unfortunately, national surveys of postsecondary students usually sample only a small number of students who received GEDs, and test scores (for example, SAT or ACT admissions tests) are typically available for only a small fraction of this already small subsample. As a result, there are usually too few data to investigate this issue directly. A comparison study of the GED and NALS scores among a representative set of GED examinees surveyed by Baldwin and colleagues (1995) does provide some useful information on this point, however.

In the NALS-GED comparison study, a representative sample of all GED examinees during a one-year period was selected to participate in the study and complete the GED tests planned anyway as well as the NALS literacy assessment and a background questionnaire (Baldwin, Kirsch, Rock, & Yamamoto, 1995). The concurrent administration of the NALS and GED instruments to a large representative sample provided analysts with data needed to cross-validate the two assessments psychometrically. They found that the two assessments measured many similar skills (such as reading and general problem solving) as well as a unique set of abilities (for example, the GED tests included writing assessment, whereas the NALS assessed familiarity with and proficiency at manipulating documents common in everyday adult life).

Figure 4.6 depicts the mean NALS literacy proficiencies of three groups. The first group, represented by the leftmost bar in each cluster of bars in the figure, contains all GED examinees who passed the GED tests, regardless of whether they planned to enter postsecondary education. The second group, represented by the middle bar in each cluster, contains GED examinees who both passed the GED tests and planned (at the time of GED testing) to continue with postsecondary education. The third group, represented by the rightmost bar in each cluster, is the currently enrolled postsecondary students within NALS. The first two groups are taken from the GED-NALS Comparison Study (Baldwin, Kirsch, Rock, & Yamamoto, 1995), and the third group comes from the original NALS study (Kirsch, Jungeblut, Jenkins, & Kolstad, 1993).

The three clusters shown in Figure 4.6 display the mean prose, document, and quantitative literacy skills for the three groups of potential and enrolled postsecondary students. Clearly the overall group of

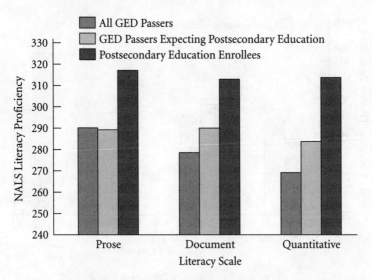

**Figure 4.6.   Literacy Proficiencies of
GED Passers and Postsecondary Students.**
Source: National Adult Literacy Survey, 1992. Author calculations.

enrolled postsecondary students has substantially higher average levels of proficiency than the GED groups. This is not particularly surprising, since the currently enrolled group includes students who have completed a range of postsecondary education and degrees, whereas the GED passer groups have not yet started any postsecondary education. Notice that the GED groups seem to have somewhat less well-developed quantitative literacy skills.

To explore this comparison further, these data were disaggregated by the level of postsecondary education that currently enrolled students and GED passers planning to enroll expected to complete. These data are shown in Figure 4.7. At each level of degree expected, two bars are shown: the left bars show the combined literacy proficiency of currently enrolled postsecondary students expecting to receive the given degree; the right bars show the corresponding average proficiency for GED passers expecting to enroll in and receive the given degree.

There is only a slight upward trend in proficiency scores among GED passers across increasing levels of degree expected. Among currently enrolled postsecondary students, a much steeper proficiency slope is evident across these levels of degrees anticipated. All groups

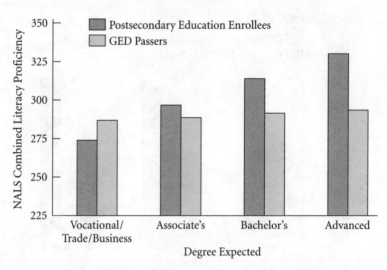

Figure 4.7.   Literacy Proficiencies of
GED Passers and Postsecondary Students by Degree Expected.
Source: National Adult Literacy Survey, 1992. Author calculations.

(with the exception of currently enrolled students in certificate programs) have mean proficiencies above the Level 3 threshold of 275. The fact that recent GED passers intending to continue with postsecondary education show relatively flat levels of proficiency across degrees expected should not be particularly surprising; unlike the currently enrolled students, they have not yet participated in the postsecondary system and its processes of literacy development and literacy selection. Perhaps these potential postsecondary students do not yet have sufficient contact with and information about postsecondary programs and the additional skills they may need to participate in them.

REMEDIAL EDUCATION FOR POSTSECONDARY STUDENTS

Recent surveys make it clear that many postsecondary students participate in basic skills training within their postsecondary institutions, in courses or programs usually labeled remedial or developmental education. These surveys have been conducted using representative samples of institutions and students at several levels of postsecondary instruction. Somewhat different pictures emerge depending on whether data are reported directly by individually sampled students or by administrators reporting aggregate data for their institutions. We will look first at data from institutional sources, then consider data reported by representative samples of individual postsecondary students.

Institutionally Reported Prevalence of Remedial Education

Lewis and Farris (1996), who described the National Survey on Remedial Education in Higher Education Institutions conducted in 1995, reported that 78 percent of institutions of higher education that enroll freshmen offered at least one remedial reading, writing, or mathematics course in fall 1995. Remedial courses were particularly common at public two-year institutions (100 percent) and institutions with high minority enrollments (94 percent).

Similar prevalence rates for remedial education have been estimated using institutional data in the federal Integrated Postsecondary Education Data System (IPEDS). IPEDS indicates, for example, that 79 percent of institutions of higher education offered remedial courses during the 1993–1994 academic year (U.S. Department of Education, 1994).

Institutions reported an average of 29 percent of their first-time freshmen enrolled in at least one remedial course. Higher remedial enrollments and lower remedial pass rates were reported by public two-year and high-minority enrollment institutions. Overall, about 75 percent of students enrolled in remedial courses successfully completed or passed those courses (Lewis & Farris, 1996).

Individually Reported Prevalence of Remedial Education

Estimates of the percentage of students taking remedial courses vary widely depending on whether individual students or their institutions report. Self-report by students yields substantially lower rates of participation in remedial courses. Whereas the institutional survey by Lewis and Farris (1996) reported that 29 percent of first-time freshmen were enrolled in one or more remedial courses, much lower participation rates are reported in surveys where students respond directly. The reasons for this discrepancy are not entirely clear. One possibility is that survey responses by administrators tend to be based on indirect information or on perceptions of the extent to which students "need" or are referred to remedial classes as opposed to direct counts of students enrolled in specific remedial courses. Another possibility is that students are reluctant to report taking remedial courses because of shame or embarrassment.[12]

Analyzing data from a direct survey of undergraduate students, the American Council on Education (1996) reported that about 13 percent of undergraduates took one or more remedial reading, writing, or math courses during the 1992–1993 academic year. Percentages for minority students were higher: 19 percent of African American, Hispanic, and Asian undergraduates and 15 percent of American Indian students took at least one remedial course, compared with 11 percent of white undergraduates. Neither the immediate degree goals nor the long-term educational goals of students taking developmental courses differed appreciably from those of other students. The two groups pursued similar majors as well.[13]

Horn and Berktold (1998), analyzing data from the National Postsecondary Student Aid Study (NPSAS), found a similar percentage (12 percent) of undergraduates in their first or second year of college who reported taking at least one remedial course during the 1995–1996 school year. Among students taking at least one such course, 70 percent took a remedial math course, 41 percent a remedial writing course, and 39 percent a remedial reading course. Younger students and those in two-year institutions were most likely to take remedial courses. In two-year and four-year institutions, 14 percent and 10 percent of undergraduates, respectively, took remedial courses during their first two years of college.

More detailed information is available from the Beginning Postsecondary Student (BPS) survey conducted by the National Center for Education Statistics. This longitudinal study followed a randomly sampled cohort of students who enrolled in postsecondary education for the first time during the 1989–1990 academic year. The cohort was followed through 1994, regardless of whether individuals stayed at their original institution, transferred to other institutions, dropped or stopped out, completed a degree, worked, and so forth. The BPS data set has particularly rich information about changes in individuals' enrollment and work status, personal and family social and economic contexts, finances, and other factors affecting individuals' decisions about their postsecondary education. The BPS also contains college admission test scores (SAT, ACT) when available, grades, type of high school diploma, and participation in remedial courses.

Analysis of the BPS data indicates that about 15 percent of beginning postsecondary students took one or more remedial courses sometime during their first two years. This represents about 387,000 basic skills students among the 2.5 million students who began their postsecondary education in a given year. The percentages for students beginning in four-year, two-year, and certificate programs are, respectively, 15 percent, 18 percent, and 9 percent. Figure 4.8 displays the percentage of beginning postsecondary students who took various types of remedial courses: math, reading, writing, and study skills. Consistent with other studies, remedial math is the developmental course most often taken: More than 8 percent of beginning postsecondary students take a remedial math course.

Figure 4.9 displays the overall percentage, by institutional type, of beginning undergraduates who took one or more remedial courses. Consistent with other research reviewed above, the highest incidence of developmental education occurs in public institutions, with public two-year institutions having slightly higher rates (18 percent) than public four-year institutions (16 percent). Private institutions have rates in the 10 to 11 percent range.

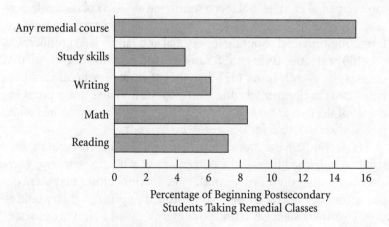

Figure 4.8.   Remedial Course Taking.

Source: Beginning Postsecondary Student Survey, 1991. Author calculations.

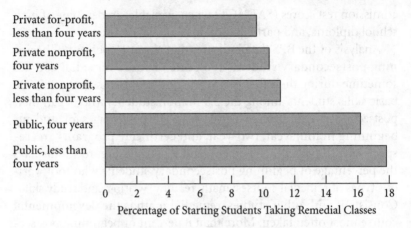

**Figure 4.9.   Remedial Course Taking by
Type of First Postsecondary Institution Attended.**

Source: Beginning Postsecondary Student Survey, 1991. Author calculations.

Men had slightly higher rates of participation in remedial courses than women: 16 percent versus 15 percent, respectively. Minorities, on the other hand, had considerably higher rates of participation: whereas 11 percent of white students participated in developmental education, 24 percent of black, 19 percent of Hispanic, 24 percent of Asian/Pacific Islander, and 18 percent of American Indian/Alaska Native students took remedial courses. Socioeconomic status (SES) plays a role here as well. Percentile SES ranks were calculated for BPS students from information provided about their personal and family backgrounds. On a 1–100 scale, the average SES rank of students who took remedial courses was slightly lower (57) than that of students who did not participate in developmental education (62). Cumulative grade point averages of the two groups were similar: 2.4 for students who had taken remedial courses, 2.5 for students who had not.

Let us compare the overall persistence rates of the two groups. Persistence is defined here as the percentage of students who, five years after beginning their postsecondary education, either had earned a postsecondary degree or were still enrolled in postsecondary education. (Nonpersistence is correspondingly defined as leaving postsecondary education without earning a degree.) The overall persistence rates are 57 percent and 64 percent, respectively, for participants and nonparticipants in developmental education.

Impact of Remedial Courses

The BPS data seem to indicate that postsecondary students who participate in remedial education are faring relatively well compared with their peers who do not participate. Their grades are about equal, and their persistence is nearly as high (which is impressive considering their somewhat lower SES). Another indicator is revealed by comparing the percentage of bachelor's degree recipients who report having taken remedial courses with the percentage of entering postsecondary students who report having taken remedial courses. McCormick and Horn (1996, p. 107) estimate, using data from the national Baccalaureate and Beyond study, that 10 percent of students who received bachelor's degrees during the 1992–1993 academic year reported having taken remedial courses as undergraduates. This percentage can be roughly compared with our BPS finding that 15 percent of all students who began their postsecondary education during the 1989–1990 school year took remedial courses during their first two years.

These numbers are not directly comparable, of course, because not all students receiving bachelor's degrees during 1992–1993 began their postsecondary education in the same year, let alone during 1989–1990. Nor did all beginning students in 1989–1990 initially enter or later transfer into four-year institutions. Nevertheless, the fact that 10 percent of students receiving bachelor's degrees had previously received basic skills suggests that developmental programs may well be assisting at least some students to develop the skills needed for academic success.

Despite such hopeful signs, such data provide a very uncertain picture of the impact or effectiveness of developmental programs as interventions to assist underprepared students. As a number of scholars have pointed out, the impact of such programs is exceedingly difficult to evaluate (Astin, 1998; Grubb, 1998). For one thing, we do not know if only those students who least needed remedial education choose to participate. The large gap between participation rates based on institutional reports and student self-reports may well reflect the gap between students judged by their institutions to need better basic skills and those who actually decide to participate in remedial courses. It is possible that students who really need remedial courses tend not to participate. We have little data about changes in students' basic skills and academic performance that can be associated with participation in these courses. Clearly, further research is needed to identify the impact of such programs on students' learning. Nevertheless, all things considered, the nearly comparable overall performance of the remedial students in the BPS data does suggest that the developmental programs are achieving at least a modicum of success. As we will see, other groups of postsecondary students show more obvious signs of academic distress within the same BPS data.

OUTCOMES FOR ADULT EDUCATION STUDENTS IN POSTSECONDARY EDUCATION

If adult education students are to pursue postsecondary education and training successfully after getting GEDs or equivalencies, they must enter programs and then successfully complete them. There is considerable evidence that adult education students neither enter nor complete postsecondary programs at rates comparable with those students earning high school diplomas or even at rates commensurate with their own expectations stated at the time of GED preparation and testing. This is particularly the case with respect to programs awarding two- or four-year degrees.

There are many reasons that individuals who did not complete high school may later find it difficult to access and complete postsecondary education after obtaining a GED. Many of the life circumstances associated with dropping out of high school may persist into adult life and serve as barriers to further education. Research on postsecondary persistence and attainment finds receipt of a GED or certificate of high school completion to be one of seven risk factors for dropping out of postsecondary education without attaining a degree. The other risk factors predicting persistence/attainment are being older than typical (delayed entry), attending part time, working full time, being financially independent, having dependents, and being a single parent (Berkner, Cuccaro-Alamin, & McCormick, 1996; Horn, 1996).

Boesel, Alsalam, and Smith (1998) reviewed follow-up studies of GED recipients, which for recent years report that 50 to 63 percent of GED recipients get additional postsecondary education or training, most of which occurs in two-year and vocational-technical colleges and most of which is focused on acquiring occupational skills.

Some relevant data are provided by the BPS survey. The first cohort studied by BPS began postsecondary education during the 1989–1990 school year. The BPS survey determined the type of high school credentials beginning postsecondary students obtained: high school diploma, GED, or other certificate of high school completion. According to the survey, there were roughly 145,000 GED graduates who began their postsecondary education in 1989–1990: 17,000 in four-year, 88,000 in two-year, and 40,000 in less-than-two-year schools. Table 4.4 displays the distribution of secondary credentials held by students beginning three levels of postsecondary institutions: four year (awarding bachelor's degrees), two year (awarding associate's degrees), and less than two year (awarding certificates).

Although nearly 20 percent of students entering certificate programs have a GED or equivalency, much smaller percentages of students beginning postsecondary education in two- or four-year institutions have a GED or equivalency certificate. About 2 percent and 7 percent of students entering four-year and two-year institutions, respectively, have a GED. Since 15 to 20 percent of all high school credentials issued at that time were GEDs, this indicates that relatively few GED recipients go on to postsecondary academic education. This pattern is consistent with research that contrasts the relatively large numbers of adult education students who report planning to pursue college degrees with the small numbers who actually enter or complete postsecondary academic programs.

Boesel and colleagues (1998) concluded that the grades of GED recipients who do enter postsecondary education are roughly comparable to those of students entering with high school diplomas. GED recipients' grades are initially lower during the first year of enrollment but rise to statistically comparable levels over time (perhaps, as Boesel and colleagues suggest, as the less able GED recipients are weeded out). The GPA ratios of the two groups rise from 0.82 to 1.06 in two-year and 0.86 to 1.00 in four-year colleges.

Institutional Level	Percentage with High School Diploma	Percentage with GED	Percentage with Certificate of Completion
Four year	98.1	1.6	0.3
Two year	92.8	7.1	0.2
Less than two year	80.2	18.8	1.0

Table 4.4.   Credentials of Beginning Postsecondary Students by Institutional Level Entered, 1990.
Source: Beginning Postsecondary Student Survey, 1991. Author calculations.

Some research indicates less persistence and degree completion among GED recipients in colleges than among students with high school diplomas. Boesel and colleagues (1998) argue that this difference is not a causal "result" of GED certification but rather of other long-established predisposing factors such as single-parent status and age-delayed entry. The BPS data can again shed some additional light on these issues.

Table 4.5 contrasts the persistence rates for beginning postsecondary students who enter various levels of institutions with a high school diploma or a GED. Overall, 63 percent of all beginning postsecondary students either attain a degree or are still enrolled and pursuing one five years after entry. The overall rate is much higher for students entering with high school diplomas (65 percent) than with GEDs (40 percent). Interestingly, there is no significant difference between the two groups' persistence rates from certificate (less than two-year) institutions. The highest persistence rates occur among students entering four-year institutions and the lowest rates for students entering two-year institutions. The biggest difference between the persistence rates of the two groups of students occurs in two-year institutions rather than in four-year institutions. It is difficult to determine whether this pattern results from the tendency of four-year schools to be more selective than two-year schools and to deny admission to students at risk (for whatever reason) of not completing programs successfully. This was suggested in Figure 4.7, where we see large differences in skills between GED passers intending to go to four-year schools and those of students currently enrolled in those four-year schools. Perhaps only the more skilled students are admitted (on the basis of college admission test scores, for example).

	Four Year	Two Year	Less Than Two Year	All
High school diploma	75	54	65	65
GED or equivalent	51	28	63	40
All	75	52	64	63

Table 4.5.   Persistence Rates for Beginning Postsecondary Students with High School Diplomas and GEDs, by Level of First Postsecondary Institution.
Source: Beginning Postsecondary Student Survey, 1989–1994. Author calculations.

To explore whether GED recipients in postsecondary education encounter more literacy-related problems than their peers with high school diplomas, I compared the relative experience of the two groups with remedial courses. Figure 4.10 displays the results of this analysis. It is clear that students with the GED are much more likely (22 percent versus 15 percent) to participate in remedial courses while in postsecondary education. The same pattern is evident for remedial reading, writing, and math courses. Although they have passed the GED tests, designed to certify their mastery of the skills and knowledge that high school graduates bring, the former adult education students may not be as well prepared for postsecondary education as students entering with regular high school diplomas. Additional research is needed to clarify the differences in skill sets that may be involved and to identify other factors that could be contributing to their different postsecondary experiences.

Other factors may be at work here as well. The two groups differ markedly in SES percentile rankings. In sharp contrast with the slight difference noted between the mean SES percentile rankings of postsecondary students who do and do not participate in developmental education, there is a substantial difference between the SES percentiles

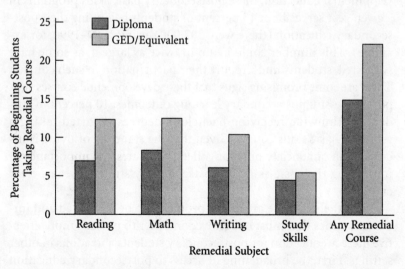

Figure 4.10.   Remedial Course Taking by Type of Secondary Credential.
Source: Beginning Postsecondary Student Survey, 1991. Author calculations.

of the GED and high school diploma groups: 35 versus 63. This difference undoubtedly is partly responsible for the observed differences between the two groups' persistence rates. At the same time, among students who manage to stay in school, SES differences appear not to influence their overall academic performance: the cumulative GPAs of the two groups are both 2.5. Further research is needed to understand better the differential influences of these factors on academic performance and persistence.

IMPLICATIONS FOR THEORY, RESEARCH, POLICY, AND PRACTICE

We have seen that nearly one in four (22 percent) of the nation's college students seeking academic degrees lacks the literacy skills to meet the designated national benchmark for adult literacy. Clearly policy and program design for improving the nation's adult literacy must focus not only on the K–12 and adult education systems but on the postsecondary system as well. An extensive set of support programs has emerged in postsecondary institutions for teaching many of the literacy skills that have traditionally been taught in adult basic and secondary education programs. Typically labeled as remedial or developmental education, these postsecondary basic skills programs in a given year serve about 15 percent of students beginning their postsecondary education (there were 387,000 during 1989–1990, for example). This number could be up to twice as large if, as some have suggested, students underreport their participation in such courses. There are some promising signs that these developmental courses support successful postsecondary learning outcomes; 10 percent of students nationwide receiving bachelor's degrees reported taking a remedial basic skills course. Given that the standard of living is increasing in our society only for college graduates, the importance of improving the basic skills of postsecondary students seems clear enough.

Nevertheless, there are major problems to be addressed and important issues that must be resolved in order to provide more effective literacy education for postsecondary students and adults in other settings. First, the broadening of access to postsecondary education and the provision of basic skills courses to college students remain controversial and politically uncertain goals in many venues. The finding that relatively few of the adult literacy students who obtain a GED eventually enroll in postsecondary education (given the large number who express an interest in doing so) is a clear concern. Even more troubling are the findings that the GED holders who do enroll have dramatically lower rates of persistence and completion within postsecondary programs. These data reflect problematic discontinuities between basic skills instruction in the adult education and postsecondary systems, as well as discontinuities between counseling, financial assistance, and other student services provided in the two systems. Such discontinuities impede the longer-term learning trajectories that adults need to follow to acquire both the literacy skills and the postsecondary degrees that they need.

To develop policies and programs that more effectively support learner progress both within and across the adult education and postsecondary education systems, a number of key policy and program issues need attention. Better theory, information, and research about adult learning and education will likely be needed to address these issues. Let us consider some implications of these results for theory and research in adult learning and literacy as well as for improved policy and practice in adult literacy education.

Implications for Policy and Practice

Despite the increasing overlap between the populations of adult education and remedial postsecondary students, surprisingly little attention has been given to developing systematic programmatic and policy bridges between the two systems. Previous reviews of policy and practice issues in adult literacy education (see, for example, Beder, 1991; Sticht, 1998; Venezky & Wagner, 1996) have not addressed the linkages between adult education and postsecondary education. Five-year state plans developed thus far for implementing the Workforce Investment Act (WIA) of 1998 have either totally overlooked coordination between adult education and remedial postsecondary education or paid scant lip-service to it. This is surprising, given that the WIA regulations recognize transition into postsecondary education as a positive outcome and require explicit coordination between adult literacy training and other services. Although there are some interesting programmatic exceptions (some noted below), the need to forge such linkages apparently has not yet been widely perceived.

Following are some recommendations on policy and programmatic issues that need careful attention:

Support learning paths from adult education into postsecondary education. It is clear that long-term increases in adults' literacy proficiencies will require developing more effective educational programs at all levels: K–12, adult education, postsecondary education, and workplace education. Given the increasingly intertwined pathways of adult education, postsecondary education, and work, more coordination in the design and implementation of basic skills programs across these sectors is needed.

Although many policymakers focus on addressing future needs through K–12 or even K–16 educational reforms, such changes will not help older and returning students in need of better skills and more education. We will be unable to meet the national education goal or provide the skills that adults need to move out of poverty if we do not create more easily traversed pathways from adult education into postsecondary education. In particular, there must be more effective types of counseling as well as financial and academic support for GED students and recipients wishing to go on for postsecondary degrees. Better transition support, delivered in a learner-centered fashion, could reduce the burden carried by learners, who already face enough difficulties, in navigating and integrating a highly fragmented and complex system.

Advance the goal of adult education from high school equivalency to college preparation. Too many students who obtain a GED or other equivalency certification apparently are not sufficiently well prepared to succeed in college. The discontinuities between adult and postsecondary education appear to be barriers to their success. Although not all adult education students may wish or choose to go to college, a more seamless learner-centered system is needed for those who do. Yet why should the target of adult education programs be high school completion rather than college readiness? There are important issues to resolve in forging such bridge programs. Where should they be located (primarily on campuses, for example, or primarily in separate locations), how should they be financed (through federal adult education funds, for example, or through tuition dollars), and who should teach these programs?[14]

Make postsecondary and adult education teachers and administrators more familiar with each other's programs. There are many compelling reasons for practitioners in developmental secondary education and adult education to familiarize themselves with each other's programs. These are the educators who must design and build the bridges across the current gaps between the two systems. In most cases, the systems operate independently of each other, even on campuses where both remedial postsecondary and adult education classes are offered.[15]

As literacy educators working in one of the settings become more familiar with the learners, instructional models, resources, and problems of programs in the other setting, they will be better prepared to design and implement more effective bridges between programs. There are currently both important similarities and differences between these programs. Grubb and Kalman (1994) describe the variety of remedial programs in subbaccalaureate institutions (especially community colleges) and point out similarities between developmental education in these institutions and other forms of adult basic skills education, such as high rates of attrition and apparent low levels of student motivation. Other common issues can be seen as well: low and uncertain levels of program funding; rumors of ineffectiveness; teacher issues, including lack of certification and reliance on part-time rather than full-time personnel; the marginality of learners, teachers, and programs; and poorly defined articulation with other programs.

There are other features that differentiate the two types of programs and keep them apart. College students taking remedial basic skills courses, for example, generally pay tuition for these classes but do not receive degree credit for them, whereas students in federally funded adult education courses receive similar instruction and assistance free of charge.

Encourage closer linkages between practitioners and professional organizations in adult education and developmental education. Practitioners currently working in the two types of programs generally belong to distinct professional organizations, have different professional identities, attend separate conferences, and read different journals. It would be helpful if these organizations jointly sponsored professional development activities and occasional publications directed to both memberships. Such joint activities could be a productive way to forge closer linkages between these two largely separate worlds of practice that find themselves serving increasingly overlapping populations of learners. More effective sharing of resources, instructional strategies and materials, and problem-solving techniques will benefit everyone, especially the students desiring more seamless learning paths leading from adult education to postsecondary education.

Share expertise across programs and settings on adult learning and literacy development. To a considerable extent, practitioners in the two settings have developed complementary expertise and approaches to adult literacy education. Adult educators have a great deal of experience with outreach and delivery models that relate to diverse individual learner goals and contexts. Instructional models have been developed specifically for delivery in workplace and family settings, for example. A range of contextualized or "functional context" models has emerged that draw on the interests, needs, and goals of individual adult learners (Sticht, 1998). These adult education models attempt to build linkages between basic skills instruction and other personal, work, family, and community contexts of interest to learners.

Developmental educators in postsecondary programs, on the other hand, have tried to create models that build contextual linkages between basic skills instruction and other academic content areas and courses. A variety of these embedded (rather than detached) models of remedial basic skills instruction have emerged. The supplementary instruction model (Martin & Arendale, 1998; Ramirez, 1997), the adjunct course model (Commander & Stratton, 1998), and the package course model (Wilcox, delMas, Stewart, Johnson, & Ghere, 1997), for example, are different approaches to linking developmental education with specific academic courses.

Thus there are models available in each domain that can be valuable resources for practitioners who are trying to bridge these two worlds of basic skills education. Important pedagogical principles shared by educators in the two domains can inform the design and implementation of these bridge programs. The central importance of learning communities, for example, is emphasized by theorists in both camps (see, for example, Street, 1995, and Tinto, 1998). The concepts of critical thinking (for example, Chaffee, 1998, and Sticht, 1998) and contextualized learning are also widely shared.

Develop better techniques for assessing the relative cost-effectiveness of different program models. There is growing need in both adult education and developmental postsecondary education to assess the impact of instructional programs on learner outcomes. Analysts have looked closely at both adult education programs (Sticht, 1998) and remedial secondary programs (Astin, 1998; Grubb, 1998) and have concluded that current data collection efforts and program evaluation methods cannot provide reliable measures of program impact on participants' basic skill gains or on other workplace or higher education outcomes. A renewed commitment to addressing the difficult assessment and program evaluation issues involved is needed.

Closely coordinate state policy and law with federal policy and initiatives. Lewis and Farris (1996), using data from the National Survey on Remedial Education in Higher Education Institutions conducted in 1995, reported that state laws or policies affect remedial offerings in about one-third of the postsecondary institutions. Typically such policies either require or encourage institutions to offer remedial education. About one in four institutions reported time limits on remedial course offerings set by either institutional policy or state policy or law. Many institutions experience external directives restricting their ability to design and implement remedial programs effectively. Conflicts arise frequently between institutional practice, state law or policy, and federal policy and initiatives in developmental education.

One issue that has not yet received much attention concerns the huge financial stakes involved with accreditation, tuition, and student financial aid as related to developmental education. Under current law and regulations, students matriculated in academic programs are eligible for Pell grants and student loans and pay tuition dollars for any remedial courses they take, but they receive no credit toward a degree for these courses. If the same students were to take basic skills courses through federally funded adult education programs, they would pay no tuition and again receive no degree credit for those courses. There are thus high financial stakes involved in changes in state policy affecting remedial education. When state university systems, for example, are discouraged from offering remedial education, many institutions can be heavily affected in financial terms as programs and students move to other institutions, such as community colleges or proprietary schools. To get a sense of scale, consider these examples reported by the American Council on Education (1996):

- In Florida, 70 percent of incoming community college students in 1993–1994 needed remedial courses, costing $53 million.
- Texas, which has one hundred two-year and four-year schools, pays an annual tab of $60 million for remedial programs.
- California State University trustees adopted a new policy in January 1996 to cut back on remedial courses costing $10 million at twenty-two campuses.

Clearly neither the students nor the public institutions involved in remedial education will be indifferent to the huge financial implications of changes in state and federal policies. The financial implications of moving large numbers of adult literacy learners (along with their tuition dollars, grants, and loans) among institutions and programs must be carefully considered as educators and policymakers strive to develop improved policies and program designs.

Attend to diversity and equity concerns. Basic skill issues are closely connected to a range of societal racial, ethnic, linguistic, and gender diversity issues. This is the case for both adult education and developmental education in postsecondary institutions. Ongoing and proposed cutbacks in remedial education will certainly have a disproportionate impact on poor and minority students. Jencks and Phillips (1998) make a strong case that when socioeconomic or basic skills differences among students are equated, race-based inequities in the eventual college completion rates of high school students disappear. Since a college education is becoming increasingly less affordable for many poor and minority students, it becomes all the more important to retain strong support for basic skills programs.

Implications for Theory and Research

Resolving many of the policy and program issues will require additional research in adult learning, adult literacy education, and postsecondary education. There are a number of topics for which further research and better theory would be particularly helpful:

Role of literacy proficiency and high school experience in entrance into and persisting in postsecondary education and lifelong learning activities. There is a growing research literature on the factors that influence students' and adults' decisions about continuing and/or returning to school for postsecondary education and about how postsecondary students manage concurrent responsibilities at work and at home. Better data are needed about these issues among adults who obtain nontraditional high school credentials such as the GED. Unfortunately, the low rates of GED recipients' subsequent enrollment in postsecondary education usually mean that there is too small a subsample of GED recipients in college within these follow-up studies to portray adequately their experiences and the unique problems they face. This makes it harder, of course, to understand the distinctive types of support that could positively influence their postsecondary experiences. In the future, it would be helpful if such studies could oversample postsecondary students with GEDs.

Interaction between literacy selection and literacy development processes within postsecondary education. There is considerable evidence in postsecondary education of both literacy development processes (through which students' literacy abilities increase) and literacy selection processes (through which students' literacy abilities weed them out of particular institutions, programs, and classes). There are many correlated characteristics at the student and institutional levels (Zemsky, 1998, in preparation; Zemsky, Shaman, & Ianozzi, 1997). The tight correlations between characteristics such as student abilities and institutional prestige are particularly difficult to interpret because they confound literacy selection and development processes happening within the postsecondary system. Improved design of developmental education will likely require an improved capacity to distinguish outcomes attributable to literacy selection versus literacy development processes at these various levels.

Transfer of learning between workplace and educational settings. The fact that a preponderance of postsecondary students concurrently work and attend school suggests that we need to understand better the factors determining how learning in one context or role influences learning and performance in the other. Ongoing efforts to restructure workplaces into learning organizations as well as efforts to restructure postsecondary institutions to fit better with workplaces will be much more effective if we understand the similarities in and differences between learning in the two contexts.

Skill gains produced by literacy education in postsecondary institutions. New research is needed to provide more direct evidence about students' skill gains resulting from various types of classes and programs supporting literacy development. There are insufficient data to allow experts to answer basic questions about what students learn in college and how such learning addresses the needs of the workplace and of adult life in general (Astin, 1998; Boylan, Bliss, & Bonham, 1997; Grubb, 1998). One promising point of departure may be to look at the distinctive characteristics and experiences of the 10 percent of bachelor of arts degree recipients who reported taking remedial courses compared with those of less academically successful students in remedial courses.

Development of literacy practices in postsecondary settings. Much of the large-scale research done on literacy education in postsecondary settings has relied extensively on standardized measures of literacy proficiency such as those drawn on in this chapter. But much student literacy development may be better understood not only through such test scores but also through detailed descriptions and analyses of how students engage in (and are sometimes excluded from access to) particular kinds of literacy practices valued by the institutions (Howard & Obetz, 1998; Hull, 1998; Smith, 1998)—for example, writing essays; searching for, compiling, and citing relevant articles for a research paper; and solving chemistry problems on an exam. Rather than investigating how best to raise students' literacy scores, a more useful question may be how to build their engagement in such literacy practices (Reder, 1994).

Follow-up studies with literacy assessments of postsecondary students. The design of improved policies and programs must be based on the results of longer-term follow-up studies of postsecondary students that include assessments of literacy skills and practices at multiple time points during and after students' postsecondary education. These studies could also assess the impact of literacy development during college on lifelong learning practices, including the use of technology and subsequent participation in continuing education, additional postsecondary education, and technical training. Existing national longitudinal studies, such as the Beginning Postsecondary Student survey or Baccalaureate and Beyond, could be used for this purpose, but their authors would need to lengthen their follow-up periods considerably and include many more students entering college with low literacy proficiencies.

Differential influences of social and economic circumstances on post-secondary persistence and performance. Further research is needed to understand better the differential interactions of social and economic factors on academic performance and persistence. The existing research base has identified a set of seven risk factors that influence persistence and attainment. One of these factors is having a GED or other nontraditional high school credential. Since we are interested in developing effective programs and policies for this particular at-risk group, it is essential to investigate how the other risk factors interact in influencing their postsecondary outcomes.

Notes

1. These "proprietary" schools typically offer certificates of completion for specific courses of study in given occupations, trades, or businesses.

2. Mean earnings for adults age eighteen and over with education, taken from U.S. Census Bureau, Current Population Survey, Educational Attainment in the United States: March 1998 (Update), Table 9 (p. 51).

3. Although the NALS assessed three scales of literacy (prose, document, and quantitative), the results of interest here are very similar for each of the three scales, so a single combined measure that averages performance across the three scales is shown in this figure for brevity (see Reder, 1998b).

4. There is a substantial amount of missing data affecting these estimates. Among the national sample of 22,548 participants entering programs between April 1, 1991, and March 31, 1992, data were missing on highest degree and/or nativity from 3,532 (15.7 percent) of the cases. Most of these data were missing because a second program intake form designed for the NEAEP was not completed. Despite the potential bias produced by these missing data (Cohen, Garet, & Condelli, 1995), it is clear that a substantial number of adult literacy students have U.S. high school diplomas or higher degrees.

5. Concurrent participation in postsecondary education was not asked in the NEAEP survey.

6. The subsample size for this identified group of postsecondary students within NALS is 2,254.

7. Since the CPS education supplement includes only individuals under thirty-five years of age, the CPS estimates were inflated by NALS-derived ratios of the total postsecondary student population over the subpopulation under thirty-five years of age. These adjustments were performed separately for the undergraduate and graduate populations.

8. CPS data were not used here because the data excluded students thirty-five years of age and older.

9. Elsewhere (1998b) I suggest the use of the combined scale in some circumstances because of the high degree of intercorrelation among the assessed prose, document, and quantitative proficiencies.

10. The subsample size for this subgroup of postsecondary students within NALS is 1,977.

11. For simplicity, this figure shows only the combined literacy score (the average of the prose, document, and quantitative scores). Table 4.3 indicates that this combined measure will probably behave the same way as the three literacy scale measures. See Reder (1998b) for further details.

12. Another explanation was suggested by a reviewer of this chapter: students underreport participation in remedial courses because they do not realize that some of the courses they took (such as "Basic Math") were in fact remedial. This seems unlikely, though; most students know

that particular courses are remedial because they must pay tuition for them but do not receive credit toward a degree for them.

13. Students taking remedial math courses were more likely to major in health-related fields than their peers who did not take any remedial classes (see American Council on Education, 1996).

14. There are examples of such bridge programs that can be resources for developing new policy and program designs. Delaware, for example, has some bridge models of college prep programs, as do participating unions in the Consortium for Worker Education in New York City.

15. In states where the community college system is the delivery system for federally funded adult education, both adult education classes (offered free of charge to students) and remedial postsecondary classes (for which students pay tuition but receive no credit toward a degree) are generally offered on the same campus. Even in such cases the two systems usually operate independently, with separate budgets, staff, and student services. There are some notable exceptions that can serve as models or resources for developing new policies and program designs. At North Iowa Area Community College in Mason City, for example, many functions and services are merged across the two programs.

References

American Council on Education (1996). *Remedial education: An undergraduate student profile.* Washington, DC: Author.

Astin, A. W. (1998, January 26–27). *Evaluating remedial programs is not just a methodological issue.* Paper presented at Conference on Replacing Remediation in Higher Education, Stanford University.

Bach, S. K., Banks, M. T., Kinnick, M. K., Ricks, M. F., Stoering, J. M., & Walleri, R. D. (forthcoming). Student attendance patterns and performance in an urban post-secondary environment. *Research in Higher Education.*

Baldwin, J. (1995). Literacy skills of adults and potential college students. *Research Briefs, 6*(4). Washington, DC: American Council of Education.

Baldwin, J., Kirsch, I. S., Rock, D., & Yamamoto, K. (1995). *The literacy proficiencies of GED examinees: Results from the GED-NALS Comparison Study.* Washington, DC, and Princeton, NJ: American Council on Education and Educational Testing Service.

Ballard, B., & Clanchy, J. (1988). Literacy in the university: An "anthropological" approach. In G. Taylor, B. Ballard, V. Beasley, H. K. Bock, J. Clanchy, & P. Nightingale (Eds.), *Literacy by degrees* (pp. 7–23).

Milton Keynes, England, and Philadelphia: Society for Research into Higher Education and Open University Press.

Barton, P. E., & Lapointe, A. (1995). *Learning by degrees: Indicators of performance in higher education.* Princeton, NJ: Educational Testing Service.

Beder, H. (1991). *Adult literacy: Issues for policy and practice.* Malabar, FL: Krieger Publishing Company.

Berkner, L. K., Cuccaro-Alamin, S., & McCormick, A. C. (1996). *Descriptive summary of 1989–90 beginning postsecondary students: Five years later* (Statistical Analysis Report NCES 96–155). Washington, DC: U.S. Department of Education, National Center for Education Statistics.

Berktold, J., Geis, S., & Kaufman, P. (1998). *Subsequent educational attainment of high school dropouts* (Statistical Analysis Report NCES 98–085). Washington DC: U.S. Department of Education, National Center for Education Statistics.

Boesel, D., Alsalam, N., & Smith, T. M. (1998). *Educational and labor market performance of GED recipients: Research synthesis.* Washington, DC: U.S. Department of Education.

Boylan, H. R., Bliss, L. B., & Bonham, B. S. (1997). Program components and their relationship to student performance. *Journal of Developmental Education, 20*(3), 2–4, 6, 8.

Campbell, A., Kirsch, I. S., & Kolstad, A. (1992). *Assessing literacy: The framework for the National Adult Literacy Survey.* Washington, DC: National Center for Education Statistics, U.S. Department of Education.

Chaffee, J. (1998, January 26–27). *Critical thinking: The cornerstone of remedial education.* Paper presented at Conference on Replacing Remediation in Higher Education, Stanford University.

Cohen, J., Garet, M., & Condelli, L. K. (1995). *Methodological review of the National Evaluation of Adult Education Programs* (draft). Washington, DC: Pelavin Research Institute.

Commander, N. E., & Stratton, C. B. (1998, January 26–27). *Beyond remediation: Adjunct courses as a new direction for academic assistance.* Paper presented at Conference on Replacing Remediation in Higher Education, Stanford University.

Cooper, S. E. (1998, August). Remediation's end: Can New York educate the children of the "whole people"? *Academe,* 14–20.

Development Associates. (1993). *National evaluation of adult education programs: Second interim report—profile of client characteristics.* Washington, DC: U.S. Department of Education.

Finn, J. D., & Gerber, S. B. (1998). Work, school, and literacy. In M. C. Smith (Ed.), *Literacy for the 21st century: Research, policy, and practice*. Westport, CT: Greenwood Publishing Group.

Gray, M. J., & Grace, J. D. (1997). *Enhancing the quality and use of student outcomes data: Final report of the National Postsecondary Education Cooperative Working Group on Student Outcomes from a Data Perspective* (NCES Statistical Analysis Report NCES 97–992). Washington, DC: U.S. Department of Education, National Center for Education Statistics.

Grubb, W. N. (1997). The returns to education and training in the sub-baccalaureate labor market, 1984–1990. *Economics of Education Review, 16*(3), 231–246.

Grubb, W. N. (1998, January 26–27). *From black box to Pandora's box: Evaluating remedial/developmental education.* Paper presented at Conference on Replacing Remediation in Higher Education, Stanford University.

Grubb, W. N., & Kalman, J. (1994). Relearning to earn: The role of remediation in vocational education and job training. *American Journal of Education, 103,* 54–93.

Harrington, P., & Sum, A. (in preparation). The post-college earnings experiences of bachelor degree holders in the U.S.: Estimated economic returns to major fields of study. In S. Reder, B. A. Holland, & M. P. Latiolais (Eds.), *Learning and work on campus and on the job: The evolving relationship between higher education and employment.*

Horn, L. J. (1996). *Nontraditional undergraduates: Trends in enrollment from 1986 to 1992 and persistence and attainment among 1989–90 beginning postsecondary students* (Statistical Analysis Report NCES 97–578). Washington, DC: U.S. Department of Education, National Center for Education Statistics.

Horn, L. J., & Berktold, J. (1998). *Profile of undergraduates in U.S. postsecondary institutions: 1995–96* (Statistical Analysis Report NCES 98–094). Washington, DC: U.S. Department of Education, National Center for Education Statistics.

Howard, J., & Obetz, W. S. (1998). Community college literacy: Is the middle right? In M. C. Smith (Ed.), *Literacy for the 21st century: Research, policy and practice* (pp. 125–138). Westport, CT: Greenwood Publishing.

Hull, G. (1998, January 26–27). *Alternatives to remedial writing: Lessons from theory, from history, and a case in point.* Paper presented at Conference on Replacing Remediation in Higher Education, Stanford University.

Jencks, C., & Phillips, M. (1998). The black-white test score gap: An introduction. In C. Jencks & M. Phillips (Eds.), *The black-white test score gap* (pp. 1–51). Washington, DC: Brookings Institution Press.

Kirsch, I. S., Jungeblut, A., Jenkins, L., & Kolstad, A. (1993). *Adult literacy in America: A first look at the results of the National Adult Literacy Survey.* Washington, DC: U.S. Department of Education, National Center for Education Statistics.

Kojaku, L. K., & Nunez, A-M. (1998). *Descriptive summary of 1995–96 beginning postsecondary students* (Statistical Analysis Report NCES 1999–030). Washington, DC: U.S. Department of Education, National Center for Education Statistics.

Levin, H. M., Koski, W. S., & Bersola, S. (1998). *A report on the conference on replacing remediation in higher education.* Stanford, CA: Stanford University School of Education, National Center for Postsecondary Improvement.

Lewis, L., & Farris, E. (1996). *Remedial education at higher education institutions in Fall, 1995* (Report NCES 97–584). Washington, DC: U.S. Department of Education, National Center for Education Statistics.

Martin, D. C., & Arendale, D. R. (1998, January 26–27). *Mainstreaming of developmental education: Supplemental instruction and video-based supplemental instruction.* Paper presented at Conference on Replacing Remediation in Higher Education, Stanford University.

McCormick, A. C., & Horn, L. J. (1996). *A descriptive summary of 1992–93 bachelor's degree recipients: One year later* (Statistical Analysis Report NCES 96–158). Washington, DC: U.S. Department of Education, National Center for Education Statistics.

Mickler, M. L., & Chapel, A. C. (1989). Basic skills in college: Academic dilution or solution? *Journal of Developmental Education, 13*(1), 2–4, 16.

Mosenthal, P. B., & Kirsch, I. S. (1994, December). *Defining the proficiency standards of adult literacy in the U.S.: A profile approach.* Paper presented at the National Reading Conference, San Diego.

National Alliance of Business. (1996, April). *Workforce Economics, 2*(1), 6.

National Educational Goals Panel. (1997). *The National Education Goals report: Building a nation of learners.* Washington, DC: U.S. Government Printing Office.

Pascarella, E. T., & Terenzini, P. T. (1991). *How college affects students.* San Francisco: Jossey-Bass.

Ramirez, G. M. (1997). Supplemental instruction: The long-term impact. *Journal of Developmental Education, 21*(1), 2–4, 6, 8,10.

Reder, S. (1994). Practice engagement theory: A sociocultural approach to literacy across languages and cultures. In R. M. Weber, B. Ferdman, &

A. Ramirez (Eds.), *Literacy across languages and cultures* (pp. 33–74). Albany: State University of New York Press.

Reder, S. (1997a). Lifelong learning and educational reform. *Journal of Higher Education and Lifelong Learning* (Japan), Special Issue, 31–38.

Reder, S. (1997b). *First level learners: Characteristics and participation of adult basic literacy learners.* Bethesda, MD: Abt Associates.

Reder, S. (1998a). Literacy selection and literacy development: Structural equation models of the reciprocal effects of education and literacy. In M. C. Smith (Ed.), *Literacy for the 21st century: Research, policy and practice* (pp. 139–157). Westport, CT: Greenwood Publishing.

Reder, S. (1998b). Issues of dimensionality and construct validity of the NALS assessment. In M. C. Smith (Ed.), *Literacy for the 21st century: Research, policy, practices, and the National Adult Literacy Survey* (pp. 37–57). Westport, CT: Greenwood Publishing.

Reder, S. (forthcoming). Literacy proficiency and lifelong learning. In N. Stacey (Ed.), *The adult learner.* Washington, DC: Government Printing Office.

Ruppert, S., Harris, Z., Hauptman, A., Nettles, M., Perna, L., Millett, C., Rendón, L., Tinto, V., Hurtado, S., & Inkelas, K. (1998). *Reconceptualizing access in postsecondary education: Report of the Policy Panel on Access* (NCES 98–283). Washington, DC: U.S. Department of Education, National Center for Education Statistics.

Smith, M. C. (Ed.). (1998). *Literacy for the 21st century: Research, policy, practices, and the National Adult Literacy Survey.* Westport, CT: Greenwood Publishing.

Spann, M. G. (1996). National Center for Developmental Education: The formative years. *Journal of Developmental Education, 20*(2), 2–4, 6.

Sticht, T. G. (1998). *Beyond 2000: Future directions for adult education.* El Cajon, CA: Applied Behavioral and Cognitive Sciences.

Street, B. V. (1995). *Social literacies: Critical approaches to literacy development, ethnography, and education.* Reading, MA: Addison-Wesley.

Tinto, V. (1998, January 26–27). *Learning communities and the reconstruction of remedial education in higher education.* Paper presented at Conference on Replacing Remediation in Higher Education, Stanford University.

U.S. Department of Education. (1994). *Characteristics of the nation's postsecondary institutions: Academic year 1993–94* (NCES 94–388). Washington, DC: Author.

Venezky, R. L., & Wagner, D. A. (1996). Supply and demand for literacy instruction in the United States. *Adult Education Quarterly, 46,* 197–208.

Wilcox, K. J., delMas, R. C., Stewart, B., Johnson, A. B., & Ghere, D. (1997). The "Package Course" experience and developmental education. *Journal of Developmental Education, 20*(3), 18–20, 22, 24, 26.

Zemsky, R. (1998, January–February). Defining the market taxonomy for two-year institutions. *Change,* 35–38.

Zemsky, R. (forthcoming). Changing the focus: New questions for the school-to-work transition. In S. Reder, B. A. Holland, & M. P. Latiolais (Eds.), *Learning and work on campus and on the job: The evolving relationship between higher education and employment.*

Zemsky, R., Shaman, S., & Ianozzi, M. (1997, November–December). In search of strategic perspective: A tool for mapping the market in postsecondary education. *Change.*

CHAPTER FIVE

Health and Literacy
A Review of Medical
and Public Health Literature

Rima E. Rudd

Barbara A. Moeykens

Tayla C. Colton

Literacy has recently emerged as a key item on the re-search agenda in medicine and public health. Researchers and practitioners are grappling with evidence that the reading ability of the average adult falls well below the reading level of educational materials, directives, forms, and informed-consent documents commonly used in the health field. The threats to effective communication and efficacious care have spurred interest in exploring strategies for more effective communication. In addition, increased attention to literacy may be driven by legal concerns for adequate protection of human subjects and ethical concerns for patient autonomy in informed-consent procedures. Methodological strides made since 1992, particularly in the form of new tools for rapid literacy measurement, have enabled a number of researchers to explore links between the literacy level of patients and health outcomes that will have critical policy implications. These investigations can best be undertaken through collaborative efforts between educators who understand the learning process and health professionals who understand the protocols used in health care and public health education. Findings will serve to enrich policy and practice.

LITERACY IN THE UNITED STATES

Studies of adult literacy in various regions of the United States have been consistent in finding that a significant proportion of adults have reading difficulties (Hunter & Harman, 1979). However, it was not until the early 1990s that a rigorous study of adult literacy in the United States was undertaken by the Department of Education (ED) at the direction of Congress. The National Adult Literacy Survey (NALS), conducted in 1992 and the most comprehensive source of data on literacy in the United States, interviewed 24,944 adults age sixteen and above (Kirsch, Jungeblut, Jenkins, & Kolstad, 1993; Chapter Four of this book). The NALS focused on functional literacy—those literacy skills most commonly put to use in everyday activities. For example, NALS reading assessments were based on newspaper stories to measure prose literacy, employment forms to assess document literacy, and bus schedules to measure quantitative literacy. Literacy skills were placed on a continuum, and findings were reported for five levels, with Level 5 reflecting the highest skills. Survey design and sampling rigor enabled analysts to estimate that more than 90 million adults in the United States (46 to 51 percent of the adult population) have extremely limited or limited reading and quantitative skills. It is also estimated that 21 to 23 percent of adults would score in the lowest of five levels and would have difficulty using reading, writing, and computational skills for everyday tasks. Furthermore, the NALS study presented the surprising finding that most of the adults performing at the two lowest literacy levels did not see themselves as having limited skills, stating their belief that they could read and write English well or very well. Many also reported that they do not seek help with reading from others (Kirsch, Jungeblut, Jenkins, & Kolstad, 1993).

NALS analysts note that those performing in the lowest two literacy levels were more likely to be poor and to report having a physical or mental disability or other health condition that keeps them from full participation in work or home activities. The NALS findings also show that older adults are more likely to demonstrate limited literacy skills than are middle-aged or younger adults. In addition, the survey indicates that members of minority populations, especially those for whom English is a second language, are more likely to perform in the lowest two literacy levels. African American, American Indian/Alaskan Native, Hispanic, and Asian/Pacific Islander adults were shown to be more likely than white adults to have limited literacy skills (Kirsch,

Jungeblut, Jenkins, & Kolstad, 1993; Reder, 1998). The population characteristics of those scoring in the lowest literacy skill groups overlap with those identified at highest risk for health problems.

LINKS BETWEEN EDUCATION AND HEALTH

Education, occupation, and income are commonly used markers of socioeconomic status and are strongly correlated with health. *Healthy People 2000*, the U.S. Department of Health and Human Services (DHHS) report of national health promotion and disease prevention objectives for the nation (U.S. DHHS, 1990), reported that people living in poverty have limited access to health promotion and disease prevention programs and to curative services; are often subject to greater environmental and occupational exposures; and have limited options in education, housing, and employment, all of which are often substandard among those with limited incomes. Consequently, *Healthy People 2000* highlighted the need to reduce the disparities in health between the more advantaged segments of the population and those groups that are disadvantaged economically, educationally, and politically. Commenting on the body of evidence establishing a strong link between socioeconomic status and health, Blane (1995) noted the "striking consistency in the distribution of mortality and morbidity between social groups. The more advantaged groups . . . tend to have better health than the other members of their societies."

A report of national trends in health statistics, *Socioeconomic Status and Health Chartbook: Health United States, 1998*, highlights a substantial body of research findings relating life expectancy as well as lung cancer and heart disease rates to family income. Similarly cited are numerous studies clearly demonstrating that death rates for chronic diseases, communicable diseases, and injuries are all inversely related to education for men and women (Pamuk, Makuc, Heck, Reuben, & Lochner, 1998).

Educational Attainment and Health

Educational attainment has become the most convenient and commonly used indicator of socioeconomic status, and the association between years of schooling and health is well established (Elo & Preston, 1996; Krieger, Williams, & Moss, 1997). Winkleby, Jatulis,

Frank, and Fortmann (1992), suggesting that education is the most judicious socioeconomic measure for use in epidemiological studies, hypothesize that education may protect against disease by influencing lifestyle behaviors, problem-solving abilities, and values. Ross and Wu (1995), demonstrating a strong association between education and health, explored three explanations for this association and hypothesize that education influences work and economic conditions, social-psychological resources, and a healthy lifestyle. Although the demonstrated evidence of the association between health and education is strong, the explanations for this association and the underlying mechanisms have not been extensively studied.

Literacy and Health

A growing number of inquiries have focused on direct measures of literacy rather than on years of schooling to explore the links between literacy skills and health. Research studies in education and adult literacy indicate that literacy influences the ability to access information and navigate in literate environments, has an impact on cognitive and linguistic abilities, and affects self-efficacy (Snow, 1991; LeVine et al., 1994; Dexter, LeVine, & Velasco, 1998; Comings, Smith, & Shrestha, 1994; Smith, 1994; Parikh, Parker, Nurss, Baker, & Williams, 1996; Baker et al., 1996). Literacy is sometimes measured in terms of comprehension skills, vocabulary, and the ability to communicate effectively across a wide variety of contexts (often discussed in terms of formal language skills). Formal language is closer to written language and can be heard in public announcements and speeches. It tends to be impersonalized and makes use of long utterances, complex sentences, and a standardized vocabulary. Estimates of formal language skills include noun recognition tests (Snow, 1991; Dexter, LeVine, & Velasco, 1998). Overall formal language relies on grammatical structure to convey meaning, unlike everyday talk, which may make use of gestures and pauses and assumes a common context (Snow, 1991; Dexter, LeVine, & Velasco, 1998).

In medical care settings, a patient's oral language skills are related to his or her ability to describe symptoms and can subsequently affect the practitioner's ability to diagnose. For example, studies have indicated that a physician's assessment of a patient's health history or test of a patient for dementia may be affected by the patient's literacy status (Weiss & Coyne, 1997). Furthermore, the patient's oral comprehension abilities may curtail his or her dialogue with the physician or ability to comprehend oral instructions.

Patients' literacy directly influences their access to crucial information about their rights and their health care, whether it involves following instructions for care, taking medicine, comprehending disease-related information, or learning about disease prevention and health promotion. Because consent procedures contain complex legal and medical jargon, a patient's literacy may influence his or her opportunities for inclusion in research and exposure to a variety of procedures. In addition, less literate patients with chronic diseases may be less well informed about the basic elements of their care plan (Ladd, 1985; Baker, Parker, & Clark, 1998). Furthermore, literacy levels may directly affect access to care. For example, difficulties in completing registration forms or applications for insurance coverage may delay the procurement of needed medical services (Baker et al., 1996). Finally, illiteracy or low literacy, which is often accompanied by feelings of embarrassment or shame, may diminish a person's capacity to express his or her concerns in our highly literate health care environment (Parikh, Parker, Nurss, Baker, & Williams, 1996).

BARRIERS TO HEALTH COMMUNICATION

Most of the medical and public health literature mentioning literacy focuses on assessing the readability levels of materials used in health care settings and for health promotion purposes. Some studies assess the readability of materials targeted at specific diseases, such as cancer or diabetes, and others take a broader approach, examining a specific type of material, such as patient package inserts or materials frequently used in institutional settings for emergency department discharge instructions or informed consent. Despite the many kinds of health-related materials analyzed for readability, a clear trend emerges from the literature: too often, the literacy demands of the material exceed the literacy abilities of the reader—that is, most adults in the United States.

The Reading Materials

Materials assessment studies clearly document that many health promotion and patient education materials, patient rights and informed-consent documents, as well as directions for medication or self-care,

are not easily accessible to the average adult. The literature shows evidence of continued efforts to assess patient information materials and ensure that the level of literacy required for comprehension is appropriate (Doak & Doak, 1987; Meade & Byrd, 1989; Spadero, 1983; Daiker, 1992).

In spite of the fact that many layout and design considerations affect readability, most assessments of health materials in the literature apply readability formulas that are designed to assign rankings to written materials and yield a score of reading difficulty based on a specific grade (Klare, 1984). Among the measures of readability commonly referenced in the literature are the SMOG Readability Formula (McLaughlin, 1969), the Flesch Reading Ease Formula (Flesch, 1948), and the Fry Formula (Fry, 1977), as well as a variety of word processing programs such as Correct Grammar (Basara & Juergens, 1994), Right Writer (Glazer, Kirk, & Bosler, 1996), and Grammatik (Davis et al., 1993b), all of which produce an overall grade-level assessment. They are most commonly based on word length and sentence length or sentence complexity, although formulas vary and they yield somewhat different reading levels. These formulas are designed to assess materials organized in paragraphs but do not measure readability for materials in other formats, such as graphs and charts, both of which are frequently used to present health facts. The assessment tool that Mosenthal and Kirsch (1998) developed provides a mechanism for measuring the readability of charts and similar documents. These can be scored on five levels of complexity and given a corresponding grade level. The use of this tool has not yet been reported in the medical or public health literature.

Informed-consent materials represent the most complex reading challenges that patients in medical care settings face and have received a good deal of attention in the medical and public health literature (Morrow, 1980; Baker & Taub, 1983; Taub, Baker, & Sturr, 1986; Spivey, 1989; Goldstein, Frasier, Curtis, Reid, & Kreher, 1996; Hammerschmidt & Keane, 1992; Hopper, TenHave, & Hartzel, 1995; Jubelirer, 1991; Meade & Howser, 1992; Tarnowski, Allen, Mayhall, & Kelly, 1990; Philipson, Doyle, Gabram, Nightingale, & Philipson, 1995; Agre, McKee, Gargon, & Kurtz, 1997; Davis, Holcombe, Berkel, Pramanik, & Divers, 1998; Brandes, Furnas, McClellan, Haywood, Ohene-Frempong, & Taylor-Watson, 1996; Gordon, 1996). Reading-level ratings ranged from eighth grade to college graduate levels, indicating that most of these materials may be incomprehensible to most adults

(Morrow, 1980; Baker & Taub, 1983; Taub, Baker, & Sturr, 1986; Philipson, Doyle, Gabram, Nightingale, & Philipson, 1995; Goldstein, Frasier, Curtis, Reid, & Kreher, 1996; Hopper, TenHave, & Hartzel, 1995; Hopper, TenHave, Tully, & Hall, 1998; Meade & Howser, 1992; Tarnowski, Allen, Mayhall, & Kelly, 1990). Findings have been consistent over the years, indicating a lack of progress or improvement. For example, in 1983 Baker and Taub evaluated the average readability of consent documents at a Veterans Administration Medical Center and found them to be written at the college level. Hopper and colleagues (1998) released their analysis of the readability of 616 surgical and procedural consent forms and reported a mean reading grade level of 12.6. Other studies have also examined consent forms and have found them to be at reading grade levels 12 through 15 (Hammerschmidt & Keane, 1992; Goldstein, Frasier, Curtis, Reid, & Kreher, 1996). Similarly, Jubelirer (1991) and Meade and Howser (1992) found consent documents for cancer patients to be written for grade levels 11 through 17.5.

Patient package inserts, which contain essential information about a medication, its use, and potential side effects, were among the first patient-oriented materials to be assessed (Pyrczak & Roth, 1976; Pyrczak, 1978; Smith & Adams, 1978; Eaton & Holloway, 1980). Certainly as self-medication with nonprescription drugs and direct-to-consumer advertising of prescription drugs become more common, the readability of these inserts becomes even more important (Basara & Juergens, 1994). As early as 1980 Eaton and Holloway suggested that package inserts be written at reading levels between grades 5 and 7. Yet in 1994, when sixty-three package inserts from pharmaceutical companies, nonprofit organizations, and commercial vendors were analyzed, the average readability was scored at grade 10 (Basara & Juergens, 1994; Ledbetter, Hall, Swanson, & Forrest, 1990; Swanson et al., 1990).

Emergency department discharge instructions have similarly been assessed for readability. The scores for instructional materials prepared for patients leaving the emergency department (emergency room discharge documents) have ranged from a grade 6 reading level to a level above grade 13 (Powers, 1988; Williams, Counselman, & Caggiano, 1996; Jolly, Scott, Fried, & Sanford, 1993).

Most of the materials assessment studies in the literature report on examinations of booklets, pamphlets, and instructional materials grouped by disease categories. Readability assessments for large groupings of cancer information and prevention materials generally score between grades 9 and 12 reading levels (Meade, Diekmann, & Thornhill, 1992; Glazer, Kirk, & Bosler, 1996; Michielutte, Bahnson, Dignan, & Schroeder, 1992; Guidry & Fagan, 1997). Meade and colleagues report that although the American Cancer Society's patient education materials had shown improvement since the mid-1980s, assessments yielded measures of reading level at grade 11 (Meade, Diekmann, & Thornhill, 1992).

Assessments of patient education materials for other diseases similarly yield readability levels well above the recommended levels of fifth to ninth grade (Dollahite, Thompson, & McNew, 1996; Ebrahimzadeh, Davalos, & Lee, 1997; Glanz & Rudd, 1990; Klingbeil, Speece, & Schubiner, 1995; Primas et al., 1992; Petterson, Dornan, Albert, & Lee, 1994; Wells, 1994; Daiker, 1992). Dollahite and colleagues (1996) found that 68 percent of 209 nutrition education pamphlets analyzed were written at the ninth-grade level or higher. Similarly, ophthalmic patient education materials (Ebrahimzadeh, Davalos, & Lee, 1997), cholesterol education materials (Glanz & Rudd, 1990), pediatric and prenatal education materials (Farkas, Glenday, O'Connor, & Schmeltzer, 1987; Klingbeil, Speece, & Schubiner, 1995; Primas et al., 1992), and materials given to diabetes patients (Leichter, Nieman, Moore, Collins, & Rhodes, 1981; Petterson, Dornan, Albert, & Lee, 1994) were analyzed and scored at reading levels well above ninth grade.

Assessments have also been conducted on various materials addressing occupational health and safety (Auerbach & Wallerstein, 1987; Koen, 1988; Bruening, 1989; Buckett & Sarri, 1991; Daiker, 1992; Wallerstein, 1992; Wallerstein & Weinger, 1992). Here too findings suggest that most worker training and safety materials are written at a level well above the literacy levels of the U.S. population and are not well suited to their intended audience (Wallerstein, 1992). Noting the need for more appropriately written health and safety materials, Wallerstein (1992) recommends that such materials be developed collaboratively by occupational health professionals, literacy educators, and language instructors.

The Readers

Determinations of reading level are valuable only if they are considered in the light of their target audience—in this case, the patient. Indeed, a shift in interest from the reading materials to the reader is evident in the literature and the development of reading assessment tools designed to offer a quick means of scoring the abilities of patients and program clients. The lack of health-related instruments, as well as the lack of time and other environmental constraints, had restricted literacy assessments in medical settings (Davis, Crouch, Wills, Miller, & Abdehou, 1990). The development of tools intended to assess health-related literacy levels has enabled researchers to examine the match more closely between the reading level of specific materials and the reading skills of the intended audience.

ASSESSMENT TOOLS. The most commonly referenced health literacy assessment tools are the Rapid Estimate of Adult Literacy in Medicine (Davis et al., 1991, 1993b) and the Test of Functional Health Literacy in Adults (Williams et al., 1995; Parker, Baker, Williams, & Nurss, 1995). Previously a number of studies applied assessment tools commonly used in educational settings, such as the reading recognition subtest of the Wide Range Achievement Test–Revised (WRATR), which requires a participant to read aloud lists of words that become increasingly difficult. When ten words have been consecutively mispronounced, the test is stopped, and a raw score, between 1 and 89, is computed and converted into a grade equivalent (Jastak & Wilkinson, 1987; Michielutte, Bahnson, Dignan, & Schroeder, 1992; Davis et al., 1994). The WRATR does not measure comprehension but simply word recognition (Davis et al., 1994). Its use is reported in several health-related studies (Jastak & Wilkinson, 1987; Cooley et al., 1995; Davis et al., 1994; Hosey, Freeman, Stracqualursi, & Gohdes, 1990; Larson & Schumacher, 1992), and it served as a model for the Rapid Estimate of Adult Literacy in Medicine (Davis et al., 1991).

For the Rapid Estimate of Adult Literacy in Medicine (REALM), participants read from a list of 125 common medical terms, arranged in four columns according to the number of syllables they contain. REALM takes three to five minutes to complete and score. Raw scores can be converted to grade ranges corresponding to lower elementary (below third grade), upper elementary (fourth to sixth grade), junior high (seventh to eighth grade), and senior high school levels (Davis et al., 1991). REALM performed well in identifying patients with low reading ability, and a shortened version was subsequently developed and assessed (Davis et al., 1993b). Analyses indicate that the shortened version, taking two minutes, performed as well as the longer version in assessments of concurrent validity.

The Test of Functional Health Literacy in Adults (TOFHLA) was developed in English and in Spanish and uses actual hospital materials, including the patient rights and responsibilities section of a Medicaid application form, instructions for preparing for an upper gastrointestinal series, a standard hospital consent form, and labeled prescription vials (Parker, Baker, Williams, & Nurss, 1995). The test includes a seventeen-item test of numerical ability and a fifty-item test of reading comprehension applying the Cloze procedure, a tool to assess reading comprehension that involves a process of deleting words from a prose selection so that the reader must correctly supply the missing word.[1] The TOFHLA takes twenty-two minutes to administer, and developers suggest that it is more useful as a research tool than as a clinical tool because of the time it takes to administer (Parker, Baker, Williams, & Nurss, 1995), although a short version, developed in 1998, may serve both purposes. The protocols for the administration of both the REALM and the TOFHLA require an eye test and offer a choice of font (or type) size.

Davis, Michielutte, Askov, Williams, and Weiss (1998) caution that these tests cannot determine the cause or type of reading or learning difficulty and thus cannot be expected to diagnose specific problems; they may, however, prove useful in identifying patients for whom standard care approaches and materials may not be effective. Researchers have not yet adequately explored the experience of patients taking these assessment tests, nor have they examined implications for patient dignity and subsequent treatment when literacy abilities are identified and documented in medical care settings. The tools have enabled researchers to measure reading skills in health care settings and subsequently contributed to the explorations of the connections between health and literacy.

HEALTH LITERACY LEVELS. Several efforts have been undertaken to obtain a profile of the health literacy levels of specific patient populations, and findings provide striking evidence of inadequate literacy skills, validating the NALS findings in medical care settings. However, low scores must not mask the inappropriate language and design of complicated materials prepared for patients noted consistently in the literature.

Williams and colleagues (1995) used the TOFHLA to assess the functional health literacy of 2,659 patients presenting for acute care at the emergency care center or acute care walk-in clinic in two urban, public hospitals. They report that a high proportion of patients were unable to read and understand basic medical instructions. Well over a third of those patients in the sample (41.6 percent) were unable to comprehend directions for taking medication on an empty stomach, and a quarter of them (26 percent) were unable to understand information on scheduling their next appointment. Of the 1,892 English-speaking patients in the sample, 35.1 percent had inadequate or marginal functional literacy, according to the TOFHLA. For the 767 Spanish-speaking patients, the figure was even higher (61.7 percent). Among the elderly (patients sixty years old or more), the difference between English and Spanish speakers virtually disappeared: 81.3 percent of English-speaking patients and 82.6 percent of Spanish-speaking patients had inadequate or marginal functional health literacy.

The TOFHLA was also used in a study of 131 African American patients with non-insulin-dependent diabetes in Georgia that was designed to assess actual and self-reported functional health literacy (Nurss et al., 1997). The functional health literacy level was scored as adequate in 47 percent of new patients at one hospital diabetes clinic and in 25 percent of established patients at three other clinics (a general medicine clinic and two satellite medical clinics). Of those with inadequate health literacy, 43 percent denied having any difficulty in reading. More than half (53.8 percent) of those with inadequate functional health literacy said they did not usually ask anyone to help them read medical forms, and only 29 percent reported asking someone (usually relatives or neighbors) to help them read the written materials given to them by the hospital. The authors note that such patients are least likely to ask their physician for help, confirming reports from earlier studies indicating that low-literacy patients are unlikely to identify themselves as such. Diabetes-related complications combined with low literacy are likely to pose a compounded threat to health, because diabetes self-management relies heavily on printed instructions.

The Mismatch Between Materials and Readers

Most of the studies examining the match between the reading level of health materials and that of those expected to read them document a clear difference. Davis and colleagues (1990) noted disparities as wide as seven gradations in their assessment of the readability of educational materials for ambulatory care patients, patients in substance abuse treatment centers (Davis et al., 1993a), and the parents and caretakers of pediatric patients (Davis et al., 1994). Many studies in the literature focus on the disparity between the reading abilities of cancer patients and the reading level of the educational materials written for them (Cooley et al., 1995; Beaver & Luker, 1997; Foltz & Sullivan, 1996; Meade, McKinney, & Barnas, 1994; Michielutte, Bahnson, Dignan, & Schroeder, 1992; Doak, Doak, Friedell, & Meade, 1998). Cooley and colleagues (1995) concluded that the reading levels of 27 percent of cancer outpatients in one study were well below that of any of the thirty cancer pamphlets analyzed with the Flesch formula. Similar findings are reported for patients with diabetes (Hosey, Freeman, Stracqualursi, & Gohdes, 1990), arthritis (Hill, 1997), and lupus (Hearth-Holmes et al., 1997). The reading levels of groups of patients with these chronic diseases fell between grade levels 6 and 10, while the readability of the materials designed for them fell between grade levels 7 and 13.

Several studies examined patient education materials designed for specific ethnic groups. Hosey and colleagues (1990) used the WRAT to measure the reading ability of a group of American Indian diabetic patients and found that although many patients scored at a reading grade level of 5, the diabetes education materials scored at a mean reading grade level of 10. Guidry, Fagan, and Walker (1998) note that less than half of the cancer education materials specifically targeting African Americans reflected the culture of African Americans and that few were written at a reading grade level for those with low literacy skills.

A substantial number of studies report on both readability and comprehension assessments of these documents, most of them deemed inappropriate (Powers, 1988; Williams, Counselman, & Caggiano, 1996; Austin, Matlack, Dunn, Kesler, & Brown, 1995; Delp & Jones, 1996; Jolly, Scott, Fried, & Sanford, 1993; Jolly, Scott, & Sanford, 1995; Logan, Schwab, Salomone, & Watson, 1996; Spandorfer, Karras, Hughes, & Caputo, 1995). Williams and colleagues (1996) analyzed the readability of emergency department discharge instructions with the Flesch and determined that about 45 percent of patients would not be able to comprehend the instructions. Jolly and colleagues (1993) found that a significant proportion of emergency room patients were not able to answer questions about their discharge instructions, which were scored between reading levels of grades 6 to 13. A follow-up study noted that patients' ability to answer comprehension questions improved when the discharge instructions were simplified (Jolly, Scott, & Sanford, 1995).

Readability formulas offer one indication of the accessibility of informed-consent documents; however, as Mariner and McArdle (1985) note, such measurements do not tell us about patient comprehension, familiarity with medical terms, or previous experience with similar forms. Cassileth, Zupkis, Sutton-Smith, and March (1980) examined comprehension and recall of informed-consent documents and report that one day after signing a consent form, only 60 percent of cancer patients understood the purpose of the consent process and only 55 percent could correctly name one major risk of the procedure. The authors attribute the limited recall to three major factors: educational attainment, medical status, and the degree of care patients said that they took while reading the form. Clearly consent documents and the consenting process must be more closely examined.

LINKING LITERACY TO HEALTH-RELATED OUTCOMES

Grosse and Auffrey (1989) highlighted a body of evidence linking literacy to health outcomes based on research conducted in developing countries. International studies continue to yield insight into the mechanisms through which literacy is linked to healthful action and health outcomes. These studies tend to focus on women, for whom literacy levels are particularly low because of traditional exclusion from schooling (Cochrane, O'Hare, & Leslie, 1980; Comings, Smith, & Shrestha, 1994; LeVine et al., 1994). The international literature is beyond the scope of the current review. However, some of these studies, particularly those examining associations between oral language and reading skills, are of increasing interest to U.S.-based research (Roter, Rudd, & Comings, 1998).

Although research on the relationship between functional literacy levels and poor health status is relatively sparse in the United States, the appearance of a number of recent, well-designed studies offers hope that more will follow. Conducting rigorous research that elucidates the mechanisms through which literacy may affect health outcomes—health status, services utilization, and behaviors—is vital to the development of effective and appropriate strategies for improving the health of those with low or limited literacy skills. Another valuable area of research concerns determining the relationship, if any, between literacy and the cost of health care.

Literacy, Health Status, and Utilization of Health Care Services

Weiss, Hart, McGee, and D'Estelle (1992) assessed the relationship between literacy and health status in a randomly selected sample of English-speaking adults enrolled in a publicly funded literacy training program in Arizona. They found that the physical health of subjects with extremely low reading levels was poor compared with that of subjects with higher reading levels (reading levels were assessed through tests of adult basic education). Even after adjusting for confounding sociodemographic characteristics, the relationship between reading level and physical health remained. The study also found a relationship between reading level and its measure of psychosocial health, indicating that low literacy is also associated with poorer psychosocial health.

TenHave and others (1997) examined the relationship between literacy scores and a reported history of heart disease and diabetes. They found that the proportion of participants reporting a history of heart disease or diabetes was inversely related to literacy scores, as measured by an assessment tool the authors developed for use in this project. In fact, the association between literacy levels and heart disease—or any one of three conditions (heart attack, hospitalization for heart condition, or diabetes)—remained statistically significant even after adjusting for educational attainment.

Baker, Parker, Williams, Clark, and Nurss (1997) examined the relationship of functional health literacy to self-reported health and the use of health services. This cross-sectional, retrospective study included a sample of 979 English-speaking patients presenting for nonurgent care at the emergency care centers and walk-in clinics at two public hospitals, one in Georgia and the other in California. At both sites, patients with inadequate functional health literacy (measured with the TOFHLA) were more likely than patients with adequate literacy to report their health as poor. In Atlanta, patients with inadequate health literacy were also more likely than patients with adequate literacy to report having been hospitalized in the past year, and this finding remained statistically significant even after controlling for sociodemographic characteristics and self-reported health.

Baker and associates' (1998) prospective cohort study of 958 English-speaking patients presenting for nonurgent care at an Atlanta emergency care center and walk-in clinic examined the literacy level of patients (using the TOFHLA) and its relationship to hospital admissions. The results of the literacy testing itself are noteworthy: 35 percent of the sample population had inadequate literacy, and an additional 13 percent had marginal functional health literacy as measured by the TOFHLA. Consequently almost half of the population studied would be unable or limited in their ability to interpret appointment slips, directions for medication, or hospital documents. Baker and colleagues found that patients with inadequate literacy were twice as likely as were patients with adequate literacy to be hospitalized during 1994–1995. After adjusting for age, gender, race, self-reported health, socioeconomic status, and health insurance status, the researchers found that the relationship between low literacy level and higher rates of admission remained at a level reaching statistical significance. On the basis of their findings, the authors concluded that patients with inadequate functional health literacy had an increased risk of hospital admission.

Literacy, Screening, and Early Detection

Davis and colleagues (1996a) assessed the relationship between health literacy levels and knowledge of and attitudes toward screening mammography with a convenience sample of low-income women from two outpatient clinics in Louisiana. Low-income women are less likely to make use of screening mammography and more likely to be diagnosed with breast cancer at later stages of the disease. Since low-income women also have disproportionately lower literacy skills than women with higher incomes, it is possible that in this case health literacy level was linked to knowledge of mammography (which would include knowledge of why women are given mammograms) and the decision to undergo breast cancer screening. The study administered the REALM to 445 women forty years of age or older who had not had a mammography in the past year. Lower reading ability was significantly correlated with less mammography knowledge. The authors conclude that limited literacy skills and lack of knowledge about screening mammography may contribute considerably to the underutilization of mammography by low-income women. This study makes an important contribution to the field by having highlighted health literacy as an influence on knowledge levels and screening decisions.

Bennett and associates (1998) assessed the relationship among literacy, race, and stage of presentation among patients diagnosed with prostate cancer. The focus of the study was 212 low-income men from two prostate cancer clinics (in Illinois and Louisiana), both of which have equal-access systems that treat primarily low-income individuals. The authors report that men with literacy levels below sixth grade were more likely to present with advanced-stage prostate cancer. Black men were more likely than white men to present with advanced-stage disease; however, race was no longer a predictor of advanced stage of disease at presentation when analysts adjusted for literacy, geographic location, and age. The authors conclude that low literacy may be an overlooked but significant barrier to the diagnosis of early-stage prostate cancer among low-income white and black men. They suggest that the development of culturally sensitive, low-literacy educational materials may improve patient awareness of prostate cancer and the frequency of diagnosis at early stages.

Literacy and Chronic Disease

Williams, Baker, Parker, and Nurss (1998b) assessed the relationship between functional health literacy (measured by the TOFHLA) and knowledge of chronic disease in a cross-sectional survey of 402 patients with hypertension and 114 patients with diabetes. Almost half (48 percent) of the patients tested had inadequate functional health literacy levels. They were less likely than those with high functional health literacy scores to know basic information about their disease and essential self-management skills. Study findings confirm that standard patient educational practices are insufficient to overcome the barriers posed by inadequate functional health literacy. The authors point out that much effort has focused on improving the quality of written materials but that research is also needed on the use of oral and visual communication to convey necessary medical information.

Williams, Baker, Honig, Lee, and Nowlan (1998a) also published a study examining the relationship between literacy and asthma knowledge and self-management skills. Asthma self-management was assessed by patient demonstrations of their use of a metered-dose inhaler. In this convenience sample of 483 patients, lower literacy levels as measured by the REALM were associated with lower asthma knowledge scores and improper asthma self-management. In fact, patient reading level was the strongest predictor of asthma knowledge score and metered-dose inhaler technique in multivariate analyses that adjusted for possible cofounders. This was the first study to demonstrate that self-management skills are poorer among patients with limited literacy skills, a finding with serious implications for the management of chronic diseases.

Literacy and the Cost of Health Care

Given the established relationship between low literacy and poor health, it is reasonable to hypothesize that low literacy levels might also be associated with higher health care costs, yet little research has been done in this area. Baker and colleagues (1998) found a statistically significant relationship between functional health literacy and the likelihood of hospital admission, one of the most costly health services.

However, a study that Weiss and colleagues (1994) conducted on 402 Medicaid enrollees, randomly selected from an Arizona Medicaid program, found no significant relationship between literacy and health care costs. The authors detected a possible relationship between literacy and costs within a particular subgroup of Medicaid patients, the medically needy, and medically indigent patients, but there were too few subjects in the subgroup to draw reliable conclusions.

STRATEGIES FOR IMPROVING COMMUNICATION

Research evidence documents health communication barriers for people with low literacy skills and an association with poor health outcomes and higher rates of hospitalization. Fortunately, research has begun on potential strategies for addressing these barriers. A number of both research and descriptive studies in the literature have included recommendations for redressing the difficulties many adults face in attempting to use health-related materials. Most of the literature focuses on educational materials, which, when written at levels beyond the reading ability of most adults, limit access to vital information.

Improving Readability

Common sense indicates that those struggling with health literacy issues would have less difficulty with materials that are written at lower reading levels. However, research indicates that this strategy by itself falls short of addressing the needs of those with low health literacy skills and instead tends to benefit most those with higher skill levels who report that they prefer such materials (Plimpton & Root, 1994).

Several research studies report on the efficacy of specifically matching the reading level of materials to the reading ability of the readers. Dowe, Lawrence, Carlson, and Keyserling (1997) randomized patients of a general medicine clinic who had a current prescription for one of two medications to a control group or to one of three experimental groups. Participants in the experimental groups were randomly assigned to receive a drug leaflet written at a low, medium, or high level of reading difficulty. Not surprisingly, among participants who had less than a ninth-grade education, those receiving the less complex materials were more likely to read the leaflet than were those who received more complex materials. Further, among those with an eighth-grade education or lower, knowledge scores were influenced by the readability of the leaflet, with the higher knowledge scores resulting when they received the less complex leaflets.

A similar study conducted by Ley, Jain, and Skilbeck (1976) addressed noncompliance issues for anxious and depressed patients taking medications. Patients were randomly assigned to receive one of three versions of an information leaflet about their medications or to receive no leaflet at all. The leaflets differed in readability levels, and the number of medication errors was employed as an outcome measure. Patients receiving easy-to-read leaflets had significantly lower medication error scores than those receiving the more difficult leaflets. This study did not analyze the results by educational level or literacy level; however, its findings are important to this discussion in that they support the link between compliance with medication regimens and readability (and presumably comprehensibility) of the information received.

The idea that simplification of emergency department discharge instructions would improve patient comprehension was tested by Jolly and colleagues (1995) with 423 adult patients who presented on randomly selected days to the emergency department of a large, inner-city university hospital in Washington, D.C. Comparisons were made against a historical control group (the authors had assessed the standard discharge instructions in the past), and analyses were done within educational groups using self-reported educational level as the only indicator of literacy. Although the mean score (of correct answers on five questions) for the current group was significantly improved over that of the control group when discharge instructions were simplified, this effect was seen only among patients in the group with a higher educational level (beyond twelfth grade). Clearly the strategy of simplifying discharge instructions for wound care and care of sprains and bruises was not sufficient to improve comprehension in patients at lower educational levels and literacy levels.

Sumner (1991) tested the effectiveness of matching patient educational material to patients' reported educational level as an influence on health behaviors. He found purposeful matching to have little effect. Sumner concluded that the 31 patients in the intervention group receiving booklets matched to their educational level were no more likely than the 213 control group patients to engage in the desired health behaviors (obtaining a sigmoidoscopy, a diphtheria-tetanus immunization, a cholesterol screening, or a smoke detector).

Davis and colleagues (1998) compared two polio vaccine pamphlets in a study of 610 parents who sought health care for their children at one of three pediatric care facilities. Parents were randomly assigned to receive one of two pamphlets, both written at a sixth-grade reading level. One was the vaccine information statement issued by the Centers for Disease Control (CDC), and the other was developed by the authors at Louisiana State University (LSU) in an easy-to-read format. The REALM was used as the measure of health literacy levels, and a structured interview elicited information about the perceptions and attitudes of the parents toward vaccination and assessed their comprehension of the pamphlets they had read. Parents at all reading levels preferred the LSU pamphlet (76 percent versus 21 percent), and more parents found it easier to read than the CDC pamphlet (58 percent versus 42 percent). However, analyses by grade-level estimates indicated that the LSU pamphlet improved comprehension scores only among parents reading on a seventh- to eighth-grade level or higher; parents with the lowest reading levels did not show improved comprehension (Davis, Holcombe, Berkel, Pramanik, & Divers, 1998). Findings indicate that the strategy of improving the readability of educational materials by bringing it to the sixth-grade level is clearly insufficient as a means of meeting the needs of patients with low literacy skills.

Additional Approaches

Informed consent has been of key concern in a small number of studies. Informed-consent processes ensure the protection of patient autonomy, the most fundamental tenet of bioethics. Here the consequences of low literacy have both legal and ethical implications. Titus and Keane (1996) examined researchers' and clinicians' attitudes toward the importance of patient knowledge and concluded that many researchers are far from proficient at ensuring the informed consent of the subject. The authors note that too often researchers use closed-ended questions, such as "Do you understand?" to hurry the consent procedure and consequently may coerce subjects into participating in studies. Taub, Baker, and Sturr (1986) suggest that informed-consent procedures may be a considerable problem for elderly patients with low education and, further, that simplifying words and sentences on consent forms may not in itself lead to greater levels of comprehension. Earlier, Taub and colleagues (1981) had examined vocabulary level and recall in a study of eighty-seven elderly adults and found a direct relationship between the elderly adults' vocabulary levels and their ability to recall consent information two to three weeks later. In addition, researchers noted the benefits of corrective feedback, throughout the consent process, as a means to improve comprehension.

One study compared the use of print materials (written at fifth-to sixth-grade reading levels) with presentation of a videotape, each containing the same information, on colon cancer. The effectiveness of the print and videotaped materials was compared in a randomized study of eleven hundred patients age fifty or older from a primary care clinic in Milwaukee (Meade, McKinney, & Barnas, 1994). WRAT II scores were used to assess reading skills, and subject selection criteria included the ability to speak and read English. Colon cancer knowledge was assessed using pre- and posttest questionnaires developed for the study. Patients were randomly assigned to one of three groups: (1) those to receive a booklet written at a reading level for grades 5 to 6, (2) those to view a videotape that contained the same content as the booklet, or (3) those to receive no intervention. Mean pretest scores were compared with mean posttest scores, and improvements in knowledge about colon cancer were observed for both the group receiving the booklet (23 percent) and the group viewing the videotape (26 percent). Reading scores, assessed by WRAT II, were used to stratify the experimental group into two groups. The first group consisted of patients with higher reading skills (grade 7 or higher) and the second of those with lower reading skills (below grade 7). No statistically significant differences in score improvements were observed; knowledge levels improved with the booklet and video for patients at both the higher and lower reading levels. The authors conclude that printed materials written at low reading levels (grade 5 to 6) can effectively substitute for videotaped materials in clinic settings without access to the more expensive audiovisual equipment. However, it should be noted that this study required participants to be able to read English and thus did not address the problem of achieving knowledge improvements among those patients at the lowest levels of health literacy.

In another fairly small study conducted in 1996, Levin looked at the value of symbols as a means of promoting healthy food choices in the cafeteria at an urban work site. The intervention consisted primarily of placing heart-shaped symbols next to targeted, low-fat entrees on the list of available food choices. At the experimental site, sales of targeted, low-fat items (as a proportion of total sales) increased significantly from baseline over the intervention period of twenty-eight weeks. At the comparison site, no significant differences were observed across the intervention period. The author notes that one of the most positive features of this promotion is its application to populations with low literacy skills, because it used no written materials other than a poster with minimal words and relied primarily on a single symbol to draw attention to recommended foods.

Roter, Rudd, Keogh, and Robinson (1987) examined the effectiveness of an educational booklet developed by construction workers on the topic of cancer and asbestos and compared this material with a National Cancer Institute (NCI) booklet on the same topic. The subject pool consisted of five hundred participants whose names were drawn randomly from each of the membership lists of ten union locals. Half of the subjects received the workers' booklet, and half received materials developed by the NCI; both groups received an evaluation questionnaire. Although hampered by a low overall return rate (21 percent), the researchers reported that readers of both materials reflected a high degree of awareness about asbestos and disease and recognized the benefits of quitting smoking and the danger of asbestos dust. However, readers of the workers' booklet had higher recall of recommended action; offered high ratings for clarity, tone, and ease of understanding; and were more likely to report that they would become more active in union health and safety issues. Furthermore, the reading level of the worker-developed materials scored from four to seven levels below that of the NCI materials. The researchers noted that in this and other instances, material developed by members of the target audience reflected their voice and their concerns (Rudd & Comings, 1994).

Delp and Jones (1996) studied the effectiveness of cartoon drawings in a prospective, randomized study of patient comprehension and compliance with discharge instructions. The study included 234 consecutive patients who presented to the emergency department of a community teaching hospital with lacerations requiring wound repair. Random assignment was used to select 105 patients to receive wound care instructions illustrated with cartoons and another 129 patients to receive release instructions without cartoons. Analyses revealed that patients given the instructions with the cartoons were more likely to have read the instructions, answer all wound care questions correctly, and actually follow the instructions in daily wound care. Especially noteworthy is the fact that even larger differences in comprehension and compliance were observed between the two groups when analyses were done on a subset of 57 patients with less than a high school education. Although this study employed educational level as the only indicator of literacy, it supports the idea of using cartoons to improve both patient understanding of discharge instructions and compliance with medical advice among patients with low educational levels and presumably lower literacy skills.

A community-based nutrition education program conducted by the Expanded Food and Nutrition Education Program (EFNEP) was designed specifically for low-literacy populations and assessed in a study with 134 participants and 70 comparison subjects (Hartman, McCarthy, Park, Schuster, & Kushi, 1997). Formative research, including focus group discussions, was used to develop the intervention with members of the low-literacy target group. Literacy levels were assessed through the Adult Basic Learning Examination Level II (ABLE), and all EFNEP participants whose reading abilities were below the eleventh-grade level were asked to participate (more than 90 percent were female). Although there are certain problems with the study design (for example, the comparison group was significantly different from the intervention group in a number of ways), the low-fat intervention designed specifically for this low-literacy population was associated with significant improvements in overall low-fat eating behaviors. This study provides partial support for the strategy of engaging low-literacy participants in formative research (for example, through focus groups) to develop interventions designed specifically to meet their needs.

A hypertension control effort described by Fouad and colleagues (1997) included an intervention program tailored to accommodate the needs of a population with low literacy skills by employing visual teaching methods, games with culturally sensitive concepts and examples, and incentives to encourage behavioral change. The findings from this quasi-experimental study indicate that the eighty-one intervention participants experienced a statistically significant decrease in mean systolic blood pressure. Although this decrease was greater from baseline to follow-up than that experienced by control subjects, the difference (between intervention participants and control subjects) did not reach the level of statistical significance.

Qualitative data are also available to guide the development of strategies for addressing the needs of low-literacy patient populations. Hartman, McCarthy, Park, Schuster, and Kushi (1994) conducted a focus group research project with forty-one participants (mostly women) to evaluate an education program promoting low-fat eating behaviors in a population in the Minneapolis–St. Paul area with limited literacy skills. The focus group participants wanted simple, practical, and relevant information about what foods to eat and how to prepare them. They considered lectures an ineffective way to receive nutrition information, preferring instead to engage in hands-on activities that allowed them to share ideas and experiences. Macario, Emmons, Sorensen, Hunt, and Rudd (1998) conducted nutrition-related focus groups with patients with low literacy skills who were clients from adult basic education programs in the Boston area. One of the key findings from this project is that patients with low literacy skills turned first to family members and friends for health information. The authors note that effective nutrition interventions must build on a patient's social networks, appear in a visually based, interactive format, and be culturally appropriate.

Overall, the literature from the health field provides limited information on research-based strategies to meet the needs of those with low levels of health literacy. Many manuals and handbooks provide guidelines for the assessment of existing materials and for the development of new materials. They highlight the importance of layout; typeface, style, and size; white space; primacy of key information; and active versus passive voice (U.S. Department of Agriculture, 1988; U.S. DHHS, 1989; Doak, Doak, Friedell, & Meade, 1998; Murphy, Davis, Jackson, Decker, & Long, 1993; Davis, Meldrum, Tippy, Weiss, & Williams, 1996b; Mayeaux et al., 1996; Szudy & Arroyo, 1994; Doak, Doak, & Root, 1996). More research is needed on strategies that complement or replace the use of written material. Suggestions have included the engagement of a surrogate reader, computer-assisted, interactive technology (Kohlmeier, Mendez, McDuffie, & Miller, 1997; Evans et al., 1998), and the communication of health information through pictorial presentations such as photo essays (Paskett, Tatum, Wilson, Dignan, & Velez, 1996) and photo novels (Harlander & Ruccione, 1993; Rudd & Comings, 1994).

TRENDS IN THE LITERATURE

Connections between health and literacy have been of concern to health educators for decades. Practitioners and researchers first turned their attention to problems with written documents, examining the reading level of drug inserts, informed-consent documents, medical care and medication instructions, and general patient education materials. Legal, ethical, and practical considerations are reflected in the many studies centered on the assessment of materials, often accompanied by insightful suggestions for reworking old and developing new materials and for dialogue and discussion. Subsequently studies were designed to examine the match between a particular population's reading ability and the reading level of health materials. Overall, studies yielded consistent findings over time—that is, the materials were written at levels inappropriate for the general public or for the specific population groups for which they were designed.

Methodological strides in the 1990s led to measures of literacy as it relates to specific health information and related tasks. The TOFHLA followed the general techniques of the NALS and validated the NALS findings among clinic and hospital patients. Both the TOFHLA and the REALM offered researchers rapid literacy assessments with high face validity for health issues and concurrent validity for more general literacy assessments. Subsequently researchers began to measure health literacy (defined as literacy skills related to the vocabulary, materials, and directions used in health care settings) and study the association between literacy and specific health-related outcomes.

Of the almost one dozen citations on literacy found in the medical and public health literature in the 1970s, two focus on barriers posed by low literacy, another two on methods for assessing and improving health education materials, and the remainder on readability assessments of health-related communications (such as the use of medical terminology and the readability of directions on nonprescription drugs).

The literature of the 1980s represents a threefold increase in literacy-related citations from public health and medical journals; the citations are both more numerous and broader in scope. Out of a total of thirty-seven articles, seven focus on general issues of literacy, comprehension, and communication. A smaller group focuses on tools for assessing materials or techniques for developing materials at more appropriate reading levels. The majority of the articles report on assessments of written material related to occupational health and safety, informed consent, hospital emergency department discharge instructions, medicine, and patient education. Many of these articles address patient education literature for a specific disease, and a few focus on health education literature for specific population groups. At the close of the 1980s, Grosse and Auffrey (1989) authored the first review of literacy and health status for the *Annual Review of Public Health*, which brought together key international studies and provided evidence of a growing scholarly interest in this area.

The number of citations available in the 1990s is evidence of the burgeoning interest in health and literacy. The first half of the decade alone produced more than one hundred citations related to health and literacy concerns. Weiss, Hart, and Pust (1991) and Weiss and colleagues (1992) called for research into the links between literacy and health. However, most of the literature from the early 1990s reflects a continued interest in health education instruction materials and medical forms. There is a continued concern with the readability of informed-consent documents.

During the latter part of the 1990s, assessments of the reading level of health-related materials (on informed consent, medical directives, patient education) continued to account for most of the public health and medical literature concerned with literacy. Numerous articles published during this period continued to draw attention to the challenge of developing valid informed-consent processes for surgical procedures and research among patients with low literacy skills. The development of specific health-related literacy assessment tools in the early 1990s advanced research inquiries into the links between literacy and health outcomes. Studies in the latter 1990s focused on health-related consequences of barriers encountered by adults with limited or extremely limited literacy skills and offered insight into issues of comprehension of basic medical instruction, management of chronic disease, and knowledge of screening and early detection. Studies have established that inadequate health literacy is associated with higher rates of hospitalization, one of the most costly medical services.

IMPLICATIONS FOR RESEARCH AND PRACTICE

Although more research is needed, the studies to date corroborate the findings from international health research indicating that lower levels of literacy are clearly associated with poorer health and that low levels of health literacy have a measurable impact on numerous intermediate factors that influence health outcomes. Recent research also highlights the fact that standard patient educational and care practices are insufficient to overcome the barriers presented by inadequate health literacy. Additional evidence is now available to awaken medical professionals to the urgent need to address the challenge of communicating effectively with patients, many of whom have limited or low literacy skills. Not only do such patients rarely identify themselves as struggling with literacy issues, but those with inadequate functional health literacy usually do not ask others to help them read health-related materials or instructions. Furthermore, studies indicate that low literacy can diminish a person's capacity to engage in fruitful interactions with the care providers in our highly literate health care environments. Findings from studies of patients in managed care organizations underscore the financial and human costs of low literacy.

Research in the 1990s also began to focus on testing strategies for meeting the needs of those with low levels of health literacy. Especially noteworthy are efforts that engage patients with low health literacy in the development of new programs intended to meet their needs better. These studies and others employing formative research methods and marketing strategies offer evidence of the influence of social marketing, with its focus on consumer wants and needs, in the field of public health (Walsh, Rudd, Moeykens, & Mahoney, 1993). When those with low health literacy are considered the target group, a social marketing approach would suggest that at least part of the challenge in effectively improving its members' health lies in developing a product that better meets their needs. A health information brochure that is written in an easy-to-read format or a chronic disease management educational session centered on a demonstration of self-care skills each represents a type of improved product for a low-health-literacy group. Participatory approaches that engage members of the population of interest and formative research methods designed to enable the clients or patients to attune appropriately programs or materials designed by others support more efficacious outcomes.

Much strategic development work, beyond improving the read-ability of materials, remains to be done. In medical settings, those with low-health-literacy skills need to participate in formulating and testing new strategies for improving their ability to communicate their concerns, their comprehension of their condition and their self-management skills, and their health behaviors. The education of health professionals needs to include information on the high preva-lence of inadequate functional health literacy and its relationship to poor health and to incorporate training on how to be effective in ad-dressing the needs of low-health-literacy patients. At the same time, the level of literacy skills demanded of patients must be modified. Pro-fessional jargon in directives, forms, signs within health care institu-tions, educational materials, and discussions must be more closely examined and eliminated where possible.

The adult education setting is another critical area for strategic de-velopment. Adult basic education (ABE) programs provide ready ac-cess to populations with low functional health literacy, and both teachers and students from these programs can be engaged in the strategic development work (formulating and testing strategies) that must take place to address fully the health-related needs of this target group. Work has already begun on the development of cancer-related teaching modules for programs in ABE, English for speakers of other languages (ESOL), and literacy programs. These and other modules serve to improve language and quantitative skills, as well as to increase health literacy, promote healthy lifestyle choices, and support health-promoting community action. Such adult education curriculum de-velopment should be expanded to include other health topic areas as well. The expertise of education and literacy professionals is vital in crafting effective health education and promotion strategies for those with low levels of health literacy, as is the perspective of those with limited literacy skills. The field has benefited greatly from the collab-orations between adult education and health professionals over the past decade, and further achievements can be expected by expanding the partnering of these two fields.

There is a critical need for additional research that will further ex-plore the relationship between levels of health literacy and health out-comes, as well as the relationship between inadequate health literacy and the intermediate factors that influence health outcomes. The mechanisms through which health literacy and health outcomes are connected are also in need of further elucidation. For example, the connection between health literacy and verbal communication has yet to be examined. In addition, strategies for addressing the special needs of those with low health literacy need to be developed and tested through well-designed research efforts with sample sizes that are sufficiently large to draw meaningful conclusions. Much progress toward weakening the association between health and literacy can be achieved if an array of research-based strategies can be employed across different health and educational contexts. Finally, the exploration of the relationship between levels of health literacy and health care costs is just beginning in the United States. It is expected to draw more attention in the future as the health care system continues to face challenges of cost containment.

MODEL PRACTICES AND NEXT STEPS

A number of exemplary projects illustrate the potential for effective collaboration between professionals in education and in health fields. The Health Team in Massachusetts, established in the early 1990s by the nonprofit organization World Education, has brought together health and literacy educators to address mutual concerns. Ideas resulting from discussions led to the design of the Health Education and Adult Literacy Program (HEAL), a collaborative effort of World Education, the Harvard School of Public Health, and the Centers for Disease Control, which brings lessons on breast and cervical cancer to adult learning centers. In addition, the team designed a program that enabled adult education centers to develop health-related curriculum, programs, and materials for adult learners. Such collaborative efforts supported the first of a series of national conferences on health and literacy that set the stage for cross-disciplinary discussions. Subsequently supported by a combination of private and public funds, yearly conferences and working groups on health literacy have served to engage researchers and practitioners from medicine, public health, adult education, and governmental and private funding agencies in the articulation of a research agenda (Giorgianni, 1998).

The Maine Area Health Education Center was instrumental in forming another collaborative project in which health education and adult education professionals were brought together, this time for a series of training sessions on how to produce easy-to-read health materials (Plimpton & Root, 1994). The materials development consortium involved a dozen health agencies and a half-dozen adult education programs. These collaborators produced dozens of easily reproducible, low-cost pamphlets focused on the *Healthy People 2000* objectives, and a model for teaching oral communication skills to health care providers who deal with low-literacy adults.

Collaborative work has been undertaken by public health and adult education researchers at the National Center for the Study of Adult Learning and Literacy (NCSALL), who are examining the topic of health and the skills adults need in health care settings as a content area for adult education. Research activities include interviews with adult learners and surveys of state directors and teachers. Findings will set a foundation for curriculum design, teacher training, and the development of laboratory sites for outcome studies. An interview study and a national survey have been implemented to engage adult educators in the process of exploring the definition and scope of functional health literacy (Rudd and Moeykens, 1999; Rudd, Zacharia, & Daube, 1998a; Rudd, Zahner, & Banh, 1998b).

Professionals at the National Cancer Institute and its Cancer Information Service have spent a decade developing cancer education strategies and materials to reach people with limited literacy skills, and they have been collaborating in this effort with representatives from ABE programs (Brown et al., 1993). The ABE and literacy networks provided the Cancer Information Service with access to the low-literacy audiences who are often described in the health literature as difficult to reach. The NCI has engaged in outreach efforts to establish regional and community linkages with literacy programs and ABE programs, and it has partnered with these programs in several states to create teaching modules on cancer-related topics for use in ABE and literacy curriculums. These modules are also expected to be useful in other settings where low health literacy is common, such as senior centers and community health centers.

A reflection of the NCI's leadership in this area is the partnership it forged in 1992 with the AMC Cancer Research Center to establish the National Work Group (NWG) on Cancer and Literacy (NWG on Literacy and Health, 1998). The group's mission was to focus national attention on the need for more effective communication with people with limited literacy skills and to provide the NCI with recommendations for effective communication with this target population. The group, which consists of professionals from the field of education as well as health, among others, was in 1996 renamed the National Work Group on Literacy and Health to reflect better the broader focus across health areas (not just cancer). An article authored by the group high-lights the pervasiveness of low literacy levels in the United States, the relationship between low literacy and health, and the need for im-proved communication between health care providers and those with limited literacy skills (NWG on Literacy and Health, 1998). The group also provided recommendations for addressing the needs of patients who have limited literacy skills.

Two subsequent developments at the beginning of 1999 may set the stage for additional collaborative research and policy development work well into the next decade. First, Healthy People 2010, the next delineation of health objectives for the nation, will include a section on health communication and health literacy (U.S. DHHS, 1998). Sec-ond, a report from the American Medical Association Ad Hoc Com-mittee on Health Literacy for the Council on Scientific Affairs reflects medicine's recognition of literacy and its role in health (Ad Hoc Com-mittee, 1999). Both developments bring health literacy to the national agenda.

More such collaborative efforts between education and health pro-fessionals are critically needed to address fully the needs of those with limited health literacy skills. There is much to be gained from pooling these areas of expertise as well as engaging those with limited health literacy skills in forging and testing new strategies for meeting the communication, educational, and health needs of this population.

Note

1. Concurrent validity was assessed by examining the correlation between the English-language version of the TOFHLA and the REALM ($r = .84$, $p < .001$) and the WRAT-R ($r = .74$; $p < .001$).

References

Ad Hoc Committee on Health Literacy. (1999). Health literacy report of the Council on Scientific Affairs. *Journal of the American Medical Association, 281*(6), 552–557.

Agre, P., McKee, K., Gargon, N., & Kurtz, C. (1997). Patient satisfaction with an informed consent process. *Cancer Practice, 5*(3), 162–167.

Auerbach, E., & Wallerstein, N. (1987). *ESL for action: Problem-posing at work.* Reading, MA: Addison-Wesley.

Austin, P. E., Matlack, R., Dunn, K. A., Kesler, C., & Brown, C. K. (1995). Discharge instructions: Do illustrations help our patients understand them? *Annals of Emergency Medicine, 25,* 317–320.

Baker, D. W., Parker, R. M., & Clark, W. S. (1998). Health literacy and the risk of hospital admission. *Journal of General Internal Medicine, 13*(12), 791–798.

Baker, D. W., Parker, R. M., Williams, M. V., Clark, W. S., & Nurss, J. (1997). The relationship of patient reading ability to self-reported health and use of health services. *American Journal of Public Health, 87*(6), 1027–1030.

Baker, D. W., Parker, R. M., Williams, M. V., Pitkin, K., Parikh, N. S., Coates, W., & Mwalimu, I. (1996). The health experience of patients with low literacy. *Archives of Family Medicine, 5,* 329–334.

Baker, M. T., & Taub, H. A. (1983). Readability of informed consent forms for research in a Veterans Administration medical center. *Journal of the American Medical Association, 250,* 2646–2648.

Basara, L. R., & Juergens, J. P. (1994). Patient package insert readability and design. *American Pharmacy, 34*(8), 48–53.

Bauman, A., Smith, N., Braithwaite, C., Free, A., & Saunders, A. (1989). Asthma information: Can it be understood? *Health Education Research, 4*(3), 377–382.

Beaver, K., & Luker, K. (1997). Readability of patient information booklets for women with breast cancer. *Patient Education and Counseling, 31*(2), 95–102.

Beckman, H. T., & Lueger, R. J. (1997). Readability of self-report clinical outcome measures. *Journal of Clinical Psychology, 53*(8), 785–789.

Bennett, C. L., Ferreira, M. R., Davis, T. C., Kaplan, J., Weinberger, M., Kuzel, T., Seday, M. A., & Sartor, O. (1998). Relation between literacy, race, and stage of presentation among low-income patients with prostate cancer. *Journal of Clinical Oncology, 16,* 3101–3104.

Blane, D. (1995). Social determinants of health—Socioeconomic status, social class, and ethnicity. *American Journal of Public Health, 85*(7), 903–905.

Bormuth, J. (1966). Readability: A new approach. *Reading Research Quarterly, 1,* 79–132.

Boyd, M. D., & Citro, K. (1983). Cardiac patient education literature: Can patients read what we give them? *Journal of Cardiac Rehabilitation, 3,* 513–516.

Brandes, W., Furnas, S., McClellan, F. M., Haywood, J., Ohene-Frempong, J., & Taylor-Watson, M. (1996). *Literacy, health, and the law: An exploration of the law and the plight of marginal readers within the health care system: Advocating for patients and providers.* Philadelphia: Health Promotion Council of Southeastern Pennsylvania.

Brown, P., Ames, N., Mettger, W., Smith, T. J., Gramarossa, G. L., Friedell, G. H., & McDonald, S. S. (1993). Closing the comprehension gap: Low literacy and the Cancer Information Service. *Journal of the National Cancer Institute, 14*, 157–163.

Bruening, J. C. (1989, October). Workplace illiteracy: The threat to worker safety. *Occupational Hazards,* 118–122.

Buckett, C., & Sarri, C. (1991). *Watch out! An ESL manual for worker safety.* Washington, DC: Alice Hamilton Occupational Health Center.

Cassileth, B. R., Zupkis, R. V., Sutton-Smith, K., & March, V. (1980). Informed consent—Why are its goals imperfectly realized? *New England Journal of Medicine, 302*, 896–900.

Cochrane, S., O'Hare, D. J., & Leslie, J. (1980). *The effects of education on health* (World Bank Staff Working Paper No. 556). Washington, DC: World Bank.

Comings, J. P., Smith, C., & Shrestha, C. J. (1994). Women's literacy: The connection to health and family planning. *Convergence 27*(2/3).

Cooley, M. E., Moriarty, H., Berger, M. S., Selm-Orr, D., Coyle, B., & Short, T. (1995). Patient literacy and the readability of written cancer education materials. *Oncology Nursing Forum, 22*(9), 1345–1351.

Daiker, B. L. (1992). Evaluating health and safety lectures: How to measure lucidity. *AAOHN Journal, 40*(9), 438–445.

Davis, T. C., Arnold, C., Berkel, H. J., Nandy, I., Jackson, R. H., & Glass, J. (1996a). Knowledge and attitude on screening mammography among low-literate, low-income women. *Cancer, 78*(9), 1912–1920.

Davis, T. C., Crouch, M. A., Long, S. W., Jackson, R. H., Bates, P., George, R. B., & Bairnsfather, L. E. (1991). Rapid assessment of literacy levels of adult primary care patients. *Family Medicine, 23*(6), 433–435.

Davis, T. C., Crouch, M. A., Wills, G., Miller, S., & Abdehou, D. M. (1990). The gap between patient reading comprehension and the readability of patient education materials. *Journal of Family Practice, 31*(5), 533–538.

Davis, T. C., Holcombe, R. F., Berkel, H. J., Pramanik, S., & Divers, S. G. (1998). Informed consent for clinical trials: A comparative study of standard versus simplified forms. *Journal of the National Cancer Institute, 90*(9), 669–674.

Davis, T. C., Jackson, R. H., George, R. B., Long, S. W., Talley, D., Murphy, P. W., Mayeaux, E. J., & Truong, T. (1993a). Reading ability in patients in substance misuse treatment centers. *International Journal of the Addictions, 28*(6), 571–582.

Davis, T. C., Long, S. W., Jackson, R. H., Mayeaux, E. J., George, R. B., Murphy, P. W., & Crouch, M. A. (1993b). Rapid estimate of adult literacy in medicine: A shorthand screening instrument. *Family Medicine, 25*(6), 391–395.

Davis, T. C., Mayeaux, E. J., Fredrickson, D., Bocchini, J. A. Jr., Jackson, R. H., & Murphy, P. W. (1994). Reading ability of parents compared with reading level of pediatric patient education materials. *Pediatrics, 93*(3), 460–468.

Davis, T. C., Meldrum, H., Tippy, P. K., Weiss, B., & Williams, M. V. (1996b). How poor literacy leads to poor health care. *Patient Care,* 94–127.

Davis, T. C., Michielutte, R., Askov, E. N., Williams, M. V., & Weiss, B. D. (1998). Practical assessment of adult literacy in health care. *Health Education and Behavior, 25*(5), 613–624.

Delp, C., & Jones, J. (1996). Communicating information to patients: The use of cartoon illustrations to improve comprehension of instructions. *Academic Emergency Medicine, 3*(3), 264–270.

Dexter, E. R., LeVine, S. E., & Velasco, P. M. (1998). Maternal schooling and health-related language and literacy skills in rural Mexico. *Journal of Comparative Education Review, 42*(2), 139–162.

Doak, C. C., Doak, L. G., Friedell, G. H., & Meade, C. D. (1998). Improving comprehension for cancer patients with low literacy skills: Strategies for clinicians. *CA—A Cancer Journal for Clinicians, 48*(3), 151–162.

Doak, C. C., Doak, L. G., & Root, J. H. (1996). *Teaching patients with low literacy skills.* Philadelphia: J. B. Lippincott.

Doak, L. G., & Doak, C. C. (1987). Lowering the silent barriers to compliance for patients with low literacy skills. *Promoting Health, 8*(4), 6–8.

Dollahite, J., Thompson, C., & McNew, R. (1996). Readability of printed sources of diet and health information. *Patient Education and Counseling, 27*(2), 123–134.

Dowe, M. C., Lawrence, P. A., Carlson, J., & Keyserling, T. C. (1997). Patients' use of health-teaching materials at three readability levels. *Applied Nursing Research, 10*(2), 86–93.

Duffy, T. M. (1985). Readability formulas: What's the use? In T. M. Duffy & R. Waller (Eds.), *Designing usable texts* (pp. 113–143). Orlando, FL: Academic Press.

Eaton, M. L., & Holloway, R. L. (1980). Patient comprehension of written drug information. *American Journal of Hospital Pharmacy, 37*(2), 240–243.

Ebrahimzadeh, H., Davalos, R., & Lee, P. P. (1997). Literacy levels of ophthalmic patient education materials. *Survey of Ophthalmology, 42*(2), 152–156.

Elo, I. T., & Preston, S. H. (1996). Educational differentials in mortality: United States, 1979–85. *Social Science Medicine, 42*(1), 47–57.

Evans, J. H. C., Collier, J., Crook, I., Garrid, P., Harris, P., MacKinlay, D. R. E., & Redsell, S. A. (1998). Using multimedia for patient information— A program about nocturnal enuresis. *British Journal of Urology, 81*(suppl. 3), 120–122.

Farkas, C. S., Glenday, P. G., O'Connor P. J., & Schmeltzer, J. (1987). An evaluation of the readability of prenatal health education materials. *Canadian Journal of Public Health, 78*(6), 374–378.

Ferraz, M., Quaresma, M., Aquino, L., Atra, E., Tugwell, P., & Goldsmith, C. (1990). Reliability of pain scales in the assessment of literate and illiterate patients with rheumatoid arthritis. *Journal of Rheumatology, 17*(8), 1022–1024.

Flesch, R. (1948). A new readability yardstick. *Journal of Applied Psychology, 32*, 2211–2223.

Flesch, R. (1951). *How to test readability.* New York: Harper & Brothers.

Foltz, A., & Sullivan, J. (1996). Reading level, learning presentation preference, and desire for information among cancer patients. *Journal of Cancer Education, 11*(1), 32–38.

Fouad, M. N., Kiefe, C. I., Bartolucci, A. A., Burst, N. M., Ulene, V., & Harvey, M. R. (1997). A hypertension control program tailored to unskilled and minority workers. *Ethnicity and Disease, 7*(3), 191–199.

Fry, R. (1977). Fry's readability graph: Clarifications, validity, and extension to level 17. *Journal of Reading, 21*, 241–252.

Giorgianni, S. J. (Ed.). (1998). Perspectives on health care and biomedical research: Responding to the challenge of health literacy. *Pfizer Journal, 2*(1).

Glanz, K., & Rudd, J. (1990). Readability and content analysis of print cholesterol education materials. *Patient Education and Counseling, 16*(2), 109–118.

Glazer, H. R., Kirk, L. M., & Bosler, F. E. (1996). Patient education pamphlets about prevention, detection, and treatment of breast cancer for low literacy women. *Patient Education and Counseling, 27*(2), 185–189.

Goldstein, A. O., Frasier, P., Curtis, P., Reid, A., & Kreher, N. E. (1996). Consent form readability in university-sponsored research. *Journal of Family Practice, 42*(6), 606–611.

Gordon, D. (1996). MD's failure to use plain language can lead to the courtroom. *Canadian Medical Association Journal, 155*(8), 1152–1154.

Grosse, R. N., & Auffrey, C. (1989). Literacy and health status in developing countries. *Annual Review of Public Health, 10,* 281–297.

Guidry, J. J., & Fagan, P. (1997). The readability levels of cancer-prevention materials targeting African Americans. *Journal of Cancer Education, 12*(2), 108–113.

Guidry, J. J., Fagan, P., & Walker, V. (1998). Cultural sensitivity and readability of breast and prostate printed cancer education materials targeting African Americans. *Journal of the National Medical Association, 90*(3), 165–169.

Guralnik, J. M., Land, K. C., Blazer, D., Fillenbaum, G. G., & Branch, L. G. (1993). Educational status and active life expectancy among older blacks and whites. *New England Journal of Medicine, 329,* 110–116.

Hammerschmidt, D. E., & Keane, M. A. (1992). Institutional Review Board (IRB) lacks impact on the readability of consent forms for research. *American Journal of the Medical Sciences, 304*(6), 348–351.

Harlander, C., & Ruccione, K. (1993). Fotoplatica: An innovative teaching method for families with low literacy and high stress. *Journal of Pediatric Oncology Nursing, 10*(3), 112–114.

Hartman, T. J., McCarthy, P. R., Park, R. J., Schuster, E., & Kushi, L. H. (1994). Focus group responses of potential participants in a nutrition education program for individuals with limited literacy skills. *Journal of the American Diabetic Association, 94*(7), 744–748.

Hartman, T. J., McCarthy, P. R., Park, R. J., Schuster, E., & Kushi, L. H. (1997). Results of a community-based low-literacy nutrition education program. *Journal of Community Health, 22*(5), 325–341.

Hearth-Holmes, M., Murphy, P. W., Davis, T. C., Nandy, I., Elder, C. G., Broadwell, L. H., & Wolf, R. E. (1997). Literacy in patients with a chronic disease: Systemic lupus erythematosus and the reading level of patient education materials. *Journal of Rheumatology, 24*(12), 2335–2339.

Hill, J. (1997). A practical guide to patient education and information giving. *Baillieres Clinical Rheumatology, 11*(1), 109–127.

Hopper, K. D., TenHave, T. R., & Hartzel, J. (1995). Informed consent forms for clinical and research imaging procedures: How much do patients understand? *American Journal of Roentgenology, 164,* 493–496.

Hopper, K. D., TenHave, T. R., Tully, D. A., & Hall, T. E. L. (1998). The readability of currently used surgical/procedure consent forms in the United States. *Surgery, 123*(5), 496–503.

Hosey, G. M., Freeman, W. L., Stracqualursi, F., & Gohdes, D. (1990). Designing and evaluating diabetes education material for American Indians. *Diabetes Educator, 16*(5), 407–414.

Hunter, C. S. J., & Harman, D. (1979). *Adult illiteracy in the United States: A report to the Ford Foundation.* New York: McGraw-Hill.

Jastak, S., & Wilkinson, G. S. (1987). *Wide range achievement test—revised.* Wilmington, DE: Jastak Associates.

Jolly, B. T., Scott, J. L., Fried, C. F., & Sanford, S. M. (1993). Functional illiteracy among emergency department patients: A preliminary study. *Annals of Emergency Medicine, 22*(3), 573–578.

Jolly, B. T., Scott, J. L., & Sanford, S. M. (1995). Simplification of emergency department discharge instructions improves patient comprehension. *Annals of Emergency Medicine, 26*(4), 443–446.

Jubelirer, S. J. (1991). Level of reading difficulty in educational pamphlets and informed consent documents for cancer patients. *West Virginia Medical Journal, 87*(12), 554–557.

Kirsch, I. S., Jungeblut, A., Jenkins, L., & Kolstad, A. (1993). *Adult literacy in America.* Washington, DC: U.S. Department of Education.

Klare, G. R. (1984). Readability. In P. D. Pearson, R. Barr, M. L. Kamil, & P. B. Mosenthal (Eds.), *Handbook of reading research* (Vol. 1, pp. 681–744). New York: Longman.

Klingbeil, C., Speece, M. W., & Schubiner, H. (1995). Readability of pediatric patient education materials. Current perspectives on an old problem. *Clinical Pediatrics, 34*(2), 96–102.

Koen, S. (1988). Functional illiteracy in today's work force. *Business and Health, 5*(3), 18–23.

Kohlmeier, L., Mendez, M., McDuffie, J., & Miller, M. (1997). Computer-assisted self-interviewing: A multimedia approach to dietary assessment. *American Journal of Clinical Nutrition, 65*(4 Suppl.), 1275S–1281S.

Kozol, J. (1985). *Illiterate America.* New York: Penguin Books.

Krieger, N., Williams, D. R., & Moss, N. E. (1997). Measuring social class in U.S. public health research: Concepts, methodologies, and guidelines. *Annual Review of Public Health, 18,* 341–378.

Ladd, R. E. (1985). Patients without choices: The ethics of decision-making in emergency medicine. *Journal of Emergency Medicine, 3,* 149–156.

Larson, I., & Schumacher, H. R. (1992). Comparison of literacy level of patients in a VA arthritis center with the reading level required by educational materials. *Arthritis Care and Research, 5*(1), 13–16.

Ledbetter, C., Hall, S., Swanson, J. M., & Forrest, K. (1990). Readability of commercial versus generic health instructions for condoms. *Health Care for Women International, 11*(3), 295–304.

Leichter, S. B., Nieman, J. A., Moore, R. W., Collins, P., & Rhodes, A. (1981). Readability of self-care instructional pamphlets for diabetic patients. *Diabetes Care, 4*(6), 627–630.

Levin, S. (1996). Pilot study of a cafeteria program relying primarily on symbols to promote healthy choices. *Journal of Nutrition Education, 28*(5), 282–285.

LeVine, R. A., Dexter, E., Velasco, P., LeVine, S., Joshi, A. R., Sruebing, K. W., & Tapia-Uribe, F. M. (1994). Maternal literacy and health care in three countries: A preliminary report. *Health Transition Review, 4*(2), 186–191.

Ley, P., Jain, K., & Skilbeck, C. (1976). A method for decreasing patients' medication errors. *Psychological Medicine, 6,* 599–601.

Logan, P. D., Schwab, R.A., Salomone, J. A. III, & Watson, W. A. (1996). Patient understanding of emergency department discharge instructions. *Southern Medical Journal, 89*(8), 770–774.

Macario, E., Emmons, K. M., Sorensen, G., Hunt, M. K., & Rudd, R. E. (1998). Factors influencing nutrition education for patients with low literacy skills. *Journal of the American Dietetic Association, 5,* 559–564.

Mariner, W. K., & McArdle, P. A. (1985, April). Consent forms, readability, and comprehension: The need for new assessment tools. *Law, Medicine, and Health Care,* 68–74.

Mayeaux, E. J. Jr., Murphy, P. W., Arnold, C., Davis, T. C., Jackson, R. H., & Sentell, T. (1996). Improving patient education for patients with low literacy skills. *American Family Physician, 53*(1), 205–211.

McLaughlin, G. H. (1969). SMOG grading: A new readability formula. *Journal of Reading, 12*(8), 639–646.

Meade, C. D., & Byrd, J. C. (1989). Patient literacy and the readability of smoking education literature. *American Journal of Public Health, 79,* 204–206.

Meade, C. D., Diekmann, J., & Thornhill, D. G. (1992). Readability of American Cancer Society patient education literature. *Oncology Nursing Forum, 19*(1), 51–55.

Meade, C. D., & Howser, D. M. (1992). Consent forms: How to determine and improve their readability. *Oncology Nursing Forum, 19*(10), 1523–1528.

Meade, C. D., McKinney, W. P., & Barnas, G. P. (1994). Educating patients with limited literacy skills: The effectiveness of printed and video-taped materials about colon cancer. *American Journal of Public Health, 84*(1), 119–121.

Michielutte, R., Bahnson, J., & Beal, P. (1990). Readability of the public education literature on cancer prevention and detection. *Journal of Cancer Education, 5*(1), 55–61.

Michielutte, R., Bahnson, J., Dignan, M. B., & Schroeder, E. M. (1992). The use of illustrations and narrative text style to improve readability of a health education brochure. *Journal of Cancer Education, 7*(3), 251–260.

Morrow, G. R. (1980). How readable are subject consent forms? *Journal of the American Medical Association, 244,* 56–58.

Mosenthal, P. B., & Kirsch, I. S. (1998). A new measure for assessing document complexity: The PMOSE/IKIRSCH document readability formula. *Journal of Adolescent and Adult Literacy, 41*(8), 638–657.

Murphy, P. W., Davis, T. C., Jackson, R. H., Decker, B. C., & Long, S. W. (1993). Effects of literacy on health care of the aged: Implications for health professionals. *Educational Gerontology, 19,* 311–316.

National Work Group on Literacy and Health. (1998). Communication with patients who have limited literacy skills. *Journal of Family Practice, 46*(2), 168–176.

Nelson, G., & Nelson, B. (1985). Are your patient education materials readable? *Health Educator, 3*(6), 10–11.

Nurss, J. R., el-Kebbi, I. M., Galliana, D. L., Zeimer, D. C., Musey, V. C., Lewis, S., Liao, Q., & Philips, L. S. (1997). Diabetes in urban African Americans: Functional health literacy of municipal hospital outpatients with diabetes. *Diabetes Educator, 23*(5), 563–568.

Pamuk, E., Makuc, D., Heck, K., Reuben, C., & Lochner, K. (1998). *Socioeconomic status and health chartbook: Health United States, 1998.* Hyattsville, MD: National Center for Health Statistics.

Parikh, N. S., Parker, R. M., Nurss, J. R., Baker, D. W., & Williams, M. D. (1996). Shame and health literacy: The unspoken connection. *Patient Education and Counseling, 27,* 33–39.

Parker, R. M., Baker, D. W., Williams, M. V., & Nurss, J. R. (1995). The test of functional health literacy in adults: A new instrument for measuring patients' literacy skills. *Journal of General Internal Medicine, 10*(10), 537–541.

Paskett, E. D., Tatum, C., Wilson, A., Dignan, M., & Velez, R. (1996). Use of a photo essay to teach low-income African American women about mammography. *Journal of Cancer Education, 11*(4), 216–220.

Petterson, T., Dornan, T. L., Albert, T., & Lee, P. (1994). Are information leaflets given to elderly people with diabetes easy to read? *Diabetic Medicine, 11*(1), 111–113.

Philipson, S. J., Doyle, M. A., Gabram, S. G., Nightingale, C., & Philipson, E. H. (1995). Informed consent for research: A study to evaluate readability and processability to effect change. *Journal of Investigative Medicine, 43*(5), 459–467.

Plimpton, S., & Root, J. (1994). Materials and strategies that work in low literacy health communication. *Public Health Reports, 109*(1), 86–92.

Powers, R. D. (1988). Emergency department patient literacy and the readability of patient-directed materials. *Annals of Emergency Medicine, 17*(2), 124–126.

Primas, P., Lefor, N., Johnson, J., Helms, S. M., Coats, L., & Coe, M. K. (1992). Prenatal literature testing: A pilot project. *Journal of Community Health, 17*(1), 61–71.

Pyrczak, F. (1978). *Application of some principles of readability research in the preparation of patient package inserts.* Rochester, NY: Center for the Study of Drug Development.

Pyrczak, F., & Roth, D. (1976). The readability of directions on nonprescription drugs. *Journal of the American Pharmaceutical Association, 16*, 242–243, 267.

Reder, S. (1998). *The state of illiteracy in America: Estimates at the local, state, and national levels.* Washington, DC: National Institute for Literacy.

Ross, C. E., & Wu, C. (1995). The links between education and health. *American Sociological Review, 60*, 719–745.

Roter, D. L., & Hall, J. A. (1992). Doctors talking with patients. In *Patients talking with doctors: Improving communication in medical visits.* Westport, CT: Auburn House.

Roter, D. L., Rudd, R. E., & Comings, J. P. (1998). Patient literacy: A barrier to quality care. *Journal of General Internal Medicine, 13*(12), 850–851.

Roter, D. L., Rudd, R. E., Frantz, S. C., & Comings, J. P. (1981). Community-produced materials for health education. *Public Health Reports, 96*, 169–172.

Roter, D. L., Rudd, R. E., Keogh, J., & Robinson, B. (1987). Worker produced health education material for the construction trades. *International Quarterly of Community Health Education, 7*, 109–121.

Rudd, R. E., & Comings, J. P. (1994). Learner developed materials: An empowering approach. *Health Education Quarterly, 21*(3), 313–327.

Rudd, R. E., & Moeykens, B. A. (1999). *Findings from a national survey of adult educators: Health and literacy.* Cambridge, MA: NCSALL.

Rudd, R. E., Zacharia, C., & Daube, K. (1998a). *Integrating health and literacy: adult educator's experiences* (NCSALL Report No. 5). Cambridge, MA: NCSALL.

Rudd, R. E., Zahner, L., & Banh, M. (1998b). *Findings from a national survey of state directors of adult education* (NCSALL Report No. 9). Cambridge, MA: NCSALL.

Smith, C. (1994). *Health education and adult literacy (HEAL) project. Final evaluation report.* Boston: World Education.

Smith, T. P., & Adams, R. C. (1978). Readability levels of patient package inserts. *American Journal of Hospital Pharmacy, 35*(9), 1034.

Snow, C. E. (1991). The theoretical basis for relationships between language and literacy in development. *Journal of Research in Childhood Education, 6*(1), 5–10.

Spache, G. (1953). A new readability formula for primary grade materials. *Elementary School Journal, 53,* 410–413.

Spadero, D. C. (1983). Assessing readability of patient information materials. *Pediatric Nursing, 9*(4), 274–278.

Spandorfer, J. M., Karras, D. J., Hughes, L. A., & Caputo, C. (1995). Comprehension of discharge instructions by patients in an urban emergency department. *Annals of Emergency Medicine, 25*(1), 71–74.

Spivey, W. H. (1989). Informed consent for clinical research in the emergency department. *Annals of Emergency Medicine, 18,* 766–771.

Sumner, W. (1991). An evaluation of readable preventive health messages. *Family Medicine, 23*(6), 463–466.

Swanson, J. M., Forrest, K., Ledbetter, C., Hall, S., Holstine, E. J., & Shafer, M. R. (1990). Readability of commercial and generic contraceptive instructions. *Image—The Journal of Nursing Scholarship, 22*(2), 96–100.

Szudy, E., & Arroyo, M. G. (1994). *The right to understand: Linking literacy to health and safety training. Labor occupational health program.* Berkeley: University of California at Berkeley.

Tarnowski, K. J., Allen, D. M., Mayhall, C., & Kelly, P. A. (1990). Readability of pediatric biomedical research informed consent forms. *Pediatrics, 85*(1), 58–62.

Taub, H. A., Baker, M. T., & Sturr, J. F. (1986). Informed consent for research: Effects of readability, patient age, and education. *American Geriatric Society, 34,* 601–606.

Taub, H. A., Kline, G. E., & Baker, M. T. (1981). The elderly and informed consent: Effects of vocabulary level and corrected feedback. *Experimental Aging Research, 7*(2), 137–146.

TenHave, T. R., Van Horn, B., Kumanyika, S., Askov, E., Matthews, Y., & Adams-Campbell, L. L. (1997). Literary assessment in a cardiovascular nutrition education setting. *Patient Education and Counseling, 31*(2), 139–150.

Titus, S. L., & Keane, M. A. (1996). Do you understand? An ethical assessment of researchers' description of the consenting process. *Journal of Clinical Ethics, 7*(1), 60–68.

U.S. Department of Agriculture. (1988*). Guidelines: Writing for adults with limited reading skills.* Washington, DC: U.S. Government Printing Office.

U.S. Department of Health and Human Services. (1989). *Making health communication programs work: A planner's guide* (NIH Publication No. 89–1493). Washington, DC: NIH Office of Cancer Communications.

U.S. Department of Health and Human Services. (1990). *Healthy people 2000: National health promotion and disease prevention objectives* (DHHS Publication No. 91–50212). Washington, DC: Public Health Service.

U.S. Department of Health and Human Services. (1998). *Healthy people 2010 objectives: Draft for public comment.* Washington, DC: Public Health Service.

Ventres, W., & Gordon, P. (1990). Communication strategies in caring for the underserved. *Journal of Health Care for the Poor and Underserved, 1*(3), 305–314.

Wallerstein, N., (1992). Health and safety education for workers with low-literacy or limited-English skills. *American Journal of Industrial Medicine, 22*(5), 751–765.

Wallerstein, N., & Weinger, M. (1992). Health and safety education for worker empowerment. *American Journal of Industrial Medicine, 22,* 619–635.

Walsh, D. C., Rudd, R. E., Moeykens, B. A., & Mahoney, T. (1993). Social marketing for public health. *Health Affairs, 12*(2), 104–119.

Weaver, C. A. III, & Kintsch, W. (1991). Expository text. In R. Barr, M. L. Kamil, P. B. Mosenthal, & P. D. Pearson (Eds.), *Handbook of reading research* (Vol. 2, pp. 230–245). New York: Longman.

Weiss, B. D., Blanchard, J. S., McGee, D. L., Hart, G., Warren, B., Burgoon, M., & Smith, K. J. (1994). Illiteracy among Medicaid recipients and its relationship to health care costs. *Journal of Health Care for the Poor and Underserved, 5*(2), 99–111.

Weiss, B. D., & Coyne, C. (1997). Communicating with patients who cannot read. *New England Journal of Medicine, 337*(4), 272–274.

Weiss, B. D., Hart, G., McGee, D. L., & D'Estelle, S. (1992). Health status of illiterate adults: Relation between literacy and health status among persons with low literacy skills. *Journal of the American Board of Family Practice, 5*(3), 257–264.

Weiss, B. D., Hart, G., & Pust, R. E. (1991). The relationship between literacy and health. *Journal of Health Care for the Poor and Underserved, 1*(4), 351–363.

Wells, J. A. (1994). Readability of HIV/AIDS educational materials: The role of the medium of communication, target audience, and producer characteristics. *Patient Education and Counseling, 24*(3), 249–259.

Williams, D. M., Counselman, F. L., & Caggiano, C. D. (1996). Emergency department discharge instructions and patient literacy: A problem of disparity. *American Journal of Emergency Medicine, 14*(1), 19–22.

Williams, M. V., Baker, D. W., Honig, E. G., Lee, T. M., & Nowlan, A. (1998a). Inadequate literacy is a barrier to asthma knowledge and self-care. *Chest, 114*(4), 1008–1015.

Williams, M. V., Baker, D. W., Parker, R. M., & Nurss, J. R. (1998b). Relationship of functional health literacy to patients' knowledge of their chronic disease: A study of patients with hypertension and diabetes. *Archives of Internal Medicine, 158*(2), 166–172.

Williams, M. V., Parker, R. M., Baker, D. W., Parikh, K., Coates, W. C., & Nurss, J. R. (1995). Inadequate functional health literacy among patients at two public hospitals. *Journal of the American Medical Association, 2714*(21), 1677–1682.

Winkleby, M. A., Jatulis, D. E., Frank, E., & Fortmann, S. P. (1992). Socioeconomic status and health: How education, income, and occupation contribute to risk factors for cardiovascular disease. *American Journal of Public Health, 82*(6), 816–820.

CHAPTER SIX

Perspectives on Assessment in Adult ESOL Instruction

Carol H. Van Duzer
Robert Berdan

⸺∿∿⸺

Assessment of outcomes and learner progress is a primary concern in federally funded adult education programs. This concern is not new, but it has gained prominence over the past decade as legislative imperatives, such as the National Literacy Act of 1991 and the Government Performance and Results Act of 1993, have required federally funded programs to be more accountable for what they do. The lack of a consistent assessment system across states and across programs within states has impeded the documentation and reporting of results to state and federal stakeholders. Such a system is needed to demonstrate the difference that adult education makes in the lives of learners, the communities in which they live, and the nation as a whole. Welfare reform and the establishment of one-stop centers for education and training underscore the need for better and more compatible accountability systems across and within states (Short, 1997).

The Workforce Investment Act (WIA) of 1998 called for the establishment of "a comprehensive performance accountability system to assess the effectiveness of eligible agencies in achieving continuous improvement of adult education and literacy activities . . . in order to optimize the return on investment of Federal funds in adult education and literacy activities" (WIA, section 212.a). States now award adult education funding to programs that provide adult education services based on twelve criteria, which include the degree to which the program establishes performance measures for learner outcomes, past effectiveness in meeting (or even exceeding) these performance measures, and the maintenance of a high-quality information management system that can report participant outcomes and monitor program performance against the performance measures (WIA, section 231.e). Adult education programs that offer English for speakers of other languages (ESOL) have much at stake in the movement to define and measure learner outcomes, for adult ESOL instruction is the fastest growing area in federally funded adult education programs in the United States (National Center for Educational Statistics, 1997).

Adult ESOL programs have always grappled with how to measure and report a range of desired outcomes and satisfy the demands of each stakeholder: learners, teachers, program administrators, funding agencies and organizations, policymakers, and the general public. Learners want to know how well they are progressing in learning English. Teachers want feedback on the effectiveness of their instruction. Program administrators want to know how well they are meeting program goals and how they can improve their services. Those funding the programs as well as the general public want to know whether funds spent are yielding results. Policymakers want to know what specific practices are successful so they can establish guidelines for allocating future funds. A single approach to assessment may not provide enough useful information to satisfy each of these demands.

Reports on testing and assessment from the early 1990s (Business Council for Effective Literacy, 1990; Sticht, 1990) show that very few of these concerns about assessment have been resolved. The tests being used in adult education—TABE (Test of Adult Basic Education), ABLE (Adult Basic Learning Examination), and CASAS (Comprehensive Adult Student Assessment System)—and in adult ESOL—BEST (Basic English Skills Test) and CASAS—are largely the same, as are the critiques of their validity and reliability. The call for research to help answer questions about the role and use of standardized tests and other assessments is still appropriate, and even the questions of what should be assessed and for what purpose are still being debated. However, the field has at the least made progress on the two following issues. First, it is generally acknowledged that tests developed for native

English speakers are not appropriate for use with English-language learners. Second, certain segments of the field have recognized that assessment is but one component in a larger instructional system that includes standards for content, program design, staff development, and assessment.

This chapter seeks to provide the field of education for adult English speakers of other languages—at local, state, and national levels—with a timely overview of the state of assessment in adult ESOL programs in the United States. It also seeks to provide a brief description of assessment reform initiatives in K–12 education and in adult language education abroad that might serve as models for adult education in the United States. Our intent is to help program staff and state and national policymakers make informed choices about assessment measures and procedures and to foster a collaborative effort to build an accountability system that addresses the needs of each stakeholder in a more effective adult education instructional system. Many decisions about assessment were being made even as we were writing this chapter. Although legislative requirements demand that states have an accountability system in place by July 1999, the field will be debating assessment issues for a long time to come.

For the purposes of this report, we are using the term *assessment* in a broad sense: *to find out what learners want, know, and can do at the beginning of instruction (needs, placement, and diagnosis), throughout instruction (ongoing progress), and at the end of instruction (achievement and outcomes).* The information presented is based on a literature review from the fields of language assessment and government policy, reviews of standardized tests currently being used in adult ESOL programs, and discussions with experienced adult ESOL educators. We explore three key issues and make recommendations based on the findings:

- What implications do legislative requirements for performance measures have for adult ESOL programs?
- What assessment tools and processes are available and how adequately do they meet the needs of all stakeholders?
- What insights can be gained from the assessment reform experience of K–12 education and adult language education abroad?

PERFORMANCE MEASURES
IN ADULT EDUCATION

The use of standardized tests to evaluate adult education programs was put into legislation for the first time in 1988, in amendments to the Adult Education Act (Business Council for Effective Literacy, 1990). In that legislation, states were required to evaluate the progress of at least one-third of their grant recipients using standardized tests (Sticht, 1990). The National Literacy Act of 1991, amending the Adult Education Act, required the U.S. Department of Education (ED) to develop indicators of program quality that would assist states and local programs in judging the effectiveness of programs that provide adult education services. The legislation specifically called for indicators in the areas of recruitment, retention, and educational gains.

The Department of Education sought input from the field of adult education by reviewing state and local practices related to program quality, commissioning papers by experts in the field, holding focus groups, and working closely with the state directors of adult education (Office of Vocational and Adult Education, 1992). A quality program indicator was defined as a variable reflecting effective and efficient program performance. It was distinguished from a measure (data used to determine the level of performance) and a performance standard (the level of acceptable performance in terms of a specific numeric criterion).

Under the area of educational gains, two indicators were identified:

• Learners demonstrate progress toward attainment of basic skills and competencies that support their educational needs.

• Learners advance in the instructional programs or complete program education requirements that allow them to continue their education or training.

Sample measures for the first indicator included standardized test scores, competency-based test scores, teacher reports of improvements in communication competencies, and demonstrated improvement on alternative assessments (such as portfolios, checklists of specific employability or life skills, and student reports of attainment). Sample measures for the second indicator included rate of student advancement to a higher level of skill or competency in the program; attainment of a competency certificate, General Educational Development credential (GED), or high school diploma; and percentage of students referred to or entering other education or training programs.

With the passage of the Government Performance and Results Act (GPRA) in 1993, more emphasis was placed on performance measurement as a requirement of government-funded program evaluations. Now, under the Workforce Investment Act, each state must negotiate acceptable target levels of performance on three core indicators with the ED that encompass the quality indicators identified as the result of the earlier legislation: (1) demonstrated improvement in skill levels in reading, writing, and speaking the English language, numeracy, problem solving, English-language acquisition, and other literacy skills; (2) placement in, retention in, or completion of postsecondary education, training, unsubsidized employment, or career advancement; and (3) receipt of a secondary school diploma or its recognized equivalent (WIA, section 212.b.2.A). The levels of performance for each core indicator are to be expressed in objective, quantifiable, and measurable form and must show the progress of each eligible program toward continual improvement of learner performance.

Within their five-year plans for adult education, each state will establish levels of performance for programs to meet. States are in the process of preparing their plans for ED approval. They became effective July 1, 1999. Each year, states will submit data on the core indicators to the secretary of education, who will issue reports on how each state is doing.

To facilitate the accountability and reporting process, the ED has been working with the state directors of adult education to establish a National Reporting System (NRS). The ED has granted funding to the American Institutes for Research/Pelavin Research Center (AIR/Pelavin) to help establish the system. The NRS will include a common set of outcome measures; a system for collecting data on these measures; and standard guidelines, definitions, and forms for reporting the data (Office of Vocational and Adult Education, 1997).

The NRS draft outcome measures for adult English-language learners are "educational functioning-level descriptors" that describe what a learner knows and can do in three areas: speaking and listening, reading and writing, and functional and workplace skills. These functioning-level descriptors appear to combine features outlined in the CASAS: level descriptors and the Student Performance Level (SPL) descriptors. States are to use the functioning levels to report educational gains of learners in the programs they fund.

Programs will determine an individual learner's entry-level and subsequent-level gains using a uniform, standardized assessment procedure that has been described in the state plan and approved by the ED (Office of Vocational and Adult Education, 1998). Illustrative examples of test benchmarks for each functioning level in the pilot NRS document include a range of CASAS Life Skills scores and SPLs. (The SPLs, developed under the auspices of the Office of Refugee Resettlement's Mainstream English Language Training Project [MELT], U.S. Department of Health and Human Services, 1985, are also descriptions of adult learners' language abilities. They are correlated to the BEST test; both the BEST and CASAS tests are reviewed below.) Unfortunately, the two test benchmark guidelines provided in the pilot draft do not cover the range of measures previously identified for the quality indicator of educational gains, nor do they allow for the flexibility that local programs may need. More examples need to be identified during the pilot field test and added to the final document. If they are not, there is a danger that in the need to satisfy the demands of policymakers and funding sources, assessment will become too narrowly focused on standardized test scores. This may lead to program designs that do not serve the needs of learners or the communities in which they live or that adequately assess what learners know and can do. The fundamental question of what is to be counted as success—and therefore what skills and proficiencies are assessed—needs to be addressed at the program, state, and national levels before the NRS is finalized.

LANGUAGE AND LITERACY ASSESSMENT IN ADULT ESOL

The Adult Education and Family Literacy Act (Title II of the WIA) defines literacy as "an individual's ability to read, write, and speak in English, compute, and solve problems at levels of proficiency necessary to function on the job, in the family of the individual, and in society." However, there have been many definitions of literacy over the years, including a school-based view of literacy as basic reading and writing skills, the functional view that is in the legislation, and a view of literacy as social practices. Even this latter definition is acknowledged in the "Family Literacy" designation noted in Title II of the WIA. The field of adult ESOL recognizes that there are many literacies, defined by how individuals use literacy in everyday life to achieve personal, family, job, and community participation goals (Crandall, 1992). Literacy includes the ability to complete a task or solve a problem, such as getting a driver's license, completing the GED, or finding a job; to support the learning of one's children; to comprehend print material (in one's first or second language); and more.

Which literacy is to be assessed: development in reading and writing, speaking, mathematical ability, social practice, or all of these? What constitutes progress in these areas, and how is it assessed? Can a gain in general language proficiency on a given measure be considered sufficient, or is a variety of assessment instruments and processes needed? These are questions that must be answered and agreed on at the local, state, and national levels if we are to establish an accountability system that captures learner progress.

Many adult ESOL programs use a combination of assessment tools to meet their program needs. These include standardized tests such as the CASAS and BEST, materials-based tests such as those accompanying text series, and program-based tools such as teacher-made tests and portfolios. However, the field of adult ESOL lacks a cohesive assessment system that enables comparison of learner achievement and program impact across the wide variety of programs (survival, pre-employment, preacademic, workplace, vocational ESOL, ESOL for citizenship, ESOL family literacy) and the wide range of delivery systems (local education agencies, community colleges, libraries, community-based or volunteer organizations, churches, businesses, and unions). The lack of consistent assessment procedures from program to program is problematic for two major reasons. One is that it impedes the documentation and reporting of results to the satisfaction of all stakeholders. The other is that it frequently impedes the movement of learners from ESOL to vocational training and academic programs because learner pathways differ from program to program.

Most programs use placement procedures to match students to the levels or courses offered. This may take the form of a standardized test, a program-developed test or interview, or a combination of these. The kinds of assessments that are used after placement depend to a large extent on the program's philosophy of language and learning, the roles of teachers and learners, and the measures of success as defined by the various stakeholders (Wrigley, 1992). Program staff need to juggle two important purposes for assessment:

- They need to assess and document the actual progress that learners are making toward English-language development and completion of learner goals.
- They must meet the legislative requirements of the WIA, which requires a standardized assessment procedure and performance measures, and the NRS, which links learner progress to proficiency descriptors.

Therefore, they must select instruments and procedures carefully and, in many cases, use a combination of standardized and alternative assessments.

Standardized Assessment Tools in Adult ESOL

For the purpose of this chapter, a standardized assessment tool is one that has been developed according to explicit specifications, has items that have been tested and selected for item difficulty and discriminating power, is administered and scored according to uniform directions, and has dependable norms for interpreting scores (Ebel, 1979). Standardized tests are used in adult education programs in most states because they are easy to administer to groups, require minimal training for the teacher, and purport to have construct validity and scoring reliability (Solorzano, 1994; Wrigley, 1992).

Standardized tests reviewed for this chapter include the Adult Basic Learning Examination, the Test of Adult Basic Education, the Adult Language Assessment Scales (A-LAS), the Comprehensive Adult Student Assessment System (components appropriate for ESOL), New York State's Placement Test for English as a Second Language Adult Students (NYS Place), and the Basic English Skills Test. Because they were designed for native English speakers, the ABLE and TABE are now regarded as inappropriate for English-language learners. We have included them here because they were used in the 1970s and 1980s in many adult education programs that had ESOL learners in classes with adult basic education (ABE) learners, and they are still used in some of these programs today. The A-LAS parallels the ABLE and TABE in that it has both language and mathematics batteries, but it was

·designed for nonnative English speakers. The CASAS and BEST are the two most widely used standardized tests in adult ESOL programs. Both were developed for assessing nonnative English speakers. The NYS Place was selected because it is the only oral assessment besides the BEST that was identified by the California Department of Education Adult ESL Assessment Project (Kahn, Butler, Weigle, & Sato, 1995) as suitable as a placement tool for assessing speaking ability in programs that were implementing the California ESL Model Standards (California Department of Education, 1992), discussed below. Ordering information for these tests is included in the chapter appendix.

ADULT BASIC LEARNING EXAMINATION (ABLE). The ABLE was designed for use with native, English-speaking adults who have limited formal education and is used primarily in ABE and GED programs and in prison education. It is an educational achievement test. It was not designed to be a language development test or even a test of language proficiency, although it does have a language subtest in Levels 2 and 3. The ABLE is available in three levels differentiated by years of formal schooling, and it has six subtests: vocabulary, reading comprehension, spelling, language (Levels 2 and 3 only), number operations, and problem solving. The first four of these subtests relate to language proficiency and are described in Exhibit 6.1. Reviews of the full battery can be found in Fitzpatrick (1992) and Williams (1992).

Although the ABLE is represented by its publisher, the Texas-based Psychological Corporation, to be an indicator of educational achievement, many of the items on it reflect a narrow concept of achievement. For example, there is a heavy preoccupation with the inflectional morphology of auxiliary verbs (for example, We are/was [verb]), which is highly differentiated across social groups. At the same time, there is a complete absence of attention to such language systems as complex nominals (for example, the combination of [noun] with [noun]), which continue to develop in adolescence and later across all groups.

The use of the ABLE with the populations for which it was designed—ABE, GED, and prison education—is problematic, and transporting the test to the adult ESOL population compounds these problems. The test does not reflect what is known about stages or sequencing of English language development. Only Level 1 would be plausible for use in most adult ESOL programs. Furthermore, because the vocabulary test is presented orally and the writing is confined to

For Level 1 (for adult learners with up to four years of schooling), all of the subtests (test items and possible responses) except reading comprehension and numerical operations are read orally by the proctor to the examinees. For Level 2 (up to eight years of schooling) and Level 3 (up to twelve years of schooling), the examinee reads all items from a test booklet. There are two forms for each level; Form E is reviewed here.

Vocabulary. There are thirty-two items at each level. Each item is a multiple-choice sentence completion with two distractors. The items are characterized by the publisher as being made up of words that adults frequently encounter in their work or other daily activities. In Level 1, however, none of the items is among the 2,500 most frequent words identified by Carroll, Davies, and Richman (1971).[a] Eight of these items come from the next 2,500 most frequent words, and half of the items come from the 10,000 most frequent words. Most of the remaining items are predicted by Carroll et al. to occur less frequently than once in 1 million words of running text. In Levels 2 and 3, at least half of the items fall into this category in Carroll et al.'s typology. Thus, across all three levels, the vocabulary tested is, with few exceptions, not the vocabulary predicted by Carroll et al. to be most important in daily life. Therefore, the ABLE vocabulary tests are largely inappropriate for use in adult ESOL programs. Some of the vocabulary is workplace based (for example, *employer, wages*), but much of it is outside both the workplace and daily experiences of many adult English-language learners (for example, *polka, monarchy*). Furthermore, because the multiple-choice items have only two distractors, guessing and chance are likely to be the primary attributes measured.

Language. Beginning with Level 2, the ABLE contains a language subtest. The first eighteen items test only capitalization and punctuation. The second part of the subtest is called applied grammar (twelve items). In Level 2, eleven of the twelve items test knowledge of inflectional morphology, principally auxiliary verb forms (for example, *we are/was*). In both Levels 2 and 3, most of the items use distractors that are characteristic of established regional or social dialects of American English (for example, *don't have no/has no* and *real good/very good*) and include constructions that seem only to be learned in school (for example, *It was they who . . .*). Very few of the distractors are distinctively characteristic of the forms used by adult English learners.

Spelling. Levels 2 and 3 ask the examinee to detect a misspelled word from among sets of four words (thirty items). All of the misspelled words are pronounceable using conventional phonics (for example, *neibor, dissapear*). Several of the items at each level have errant spellings that reflect contemporary colloquial pronunciation (for example, *hunderd, hankerchief*).

Exhibit 6.1.   Review of ABLE Language Subtests.
[a]We recognize that although Carroll, Davies, & Richman (1971) may be thought of as a dated source, it continues in use. It seems highly unlikely that the passage of time has changed the basic argument that tests designed for adult native speakers of English employ vocabulary that is inappropriate for adult populations learning English.

words in isolation (a spelling test), the ABLE has very few items that actually measure literacy skills.

TEST OF ADULT BASIC EDUCATION (TABE). The developers of the TABE made a conscious attempt to assess the basic skills taught in adult basic education programs. The publisher, CTB/McGraw-Hill in California, reports a systematic effort to limit cultural, gender, and ethnic bias; construct items with content appropriate for adults; and include items developed through item response theory (IRT) modeling (see Hambleton, 1991), with desirable psychometric properties such as item discrimination and range of difficulty. That effort has resulted in content that is generally accessible to immigrant adults.

The TABE has three basic levels: E (easy, grade equivalents 1.6–3.9), M (medium, grades 3.6–6.9), and D (difficult, grades 6.6–8.9), with an upward extension to A (advanced, grades 8.6–14.9). There are also a downward extension, L (literacy), a Spanish-language version, a computer-based version, a placement test, and several other associated products. Levels E through A consist of two mathematics tests (computation and applied mathematics), a reading test, a language test, and an optional spelling test. There is no writing test. The language tests are reviewed in Exhibit 6.2.

The TABE is not suitable for learners in beginning-level adult ESOL classes. If given the locator test, many ESOL learners will be assigned to take the Level L test. That test, with its high proportion of literacy readiness items (twenty-three), may be useful for testing adults with little or no previous alphabetic literacy experience, but it is not appropriate for beginning English learners who are literate in their native language. The remaining twenty-seven items of the test, with too few items at the lower range of language development, will not detect the learning that can reasonably be expected in early levels of ESOL instruction. However, for the most advanced levels of adult ESOL instruction, the TABE may prove useful.

ADULT LANGUAGE ASSESSMENT SCALES (A-LAS). The A-LAS, published in New York by McGraw-Hill, is designed to test the English-language skills needed for "entry level functioning in a mainstream academic or employment environment" (Duncan & DeAvila, 1993, p. 1). The A-LAS consists of two test batteries: a set of oral tests and tests of reading, writing, and mathematics, available in two forms. The reading and writing tests are described in Exhibit 6.3.

Each of the three levels (easy, medium, and difficult) is available as a full battery of about two hundred items or as a survey of about half that many items. There is a separate locator test for selecting the appropriate level. All of the items are multiple choice. Many are embedded in authentic—or, perhaps more accurately described, quasi-authentic—content. That is, the items are specifically constructed for the test in formats resembling advertisements, letters, articles, or product labels but are not actual documents.

The TABE does not contain a separate vocabulary test but embeds vocabulary testing into short reading passages. The language test uses a variety of item types, and the complexity of content increases across higher test levels. Verb and auxiliary inflection are the focus of a relatively small proportion of the items. Each level contains a series of sentence-combining tasks. Most of the punctuation and capitalization items are embedded in paragraphs or short documents such as business letters.

The TABE has become a highly elaborate testing system that reflects much of current thought about language and literacy testing in the content and formatting of the items and the use of item response theory modeling for the selection of items. This does not guarantee, however, that the test can be used effectively with adults learning English. Many students in adult ESOL programs will not be able to respond to the items on the locator test. Most of these items are based on multiparagraph prompts that are more complex than the materials taught in beginning adult ESOL instruction.

The TABE provides, as an alternative to the locator list, a list of forty one- and two-syllable words to be read aloud by the examinee. As a result of the examinee's performance in reading the words, he or she may be referred to the literacy level (L) test. The L test consists of two parts. The first (twenty-three items) is chiefly a literacy readiness test with letter- and word-matching items and identification of sound-letter correspondences. The second part (twenty-seven items) is a reading test of words in isolation, words matched to pictures, and brief sentence or sentence pair items.

Exhibit 6.2.   Review of TABE Language-Related Subtests.

The A-LAS was constructed for testing the language and literacy of adults learning English. That it was not adapted from another test is apparent in the vocabulary employed (carefully selected for English learners) and the adult level of the item content (for example, concerning employment). None of the items, however, seeks to differentiate stages of English-language development. Because the A-LAS attempts to test the full range of English skills, from no English to entry-level functioning for employment and academic work, it must contain items that range in difficulty from monosyllabic word recognition to essay construction. However, the reading test has relatively few items at any particular level of development. This may be sufficient for a placement instrument, but if used for assessing achievement, it will be difficult to detect the increment of learning that many

The A-LAS reading test has four components: vocabulary (ten items), fluency (ten items), reading for information (ten items), and mechanics and essential structures (twenty items). All of the items are multiple choice. The writing test has two components: sentences in action (five items) and adventures in writing (one essay). All of the items in the writing test involve constructing responses, ranging from writing a sentence to writing and sequencing paragraphs, and are scored holistically. The test instructions allow a wide range of time for test completion, suggesting that examinees work on each section until they have finished.

Vocabulary and Fluency. The first ten items are picture-cued vocabulary items; the fluency items call for sentence completion with multiple-choice response. Overall half of the vocabulary is drawn from the most frequently used English words and 90 percent of it from the 2,500 most frequently occurring words (Carroll, Davies, & Richman, 1971). The A-LAS uses four distractors rather than the three used in many other tests, to lessen the chance of guessing, an important factor in tests with few items.

Reading for Information. All of the items involve a response to questions about a document. In Form 1A, the document is a letter from a utility company, and the questions test comprehension of the content and knowledge of the conventions of a business letter.

Mechanics and Essential Structures. This section contains questions about punctuation (three items); verb and auxiliary tense and number inflection (five items); and a variety of other constructions, including pronouns, articles, possessives, prepositions, and capitalization (twelve items).

Sentences in Action. This section consists of five picture prompts that show an adult engaged in an everyday activity. For each picture, examinees are directed to write a sentence that explains what is happening in the picture. Responses are scored holistically on a scale of 0 (no response) to 3 (no errors; contextually appropriate). The test manual provides a detailed scoring rubric and multiple examples of writing at each level. Considerable attention is given to selecting and training scorers and achieving acceptable levels of interscorer reliability.

Adventures in Writing. Examinees select one of five written prompts (for example, My First Day in the United States, The Happiest Day of My Life, A Day in My Life 15 Years from Now) and write an essay. They are directed to try to fill up an entire page. They are reminded to attend to punctuation, capitalization, paragraph form, and spelling. Responses are scored holistically on a scale of 0 (no response) to 5 (vivid, precise vocabulary; well organized; fluent, varied sentence structure). The test manual provides multiple examples of writing at each level for each prompt.

Exhibit 6.3.   Review of the A-LAS Reading and Writing Subtests.

adults display in the relatively short time they stay in programs. The A-LAS would be a much stronger tool for assessing achievement if it were available in multiple levels, allowing more items at each difficulty level.

COMPREHENSIVE ADULT STUDENT ASSESSMENT SYSTEM (CASAS). The CASAS Web site (http://www.casas.org) lists the availability of more than one hundred standardized assessments and a variety of instructional and supporting materials developed by CASAS. The system was designed for adult basic education, workforce learning, special education, adult ESOL, and various other state and federal programs. CASAS began in the early 1980s as a collaborative effort between adult educators in California and the State Department of Education. Their goal was to develop an assessment model that would help adult education programs to implement competency-based education, as mandated by the 1982 California state plan for adult education (Center for Adult Education, 1983). Over the years, the system developers have identified more than three hundred competencies (that is, statements that describe adult functioning in employment and in society). They then developed and field-tested more than four thousand life skills reading items that assess those competencies. These items are the basis for the array of assessments now available from CASAS. Extensive training is required as part of the CASAS purchase agreement to ensure proper administration and use of the assessments. See Exhibit 6.4 for a descriptive review of the assessments for ESOL populations, particularly the series of tests characterized as life skills.

CASAS tests multiple modalities at multiple levels with multiple forms. Some of the tests are specifically constructed for the adult English-language learner population. In general, the item content is accessible for immigrant populations. All of the items are tied to a list of competencies, and all of the tests are scaled to a single, uniform scale of proficiency. Ranges of the scale are associated with highly generalized statements of language proficiency or skill levels.

The CASAS system provides the instructor with a chart to construct an item-by-item, student-by-student summary, or class profile, for some of the assessments. The student-by-student class profile is keyed to corresponding CASAS competencies rather than directly to test item. Constructing such class snapshots of student performance allows teachers to see where students are performing well and where

Language proficiency is measured using a series of reading and listening tests. To determine the appropriate level of assessment to be used with ESOL students, CASAS provides a brief screening test to assess all four modalities: listening, speaking, reading, and writing. The speaking test consists of six oral questions that can be answered with a single sentence or phrase (for example, "What country are you from?"). The writing test consists of two short sentences written from dictation. The listening test (twenty-three items) is cued from a tape recording with multiple-choice printed responses. The reading test consists of items ranging from identification of signs to complex paragraphs (twenty items). In each case, the items cover a wide range of proficiency levels, as is appropriate for a screening or locator test.

The screening test is keyed to a series of reading and listening tests, each available in multiple levels and multiple forms. Each level contains items of a fairly broad range of difficulty. The reading test is available at five levels. Level A (twenty-three items) tests functional literacy: highway signs, coins, maps, addresses, and so on. At Level C the reading items (thirty-eight of them) are much more complex and embedded in a variety of documents, including letters, advertisements, instructions, and forms. Level D (forty items) includes some documents, but most items test comprehension of multiparagraph expository prose selections. There is also a beginning literacy level, below Level A, that tests alphabetic correspondences and a variety of signs and labels (thirty items).

The life skills listening tests are administered by audiotape. At Level A, all twenty-seven items require the student to listen to the item on the tape and then select an appropriate picture. By Level C most of the items require the student to select from among brief written responses to a prerecorded stimulus. Each level is available in two forms for pre- and posttesting.

In addition to these general tests, which are designed to assess a wide range of proficiency levels, CASAS has an exit-level completion test designed for adult students who have completed initial ESOL instruction. Content is aligned with the California ESL Model Standards (California Department of Education, 1992). This test contains three subtests: reading, listening, and grammar. The reading subtest is based on multiparagraph texts or brief documents and presumes well-established literacy. Material for the listening subtest (ten items) is presented on audiotape. The multiple-choice questions concern direct comprehension of content. For each set of questions, the material is repeated on the audiotape so that memory problems are minimized. The grammar subtest is a set of thirteen multiple-choice cloze items embedded in dialogue. The items principally test verb tense and agreement and the use of auxiliaries in questions and negation. Unlike the ABLE and TABE, the distractors are drawn largely from early stages of adult learner English rather than from established dialects of English. Completion tests for other levels are under development.

Exhibit 6.4.   Review of the CASAS Tests for the ESOL Population.

they need continued instruction. However, one might hesitate to provide instructors with such information because they might limit instruction to the content of the test, and this might pose a problem with the relationship between parallel forms of the tests. At any level, the items are selected not only to be of comparable difficulty across forms but to have a very high overlap of the competencies they represent. For example, at Level A, Life Skills Listening, twenty-six of the thirty-four items are drawn from competencies shared across the two forms (form 51 and form 52). Many of the competencies are very narrowly defined (for example, "Interpret clothing and pattern size"). When the class profile shows that many students did not get the item for a particular competency correct, there will be a tendency to focus instruction in that area. When that same competency is retested on the parallel posttest form, improvement could be expected, but this does not mean that there would be similar growth in all comparable competency areas.

Another problem could develop if the instruction and testing are drawn into narrow content domains or competencies while the test results are being interpreted in very broad proficiency ranges. Because the posttests do not sample broadly across the competencies but rather concentrate on the taught areas, they will overstate proficiency when it is then interpreted in terms of broad skill levels. (For example, the test results may state that a person is low intermediate ESL, meaning she can satisfy basic survival needs and very routine social demands and can understand simple learned phrases easily. What the results do not state is that she may have this competency only in the area of clothing.)

BASIC ENGLISH SKILLS TEST (BEST). The BEST, published by the Center for Applied Linguistics in Washington, D.C., is designed as an adult English-language proficiency test, focusing primarily on survival and preemployment language skills. It consists of two parts: oral interview and literacy skills.

Like the CASAS assessments, the BEST was an outgrowth of the movement toward a competency-based approach to instruction for adult English-language learners in nonacademic programs. The development of the BEST was funded principally by the Office of Refugee Resettlement (ORR) of the U.S. Department of Health and Human Services (HHS). Teachers and administrators from ORR's Region 1 in

Boston and the National Office in Washington, D.C., worked with test developers from the Center for Applied Linguistics (CAL) to develop the original 1982 version (form A). Three additional forms (B, C, and D) were developed and field-tested in 1984 with the help of staff from seven geographically diverse programs that were participating in the ORR Mainstream English Language Training (MELT) Project (National Clearinghouse for ESL Literacy Education, 1989).

The primary goals of the MELT Project were to provide consistency among ORR-funded programs in the United States, continuity between the domestic and overseas training programs (mostly in Southeast Asia), and guidance for curriculum development, establishment of instructional levels, and assessment. Products other than the BEST included the Student Performance Levels (SPLs) (cited as test benchmarks in the NRS) and a core curriculum document that correlated topics and competencies to the SPLs (U.S. HHS, 1985). Although the BEST was primarily developed for use with English-language learners from Southeast Asia, many of the programs participating in the field test of the BEST also provided other refugee and immigrant populations with services and included those populations in the field test (Allene Grognet, director, BEST Development Project, personal communication, January 14, 1999). However, the test population data reported in the MELT documents includes only refugee populations.

The BEST was made available to ORR-funded programs from the ORR Refugee Materials Center in Kansas City, Missouri, until it closed at the end of 1987. At that time, CAL decided to reprint form B and make it available through CAL. Form C was eventually reprinted as well. The form B oral interview section is described in Exhibit 6.5.

Using only forty-nine items, the BEST oral interview attempts to assess language proficiency from eight topic areas or domains, across eight proficiency levels, using the four response modalities of speaking, listening, reading, and writing. The result is that very few items are actually related to the theoretical model at each proficiency level. The length of the test and the number of items are constrained by the need to administer each interview individually. The consequence of this time constraint and the desire to develop a broadly defined scale of performance levels in a single test is that the test loses stability when used to predict the exact proficiency level of individual students. In fact, the test developers recognized that the BEST discriminates better at the lower SPLs (0–VI) than the higher ones (VII–X). In 1992, CAL convened a meeting with potential users of a higher-level BEST

Underlying the BEST was a major effort to identify grammatical and situational proficiency levels described by the SPLs. Items are contextualized in functional tasks that relate to a wide range of daily life situations (for example, asking the price of something, describing an injury). Because the interview requires oral responses, it is administered individually. Most items are picture cued. Items that focus on listening comprehension require the examinee only to point or to give some other nonverbal response and are scored 0 (incomprehensible, inappropriate, or no response) or 1 (appropriate response). Items that focus on communication usually require a sentence or phrasal response and are scored 0 (incomprehensible, inappropriate, or no response), 1 (appropriate response but not grammatically accurate), or 2 (appropriate and grammatically accurate). Items that focus on fluency allow the examinee to construct extended responses and are scored 0 (incomprehensible or no response), 1 (terse and unelaborated response, a minimum response), 2 (shows some effort in going beyond the minimum), or 3 (elaborated response). These latter items are scored only for the extensiveness of the language the examinee provides, not for grammar. In addition to listening comprehension, communication, and fluency, the BEST has four items that require the student to match a sight word to a picture and a brief form of four items asking for personal identification information and the date, which can be used as a screening device for the literacy section. The scores on these eight items are not figured into the total score for the oral interview.

Exhibit 6.5.   Review of the BEST Oral Interview, Form B.

to explore the general design and preliminary specifications of a test that would discriminate at the higher levels (CAL, 1992, summary of the higher-level BEST test meeting). Lack of funding prevented the test development from proceeding. The BEST, however, does elicit extended responses for fluency questions so that the proficiency level of the learners can be probed more deeply than is allowed for in the NYS Place.

NEW YORK STATE PLACEMENT TEST FOR ENGLISH AS A SECOND LANGUAGE ADULT STUDENTS (NYS PLACE). The NYS Place is primarily an oral picture description task, cued by brief oral questions from the examiner. The test has an optional initial oral screening component, or oral warm-up, to determine if the examinee has sufficient English to proceed with the test. These seven items are simple greetings and directives. If the examinee fails to answer three items in a row, testing is suspended. There is also a literacy screen with items asking the test taker to read letters, numbers, and words in isolation as well as one short sentence. Exhibit 6.6 presents a description of Form B, the only form currently available.

The test consists of three sequences of three or four drawings showing adults dealing with some problem. Examinees are asked to describe certain characteristics of the pictures, explain the feelings of characters, or suggest what they might be saying in such situations. The vocabulary in the questions in Form B is all high frequency, virtually all drawn from the 2,500 most frequently used words. The test is administered individually. Responses are scored on a 0–2 scale for their content and grammatical correctness. The elliptic responses that characterize native English dialogue receive full credit. The administrator's manual presents a scoring rubric for only one item. There is also a videotape with additional scoring and test administration information. If at any point in the administration a student scores 0 on three consecutive items, the test administration is stopped and diverted to a fail-safe question to end the session. Raw scores are keyed to a set of four student performance levels. These correspond roughly to the lower three to four levels of the California Model ESL Standards (California Department of Education, 1992).

Exhibit 6.6.   Review of the New York State
Placement Test for English as a Second Language, Adult Students.

The NYS Place, developed by the State Education Department of New York, is available from the City School District of Albany. It was developed specifically for the initial placement of adults in ESOL programs, and the content is generally accessible to immigrant populations. The NYS Place, along with the BEST, is one of the few tests of spoken English for adults. It is a highly structured test. Unlike the BEST, it does not give the examinee an opportunity to initiate or elaborate at any time. Therefore, the test protocol cannot be represented as eliciting authentic conversation.

GENERAL OBSERVATIONS ON TESTS. There are probably as many definitions of language proficiency as there are programs. Because language has so many facets and so many uses, different tests approach different aspects of language proficiency. Over the years, proficiency testing has reflected changes in our understanding of language theory. It has moved from a structural view (for example, discrete point tests of grammar, phonology, and other components of language), through a sociolinguistic view (integrative tests such as cloze and dictation), to a communicative view (for example, oral proficiency interviews that assess the learner's ability to use language to carry out communicative tasks) (Manidis & Prescott, 1996). Today, given the focus on real-life, practical content in adult ESOL instruction and the goals of the learners, if a test does not in some way look at language as communication, it would seem to be missing much that is important.

Nevertheless, most items in most tests do not relate directly to either theoretically or empirically derived understandings of adult English-language proficiency development. One might assume that if a test is constructed in English and requires responses in English, then higher scores will correspond to higher levels of English proficiency. But this is a very shaky foundation on which to build proficiency assessment. To the extent that the content of the items is known to and within the experience of all examinees, score differentials will more directly reflect language proficiency differentials.

A number of the tests designed for English-language learners reviewed here relate scores to some broadly defined scale of proficiency levels. These proficiency levels tend to be described in very global terms, often corresponding to the complexity of communicative situations (for example, greetings and leave-takings contrasted to explanation and persuasion). The actual items in a test, however, may be particular to a competency area and may sample very narrowly from the broad ranges of behavior described by the proficiency levels. The generalizability from performance on the test items back to all situations consistent with a particular level description may be difficult to establish. When there is only one form of a test or a very small set of alternate forms, the possibility increases that learners begin to learn the test or that teachers teach to the test.

The use of a single test form to assess the full spectrum of proficiency levels also means that most items will not match any particular test taker's current level of functioning—that is, there are too few items at any one level of proficiency. Tests with multiple levels usually make more accurate assessments of functioning level. This can also be achieved in direct measures of proficiency, such as oral interviews, if the items engage the examinee in extended dialogue so that proficiency is assessed based on learner response and not the difficulty of the question.

Alternative Assessment in Adult ESOL

In the reviews of standardized tests, we pointed out the difficulty of using a single assessment instrument to provide information useful for placement, instructional decisions, and accountability. This fact has led many adult ESOL program staff to develop program-based alternative assessments. Alternative assessment is "any method of finding out what a learner knows or can do, that is intended to show growth and inform instruction, and is not a standardized or traditional test (Valdez-Pierce & O'Malley, 1992, p. 1).

Alternative assessments may take the form of performance assessment, portfolio assessment, or learner self-assessment. In performance assessment, the learner uses prior knowledge and recent learning to accomplish a task related to general language use or relevant to a specific context (Lumley, 1996). The learner response to, or outcome of, performance assessment may be an oral or written report, an individual or group project, an exhibition, or a demonstration (O'Malley & Pierce, 1996). A portfolio is a systematic collection of learner work that represents progress and achievement in more than one area (Fingeret, 1993). In learner self-assessment the learners monitor their own progress and accomplishments in order to select learning tasks and plan their use of time and resources to accomplish those tasks (O'Malley and Pierce, 1996).

Alternative assessments are consistent with emerging models of language acquisition. These models examine how people acquire language competence as they use the language in social interaction to accomplish purposeful tasks, such as to give and receive information and to make requests (August & Hakuta, 1997).

During the past decade, several studies and publications on best practices have guided the development of alternative assessments. The most comprehensive that was written specifically for adult ESOL is *Bringing Literacy to Life,* a document prepared for the U.S. Department of Education by Aguirre International (Wrigley & Guth, 1992). Other publications include the following:

- *Assessing Success in Family Literacy Projects: Alternative Approaches to Assessment and Evaluation* (Holt, 1994)

- *Adventures in Assessment* (McGrail & Simmons, 1991–1998)

- *Making Meaning, Making Change: Participatory Curriculum Development for Adult ESL Literacy* (Auerbach, 1992)

- *It Belongs to Me: A Guide for Portfolio Assessment in Adult Education Programs* (Fingeret, 1993)

- *Authentic Assessment for English Language Learners: Practical Approaches for Teachers* (O'Malley & Pierce, 1996)

The last book, though focused on K–12 education, can be helpful to adult ESOL programs as well. It devotes considerable attention to assisting teachers in developing assessment tasks and scoring rubrics (that is, rating scales) that ensure the reliability and validity of alternative assessments. Examples of assessment tools and processes advocated in these materials include learner-teacher conferences; questionnaires and surveys; teacher observation forms; checklists of communication skills and behaviors (Crandall & Peyton, 1993); and learner reading, writing, and speaking logs. Learners might prepare narrative writings or keep journals in which they express what they have learned in class; what changes they have made in their language and literacy practices or interactions; and how their goals, needs, and interests have been met or modified (Auerbach, 1992).

Although these alternative assessments are not standardized, they should be consistent with the following principles:

- They are program based, reflecting the program's underlying philosophy of instruction.
- They are learner centered, reflecting the strengths and goals of individual learners.
- They are done with the learner, not to the learner, so that learners are actively involved in setting goals, discussing interests, deciding what to evaluate, and reflecting on their accomplishments.
- They focus on the learning process as well as outcomes, allowing learners to reflect on their progress and make changes in how they are using their time and resources.
- In addition to the linguistic dimension of language and literacy development (for example, vocabulary and grammar), these assessments focus on the metacognitive (for example, developing learning strategies) and affective (for example, increased confidence) dimensions.
- They involve a variety of procedures, not just a single process or tool.

Alternative assessments provide teachers and learners with valuable feedback on learner progress and instructional changes that may need to be made.

Despite the fact that alternative assessment is guided by these principles and affords greater flexibility than standardized tests in gathering a more complete picture of what learners know and can do, its use as a means for accountability has raised serious questions. Without the development of guidelines and rigorous procedures for the collection and evaluation of evidence of learner performance and without the proper training of staff in how to carry out the assessments, alternative assessments do not produce the reliable, hard data that sources of funding require. To dispel the uncertainty of the subjectiveness associated with such assessments, administration procedures and conditions would have to be strictly monitored and a minimum of two raters involved in assessing student performance (Lumley, 1996). Furthermore, the program-specific nature of the assessments, along with difficulty in aggregating the data across programs, make program comparisons difficult.

EDUCATION REFORM INITIATIVES
THAT INFORM ADULT ESOL ASSESSMENT

The issues of what and how to assess in language and literacy development are not unique to adult ESOL education. Assessment reform movements in K–12 education and language education abroad face similar challenges, although in some respects they are ahead of adult education in the United States, and the field can learn from their experiences. The next two sections briefly review some initiatives in K–12 education and abroad.

K–12 Education

In K–12 education in the United States, the assessment reform of the early 1990s was tied to the K–12 standards movement, which resulted from the passage of Goals 2000 legislation and the Improving America's Schools Act of 1994. A number of national, state, local, and professional groups have been developing content standards—what students should know and what schools should teach and assess—in a broad array of subjects, including art, foreign language, geography, history, language arts, mathematics, science, and social studies. In some content areas, performance standards—what students must know and be able to do to demonstrate proficiency in the content area—are also being developed. Performance standards can be used to guide the development of assessment tools and processes. A third type of standard, referred to as opportunity to learn, defines what resources (for example, staffing and materials) are needed to make sure students will be able to meet the content and performance standards (August & Hakuta, 1997).

Early in the standards movement, Teachers of English to Speakers of Other Languages (TESOL) formed a task force to ensure educational equity and opportunity for students learning English as a second or additional language. The task force became concerned that many of the K–12 academic content standards did not take into account the important role of language in academic achievement. The task force developed ESOL standards for pre-K–12 students that specify the language competencies English-language learners need to become fully proficient in English, both socially and academically (TESOL, 1997).

The framework for the standards is based on three overarching goals: developing competence in English in social language, academic language, and sociocultural knowledge. These goals are supported by nine standards, organized by grade-level clusters (pre-K–3, 4–8, and 9–12), that can be used to guide curriculum development at the state or local level. Descriptors of representative behaviors that demonstrate a standard is being met, along with sample progress indicators, are included in the document to assist in the development of curricular objectives and benchmarks for reporting student performance. Examples are included of how the sample progress indicators can be used across grade-level clusters to account for different English-language proficiency levels (beginning, intermediate, advanced, and limited formal schooling).

Exhibit 6.7 shows how tasks can be constructed across proficiency levels to demonstrate the same standard. It can be used to guide the development of assessment tasks to monitor the progress not only of K–12 English-language learners but also of adults. The goal in the example, "To use English to achieve academically in all content areas," is admittedly geared toward academics in pre-K–12 education. But the standard, "to obtain, process, construct, and provide subject matter information in spoken and written form," describes uses of language that adult learners identified as important to their own literacy development in the adult-focused Equipped for the Future Project (Stein, 1997) and that employers defined as important in a high-performing workforce (Secretary's Commission on Achieving Necessary Skills, 1993). The TESOL pre-K–12 standards document, along with its accompanying *Scenarios for ESL Standards-Based Assessment* (TESOL, 1999),

Goal 2, Standard 2

To use English to achieve academically in all content areas:

Students will use English to obtain, process, construct, and provide subject matter information in spoken and written form

Sample Progress Indicator (SPI): Construct a chart or other graphic showing data

	Beginning	Intermediate	Advanced	Limited Formal Schooling (LFS)
Grade 1 Vignette In math class, students read counting stories, and use unifix cubes to understand basic number theory.	Draw unifix towers in descending order and write the numeral underneath each.	Construct a picture graph illustrating the number of food items that the caterpillar ate and describe the graph orally, using simple sentences.	Draw storyboard pictures to summarize the plot and include unifix pictures for each food item eaten. Describe storyboard orally or in writing.	Participate in a "physical human chart" that illustrates the number of food items the caterpillar ate in the story, *La Oruga Muy Hambrienta*.
Grades 4–5 Vignette Students read a Native American myth and share myths from their own cultures.	Draw a sequence chart to illustrate the story line of the myth that was read and describe the chart orally, using words and phrases.	Draw a sequence chart to illustrate the story line of the myth that was read and write simple sentences describing the chart.	Develop a comparison chart to compare two nature myths with regard to characters, setting, and conflict resolution.	Make rebus symbols for key vocabulary and then copy part of the myth using rebus symbols for appropriate words.
Grade 11 Vignette Students research a position on the development of a neighborhood toxic waste dump.	Survey neighbors to learn if they are for or against a potential dump site and represent results in a graph.	Illustrate in a chart the advantages and disadvantages of various waste management options.	Using a computer model, generate a graph on the decomposition of different waste material over time and summarize.	Create a photo essay or magazine picture collage to reflect the pros and cons of a dump site and write captions.

Exhibit 6.7. Tasks Constructed Across Proficiency Levels That Demonstrate the Same Standard.

Source: From *ESL Standards for Pre-K–12 Students* (1997). Alexandria, VA: Teachers of English to Speakers of Other Languages, Inc. Copyright © 1997 TESOL, Inc. Used with permission.

can serve as a model for creating performance assessment tasks that probe the functioning proficiency level of the adult learner.

Adult Language Education Abroad

Developments in assessing language learners in Australia, Canada, and Europe can inform efforts in adult education in the United States. Stakeholders in each country have expressed the need for a common way to measure and describe learner outcomes across a wide variety of programs. In Australia and Canada, there are strong links between immigration policy and economic and labor policy. As Europe moves toward closer ties under the European Union, educators face the daunting task of linking assessments in various member languages to a common framework in order to compare language certification across member countries.

AUSTRALIA. Australia traditionally has welcomed immigrants. Before World War II, most immigrants to Australia came from Ireland and the United Kingdom. After the war, Australia's immigration policies looked to non-English-speaking countries to meet the demands for new settlers. As a consequence, the Adult Migrant Education (now English) Program (AMEP) was established to provide these new settlers with English-language instruction and settlement information.

The AMEP has become the largest government-funded English-language training program in the world. At first a centralized curriculum was designed by the government, but in the 1970s curriculum development was decentralized so that teachers at individual programs became the primary developers of curriculum, learner placement, needs assessment, and procedures for monitoring progress (Burns, 1994). In the 1990s, a collaborative initiative was undertaken by the Australian government, industry, and unions to develop a curriculum framework linking industry needs with training in workplace competence (Hager, 1996). This occurred in response to changing world economic conditions, a need for increased continuity between language-training programs and vocational and job-training programs, and a demand for measurable outcomes. The result has been the development of a number of competency-based curriculum documents that are nationally or state accredited. Among the most well known is the Certificate in Spoken and Written English (CSWE), developed by the New South Wales Adult Migrant English Service and the National Center for English Language Training and Research (NCELTR).

The aim of the CSWE is to enable adult English-language learners to develop the language and literacy skills that will enable them to participate in further education or training, seek and maintain employment, and become contributing members of the community. Competencies that describe what learners can do at the end of study are identified at three stages of proficiency (beginning, postbeginning, and intermediate), based on the Australian Second Language Proficiency Ratings (ASLPR). Within each stage, learners can be grouped by a slow, standard, or fast learning pace to accommodate for differences in educational experiences and native language literacy abilities.

The CSWE document is considered a curriculum framework rather than a syllabus, from which individual programs can create their own courses of study. However, the document specifies the explicit criteria under which the competencies must be assessed. Within these criteria, the competencies may be assessed through teacher observations, interviews, role plays, learner self-assessments, and other means, following the guidelines. Possible exit points occur at the end of each stage, but the certificate is issued only after Stage 3 competencies have been achieved. It takes a learner approximately 250 to 300 hours to pass through a stage. (For a detailed description of the CSWE, see New South Wales Adult Migrant English Service, 1993.)

Initially teachers were concerned about the appropriateness of formal assessment with their learners, the time it takes to assess performance, and validity and reliability issues among teachers and across programs. After an initial adjustment period, teachers found that the new system enabled them to focus their teaching in a way that provided clearer direction and more explicit feedback to learners on progress (Burns & Hood, 1995). Issues of validity and reliability continue to concern Australian adult educators as proficiency assessments based on rating scales are increasingly used for accountability purposes (Manidis & Prescott, 1996; Brindley, 1999).

Another concern is the apparent inadequacy of the system for assessing the progress of learners who have limited experience with formal learning, low literacy levels in both their native language and English, and difficulty adjusting to new cultural expectations (Jackson, 1994). These same concerns for the low-level learner have surfaced in the United States as well. These learners tend to require longer periods of instruction and make smaller language gains than more literate learners. The gains they make tend to be nonlinguistic outcomes in the affective, cognitive, and sociocultural domains.

A research project undertaken by the NCELTR identified eight major categories of nonlinguistic outcomes: confidence; social, psychological, and emotional support in one's living and learning environments; knowledge of social institutions; cultural awareness; learning skills; goal clarification; motivation; and access and entry into further study, employment, and community life (Jackson, 1994). Despite the incorporation of nonlanguage outcomes in the knowledge and learning competencies of the CSWE (New South Wales AMES, 1993), teachers lack adequate tools to assess and document these outcomes. Research has shown that these outcomes reflect characteristics of good language learners and appropriate language teaching methodologies (Jackson, 1994). They also reflect characteristics and skills favored in the workplace (Hager, 1996; Secretary's Commission on Achieving Necessary Skills, 1993). They should be considered in every assessment system, and teachers need help in finding ways to assess and record them.

CANADA. In response to the field's expressed need for a common set of standards to measure and describe language development of learners in Canadian adult ESOL programs, Employment and Immigration Canada (now Citizenship and Immigration Canada [CIC]) developed national English-language benchmarks with the assistance of a working group of ESOL learners, teachers, administrators, immigrant service providers, and government officials (CIC, 1996; Pierce & Stewart, 1997).

The Canadian Language Benchmarks (CLB) project, launched in spring 1996, is a task-based descriptive scale of ESOL proficiency. It identifies twelve benchmarks across three stages of proficiency (basic, intermediate, and advanced) in three skill areas: speaking/listening, reading, and writing. Each benchmark describes a person's ability to use English to accomplish a task and includes information on the abilities of the person (for example, "Can copy information, describe personal situations"), performance conditions (for example, "Copies words and numbers clearly and accurately"), situational conditions (for example, time limit, length of text, number of mistakes allowed), background knowledge helpful to completing a task (for example, cultural expectations, availability of community services, note-taking conventions), and sample tasks. As compared with the American SPL descriptors, the level of detail in the Canadian benchmarks makes the document more useful for creating assessment tasks. The CLB does not purport to be a proficiency test or a syllabus, but curriculum writers, materials developers, and practitioners can use it as a guide for syllabus development, instruction, and monitoring of learner progress. (For a detailed description of the benchmarks see CIC, 1996.)

Concurrent with the field testing of the draft CLB document, CIC contracted with the Peel Board of Education in Ontario to develop the Canadian Language Benchmarks Assessment (CLBA) to assist in placing learners in programs and assessing learner progress. It was to be a task-based assessment instrument that addressed Benchmarks 1 through 8 (Stages 1 and 2) in each of the three language skill areas. The developers faced many challenges: the instrument had to consist of tasks representative of those identified in the CLB document, reconcile the assessment of each separate skill area with the holistic approach implicit in task-based assessment, balance cultural bias and authenticity of task, and be user friendly—for both the test giver and the test taker—across a wide range of program types and settings (Pierce & Stewart, 1997).

The resulting CBLA consists of three separate instruments—one for each of the skill areas. The listening/speaking assessment is administered one-on-one and is scored by the interviewer as it is being administered. It takes ten to thirty minutes to complete. The reading and writing assessments can be administered individually or in a group setting and take at least another one to two hours to administer. There are parallel forms of the reading and writing assessments— two to be used for placement and two for assessing outcomes.

The developers consider the CBLA a work in progress. Assessors are being trained, and an interrater reliability study is underway. They caution, however, that it remains a low-stakes instrument that would need to have its validity and reliability enhanced before it could be used for a high-stakes assessment such as job entry, academic opportunity, or immigration (Pierce & Stewart, 1997).

EUROPE. The assessment reform effort in Europe is perhaps more complex than the efforts in Australia, Canada, and the United States because the Europeans are attempting to correlate assessments in many languages to a common set of standards. Two projects in particular, the Council of Europe's Common European Framework and the Association of Language Testers in Europe's (ALTE) Framework Project, are worth noting. The first establishes a comprehensive framework for the description of language proficiency and its relationship to content. The second then applies this framework to the various examinations and certificates offered in member countries to promote the recognition of language certification across Europe.

Common European Framework. The Council of Europe assists its forty-four member states in encouraging all citizens to learn nonnative languages to promote mutual understanding, personal mobility, and access to information in a multilingual, multicultural Europe (van Ek & Trim, 1996). The second draft of the *Modern Languages: Learning, Teaching, Assessment—A Common European Framework of Reference* (Council for Cultural Cooperation Education Committee, 1996) represents the council's latest effort in a collaborative process that began in 1971. The document identifies four contexts for language use (personal, public, occupational, and educational) and specifies ranges of language knowledge and skills. Language programs can use the document to develop curricula, select instructional approaches and techniques, and establish assessment procedures. It includes information on the purposes of communication (for example, completing insurance forms, taking public transportation, reporting an accident); communication activities (productive, receptive, interactive) and processes (for example, plan, organize, execute); texts (for example, spoken: public speeches, news broadcasts; written instructions, letters, signs); learning strategies; the processes of language learning and teaching; establishment of levels and scales; and assessment purposes and types. It is not prescriptive in the sense of telling practitioners what to do or how to do it. Rather it provides a range of elements for programs to choose from and establishes principles for language teaching, learning, and assessment to facilitate program design. It thus provides a common basis for discussing these choices among programs.

ALTE Framework Project. The ALTE, established in 1989, is an association of European institutions that offers learners language training and certification in the language of the institution's country or region. Fifteen languages are represented among the association's eighteen members. As the European workforce becomes more mobile within the European Union, both employees and employers need to know what language qualifications mean across countries. To meet this need, ALTE members are establishing common levels of proficiency and common standards for the language testing process (ALTE, 1998).

They have drawn from previous work of the Council of Europe that specified the descriptions of language ability (van Ek & Trim, 1996) as well as from their collaboration with the council on the Common European Framework project.

The ALTE framework identifies five main levels of proficiency, each defined by statements of what a user can do at that level across the productive (speaking and writing) and receptive (reading and listening) skill areas. Examinations given by ALTE members have been charted along this continuum by comparing the content and the demands each examination makes on the examinee (ALTE, 1994); this allows for comparisons of skill level attainment across language tests. For example, a learner of French as a foreign language achieving the Diplome de Langue Française issued by Alliance Française would have the same proficiency in French that a learner of Italian would have in Italian upon achieving the Certificato di Conoscenza della Lingua Italia, Livello 3. The "can do" statements for each level are currently being validated so that they can be used to describe what a language test score actually means in the real world (for example, "Can offer help to a client or customer: 'I'll give you our new catalogue'") (Jones, 1999).

Works in Progress. Both the Council of Europe and the ALTE consider their frameworks to be works in progress—to be used, commented on, and further developed in response to experience gained from using the documents, to developments in research in language acquisition and learning, and to new needs that may arise.

Lessons from These Assessment Initiatives

Assessment initiatives in adult education in the United States can apply the lessons learned from K–12 efforts and adult-language education efforts abroad. The primary lesson to be drawn from these efforts is that in the overarching structure, assessment is but one component in a larger instructional system. The K–12 system is well established in the United States. Australia's Adult Migrant English Program was strongly backed by government funding initiatives and linked to a major government-funded research institute, the National Center for English Language Training and Research (NCELTR), which works with practitioners to produce research and provide training that reflect the practical classroom issues language teachers face (for example, assessing oral proficiency [Manidis & Prescott, 1996]). The Common European Framework project is producing a comprehensive compendium of elements of a language instructional system so that programs can base their instructional designs on solid knowledge about language acquisition and principles of language teaching and assessment.

These initiatives also show that assessment reform does not begin with assessment procedures but with content standards—what learners need to know and be able to do to function successfully in the communities in which they live. Once the content is identified, curriculum and instructional approaches are chosen and performance standards and assessment procedures developed. This does not mean that every program that uses the pre-K–12 TESOL standards document, the Canadian Language Benchmarks, or the Common European Framework will be teaching and assessing the same things in the same way. However, these documents enable individual programs to select elements that match program and learner purposes and goals, while at the same time providing a common frame of reference among the programs.

Although the requirements of the Workforce Investment Act and the development of the National Reporting System represent strong moves toward a national accountability system in the United States, by and large, there is no national comprehensive learning system for adult education (Merrifield, 1998) with which accountability and assessment fit coherently. What to assess, how to assess, how to report the data, what they mean, and how to use them are questions that still need to be agreed on. This does not mean that traces of such a system do not exist. In fact, there are initiatives at local, state, and federal levels that indicate the field is lurching toward building a system. For example, many programs have developed instructional designs with articulated mission statements and goals, approaches to curriculum and instruction, and procedures for assessment. The way these components are defined varies, depending on the type of program and the goals of the program and its learners. What is lacking is a common framework, as in the European model, to enable programs to compare what they are doing across their varying types and missions.

Several states, including Massachusetts and California, have elements of statewide systems in place. California was the first state to identify standards for adult ESOL. The *English-as-a-Second-Language Model Standards for Adult ESL* (California Department of Education,

1992) provides standards for program design, curriculum, instruction, and student evaluation. The document also identifies proficiency levels and describes course content and sample lessons for each level. The Massachusetts effort to establish standards is part of a larger effort across the state to implement standards in all of adult education. The first step in the process is to establish a curriculum framework that identifies what learners need to know and be able to do. From this framework, assessment and implementation phases will follow (Massachusetts Department of Education, 1998).

On the national level, the National Institute for Literacy's Equipped for the Future (EFF) project is attempting to answer the question, "What is it that adults need to know and be able to do in order to be literate, to compete in the global economy, and to exercise the rights and responsibilities of citizenship?" (Stein, 1997, p. 2). The goal is to establish content standards that articulate what adults need to know and be able to do to be effective family members, community members, and workers. These standards will cut across the four purposes of literacy identified in phase 1 of the project: gain access to information, give voice to ideas, act independently, and build a bridge to the future by learning how to learn. ESOL programs in several states have been involved in the development and pilot testing of the content standards. These standards can provide the basis for establishing performance standards from which programs and states can develop assessment systems. In fact, the EFF team is already beginning to conceptualize what an assessment system for the standards might look like (National Institute for Literacy, 1999).

Another project at the national level is the "What Works" Study for Adult ESL Students Evaluation, a five-year study sponsored by the U.S. Department of Education and being conducted by the Pelavin Research Center and Aguirre International. Its purpose is to evaluate the effectiveness of instructional approaches for adult English-language learners with limited literacy skills and then make recommendations to the field. A small part of the study will examine the types of assessment and outcome measures that are being used and identify those that are most appropriate for these learners.

Finally, TESOL has appointed a task force to develop adult education program standards and sample performance measures that will address program goals, structure, implementation, curriculum, instruction, and assessment (Bitterlin, 1997). This document will be a useful guide for program staff and policymakers in establishing performance measures to ensure high-quality educational services for adult learners of English.

RECOMMENDATIONS FOR POLICY, PRACTICE, AND RESEARCH

The field of adult education in the United States is in the midst of implementing accountability systems, as is the field of K–12 education. However, in adult education this is being done without the benefit of the infrastructure of the K–12 system. Programs and states need support from both researchers and those providing funds to develop accountability systems that are part of a larger adult education instructional system, effectively capture what learners know and can do, and can be efficiently and realistically carried out at the program level. The following recommendations focus on the policies, practice, and research needed to make this possible.

Policy

The Workforce Investment Act (with its emphasis on performance measures) and the National Reporting System (with its emphasis on functioning levels) are driving the types of accountability systems that states are formulating. The NRS gives only limited examples of test benchmarks—ranges on CASAS tests and SPLs—to assess learner functioning levels. The SPLs are descriptors of learner abilities and not a test. Determining the SPL of an individual learner can be accomplished by correlating the local program level to which the learner is assigned to the SPL or assigning the SPL according to teacher judgment and verifying with the BEST test (U.S. HHS, 1985). Also, although not as detailed as the Canadian Language Benchmarks, the SPLs can guide the development of informal performance-based assessments (Grognet, 1998). However, it is doubtful that these two benchmarks (CASAS ranges and SPLs) are adequate for assessing the functioning level gains of learners for accountability purposes in all types of adult ESOL programs. The BEST test or formal performance-based assessments (valid, reliable, consistently administered, and perhaps using multiple raters) correlated to the SPLs would need to be administered to ensure that a standardized assessment procedure was used to assess learner gains using the SPLs. Furthermore, the assumptions about curricular content and instructional approaches that underlie the CASAS, and to some extent the BEST, are not necessarily the assumptions that undergird all adult ESOL programs. In this chapter we have also pointed out the dangers of assuming that a higher test score translates into increased language proficiency when the tests contain too few items at any single proficiency level or assess too few contexts to ensure an accurate proficiency level assessment.

First, agreement needs to be reached as to what constitutes literacy development among adult ESOL learners and how it can be measured for accountability purposes as learners progress. Assessment measures should reflect one's view of literacy and be comprehensive enough to show the full range of learner achievement. If the measures are to be made into tests, the resources are needed to improve the instruments now being used. The SPLs should be revised and revalidated in view of increased knowledge of language development and changing practices since they were first formulated in the 1980s (Grognet, 1998). Sample tasks for each proficiency level, such as those given in the TESOL standards document and the CLB, need to accompany the descriptors. If new standardized instruments are to be developed, they should be able to accommodate learners at every stage of language and literacy development. If alternative measures are acceptable, programs will need clear guidelines on how to select or develop those measures that are most appropriate for their learners and meet the legislative requirements for a standardized and rigorous process.

In addition, consideration must be given to the long time adults need to become fluent in another language. SPL studies indicate that a low-level learner (SPL 1) needs between 110 and 235 hours to advance to the next proficiency level, depending on the characteristics of the program (for example, intensity of instruction and class size) and the learner (for example, educational experience, health, and motivation) (U.S. HHS, 1985). Australian studies support the need for many instructional hours, especially for learners with low literacy skills, to show gains in proficiency level. The National Evaluation of Adult Education Programs (NEAEP) study, conducted between 1990 and 1994, reported that the median amount of time that ESOL learners stay in programs is 113 hours (Fitzgerald, 1995). Furthermore, the initial gains that low-level learners make tend to be nonlinguistic. As mentioned earlier, these are the skills and knowledge that may make it possible to continue learning and may be important in the workplace, but they do not show up on existing tests. Any test or proficiency scale needs to describe sufficiently the benchmarks on the way to achieving the next level, so that even learners with limited literacy skills or little time available to devote to formal instruction can show progress.

Programs need additional resources to implement assessment requirements—whether in the development of rigorous performance assessments, teacher training on using the assessment tools and procedures, or the ability to compensate teachers for time to assess learners and document results. Policymakers at the federal, state, and local levels must work with program administrators to determine how resources can be allocated to provide this support.

The first few years of WIA implementation will yield rich data for analysis of what is working, for whom, and what adjustments may have to be made to make the system work for everyone. The development of databases about what works best for various types of learners can identify elements of program design that will meet the needs of each stakeholder. Program staff need this information in clear and understandable language and in a timely fashion if they are to make well-informed decisions. Researchers need this information to guide their research and development efforts.

The development of an accountability system should be just one component in an educational system that also encompasses guidelines for curricular content and instructional practice. A comprehensive system such as the Common European Framework presents a model for policymakers, program administrators, practitioners, and researchers to consult as results from EFF, the "What Works" Study, the NRS, and various research studies are reported.

Practice

Practitioners need to be aware of efforts such as EFF, the "What Works" Study, and TESOL's Task Force on Program Standards. EFF can provide program staff with information for evaluating curriculum content, thereby helping to increase their awareness of what counts as success to learners across a spectrum of program types and, therefore, what should be taught and assessed. The "What Works" Study can shed light on best practices for learners with limited literacy skills in both instruction and assessment. TESOL's program standards can be used to guide the development of assessment procedures within adult education programs. These three efforts can work together to provide the types of programs that meet the needs of each stakeholder.

As practitioners consider what counts as progress and how it can best be measured for the learners they serve, they must be able to present and support their decisions before administrators and funding agencies and organizations. Selection of assessment measures should be made with solid knowledge about the proficiencies of learners, the educational context of the program, and the adequacy of the assessment measures being considered to carry out the purpose of the assessment.

Research

To inform both policy and practice, research efforts should address issues that the field itself has identified as critical in the area of assessment and outcomes. These issues are compiled in the Research Agenda for Adult ESL (CAL, 1998, p. 11), in which the following questions are raised:

- What immediate and long-term impact can be expected from the various types of adult ESOL programs? What impact does learner participation in such programs have on the learners and their communities?

- How can adult ESOL programs best capture what learners know and what they have learned?

- What is the cost in time, staffing, and funds to assess and document learning outcomes effectively?

- How can each of the stakeholders in a program participate in determining what counts as progress?

- How do measures of program impact, such as an increase in reading to one's children or a job promotion, correlate with increases in English-language proficiency?

- How might a national proficiency scale facilitate the reporting of learner progress and program impact? How effective is the NRS scale in reporting learner gains?

- Which assessment instruments can reliably document changes in learner performance at what levels? Can these instruments serve all types of adult ESOL programs?

- What changes in program design and staff development are needed to ensure that current and new assessment tools are reliably used?

• How can technology facilitate the implementation of a system for documenting learner outcomes and program impact?

• How do local, state, and national policies affect assessment tools and practices, and what policies need to be created?

CONCLUSION

Whatever the decisions that will be made in the near future about assessment in adult ESOL, it is clear that policymakers, practitioners, and researchers must engage in a collaborative effort to produce substantive, purposeful, and effective change in the field. The U.S. Department of Education's (ED) Office of Vocational and Adult Education continues to make efforts to listen to stakeholders through such venues as the biannual meetings of the State Directors of Adult Education and the studies and the clearinghouse it funds. The ED also sponsors a National Forum on Adult Education and Literacy, which in 1997 brought in learners from across the United States and, in 1998, teachers, to discuss adult education issues. However, more substantive efforts are needed to create an infrastructure that can sustain a comprehensive adult education system. At local, state, and national levels, representatives from each stakeholder group (policymakers, practitioners, researchers, and learners) should develop a plan of action that supports the implementation of the new legislative imperatives and program designs that effectively and efficiently serve the needs of the community and the learners.

Appendix: Ordering Information for Selected Standardized Tests

ABLE (Adult Basic Learning Examination)

Psychological Corporation
Order Service Center
P.O. Box 839954
San Antonio, TX 78283
(800) 211-8378

A-LAS *(Adult Language Assessment Scales)*
McGraw-Hill
1221 Avenue of the Americas
New York, NY 10020
(800) 624-7294
http://www.mhcollege.com

BEST *(Basic English Skills Test)*
Center for Applied Linguistics
4646 Fortieth Street, N.W.
Washington, DC 20016–1859
(202) 362-0700
http://www.cal.org

CASAS *(Comprehensive Adult Student Assessment System)*
8910 Clairemont Mesa Boulevard
San Diego, CA 92123
(619) 292-2900
http://www.casas.org

NYS Place Test *(New York State Placement Test for ESOL Adult Students)*
City School District of Albany
Albany Educational TV
27 Western Avenue
Albany, NY 12203
(518) 462-7292, ext. 30

TABE *(Test of Adult Basic Education)*
CTB/McGraw-Hill
20 Ryan Ranch
Monterey, CA 93940
(800) 538-9547
http://www.ctb.com

References

ALTE. (1994). Using the ALTE framework. *ALTE News, 3*(1), 1–3.
ALTE. (1998). *ALTE document 1: European language examinations and examination systems.* Great Britain: Author.

Auerbach, E. (1992). *Making meaning, making change: Participatory curriculum development for adult ESL literacy.* Washington, DC, and McHenry, IL: Center for Applied Linguistics and Delta Systems.

August, D., & Hakuta, K. (Eds.). (1997). *Improving schooling for language-minority children: A research agenda.* Washington, DC: National Academy Press, 1997.

Bitterlin, G. (1997). Program standards for adult-level ESL programs. *TESOL Matters, 7*(5), 9.

Brindley, G. (1999, March). *Task effects in second language assessment.* Paper presented at Teachers of English to Speakers of Other Languages, Thirty-third Annual Convention and Exposition, New York.

Burns, A. (1994). Adult ESL in Australia. *Digest of Australian Languages and Literacy, 7,* 1–4.

Burns, A., & Hood, S. (Eds.). (1995). *Teachers' voices: Exploring course design in a changing curriculum.* Sydney, Australia: National Center for English Language Teaching and Research.

Business Council for Effective Literacy. (1990). Standardized tests: Their use and misuse. *BCEL Newsletter, 22,* 1, 6–8.

California Department of Education. (1992). *English-as-a-second-language model standards for adult education programs.* Sacramento, CA: Bureau of Publications.

Carroll, J. B., Davies, P., & Richman, B. (1971). *American heritage word frequency book.* Boston: Houghton Mifflin.

Center for Adult Education. (1983). *Handbook for CBAE staff development.* San Francisco: San Francisco State University.

Center for Applied Linguistics. (1998). *Research agenda for adult ESL.* Washington, DC: Center for Applied Linguistics.

Citizenship and Immigration Canada. (1996). *Canadian language benchmarks: English as a second language for adults and English as a second language for literacy students.* Ontario: Ministry of Supply and Services Canada.

Council for Cultural Cooperation Education Committee. (1996). *Modern languages: Learning, teaching assessment: A common European framework or reference.* Strasbourg, France: Council of Europe.

Crandall, J. (1992). Literacy, language, and multiculturalism. In J. E. Alatis (Ed.), *Linguistics and language pedagogy: State of the art.* Washington, DC: Georgetown University Press.

Crandall, J., & Peyton, J. (Eds.). (1993). *Approaches to adult ESL literacy instruction.* Washington, DC, and McHenry, IL: Center for Applied Linguistics and Delta Systems.

Duncan, S. E., & DeAvila, E. A. (1993). *Adult language assessment scales: Administration and scoring manual.* Monterey, CA: CTB/Macmillan/ McGraw-Hill.

Ebel, R. I. (1979). *Essentials of educational measurement.* (3rd ed.). Englewood Cliffs, NJ: Prentice Hall.

Fingeret, H. (1993). *It belongs to me: A guide to portfolio assessment in adult education programs.* Durham, NC: Literacy South, 1993.

Fitzgerald, N. B. (1995). *ESL instruction in adult education: Findings from a national evaluation.* Washington, DC: Center for Applied Linguistics.

Fitzpatrick, A. R. (1992). Review of the adult basic learning examination, second edition. In J. J. Kramer & J. C. Conoley (Eds.), *The eleventh mental measurements yearbook.* Lincoln, NE: Buros Institute of Mental Measurements.

Grognet, A. (1998). *Performance-based curricula and outcomes: The mainstream English language training (MELT) project updated for the 1990s and beyond.* Denver: Spring Institute for International Studies.

Hager, P. (1996). The development of competency-based training: Government, industry, and union pressures. *Prospect: A Journal of Australian TESOL, 11*(1), 71–78.

Hambleton, R. (1991). *Fundamentals of item response theory.* Thousand Oaks, CA: Sage.

Holt, D. (Ed.). (1994). *Assessing success in family literacy projects: Alternative approaches to assessment and evaluation.* Washington, DC, and McHenry, IL: Center for Applied Linguistics and Delta Systems. (ERIC Document Reproduction Service No. ED 375 688)

Jackson, E. (1994). *Non-language outcomes in the adult migrant English program.* Sydney, Australia: National Center for English Language Teaching and Research.

Jones, N. (1999, March). *Validating can do scales.* Paper presented at Teachers of English to Speakers of Other Languages, Thirty-third Annual Convention and Exposition, New York.

Kahn, A. B., Butler, F. A., Weigle, S. C., & Sato, E. (1995). *Adult English-as-a-second-language assessment project: Final report: Year 3.* Los Angeles: UCLA Center for the Study of Evaluation.

Kenyon, D., & Stansfield, C. (1989). *Basic English skills test manual.* Washington, DC: Center for Applied Linguistics.

Lumley, T. (1996, June). Assessment of second language performance. *Digest of Australian Languages and Literacy Issues.*

Manidis, M., & Prescott, P. (1996). *Assessing oral language proficiency: A handbook for teachers in the adult migrant English program.* Sydney,

Australia: National Centre for English Language Teaching and Research.

Massachusetts Department of Education. (1998). *Framework for adult ESOL in the Commonwealth of Massachusetts.* Rev. draft. Boston: Author.

McGrail, L., & Simmons, A. (Eds.). (1991–1998). *Adventures in assessment.* Boston: SABES.

Merrifield, J. (1998). *Contested ground: Performance accountability in adult basic education.* Cambridge, MA: National Center for the Study of Adult Learning and Literacy.

National Center for Educational Statistics. (1997). *Participation of adults in English as a second language classes: 1994–1995.* Washington, DC: U.S. Department of Education.

National Clearinghouse for ESL Literacy Education. (1989). *Basic English skills test manual.* Washington, DC: Author.

National Institute for Literacy. (1999, January 6–7). *Developing national qualifications framework for adults.* Paper provided for Equipped for the Future Expert Review Session, Washington, DC.

New South Wales Adult Migrant English Service, and National Center for English Language Training and Research. (1993). *Certificate in spoken and written English.* Sydney, Australia: Authors.

Office of Vocational and Adult Education. (1992). *Model indicators of program quality for adult education programs.* Washington, DC: U.S. Department of Education.

Office of Vocational and Adult Education. (1995). *Adult education for limited English proficient adults.* Washington, DC: U.S. Department of Education.

Office of Vocational and Adult Education. (1997, October 9). Thursday notes: A weekly fact sheet on adult education issues. Washington, DC: U.S. Department of Education.

Office of Vocational and Adult Education. (1998, August). *Measure definitions for the national reporting system for adult education.* Washington, DC: U.S. Department of Education.

O'Malley, M., & Pierce, L. (1996). *Authentic assessment for English language learners: Practical approaches for teachers.* Reading, MA: Addison-Wesley.

Pierce, B. N., & Stewart, G. (1997). The development of the Canadian language benchmarks assessment. *TESL Canada, 14*(2), 17–31.

Secretary's Commission on Achieving Necessary Skills. (1993). *Teaching the SCANS Skills.* Washington, DC: U.S. Department of Labor.

Short, E. (1997). Why a statewide assessment system? *Developments, 1*(2), 2–3.

Solorzano, R. (1994). *Instruction and assessment for limited-English-proficient adult learners.* Philadelphia: National Center on Adult Literacy. (ERIC Document Reproduction Service No. ED 375 686)

Stein, S. (1997). *Equipped for the future: A reform agenda for adult literacy and lifelong learning.* Washington, DC: National Institute for Literacy.

Sticht, T. G. (1990). *Testing and assessment in adult basic education and English as a second language programs.* San Diego: Applied Behavior and Cognitive Sciences.

Teachers of English to Speakers of Other Languages. (1997). *ESL standards for pre-K–12 students.* Alexandria, VA: Author.

Teachers of English to Speakers of Other Languages. (1999). *Scenarios for ESL standards-based assessment.* Working draft.

U.S. Department of Health and Human Services. (1985). *Mainstream English language training project (MELT) resource package.* Washington, DC: Author.

Valdez-Pierce, L., & O'Malley, M. (1992). *Performance and portfolio assessment for language minority students.* Washington, DC: National Clearinghouse for Bilingual Education.

Van Ek, J., & Trim, J. (1996). *Vantage level.* Strasbourg, France: Council of Europe.

Williams, R. T. (1992). Review of the adult basic learning examination, second edition. In J. J. Kramer & J. C. Conoley (Eds.), *The eleventh mental measurements yearbook.* Lincoln, NE: Buros Institute of Mental Measurements.

Workforce Investment Act of 1998, Public Law No. 105–220, sec. 212, U.S. Government Printing Office.

Wrigley, H. S. (1992). *Learner assessment in adult ESL literacy.* Washington, DC: Center for Applied Linguistics.

Wrigley, H. S., & Guth, G. (1992). *Bringing literacy to life: Issues and options in adult ESL literacy.* San Mateo, CA: Aguirre International. (ERIC Document Reproduction Service No. ED 348 896)

CHAPTER SEVEN

Adult Learning and Literacy in the United Kingdom

Mary Hamilton
Juliet Merrifield

━◆◆◆━

Like the United States, the United Kingdom[1] started a literacy campaign in the early 1970s characterized by dependence on volunteers, one-to-one tutoring, and ad hoc, often creative approaches to teaching and learning.[2] The British Right to Read campaign, initiated by volunteer activists and supported by politicians and the broadcasting services, aimed to mobilize national and local government resources, raise public awareness, and achieve widespread involvement in the teaching and learning of adult literacy. Although first seen as a temporary response to a short-term crisis, the campaign in fact laid the groundwork for a new, publicly funded adult basic education (ABE) service. In the process, some distinctive styles of provision were created, including an emphasis on writing as a way to develop reading ability and self-empowerment, a commitment to equality between students and teachers (or tutors),[3] and informal approaches to working with adults in small groups and community settings.

The Further and Higher Education Act of 1992 made ABE part of the system of further education in England and Wales, the primary purpose of which had been vocational training for school leavers[4] in the age

243

group sixteen to nineteen. As a result of these developments, ABE has become more firmly established and also increasingly formalized.

In this chapter our primary aim is to describe the general workings of the system of adult literacy and learning as it exists in the United Kingdom today. To better illuminate that system, we take a little time delving into its past—that is, showing how it arrived at its current state of operation. A secondary aim is to compare and contrast aspects of the U.K. system with that in the United States, which has experienced shifts in practice, similar to those just described, from a patchwork of community programs relying on volunteers, diverse institutions, and varied funding streams to ever-greater moves toward national accountability, documented performance, and systematic standards. In conducting this analysis, we hope to broaden the reader's understanding of the two systems as well as our own.[5]

THE ECONOMIC, POLITICAL, AND CULTURAL CLIMATE SHAPING ABE

Adult basic education is inevitably influenced by the broader economic, political, and cultural climate that shapes policy options. Since the 1970s, the United Kingdom has undergone profound changes, both internally and in its sense of nationhood and place in the world. It has been placed firmly within a new world order, experiencing a reorientation from empire to equal partner in the European Union. Its population is increasingly multiethnic. The gap between rich and poor has widened as global economic changes have affected the economy, employment, and social divisions, and as a radical Conservative agenda called for cutting the social safety net and weakening collective action through trade unions. Although policy changes designed to affect these areas have not, on the whole, been directed at ABE, they have had consequences for ABE and shape the space within which it operates (Fullan, 1991; Derrick, 1996).

The Economy: Widening Inequality

While successive U.K. governments have argued that the United Kingdom is, in contrast to some of its European neighbors, an economic success story, that story is also characterized by increasing poverty, social inequality, and unemployment. Nearly a quarter of all households with children are living in poverty (Oppenheim & Harker, 1996).

Chancellor Gordon Brown says that the United Kingdom is "more unequal [now] than in 100 years" (Brown, 1997). The richest 1 percent
of the population owns 19 percent of the United Kingdom's wealth,
while the poorest 50 percent owns just 7 percent (Office for National
Statistics, 1998).

A split has opened up between "working rich" and "working poor"
households (Howarth, Kenqay, Palmer, & Street, 1998, p. 38). Almost
one working-age family in five—19 percent—has no wage earner
(Brown, 1997). This contrasts with 11.5 percent in the United States,
15 percent in Germany, and 16 percent in France. In some urban areas,
about one-third of working-age families have no wage earner. Unsur-
prisingly, in the context of such poverty and inequality, the prison population has risen sharply. Another sign of trouble, which is of direct
concern to future adult literacy, is the sharp rise in the number of
children permanently expelled from English secondary schools: in
1996–1997 the number amounted to more than 12,500, a fourfold increase since the beginning of the decade (Howarth, Kenqay, Palmer, &
Street, 1998, p. 55).

Education and training is the primary policy tool with which the
Labor government can address the effects of these economic and social
changes. It has implemented new welfare reform programs, which,
emulating earlier U.S. policies, aim to use training and job placement
to move people off welfare and into work. National education targets
have been established for the general population, designed to raise
competence in key skills (including reading and math). The central
focus of literacy policy, too, whether for adults or schoolchildren, is
on upgrading skills for international competitiveness.

Governance: Devolution and Centralization

The U.K. central government has always had much greater control than
its U.S. counterpart over public services such as education, training,
and welfare. At the same time, regional governance variations in England, Wales, Scotland, and Northern Ireland have resulted in somewhat different educational structures. New constitutional changes are
rapidly affecting all of these. Wales has a bilingual educational system
and has recently gained its own regional assembly (though with limited powers). Northern Ireland has retained a system of selective secondary schooling and has just regained its regional assembly. Scotland
has recently gained its regional parliament, with powers to raise taxes,

and has always had educational qualifications and administrative and funding structures distinct from those of England and Wales.

A decade ago it could be said that the educational system of England and Wales was a "national system, locally administered" (Cantor & Roberts, 1995, p. 11), but since then the powers of local governments and their local education authorities (LEAs) have been radically reduced by a Conservative central government distrustful of their influence. (LEAs are comparable to local school systems in the United States and are made up of elected representatives and paid staff.)[6] Individual schools and colleges now have boards of governors who control their budgets, similar to the site-based management systems in some areas of the United States. This system may appear to be more democratic, but it actually increases the control of the central government. Because there are no mechanisms through which individual schools and small local authorities can coordinate their activities, it is difficult to form powerful enough associations to challenge the central government or to develop local or regional strategies (Tuckett, 1991). It seems unlikely that the current government will reverse these trends, but it is looking for new ways of addressing the need for local and regional coordination. Collaboration and partnerships have become the new order.

Public Services: The Contract Culture

During the 1980s the notion of public service was replaced by the metaphor of the marketplace, in which competition is promoted as a positive value (Ball, 1994). Users of public services are referred to as customers or consumers, and collective action and representation have been replaced by the idea of consumer power at the individual level. Even the term *citizen* has been appropriated: the citizens' charters developed by the Conservative government were essentially public service consumers' bills of rights.

All public services—transportation, health, education, social services, prisons—have been reorganized within the new contract culture. Internal markets have been developed, whereby different parts of a public service are encouraged to act like independent businesses and buy goods and services from one another or elsewhere in a system of competitive tendering. This pseudomarket has particularly affected further education, which now has primary responsibility for ABE in England and Wales.[7] Since 1992 further education colleges have been set up as quasi-businesses, expected to compete for students.

Vocational Education:
Expansion and Unification of Qualifications

Since the 1970s, there has been growing government concern about the changing structure of employment and the perceived need for new training strategies to promote global competitiveness. The decline of manufacturing in the United Kingdom has resulted in the collapse of the traditional apprenticeship system. The increasing call for flexible workers who can move easily from job to job in response to economic demand has brought the issue of vocational training, including basic skills for employment, to the center stage of government policy.

During the 1980s there was a massive expansion of vocational education and training, primarily directed toward school leavers in the age group sixteen to nineteen years and adults with a long history of unemployment. Local business-led consortia, called Training and Enterprise Councils (TECs), were explicitly modeled after the Private Industry Councils (PICs) formed in the United States, as were a number of other social policy initiatives at this time (Finegold, McFarland, & Richardson, 1993). TECs decide on local priorities for vocational training within broad criteria and very tight financial constraints established by the central government. They are encouraged to make profits and reinvest these profits in their localities. They may provide training themselves or contract with a wide range of private and public sector providers.

Training for people already at work has received much less financial support from public funds. "Flexible working" has led to a huge increase in temporary and part-time jobs, which do not offer access to training (Frank & Hamilton, 1993; Gee, Hull, & Lankshear, 1996; Hull, 1997). No legislation compels employers to contribute to the training of their employees, although they are encouraged to do so through the Investors in People program, founded in 1990. This government-led partnership with business, employee, and training organizations aims to establish national standards for effective staff development. It rewards employers who provide training with publicity and a special "quality mark" logo.

As in Australia (Lo Bianco & Freebody, 1997), the central government has put a great deal of effort into developing a unified system of national vocational qualifications (NVQs) that are tied to a set of national training targets and quality assurances. This system is designed to provide a means of determining equivalence amid the maze of different vocational qualifications and bridge the divide between academic and vocational qualifications. In England, ABE learner and teacher credentials have both been linked with the NVQ system.

Higher Education: More Flexible Pathways and Expansion

Alongside these reforms of education and training have been major developments in degree-level higher education, with more adult and part-time students entering the system and a doubling of the quota of students. (The number of student places allowed at various institutions is tightly controlled through public funding, with penalties for universities that overstep the quota.) The traditional route from secondary school to higher education is through the General Certificate of Secondary Education (GCSE) exams (taken at age sixteen) and A-levels (exams taken at age eighteen). These examinations are also available to older students in further education colleges, but many adults prefer the more flexible routes that have been developed for them. These include alternative entry programs through one-year linked access courses and the creation of alternative pathways through the Open College Networks system (Davie & Parry, 1993).[8]

Lifelong Learning: The New Mantra

Although both the U.K. government and the European Union now give strong rhetorical support to the concept of lifelong learning, they still appear reluctant to invest public money to promote it effectively (Tuckett, 1997). The Labor government has created a ministry responsible for lifelong learning and has consulted widely with interested organizations and individuals about how to promote it (Department for Education and Employment, 1998). However, it is unclear whether strong new policy initiatives will result from these efforts, and there still appears to be little support for a broad program of adult education that could serve purposes other than employment, such as education for citizenship. The government's lifelong learning flagship, the University for Industry, is intended to promote opportunities to learn basic skills and to become one of the primary vehicles for increasing access to lifelong learning (Department for Education and Employment, 1998).[9]

Information Technology and Broadcast Media

In contrast with the media in the United States, British broadcast media, and in particular the British Broadcasting Corporation (BBC), have a well-established educational mission (Robinson, 1983; Sargent &

Tuckett, 1997). The BBC played an important role in the literacy campaign of the 1970s and has been involved in the development of the Open University, a distance-learning institution (distinct from the Open College Networks), and other innovative forms of programming (Sargent & Tuckett, 1997).

Television broadcasting has also been used as a means of raising awareness of social issues, from incest to literacy. In the most recent of these efforts, linked to the National Year of Reading 1998–1999, story lines relating to adult literacy have been written into popular soap operas and a national help line set up and advertised to provide callers with information about ABE programs in their area.

A BRIEF HISTORY OF ADULT BASIC EDUCATION IN THE UNITED KINGDOM

Until the early 1970s, adult literacy was not an issue for educational and social policy in the United Kingdom. Since the advent of compulsory schooling at the end of the nineteenth century, policymakers had been preoccupied with children's education. Ad hoc provision of adult literacy education by community groups and local education authorities had been rising unremarked during the late 1960s. By 1972, the eve of the campaign, more than 230 literacy schemes in England and Wales served about five thousand learners (Haviland, 1974).

Right to Read Campaign

In 1973 the national literacy campaign for the Right to Read was launched under pressure from the British Association of Settlements (BAS), a coalition of longstanding voluntary associations working in local communities to alleviate the social problems of the poor (British Association of Settlements, 1974). This was the first adult literacy campaign to take place in a Western European country. The BAS led the political side of the campaign, while the BBC organized a public awareness campaign and referral service (Hargreaves, 1980). The campaign grew out of a political climate that was still committed to expanding welfare and equal educational opportunities.

In 1974, the central government released £1 million (then about $2 million) to the campaign. This, combined with an enormous volunteer effort, quickly established adult literacy services throughout England and Wales. Local governments provided the greater part of funding for these services, with limited money coming from the central government. LEAs recruited both volunteer and paid teachers and organized part-time literacy classes to respond to the demand created by the campaign. Most were set up within existing adult and community education centers (for details see Hamilton, 1996; Withnall, 1994; Street, 1997; Jones & Charnley, 1978).

Now as then, the majority of those working in ABE continue to do so in part-time or voluntary posts. There is, however, a general trend toward decline in the number of volunteers and growth in number of paid staff, reflecting an increasing emphasis on professionalism in the field of ABE. In 1995–1996, approximately 10 percent of adult literacy/numeracy staff in England were full-time—1,290 out of a total of 12,893 (Basic Skills Agency, 1997a). The rest were part-time, many spending only a few hours per week on basic skills work as temporary, hourly paid teachers. In the same year, there were 13,374 volunteers.

The U.K. mass media, such as radio and television, have since the beginning of the campaign been used mainly to raise awareness about literacy issues and refer people to opportunities for learning, not as a means of directly teaching ABE. Program developers have had to be careful to work with local ABE providers to make sure that sufficient resources exist to respond to the interest generated by publicity on television and radio. The BBC was the first to develop a series of programs, *On the Move,* intended to publicize learning opportunities and help recruit learners. Both the BBC and commercial television channels have periodically produced programs on literacy, English for speakers of other languages (ESOL), numeracy, and computer skills. The creators of these programs have made efforts to overcome the stereotype of the illiterate as a stigmatized "other" and to present literacy as an issue that affects everyone.

A central resource agency for adult literacy was set up by the central government in 1975–1976 to fund special development projects (for example, innovative programs for special groups of learners), publish resource material, and develop staff training programs. Originally called the Adult Literacy Resource Agency (ALRA), in 1980 it was renamed the Adult Literacy and Basic Skills Unit (ALBSU).[10]

In the late 1980s, the ALBSU and the BBC played a key role in establishing a new accreditation framework for ABE: Wordpower and Numberpower. This is related to the NVQ system and establishes a framework of basic skills standards and an assessment system.

The rhetoric of the Right to Read campaign—with its call to eradicate illiteracy—and the use of contemporary definitions of functional literacy,[11] derived from UNESCO, along with the campaign's style of mobilizing public interest and volunteers, were typical of mass campaigns in countries such as Cuba and the Soviet Union (Limage, 1986, 1990).

The priorities of ABE are very much determined by the nature of its affiliation—whether with employment, social services, or citizenship and immigration. Comparisons with other countries, such as France and Canada, show that this arrangement can lead to a number of different situations (Hamilton, 1989). Indeed, in England and Wales, ESOL was developed under the Home Office (Department of Internal Affairs) as a response to immigration and took a path separate from literacy.

In the United Kingdom, ABE was linked with the central government Department for Education (now the Department for Education and Employment), but only indirectly. The effect of this arrangement (whether deliberate or not) was to separate the campaign from debates about the quality of schooling and differences in educational achievement among different social, cultural, and linguistic groups, which are in fact highly relevant to an understanding of the need for an ABE service. The ABE that developed has never fully engaged with issues concerning gender, class, or cultural diversity in relation to literacy. Policy documents and practices have operated with an undifferentiated view of the typical ABE learner.

ABE initially became part of the existing adult education service, funded and led by LEAs. It took on the ethos of that service: a broad liberal curriculum aligned with personal self-development rather than social goals. Along with that sense of purpose it adopted its basic characteristics: informal, student-centered teaching and assessment, part-time staff, and mainly evening classes without dedicated space or facilities (often housed in schools) (Keddie, 1980; Fieldhouse, 1996).

There are several interwoven and contradictory philosophical strands within ABE's development in England. Among those drawn into teaching ABE were people with a more political commitment to the emancipatory potential of adult literacy. Their focus was not just personal development but social change. They were influenced by community development, working-class and community publishing, and the ideas of Paulo Freire and deschooling society (Freire, 1972, 1985; Illich, 1973; Lister, 1974).[12] Some of the most innovative work initially came from these directions, especially from those working with voluntary organizations who saw literacy primarily as a social rather than an educational issue (Mace, 1979; Street, 1997).

Two other major philosophical strands were from the start intertwined in U.K. literacy work: the functional view of literacy associated with social control of an undereducated population (always important in vocational, army, and prison settings and later to become the most prominent view in mainstream ABE) and a deficit view of literacy, inherited from special education in schools and focused on what adults *cannot* do—that is, read, write, or speak in ways deemed appropriate by mainstream institutions.

Consolidation and Formalization

In 1973, when the Right to Read campaign began, the consensus was that the issue of adult literacy was a temporary problem, requiring only short-term funding for its solution. By 1979 adult educators were arguing that ABE should be funded as a permanent part of adult continuing education (Advisory Council on Adult and Continuing Education, 1979). More than a decade later, with the passage of the Further and Higher Education Act of 1992, ABE was made a permanent part of further education in England and Wales.

By this time, a policy rationale very different from that of Right to Read was in ascendance: that of economic efficiency (Hamilton, 1996). Central government funds for adult education were clearly targeted toward helping adults "improve their qualifications, update their skills, and seek advancement in their present career or in a new career" (Department for Education, 1991, p. 8). Courses for the "leisure interests" of adults were to be provided elsewhere and financed through fees charged to individuals, not paid for by the government.

Although ABE thus became a statutory program, required by law, with stable funding and a clear mandate, it was placed within an institutional sector whose primary business is vocational training for sixteen to nineteen year olds. LEAs may choose to continue their ABE provision, but there is no longer any overarching institution charged with local or regional strategic planning for adult basic education.

The context of further education has continued to change throughout the 1990s. In the wake of a series of influential reports on further and higher education (Kennedy, 1997; Dearing, 1997; Tomlinson, 1996), the focus in further education has shifted from simply growing to targeting learners, particularly those from areas of social and economic deprivation. To attain targets, further education colleges are increasingly forming partnerships (sometimes with community groups and voluntary organizations) and joining in local and even regional planning efforts.

Services in Scotland developed in a similar way to those in England and Wales in the early years, but the Scottish Adult Basic Education Unit was integrated into the Scottish Community Education Council in 1991, and ABE has always been part of Scotland's strong community education service rather than the (vocational) further education system (European Bureau of Adult Education, 1983; McConnell, 1996). Its ethos has been characterized by a firmer commitment to social and political change than in England and Wales. At the same time, it has had a less distinct presence.[13]

Literacy Provision for Speakers of Languages Other Than English

ESOL was not included in the Right to Read campaign. Concern for the language needs of linguistic minority groups, whether immigrant or indigenous, has always been quite limited at the policy level in the United Kingdom. Alan Wells, director of the Basic Skills Agency (BSA), the central resource agency for adult education in England and Wales, acknowledges that no real policy has ever emerged and that there are no universal opportunities for new citizens to learn English (Wells, 1996). Although England has always had a population whose mother tongue is not English, it was not until the 1960s, when large numbers of East African Asians began to arrive, forced out of their homes by the Ugandan government under Idi Amin, that the need for English-language provision for adults was officially recognized and ESOL schemes came into existence.

Official recognition came in the shape of funding from the Home Office to LEAs to set up ESOL courses in areas where demand was greatest. The fact that funding was entirely separate from ABE and was never offered in terms of a public awareness campaign meant that what should have been overlapping provision developed quite separately. Only gradually were connections made.

Until the early 1990s, funding for ESOL was restricted to immigrant groups from the New Commonwealth[14] and therefore did not cover many ESOL groups that arguably had equal or greater language needs (such as those from Eastern Europe or Vietnam). Unlike ABE, which was addressed as an educational problem, ESOL was treated as a social problem resulting from immigration. Within mainstream services, the only aim was for adults to learn the English language. Bilingual adults and their children have been pathologized and treated as deficient rather than as a resource. There is little recognition of the diversity of bilingual learners, who range from those who have had no access to education to those who are already highly literate in their native tongue and other languages.

Native tongue and bilingual literacy programs have never been officially sanctioned and funded (Hartley, 1992). The literacy needs of speakers of minority dialects, such as African Caribbean adults, were addressed by neither national ESOL funding nor mainstream literacy programs. The most notable work was done without central government funding. Such was the case with the Sheffield Black Literacy campaign (Gurnah, 1992), the Kweyol project (Morris & Nwenmely, 1994; RaPAL Bulletin, 1994), and other local projects developed with African Caribbean speakers in London and Manchester (Schwab & Stone, 1987; Craven & Jackson, 1986).

Approaches to Teaching and Learning

Teaching and learning methods in the days of Right to Read were eclectic. Student writing and publishing were characteristic of these early programs. Teachers and students took part in residential writing weekends and reading evenings (Gardener, 1985). They established links with community bookstores, and undertook publishing projects, such as Gatehouse Books (see Gatehouse Books 1985, 1992) and *Write First Time,* a collectively produced newspaper that closed after ten years amid political controversy (see Mace, 1979, and the appendix at the end of this chapter, under "Useful Contacts"). The use of student writing not only provides a creative solution to the problem of what adult learners should read, it also supports the value placed on student participation and the validation of their experience.

The principles of flexible, negotiated, student-centered teaching favored by participants in the original literacy campaign were supported by high-quality materials published by the central resource agency, the ALBSU. To its credit, the ALBSU never produced primers or a fixed ABE syllabus. Instead it published resource packs that teachers could draw from according to individual student need. Nevertheless, the ALBSU's accreditation system, Wordpower and Numberpower, in practice amounted to a curriculum, as inexperienced teachers looked to it to structure their teaching.

Later the ALBSU led a move toward drop-in workshops (known as open learning centers) offering supported self-study (ALBSU, 1992; Bergin & Hamilton, 1994). This move toward open learning in ABE fits with more general trends in further education colleges, where open learning centers, equipped with computers and self-access worksheets, are now pervasive. These are seen as forward looking in their use of new learning technologies and cost-effective in that they reduce the need for teacher contact time. After 1992 student writing and publishing still existed, but there was little staff training to support it and few opportunities for weekend workshops or national circulation of the work (O'Rourke & Mace, 1992).

THE NEED FOR ABE IN ENGLAND

It is notoriously difficult to estimate the extent of the need for adult basic education. Statistics from the International Adult Literacy Survey (IALS) indicate that the proportion of the population with basic skills difficulties is smaller in the United Kingdom than in the United States, but it is still a major issue in terms of public perception (OECD, 1997). The IALS measures literacy along three dimensions of literacy—prose literacy, document literacy, and quantitative literacy—at five levels. About 22 percent of the U.K. population scored at the lowest level on all three dimensions. There are, however, methodological reasons for treating these results with caution (see Hamilton & Barton, forthcoming).

The United Kingdom is fortunate in having some major longitudinal cohort studies, which have been used to collect data on adult literacy and numeracy. Recently these studies have included interviews and formal tests as well as self-reports of difficulties with reading, writing, and numeracy. Bynner and Parsons (1997) report some research using the National Child Development Study (NCDS), which has followed more than 17,000 people born in the United Kingdom in one week in 1958. This research took a representative sample of 2,144 cohort members at the age of thirty-seven. Just over 1,700 cohort members completed interviews and undertook eight literacy and numeracy tasks designed to test everyday literacy and numeracy skills of increasing difficulty (four levels). The results revealed that 19 percent of those tested scored at the lowest literacy levels, 1 or 2, and 48 percent scored at the lowest two levels on the numeracy tasks.

In contrast, a much lower percentage, only about 15 percent of the cohort, reported that they had problems with reading, writing, spelling, or numeracy. Most of these problems were concerned with writing or spelling, for example, when completing a job application form. If we take even this very conservative estimate, of 15 percent of the adult population reporting basic skills difficulties, it suggests that around 6 million people in the adult population believe that their basic skills are not adequate to meet the demands of everyday life.

The International Numeracy Survey, comparing the basic numeracy skills of adults ages sixteen to sixty in seven countries (the United Kingdom, France, the Netherlands, Sweden, Japan, Australia, and Denmark) found that U.K. respondents performed the least well; only 20 percent accurately completed all twelve tasks. Overall, the U.K. respondents achieved an average of 7.9 correctly completed tasks, while all other nations in the survey achieved an average of 9 or more (BSA, 1997b). "Comparisons between the skill and educational capacity of our workforce with those of our principal competitors quickly established that, broadly speaking, our workforce was worse educated and worse trained than our competitors" (Atkinson & Spilsbury, 1993, p. 9).

An ALBSU survey in 1989 estimated that about 500,000 people in England and Wales who did not speak English as their native tongue needed help to speak, understand, and read or write English (this is less than 1 percent of the total population). Forty percent of the non-native English-speaking population said they could read and write English only a little or not at all. Almost 30 percent said they had real difficulty understanding or speaking English.

One clear trend in the numbers is the increase in program enrollment. In 1973 only 5,000 people were receiving help with reading and writing in England and Wales. By 1985 the total had risen to 110,000 (see ALBSU, 1985), and by 1995–1996, 319,402 people were receiving help with literacy and numeracy in England (BSA, 1997a). The assistance they received can be broken down as follows:[15]

Literacy only: 108,813

Numeracy only: 43,035

Literacy and numeracy: 79,437

ESOL: 88,117

These figures compare with an estimated 6 million people in need of help.

The Basic Skills Agency does not collect statistics on gender participation in ABE. However, a gender breakdown is available for the two-thirds of ABE learners who study in the further education colleges. These figures show somewhat more women than men in the middle and older age groups. Table 7.1 shows the breakdown by gender of the basic education student population studying in further education colleges (205,200 students) in 1995–1996 (FEFC, 1998).

Another measure by which the system's ability to meet adult learners' educational needs can be judged is progression and dropout rates. The notion of dropping out is a complex one requiring flexibility in program definitions, since many part-time students attend irregularly and drop back in to courses at a later date, depending on the other demands in their lives. The most comprehensive figures about progression and dropout rates from the 1998 FEFC report cover only ABE students enrolled in further education colleges in England. This report estimates that 81 percent of ABE students stay to the end of the course, and of these, 60 percent achieve the qualifications or learning goals they were aiming for (FEFC, 1998).

A small-scale ALBSU 1992–1993 survey based on seven LEAs gives a more pessimistic picture and points out the dearth of information on outcomes (Kambouri & Francis, 1994). This study found that more than half of the students enrolled in literacy and numeracy programs leave during the year—most of them during the first two or three weeks because they feel the course is unsuitable. One-third of learners progressed to further courses or into employment. Information about why students leave class is incomplete, and the survey also found a significant discrepancy between teacher and student reports on reasons for leaving. For example, teachers said that 10 percent of

Age	Percentage Female	Percentage Male	Percentage All Students
Under 19	19	28	23
19–24	17	17	17
25–39	39	34	37
40 or over	25	21	23

Table 7.1.   Basic Education Student Population Studying in Further Education Colleges, 1995–1996.
Note: N = 205,200.
Source: Further Education Funding Council (1998).

their students left for employment-related reasons, while more than 16 percent of their students said they left for such reasons.

A later study of ESOL learners found similar dropout rates (Kambouri, Toutounji, & Francis, 1996), although the rate was cut in half for intensive classes (seventeen to twenty-one hours per week) compared with part-time classes (two to six hours per week).

TOTAL FUNDING

Total funding of ABE programs is hard to estimate. There is the dedicated government budget for basic skills, but further funding is hidden within other programs (for example, those offering more general training for unemployed groups and those partly funded by the European Union or other national and local government funds). The BSA budget (just over £5 million, or $7.5 million), which used to be a good guide to spending on ABE, now covers basic skills in secondary schools as well. Estimates of the full costs of provision would be much higher than this.

The main source of funding for ABE is now the Further Education Funding Council (FEFC), which in turn is funded by the Department for Education and Employment. The FEFC funds further education colleges through a complex formula based on the number of students who are enrolled, attending class, and gaining credentials. Other organizations may apply for FEFC funds to provide ABE services, but they must do so through a further education college, which then becomes a gateway to these funds.

Funding for prison education and ESOL for immigrants is distributed from the Home Office to LEAs, which offer services directly and further distribute funds to public, private, and voluntary organizations to provide the services. Some LEAs still support ABE services along with other adult education programs, but the scale of LEA basic skills programs is much diminished.

The BSA is nominally independent but is funded almost entirely by the central government for its monitoring and control functions, special projects, and research.

Special project funding is also available from other national and international sources. One source is single regeneration budget funds, provided by the central government to local partnerships in areas with a high level of economic and social problems. Within an area, different agencies compete with one another to bid for funds, and agencies offering educational services, such as literacy, must compete with social welfare and housing projects. The short-term nature of such project-based funding (contracts are often reviewed and renewed on a yearly basis) creates insecurity among staff and discourages long-term planning.

European Union funds are particularly important for innovative community-based projects. The European Union focuses on particular target groups, such as women, migrant groups, and unemployed youth. Women's organizations and communities with high unemployment have particularly benefited. Special funding is available to Northern Ireland through the European Union's Peace and Reconciliation program. Exchanges and visits between students and teachers in different European Union countries are often part of such programs, reflecting the effort to create a new European identity. Massive paperwork demands and requirements for matching funds create problems for small community groups.

Since 1992, many ABE programs, including nonvocational community initiatives, have relied increasingly on funding that combines the above sources with others, such as the national lottery, philanthropic foundations, and corporations.

THE SYSTEM AT WORK TODAY

The many faceted system for the provision of adult education is the product of all the forces that came before it: from the earliest literacy campaigns to shifts in the overall economy to the diminished power of local governments and education authorities to fluctuations in the amount and nature of funding. This section represents our attempt—given the limitations on space in this one chapter—to portray ABE as it is today. For a start, Exhibit 7.1 lists the types of organizations providing ABE programs and provides a breakdown of the overall number of ABE programs and the percentage of ABE learners in each.

National Organizations

Over the years, the government has exerted strong pressures on literacy programs for accountability, quality control, and accreditation. It exerts these pressures by means of the BSA, whose primary mission is development: "We provide a wide range of organizations with advice and support to develop high quality programs to help children, young

The following types of organizations provide ABE programs:

FE sector college: 59.8 percent of ABE students
LEA adult college:[1] 23.2 percent
Prison: 12.6 percent
Training organization (for example, TECs): 1.8 percent
Voluntary organization: 0.7 percent
Employer: 0.2 percent
Other: 1.8 percent

Following is a breakdown of the number of ABE programs and the percentage of all ABE learners in those programs:

ABE Programs	Literacy and Numeracy	Percentage Learners	ESOL	Percentage Learners
Dedicated basic skills	395	58.9	322	78.8
Basic skills support	384	30.7	242	15.3
Family literacy	134	2.3	31	0.6
Youth training	154	2.8	13	0.2
Training for work	104	1.6	36	0.8
Workplace training	71	1.615	0.7	
Other	65	2.1	47	3.4
Total	1,307	100	706	100

Exhibit 7.1.   ABE Programs and Learners.

[1]Adult colleges are dedicated colleges for adults, run by LEAs and providing nonvocational courses. There are few of them left now that further education colleges offer a broader provision that includes adult and continuing education.

Source: BSA (1997a).

people and adults to improve their basic skills" (BSA, n.d.). Closely associated with this mission is its role in quality assurance: as mentioned earlier, it has established a quality mark for basic skills programs for adults. The BSA has developed in-service qualifications for basic skills teachers but does not itself provide staff development. It also supports research into the level of need and effectiveness of basic skills programs.

The BSA's mission currently overlaps somewhat with that of the Further Education Development Agency (FEDA), which provides further education colleges in England and Wales with services to promote quality, guide curriculum design and development, and enhance effective governance and management. It offers resources, research, technical assistance, and staff development across the whole range of further education (including basic skills). The FEDA, for example, is developing its own good practice guidelines for basic skills work in colleges and organizes seminars for staff working in ABE.

The National Literacy Trust (NLT) was launched in 1993 with the twofold aims of encouraging more reading and writing for pleasure and improving literacy standards across the United Kingdom. It is supported by corporate and foundation sponsors and has established a central information service with a large database. The trust also publishes a newsletter highlighting the full range of cradle-to-grave literacy-related activities. The NLT works with the media and encourages partnerships with other cultural organizations (libraries, publishers, newspapers, the British Film Institute, arts councils) and with charities and businesses to find ways in which all of these groups can put their resources to work for literacy in local communities. One of its main strengths is its freedom to work across the boundaries imposed by funding streams and mission statements.

The National Institute for Adult Continuing Education (NIACE) is the national organization for adult learning. It has a broad mandate to advance the interests of adult learners generally and to work with government, education providers, Training and Enterprise Councils, employers, and voluntary associations to promote equal opportunity access to lifelong learning. In its original form, the Adult Literacy and Basic Skills Unit was a subsidiary of the NIACE but later became independent. As a result, the NIACE has had only minor involvement in basic skills education, except as it relates to lifelong learning.

Professional associations, such as the National Association of Teachers of English, the National Association of Teachers of English and Community Languages to Adults, and the National Association of Teachers in Further and Higher Education all have some interest in working with staff involved with adult basic skills education.

The RaPAL (Research and Practice in Adult Literacy) Network is the only membership organization devoted to adult literacy that operates across the whole of the United Kingdom. It is quite small (with around three hundred members) and is run almost entirely by volunteers. The Workplace Basic Skills Network, made up of practitioners and others involved in workplace basic skills training, aims to pool information, ideas, and best practices. It runs regular seminars throughout the United Kingdom and publishes a newsletter. There is currently no national association for ABE students.

Research

Although the research base on adult literacy in the United Kingdom has grown since the early 1980s, it has had a limited impact on practice. The BSA limits itself to "research into the scale and characteristics of basic skills need and the effectiveness of basic skills programs" (BSA, 1995). It has tended to fund quantitative, policy-driven research that assumes, rather than explores, the needs and interests of learners and communities. Researchers in universities, often in partnership with practitioners, have been developing alternative notions of literacy as social practice, an approach that has become known as the new literacy studies (Mace, 1993; Barton, 1994; Street, 1995; Barton & Hamilton, 1998). These ideas form the underpinnings of much community-responsive literacy work, especially among nongovernmental voluntary organizations in the United Kingdom and internationally.

This cultural approach to literacy emphasizes the significance of local contexts and purposes to literacy students, but it has not found a sympathetic climate in government policy circles. The entrenched views of the media reporting on literacy and the traditionally distant and mistrustful relationship between higher education and ABE practice in the United Kingdom have made it difficult for this new research to reach and influence mainstream practice.

Service Delivery

ABE services are delivered in a variety of ways. The examples presented here are not necessarily meant to be typical of the kinds of programs available but rather to indicate the broad range of activities and services in which adult students can participate.

FURTHER EDUCATION COLLEGES. About two-thirds of the approximately 320,000 ABE students in England and Wales are in further education colleges, with less than a quarter in LEA programs—a reversal of the proportions at the start of the 1990s (BSA, 1997a). At the same time that colleges have assumed greater responsibility for the provision of specific basic skills courses, they have also developed their basic skills support of students engaged in other courses. An FEDA staff person suggested that about 80 percent of students in further education colleges in London need basic skills support (Ursula Howard, personal communication). These are often sixteen to nineteen year olds enrolled in vocational courses. Given the huge need for basic skills education for younger students, it is tempting for colleges to redirect their basic skills effort toward these students rather than focus on the adults in the wider community (FEFC, 1998).

The diversity of further education colleges makes it difficult to illustrate the situation with a single example. Some remain focused on their traditional role of providing vocational education for school leavers in the age group sixteen to nineteen. Others, like Knowsley College, are much more actively involved in their communities, offering innovative programming for students of all ages.

Knowsley College, located near Liverpool, has traditionally focused on students sixteen to nineteen years old, but now concerns itself with a wider range of students. It manages the Learning in Neighborhood Centers (LINC) program, originally funded by a bequest from a company that had been a major local employer but later pulled out of the area. The program is now run jointly by the college and the LEA, with support from the European Union.

The aim of the LINC program is to make adult education and training accessible in the heart of local communities. Part-time courses are run in a range of centers, including primary and secondary schools, churches and community centers, and college campuses. The basic education program includes courses on English improvement, math, computer skills, local history, creative writing, ESOL, and parenting. LINC also includes a range of nonvocational courses on subjects such as textile crafts, health and beauty, assertiveness, music, and computers. There is a full-time Return to Learn program for women as well as other courses designed to prepare all students for progression within further and higher education. LINC employs a team of outreach workers who talk to people in their communities and work with other organizations in Knowsley to develop new courses. Courses are free and offer accreditation through the Merseyside Open College Federation and other national accreditation systems (Hamilton, Machell, & McHugh, 1997).

LOCAL EDUCATION AUTHORITIES. LEAs have been influential in ABE in the past, and some have continued to be significant providers as well as funders of services. The range of activities available is enormous, and some are quite traditional in their approaches. A variety of local government–funded agencies whose primary function is not education are involved in basic education, such as homeless organizations, foyers (housing and job placement services for young unemployed people), housing associations, and health centers. After the period following the 1992 ABE legislation, during which ABE was forced to move out of such venues, these partnerships are again becoming more popular. A BSA spokesperson told us, "There is the idea that basic skills should be in a lot of other agencies, maybe with the support of basic skills people—you have to be there 'at the right moment' for people, when literacy becomes of importance to them."

One example of an innovative partnership is Read On Write Away! (ROWA!), a literacy campaign initiated by an LEA in Derbyshire that aims to develop a more literate community by coordinating initiatives in different institutions and groups. ROWA! is a partnership between two LEAs, two Training and Enterprise Councils, and two national literacy agencies (the BSA and the National Literacy Trust), which together bid for funding from the single regeneration budget. In its first year, 1997, ROWA! sponsored a series of consultative forums to bring together representatives from all local agencies involved in literacy efforts with different groups in the community. As a result of these consultations, ROWA! has developed five initiatives: books for babies, family literacy, reading interventions in primary and secondary schools, vocationally related basic skills work with unemployed adults, and basic skills courses in workplaces. Each of the five initiatives works toward a well-defined set of objectives and has built-in staff development, research, and evaluation components. ROWA! aims to reach across the age range from birth to ninety and to offer the best possible opportunities for all members of the community who have literacy needs.

LEAs also have responsibility for basic skills services in prisons. Prisoners account for about 12 percent of basic skills students (BSA, 1997a). Educational programs in prison have been contracted out to a variety of training providers, including some U.S. organizations (BSA, 1994). All incoming prisoners are given the BSA screening test to determine their level of literacy and are then offered Wordpower or Numberpower or an Open College alternative accreditation.

Literacy programs organized by community-based voluntary organizations have been hit hard by the shift in funding away from LEAs to further education colleges. Although they survive and continue to make innovative contributions, these groups have become increasingly marginalized as the state-funded sector has grown stronger. BSA statistics suggest that these kinds of services currently reach a tiny proportion of basic skills students in England and Wales (around 2 percent). However, it is difficult to document the full extent of such services because they are not part of statutory services and may not even use the term *basic skills* to describe what they do. Many of these organizations work with ethnic and cultural minority groups, adults with special learning needs, addicts, the mentally ill, ex-offenders, rural and inner-city populations, older adults, and young people who are alienated from mainstream services. Two very different examples of innovative, community-based programs are the one at Pecket Well College and an ESOL program working in an untraditional venue.

Pecket Well residential college for adults opened in 1992 in a rural area near Halifax in the north of England. Courses are run for and by students, and the college welcomes adults with physical or learning disabilities. The college was created by a small group of people committed to principles of democratic learning that show themselves at all levels of college operations: learning methods, course design, relationships between workshop leaders and participants (who at different points in time may be the same people), management, and community outreach.

One of Pecket Well's strengths is its emphasis on developing a public voice for students through collectively documenting and publishing the writing they do in courses (Pecket Well, 1994, 1995). In this, the college is supported by a national network, the Federation of Worker Writers and Community Publishers, which hosts both national events and exchanges contacts and ideas with other groups and organizations that promote student writing.

The college raises money for its activities from a range of sources, including trusts and the European Community. So far it has been able to operate independently, but even so it cannot escape the effects of bigger changes in policy. Increasingly, it is under pressure from funders to fit learners into particular target categories and to measure learning outcomes in terms that funders will recognize.

The ESOL project, based in London, is funded by short-term grants from multiple sources (currently two LEAs, a TEC, and single regeneration budget funding). The project has two part-time, temporary, basic skills teachers and one vocational guidance worker who is shared with another project. It is based in a community center, on the ground floor of one of the housing blocks in a public housing complex where there is a high crime rate, a large number of refugees, and many incidents of racial abuse. Other projects share the facilities, including a dance project for disabled people, a day care center, a play group, and a vocational guidance service. ESOL students make up 80 percent of those in the literacy project and originate from twelve countries. The literacy project responds to the needs of these students, who want advice on civil rights, welfare, and immigration issues. Also, because many of the students have mental health problems, it has been important to establish an atmosphere of trust and emotional safety before any learning takes place.

Teachers feel isolated and ill prepared by their training to address the problems their students bring to them and to do the outreach work necessary to make the project successful. The teachers have no support network and have access to few of the resources enjoyed by college-based programs. Yet they believe they are doing essential work with a group of people who are hard to reach by any other means (Deigan & McArthur, 1997).

WORKPLACE PROGRAMS. A number of ABE programs have been developed at large and medium-sized companies—some initiated by the employers themselves, some by outside training providers, and some by trade unions. It is hard to put a precise figure on the number of such programs, but according to the BSA (1997a), they constitute less than 1 percent of all basic skills provision. Frank and Hamilton (1993) describe a range of case studies of workplace programs in both the private and public sectors. Broad-based employee development schemes, similar to those instituted by Ford, have been set up in some major companies. These schemes encourage employees to get involved in a wide variety of learning activities—vocational, academic, and recreational—and provide access to basic skills courses (Beattie, 1997).

Trade unions have been involved with promoting basic skills in the workplace since the beginning of the literacy campaign in the early 1970s, although their contribution has always made up a small part of basic skills work (Mace & Yarnit, 1987). UNISON (this is not an acronym), the public employees union, has developed its own Open College accreditation framework, which includes a program of basic skills courses in partnership with WORKBASE (UNISON, 1994). WORKBASE is an organization of consultants set up by a trade union in the 1980s to carry out training needs analyses in the workplace and to custom-design courses for business. It has a range of other educational partners and has developed a widely used collaborative methodology for setting up workplace programs (Bonnerjea, 1987; Bonnerjea & Freud, 1988).

Training and Enterprise Councils are local business-led consortia that receive funding from the central Department for Education and Employment (and other sources) to provide courses for unemployed people. Usually they subcontract these services to private training organizations. Two major programs exist: one for unemployed sixteen to seventeen year olds and another for unemployed adults.

FAMILY LITERACY PROGRAMS. The BSA family literacy initiative established in 1993 included five demonstration projects that have been extensively evaluated (Brooks, Gorman, Harman, Hutchison, & Wilkin, 1996). The aims of the family literacy programs, which are mainly located in or near primary schools, are to improve the literacy of both children and parents and to increase parents' capacity to help their children with reading and writing. They typically involve some joint learning sessions for parents and children and some separate ones. The evaluation of the demonstration projects found that 96 percent of the parents participating were mothers, most between the ages of twenty and thirty-four. The parental dropout rate was low, at 9 percent, and 95 percent of parents who completed the course gained a qualification. Children also progressed on a variety of literacy measures.

Although they currently constitute only 2 percent of ABE programs, family literacy programs have been a high-profile development. One report recommends that these programs be expanded to the point where every infant (preprimary) and primary school in disadvantaged areas has one by the year 2002 (Moser, 1999).

COLLABORATIVE PARTNERSHIPS. Recently an assortment of collaborative partnerships has been developed between adult education and other statutory agencies (documented in the National Literacy Trust database). One such is a literacy project for sixteen to twenty-five year olds in partnership with the government-funded Youth Service, which organizes leisure and vocationally related activities for people in this age group. The practitioners working on these pilot projects, supported by corporate funding and operating in ten different locations around England, have developed innovative ways of encouraging young people who are unemployed, alienated, and disenfranchised to develop literacy skills, using such stepping-off points as pop music, car maintenance, and video production.

FLASHPOINTS AND EVALUATIONS FROM THE FIELD

A flashpoint is created when there are strongly held but conflicting points of view on an issue of importance. Different parties may disagree on the true nature of the issue or on how to change it. Often people with different roles have different perspectives. We identified such flashpoints in our interviews in 1996–1997 with thirty-five professionals in the field: teachers, local program managers, and staff with national organizations. A discussion with practitioners at the 1997 RaPAL conference clarified and refined the flashpoints. Here we focus on accreditation of learners, professionalization of teachers, the efforts among stakeholders to form partnerships while at the same time having to compete for funds, and the changing culture of ABE.

Accreditation of Learners

Learner accreditation (the award of a credential for work completed) has become a flashpoint for many practitioners because they accept its purpose but are uncomfortable with its dominant forms and its impact on students and teachers.

BACKGROUND. In the late 1980s the ALBSU developed national accreditation for adult basic education learners: Wordpower (for literacy) and Numberpower (for numeracy). These schemes were consistent with the framework of NVQs, which had been developed to harmonize both academic and vocational qualifications and to simplify the mazelike world of postcompulsory education and training. Like NVQs, Wordpower and Numberpower are based on a national set of standards that identifies competencies. The competencies are organized by level—for example (ALBSU and Institute of Manpower Studies, 1993):

Foundation Level

• Use and act on a simple text (up to six sentences or one
   paragraph)

- Write a short simple note or letter conveying up to two separate ideas
- Use a simple list

Level 1

- Understand and act on a graphical source up to one page long (for example, a town map)
- Write reports, letters, or notes conveying up to four separate ideas
- Consult a reference source to obtain simple information (for example, the Yellow Pages)

Level 2

- Choose and use appropriate materials from more than one written source
- Complete an open-ended form (for example, an accident report form)
- Use a reference system to obtain specific information (for example, find a book in a library)

Level 3

- Select and evaluate material from several graphical sources for a specific need
- Write material in a variety of appropriate styles and formats according to need
- Select and use appropriate reference systems for a purpose (for example, research an issue)

Wordpower is a framework of performance indicators based on these standards, which assess reading and writing, speaking and listening. Wordpower is organized in stages that match the levels of the standards, from Foundation through Stage 3. Each stage has a set of fifteen to sixteen elements to be demonstrated, divided into sections on addressing reading, writing, and oral language (and in Stage 3 also study skills). Following are examples of the elements to be demonstrated at Stages 1 and 2 in Wordpower:

Stage 1

- Provide information to one person (Unit 308 E1)
- Convey information and opinions in writing (Unit 305 E2)
- Extract information and meaning from a variety of written sources (Unit 304 E1)

Stage 2

- Provide introductions and farewells (Unit 309 E1)
- Convey information in writing—report writing (Unit 308 E2)
- Evaluate an argument in a piece of writing (Unit 307 E2)

Students build up a portfolio to demonstrate mastery of each element in a stage. There is choice of content in the sense that elements such as "make a phone call" and "write a short note" can be demonstrated in any context: work, home, or community. The portfolios are then examined by an independent "assessor" who is paid by the accrediting agency, the City and Guilds.[16]

Performance indicators provide a snapshot of the knowledge and skills a learner has at a particular moment in time. The Basic Skills Accreditation Initiative, which designed the Wordpower/Numberpower scheme, intended it to be applied flexibly:

> [There is] no prescribed teaching course or time limit. There are no set tasks to perform so the learner-centered approach can be readily accommodated. Students or trainees work at their own pace and activities may be chosen which relate to individual needs and interests. Most important of all, the student can be fully involved, at all stages, in deciding what needs to be done and how to go about it. [Hulin, n.d., p. 6]

An alternative to Wordpower and Numberpower, which dominate learner accreditation, especially in the further education sector, is the Open College Network, a system of regional accrediting networks designed as a pathway to higher education. Institutions can apply to have a specific course accredited, declaring how they will verify student competence in certain skills and knowledge. The Open College Network also has a set of standards that allow it to place skills and knowledge within a consistent framework.

Although accreditation is not specifically required by legislation, most classes do involve learners who are working toward a certificate of some kind, especially in the further education sector. Further education colleges benefit financially from accreditation, because part of the complex government funding formula for further education is based on the number of students gaining a credential. The BSA's quality standards for programs also require that learners have access to accreditation (but not that all learners must be working toward accreditation).

PERSPECTIVES. Accreditation addresses policymakers' concerns about accountability and control of program outcomes. Most practitioners accept that many students want credentials, both to boost their self-confidence and to gain access to further training and education. The tensions lie in the way the system actually works and in the impact it has on teachers and students.

Part of the rationale for the framework of performance indicators is that it serves as a clear conceptual map for both teachers and learners as to what is expected to be taught and learned in basic skills programs. As one staff member at a national organization told us, "People should know where they are going and how long to expect it to take." The U.K. road map for learners focuses on everyday literacy activities, such as writing letters and reading for information. It differs radically from the academic roots of the General Education Development (GED) credential, which is derived from what U.S. high school students are taught. The portfolio approach enables students to choose real-life literacy activities to demonstrate their skills and knowledge. One teacher told us about a man who used the work he did in planning his daughter's wedding in his Wordpower portfolio.

With Wordpower and Numberpower being such powerful drivers of the field, it seems odd that their definitions of competency should be rooted in obscurity. Most practitioners we talked with did not know the process by which competencies were identified and validated, whether they are based on theory and research, or how they might be modified to keep them up-to-date.

Some practitioners were concerned about the conception of literacy embedded in Wordpower as a set of skills, with learning then becoming the accumulation of discrete competencies. Newer literacy research emphasizes practices rather than skills and sees these as embedded in broader social and cultural settings (Mace, 1993; Barton,

1994; Street, 1995; Barton & Hamilton, 1998). Literacy practices are intrinsically shaped by power relationships. Some practitioners argue that literacy education should support learners in critically examining their own and society's literacy practices. The Wordpower approach to literacy in terms of skills inhibits critical reflection. One national organization leader told us, "At its best, it's just another tool, not an inhibitor of learning—but at its worst, it narrows the world into a mean place."

Many practitioners expressed concerns about the practice of learner accreditation. Rather than a clearly understood road map for learners, competency frameworks seem to some practitioners to be so complex that they foster learner dependency on teachers. Some practitioners noted particular issues for certain students. The foundation stage, designed for people with learning difficulties or disabilities, is seen as insulting to other adults. Several practitioners said that because Wordpower assumes native English speaking, cultural knowledge, and familiarity with grammar, ESOL students are always kept at the bottom levels.

Time issues were of concern for both learners and teachers. Although the idea that the time individual learners take to advance through levels should be open-ended would seem inherent to the portfolio approach, in practice there is a strong push to move students on quickly because of funding formulas. Practitioners repeatedly voiced their frustrations about the heavy demands that the paperwork of accreditation places on their time. Tracking learners' progress is time-consuming. Not only are different learners within a class at different levels, but individuals may be at different levels in different skill areas. The framework tends to assume that each learner has oral, written, and reading skills at the same level, but in practice this is not so.

Student accreditation issues are linked with another flashpoint: teacher accreditation. Inexperienced and inadequately trained teachers look for a curriculum to guide their teaching, and although the accreditation framework was not intended to serve as a curriculum, that is what it often becomes. Teaching then consists of "checking off the boxes" of the accreditation tool rather than helping students identify and master what they want to learn. We were often told that highly skilled, experienced, and creative teachers could create a good curriculum that also provides learners with accreditation. But the problems with provision of teacher training in Britain mean that many teachers are not highly capable. One practitioner told us, "Wordpower is not the worst thing that has happened, but you have to think hard to find creative ways of teaching with Wordpower."

The role of assessors and verifiers can also be problematic for teachers. They provide external validity, but they are seen as interpreting their role in different and inconsistent ways. Some assessors, perhaps inadequately trained, are seen by teachers as less flexible than others in their interpretation of when a competency has been demonstrated.

For learners, a vital issue is that Wordpower credentials appear to have no currency in the labor market. Indeed, some teachers told us they advise students not to put their Wordpower certificates on their résumé because it would label them as a literacy student and thus put them at a disadvantage. We heard a story about one literacy program manager who was unwilling even to interview a candidate for a secretarial job in the program because she had a Wordpower certificate.

LESSONS FOR THE UNITED STATES. The NVQ approach that underlies Wordpower and Numberpower has strengths from which U.S. adult basic education could draw. It is tied to everyday use of literacy and numeracy rather than an academic framework of what children are expected to learn in school. It lays out a clear set of expectations for teaching and learning that spread from foundation levels of literacy to more advanced levels. It enables students to demonstrate what they know and can do from the beginning and to build up tangible evidence of their accomplishments in their portfolio. This is unlike the U.S. system, in which the GED can be a distant goal, with no intermediate credentials except in states that have adopted basic skills certificates. The portfolio approach combines flexibility and individual choice with national standards and reporting.

The United States can also learn from the problems associated with this approach to accreditation. Teacher training in particular is a crucial aspect of the system that has been neglected. When working in an open framework, teachers need solid training that will allow them to develop the confidence, knowledge, and skills needed to create good teaching practices. They need the theoretical understanding of literacy to help students reflect critically on literacy practices.

Professionalization of Teachers

There is increasing demand from government for a more professional (that is, trained and accountable) workforce, and practitioners often support this. But many practitioners are concerned about the amount and form of teacher training provision, the lack of a professional organization to give them voice in national policy matters, and an apparent contradiction between the demand for trained and credentialed teachers and the actual working conditions offered.

BACKGROUND. According to the BSA's quality standards, all teachers in a program should be trained "to nationally recognized standards." The dominant teacher accreditation framework parallels that for literacy learners (via Wordpower and Numberpower). Both draw on the NVQ model of a competency framework, demonstration portfolio, and external verification. Both are based on ALBSU-developed standards and mesh with NVQ levels. Both provide opportunities to document experience and learning. Both are administered by the City and Guilds organization.

Yet despite the BSA recommendations for certified teachers, there is no standard provision or funding set-aside for teacher training, and in-service training is left to the discretion of each institution. Initial teacher training is at a minimal level; one national organization staff person said it "stops you from being dangerous." Advancing in skills and understanding is left up to individual teachers on their own time or, haphazardly, to their employers.

Perhaps related to the lack of consistency in teacher training is the lack of teacher organization and representation. Unlike the United States, the United Kingdom has no national membership organization devoted to the representation of ABE staff. The NIACE is a membership organization, but it is more broadly concerned with the general interests of adult educators than with those of basic skills teachers in particular, and it has no remittance on literacy and language concerns. The major voice in basic skills policy outside the government, the BSA, is not a membership organization and receives the bulk of its funding from the government. Deputy director Annabel Hemstedt says that although she sees the BSA's role as being "in partnership with the field, sometimes we have to do things that are not popular with the field, because that is our job as national leader" (personal communication).

Other organizations with visibility at the national level are not membership organizations and are not accountable to the field of ABE. An example is the National Literacy Trust, which is accountable to its board of trustees. RaPAL is the only national membership organization specifically for literacy practitioners, and because it has no external funding, it remains small. Practitioners have had little systematic input into ABE policy changes and have few opportunities to meet. The local and regional networks developed in the 1970s and 1980s, which brought together practitioners (and often students) for training, exchange of ideas and approaches, and discussion of policy, were virtually destroyed when the LEAs were dismantled as the main providers of ABE.

ABE has always had a marginalized status within education. Its mostly female workforce helps explain the poor conditions of service and the part-time nature of most teaching jobs. The institutionalization of ABE within the further education sector might have been expected to lead to better working conditions, greater job security, and more full-time jobs. But the statistics still suggest that only one in ten adult literacy or numeracy staff in England and Wales is full time (BSA, 1997c). Further education colleges are more likely to have full-time staff, though often as managers, with teachers still working part-time.

Pressure to cut costs, now that further education colleges are expected to behave as businesses, means that local negotiations have replaced national bargaining for wages and working conditions. Increasingly, staff are provided by private agencies who hire teachers on a temporary basis. One practitioner commented that when the European Union decided part-timers should get the same conditions of service as full-timers, "Some colleges didn't want to pay them holiday and sick leave, so they sacked all their part-timers, and then hired them back through an agency. They're all now self-employed. Instead of getting £15 an hour [about $24], they're getting £10 an hour [about $16]. Everyone is so beaten up they will accept anything."

Funding cuts associated with the shift of ABE to the further education sector have particularly affected staff in voluntary organizations. Many now depend on project-based funding, which is often short term and insecure, while also providing few resources for staff development. The use of volunteers in the field has long been a source of tension, and although their numbers are declining, volunteers continue to provide substantial support.

There are a few new models of volunteer involvement. In the Sheffield Black Literacy campaign, for example, young people of color are trained and accredited so that they can get on a track to higher education and serve as volunteer outreach workers in their own communities (Gurnah, 1997).

PERSPECTIVES. As with learner accreditation, there seems to be wide-spread agreement on the theory of teacher professionalism but dis-agreements over its practice. National policy organizations and teachers have different perspectives. While the BSA sees teacher certi-fication as an essential element of high-quality programs, a number of practitioners have concerns that have not been addressed by the BSA—about the theoretical underpinnings of certification and the gap between the high level of sophistication needed to teach in an open learner accreditation framework and the minimal level of the actual qualifications.

One experienced teacher suggested that the process of certification should have a more philosophical and theoretical underpinning: "Whilst 'how to' training is vital, it needs to be balanced with 'why?' and 'in what context?' but also 'for what purpose?' and 'to whose ad-vantage?'" To many practitioners, the competency framework of the teaching certificates, like that for learners, is a mechanistic, incremental approach to skills and knowledge. Another teacher said that dividing teaching into tiny bits without an overarching theoretical context is a mistake. "You can end up with structured assignments in order to tick the boxes. In the end, something designed to assess your practice ac-tually assesses your literacy and study skills." One teacher-trainer said of the City and Guilds certificates: "You could be a lousy teacher and still pass." They certify minimal qualifications rather than full profes-sional growth and development.

A strong approach to teacher training is particularly important for managing the very sophisticated learner accreditation approach in-troduced with Wordpower and Numberpower. Again and again prac-titioners told us that creative teachers can do a good job with Wordpower but that the kind of training and support now provided cannot be relied on to produce good, creative teachers. "The more cre-ative people can see how to fit what we're doing around it," a practi-tioner explained. "For others, Wordpower is very atomized—how does it all fit together? There is an advantage for inexperienced tutors: it gave them an agenda, told them what needs to be addressed. But the agenda is too narrow. There's a desperate need for training for people to use the accreditation system to meet student needs."

Problems with training are exacerbated by the lack of ongoing op-portunities to learn from other teachers. Now that regional networks have almost disappeared, in-service training happens within institu-tions (if at all). We heard practitioners say, "There is no meeting with others, no discussing, sharing ideas." The important thing lost is the staff networking. Another said, "People feel very cut off. People are reinventing the wheel—a whole body of knowledge is being lost because it isn't being passed on."

The BSA has a different perspective on the regional networks, which it once funded. A BSA staff person argued that the networks did not work well: "We found that access and effectiveness were poor—the same people went to everything, and not all providers took part." The BSA now focuses instead on its quality standards as a way to ensure that each program meets minimum standards of teacher certification.

The national emphasis on professionalism is at odds with another part of the picture: a marginalized workforce. Some practitioners told us their job is increasingly fragmented and consumed with "busyness." As paperwork has increased, teachers have less time to plan and teach well. But there are few complaints, because many fear losing their jobs, given the restructuring of colleges and other institutions to meet funding constraints. "There's a lot of passivity," someone told us. "Everyone is scared about losing their job, everyone is doing three people's jobs, and they can't, so they feel guilty about it." The BSA sees the credentials as a way of increasing the value of these marginalized workers, emphasizing the skills and training required to teach ABE. That payoff is not yet apparent, though it may still come. Without a strong professional organization, however, teachers will not acquire a national voice, and they will have no formal place at the table during policy consultation.

LESSONS FOR THE UNITED STATES. The approach to teacher training in the United Kingdom, based on a portfolio of demonstrated competencies, should be of interest in the United States. Rather than depending on experienced teachers enrolling in college courses (which are themselves subject to little quality control and may have only indirect application to ABE practice), the model allows teachers to demonstrate what they know. However, it also suffers from the same potential problems as the student accreditation approach: the dangers of dividing a holistic ability—teaching—into so many little skills and bits of knowledge that the whole gets lost. But the consistency of approach with learner accreditation is a strength, and the national scope of the accreditation system allows teacher movement and flexibility. It may also increase the value and status of ABE teachers in the long run, although that is not yet clear.

The British system does not appear to be as strong as the U.S. system in its provision for ongoing professional development. Staff development depends on each institution, and there are few opportunities for British teachers to meet and learn from one another across institutions.

The absence of a strong voice in the field at a national level in England should lead U.S. practitioners to value their tradition of advocacy and recognize it as an essential part of a high-quality system of ABE. Perhaps the United States will be able to avoid the contradictions the United Kingdom faces as its emphasis on professionalism increases while the working conditions for many staff continue to deteriorate. However, many ABE and ESOL teachers in the United States already feel like migrant workers, moving from class to class with little institutional attachment. Like many of their students, they are part of the growing global trend toward contingent workforces that offer temporary jobs with low pay.

Partnerships and Competition

In our discussions with practitioners and policymakers alike, ideas about partnership were on everyone's lips. However, at the same time that partnerships are encouraged for the purpose of coordinating local services, funding and governance structures for ABE actively promote competition between providers, the very antithesis of partnership. The resulting tensions have been problematic for responsive and democratic service provision.

BACKGROUND. Partnerships have been encouraged by central government policy over the 1990s. Adult literacy educators have forged links between the voluntary and statutory sectors, between different education and training sectors (such as schools and ABE through family literacy programs), between further and higher education (for example, through concerns for students who find academic writing difficult), and between education and training providers and the workplace. There are also links with vocational training and other further education courses.

However, the legal and financial governance of ABE, established by the Further and Higher Education Act of 1992, encourages competition between providers, replacing a more cooperative culture in which expertise and other resources were shared with an expectation that learning institutions will behave like businesses. Further education colleges have been designated the primary receiver of government funding for ABE, and local coordination by LEAs has been dismantled. Colleges compete with each other for students and so are unable to share information or develop referral systems that would put the interests of students first. One practitioner describes the situation in her college in this way: "We are a small college in a competitive area. There is no LEA, community-based adult education left, and there are many colleges competing for students. This makes cooperative referrals more difficult."

As one observer pointed out, "Against a background of thinly spread educational resources, widespread social deprivation, and educational underachievement, the idea of encouraging competition between educational institutions makes little sense" (Reeves et al., 1993, p. 10).

PERSPECTIVES. Although everyone seems to agree on the desirability of genuine partnerships, the difficulty of achieving them lies in the breakdown of earlier networks and the competition between educational providers. Even the BSA acknowledges that "the effects of the [Further and Higher Education] Act have been fragmentation," but the agency also sees a good side, claiming that more agencies are now involved in organizing a wider range of learning opportunities for more students than ever before. The claim is not verifiable, for although student numbers have grown over the 1990s, there are few data on the range of agencies involved in provision of services.

At the time the act was passed, the Conservative government saw competition as a way of livening up moribund educational institutions and freeing them to develop enough independence to innovate. There is some acknowledgment that this has happened for at least some institutions: "Good further education colleges are operating with a new spirit of freedom and being entrepreneurial," said one staff member at the National Literacy Trust. But there have been costs for other institutions, particularly in terms of local coordination. A number of practitioners vividly described the unintended consequences of this strategy: difficulty in referrals between institutions that are competing for student numbers to boost their own funding, difficulty in joint community-wide planning and coordination, and the decimation of the fragile community-based program sector.

Another practitioner describes the effects of reorganization on her program, which is located in a multiethnic area: "Our service has been reorganized as a business unit, and inevitably this has changed the relationship of the service to the community as a whole. The days when we could develop provision—whether community based or in formal institutions—in equal partnership with community workers are well and truly over."

The voluntary sector has been particularly hard hit by the reorganization of funding in 1992 and the new base for ABE in the further education sector. Voluntary organizations have found their funding base to be increasingly fragile. Neil McLelland, director of the National Literacy Trust, says, "The voluntary sector was decimated. They were able to offer flexible response to local needs, but they were never properly funded from that point onward." It is not surprising that these fragile groups have found it most difficult to establish effective and equal partnerships.

The local and regional networks that used to be an important part of informal cooperation have been dismantled in the face of competition for students and funding. People affiliated with different projects may keep in touch by informal means, but they often feel isolated or invisible. As one practitioner said, "We don't have connections with each other—no networks, no time. I used to feel in the center; now I feel marginalized."

When they speak of partnerships, policymakers usually mean learning institutions, not the learners and communities of which they are a part. There is no national organization that represents the views of ABE students, although some local programs have student councils and management committees on which ABE students are represented. Students may not be aware of the ways in which the courses they arrive at are funded and organized, although there are some examples of student groups' mobilizing to save programs threatened with closure.

Practitioners and learners usually find themselves to be the least powerful players in unequal partnerships. Dominant partners are typically colleges and schools, and as a result, formal, school-oriented agendas are more powerful than community development agendas. As an organization brokering these partnerships, the National Literacy Trust is well aware of these inequalities. Its director told us, "The school sector dominates all. The bits of adult education remaining in LEAs are low status, powerless in decisions and in budgeting. They are the first to get hit to protect the school sector." Such problems highlight the need for adult learners and practitioners to have an effective voice to lobby for their interests.

LESSONS FOR THE UNITED STATES. *Partnership,* like *community,* is a positive term that implies some level of consensus and equality between parties. However, some partners are patently less equal than others. There are significant power differentials between the school and business lobbies on the one hand and community-based ABE programs on the other. The agendas of some partners are more visible and influential than others and come to dominate the provision of services. This is as true in the United States as it is in England, although there has been less emphasis in the United States on either partnership or competition in the ABE structure.

The lack of strategic local planning that has resulted from British government policy is starting to be remedied. An increasing number of initiatives are starting up with the goal of finding ways to bring people together. An FEDA staff person told us that "the colleges' initial euphoria at being set free from LEAs wore off, and they saw there had been a useful role of regional planning. And the colleges want to be recognized as major players in regional development."

To be effective, partnerships must be supported by stable networks at many levels, which can address inequalities of power and capacity. In particular, there is a need to sustain voluntary organizations in the community as a vital link between top and bottom. England had to learn the hard way a lesson about the vital role of community-based provision and the need to support and promote egalitarian partnerships that include learners and practitioners. As the provisions of the Workforce Investment Act of 1998 begin to take hold in the United States and the demands of performance accountability begin to affect its voluntary sector, the United States should take note of England's hard-earned lesson.

The Changing Culture of ABE

People who have been involved with literacy work since the early campaign have seen a major shift in the culture of the field. Changes in accreditation, professional status, and the institutional location of ABE have inevitably led to changes in the discourse of literacy, what is defined as good or bad practice, and what counts as goals for literacy work.

BACKGROUND. Literacy work in the United Kingdom has been shaped by several ideologies, which are often contradictory. Literacy education has been seen sometimes as emancipatory (literacy as empowerment of individuals and groups) and sometimes as a form of social control (literacy to develop a competitive workforce and families that support children's success in school). Sometimes literacy education has been seen as cultural missionary work (bringing the light of reading to the darkness of the illiterate) and sometimes as remediating deficits (derived from special education's ideas about filling developmental gaps). These contradictory ideologies continue to be reflected in institutions, policy, and practice, and they often coexist within a single program. As Street notes (1997), these ideologies reveal the contested nature of literacy by different interest groups. The balance of power between the different ideologies shifts as political climates change.

When the literacy campaign began, an ideology of emancipation (or empowerment) dominated. The approach was practical rather than theoretical or research driven, emphasizing student definitions of literacy needs and informal, democratic relationships between teachers and learners. There was little specialist training and few teaching materials, so practice was exploratory and improvised. "In the beginning it was well-meaning, do-gooding people volunteering," one practitioner explained. "We had a climate in the 1960s and 1970s with big literacy movements—a lot of emphasis not on literacy for vocational preparation but for self-fulfillment, empowerment, being somebody."

This early work emphasized the diversity of learner needs and valued institutional responsiveness. There was a conscious philosophy that ABE should not replicate the experience of traditional schooling. Central to this approach was support for student-centered learning, enabling students to make active and informed decisions for themselves. The ALBSU endorsed this view: "A participatory approach has been the 'bedrock' of adult literacy tuition . . . students not as passive receivers but as active participants in their own learning" (ALBSU, 1985, p. 9). Entry to ABE was open, and there were no screening tests or eligibility criteria. Literacy for empowerment was reflected in the nature of teacher-student relationships, which were built on "a sense of equality" and mutual exchange and were characterized by a blurring of the roles of teacher and learner, with the implied possibility of movement between them.

Through the 1980s an ideology of social control became more dominant. Public discussions about literacy increasingly invoked the vocational discourse of human resource investment. In areas such as prison and army education, the functional-instrumental aspects of literacy had always been stressed, but during the 1980s and 1990s these came to dominate mainstream ABE. Literacy came to be linked with unemployment and social problems. No longer a service open to any who chose it for their own purposes, ABE has redefined itself by targeting specific vocational purposes and particular groups of learners.

PERSPECTIVES. There is a shared perception among all stakeholders that the field of ABE has changed dramatically and a broad agreement on the nature of these changes. Disagreement centers on the impact of the changes.

Some people emphasize the benefits of change—the importance of structure and progression, the positive effects of quality standards and statutory status for ABE, which encourage better resourcing and create pathways for people to continue their education and training rather than ghettoizing them within basic education. Jim Pateman of the BSA says:

> The predominant mode in 1987 when I came to the agency was part-time, group work, mostly evening but some daytime. There has been a growth in the kinds of opportunities available. More short courses, or full-time courses. Open Learning Centers allow different kinds of [independent work]. Workplace provision, family literacy. From our perspective these kinds of developments have opened up opportunities for people.

Some practitioners we interviewed also support the changes and point to the limitations and uneven access that were features of earlier provision. "There were large numbers of people not getting a fair crack at the education system; their needs were not targeted," explained a practitioner who was involved in the development of Wordpower and Numberpower. "There was no feeling of progression. Some people stayed in the same class with the same tutor for years. It was very cozy, which was both its strength and its weakness." The new frameworks, she thinks, offer a much broader range of contexts for literacy and consider it to be "a journey, not a staying place. A range of options have opened up—we have got much clearer."

Movement into the mainstream has clearly been supported by some. As one former practitioner, now working in the FEDA, put it,

"There are dangers to being absorbed, but it was out of the margins into the mainstream. I am more on the side now of incorporating ABE into other provision, because you are not as likely to define people as 'basic skills students.'"

Other practitioners, and some policymakers, regret the loss of an approach to literacy as a right and a means of empowerment. They also regret the loss of the flexibility and openness of relationships that characterized the old approach, even if these ideals were not always realized in practice. Alan Tuckett of the NIACE observes, "There has been a disappearance in the faith in learning without an obvious next step. LEAs have found it harder and harder to fund that [faith in learning]"—what Tuckett also refers to as "seriously useless learning." For some of those whose experience stretches back to the early campaign years, ABE's aims have become less democratic and student centered. These educators see a significant shift toward more rigid and hierarchical relationships with students: "The changes have been about a changed concept of knowledge" says Tuckett. "In the 1970s adult literacy education was about dialogue, about including excluded voices. In the 1980s it was about incorporation of those voices. The power relations between tutors and learners is at the heart of it."

Rather than being negotiated, provision is now standardized. One teacher in an ESOL program said: "No effort was made to find out who the students were. It was assumed that what they needed was to learn English. Their languages, cultural values, previous experience, existing skills, knowledge, and qualifications were ignored." As a result, she believes, students have been referred to inappropriate courses. Certain strands of work that used to be considered good practice are now dismissed as "woolly" and "unaccountable," including the use of various community-based locations, group-based writing weekends, and other residential courses. (For examples see Mace, 1995.)

The closer alignment of ABE with a formal system of vocational education means that there is more targeting, screening, and classifying of adults in programs, and the result may be discrimination against particular groups of adults (such as retired people). There are problems in finding resources for adults with serious disabilities or learning difficulties. Targeted funding is now very widespread, whether for family literacy programs, "disaffected youth," unemployed adults, or workplace literacy. According to practitioners who responded to a questionnaire survey in 1991, one of the early effects of these practices was the exclusion of "students with very basic educational needs and those lacking in confidence who need long-term support rather than instant success" (Bergin and Hamilton, 1994). The services provided were increasingly catering to mainstream college students. There has been a real "pressure to move provision toward students likely to show satisfactory outcomes and accreditation."

LESSONS FOR THE UNITED STATES. Moving adult literacy into the mainstream of continuing education in England has imposed strong statements of what literacy is and who it is for. ABE has become part of foundation studies leading to vocationally oriented further education. The only alternative, it was thought, was to leave it in a weakened and isolated literacy ghetto from which students cannot escape.

The division between vocational and nonvocational courses in the 1992 legislation was particularly important in changing the culture of ABE. It contradicts a long tradition of viewing education as having many simultaneous functions—as part of cultural and community development, of citizenship as well as employability (Tuckett, 1991; McConnell, 1996). The Further and Higher Education Act redefined nonvocational education as a less important "leisure" activity. One practitioner argued that while the vocational courses have been "highly resourced and monitored for quality," those defined as nonvocational have become fragmented, "more than ever marginalized and devalued and subject to the often conflicting agendas of individual tutors, managers, and community workers."

It has been difficult to sustain public debate about these changes in the definitions and purposes of ABE. Without a strong public voice, practitioners who have been in the field for a long time worry in private about how their role has been redefined and what the effects are on students and programs. Others, new to the field, have little sense that ABE could be anything other than what it is now and have little knowledge of the history of the original campaign. One practitioner who was among the old guard observes the following:

Teachers and organizers still draw on old learnings or have a sense that it must be possible to work from other discourses than the dominant ones without really knowing if they exist in anyone else's mind. What is surely the case is that the slow and dispersed work of building shared discourses with the participants in literacy programs has taken a huge setback.

Change is not necessarily a straight line of progress but a contested process, the outcomes of which depend on the relative power of the interest groups involved. The benefits identified here include improved structure and progression within the curriculum, quality standards and statutory status for ABE that secure better resourcing, and integration with further education and training. But the costs of mainstreaming in the United Kingdom have been identified by many in the field.

Some see an undermining of the long-standing philosophy of open access, which may unintentionally lead to the exclusion of certain groups of adults. Some see the loss of certain kinds of flexibility in pursuit of others; provision has become more flexible in areas such as timing of courses and options for progression to other courses, while standardization has resulted in less flexibility—for example, in negotiating learner goals and curriculum. The notion of flexible provision is a complicated one with many dimensions that need to be balanced. Some see a conflict between the move toward standardization and the need to consult and negotiate with students and tutors in ABE. Some argue there has been a devaluing of aspects of good practice in ABE that is hard to quantify or does not demonstrate itself in immediate, short-term effects. Finding ways to value process as well as outcomes is a challenge to the current system. These dilemmas are surely recognizable to educators in the United States.

SUMMARY AND ASSESSMENT

The United States could learn much from the United Kingdom, for the changes that have produced the current British system have parallels in the United States. Our concerns about the underlying purpose of ABE, the discourse about literacy, and the ways in which these can be overtaken by other political and social policy agendas could as easily be expressed about adult literacy in the United States.

Strengths of the U.K. System

Particular strengths in the U.K. system include much practice at the classroom level, innovative partnerships, aspects of the accreditation system, the alternative routes and progression for learners into further and higher education, and ABE's established place as a statutory requirement.

TEACHING. Despite recent changes, classroom practices in the United Kingdom at their best continue to provide outstanding examples of good practice. Many practitioners remain committed to participatory learning and have experience in nurturing it. Particularly notable are the use of learning contracts, group discussion and projects, the incorporation of student interests in teaching content, and the emphasis on student writing.

PARTNERSHIPS. After a period in which competition has been emphasized, many partnership possibilities are being explored. They have the potential to widen participation and increase community accountability.

NATIONAL ACCREDITATION SYSTEMS. These systems are independent of school-based learning and provide a degree of flexibility and learner choice. In comparison with U.S. practices, which are dependent on standardized tests and school-based definitions of what adults need to learn, the British NVQ approach takes more account of everyday literacy practices, especially those related to the workplace.

ALTERNATIVE ROUTES FOR LEARNERS INTO OTHER SECTORS OF EDUCATION. The Open College Network provides a pathway for accreditation that has the advantage of being tailored to local needs and interests, and it is linked all the way to higher education.

ABE'S STATUTORY STATUS. As a service mandated by legislation, ABE has a secure funding and institutional base that is still lacking in the United States.

The Downside

There are problems with the development of partnerships and the accreditation system, and the ABE's assured place in the further education system does not come without a cost. In addition, the continuing separation of ESOL from ABE in practice is an ongoing concern.

PARTNERSHIPS. Partnerships are valuable, but adult education does not always enter these from a position of strength or with a clear sense of the skills and knowledge it can contribute. The formation of partnerships across sectors brings with it the risk that the powerful lobbies of schools and businesses will overshadow community interests.

ACCREDITATION. Concerns about the accreditation system include the underlying theory of literacy as a bundle of separate skills, the lack of widespread understanding of the origin and purpose of the skill standards, and the lack of a strong staff development system, which is needed to implement the accreditation system effectively.

STATUTORY STATUS. The security that ABE derives from the statutory requirement has costs, especially in terms of the loss of a separate space for this education. In further education settings, ABE for adults is blurred by the learning support offered to younger, full-time college students. Community-based programs have been much weakened.

A PLACE FOR ESOL. ESOL is still in many ways seen as separate from ABE, and this separateness does not serve the needs of an increasingly diverse society. This is an area where international comparisons are sobering: many other countries have recognized and debated the relationship between literacy and language variety, the underlying social relationships of power and subordination, and the need to address these relationships in a coordinated fashion. There is silence on this issue in the United Kingdom, accompanied by policies that emphasize "English First" or "English for All" rather than multilingual or bilingual literacy. In Canada and Australia (societies not devoid of racism), literacy and ABE policy have recognized the relationship between literacy and language variety, the underlying social relationships of power and subordination, and the need to address these relationships in a coordinated fashion.

REPRESENTATION OF THE FIELD. An important lesson for the United States can be derived from the question of how a national policy organization relates to the field. The BSA can be credited with keeping ABE on the policy agenda and securing its statutory basis. At the same time, it has become part of the monitoring and control function rather than a promoter of grass-roots innovation. Many practitioners accuse it of selling out. Whatever the history, it is clear that responsive policy requires representative organizations to encourage dialogue between practitioners and learners. In contrast with the BSA, the membership organization NIACE (though not involved specifically in ABE) has pursued a different path, keeping equality of opportunity for adult learners at the forefront and maintaining the importance of nonvocational adult learning along with vocational.

Underlying Issues

Beneath much of the debate in the United Kingdom are deeply political questions about the purpose of ABE. Finch (1984), in looking at education and social policy in the United Kingdom since the 1940s, noted the tension that has existed between the aim to serve the interests of individual good on the one hand and society as a whole on the other. Finch claims that policy proposals that address individual needs and benefits—the right to read—are less likely to get implemented than those appealing to the social good—a productive workforce or a prosperous economy.

These questions are also at the heart of ABE in the United States. Is it the goal of ABE to make everyone middle class? To provide individuals with the skills and credentials they need to realize the American dream of a good job, nice house, and a flashy car? Or is the purpose of ABE to extend participatory democracy and promote social justice, to enable people to develop their own voice and create new visions of what is the good life? Can it do both?

In both the United States and the United Kingdom, the arguments used to justify the need for ABE have often been framed in terms of global economic competitiveness: creating a skilled workforce rather than an informed citizenry. European experience counters this with the concept of social exclusion, arguing that society is threatened by a dispossessed minority who are systematically excluded not only from the good jobs but also from participation in their community. Using arguments that are recognizable today but that date from two hundred years ago in England, Martha More tried to convince farmers to allow their workers to attend reading classes: "We . . . said that we had a little plan which we hoped would secure their orchards from being robbed, their rabbits from being shot, their game from being stolen and which might lower the poor-rates" (Kelly, 1992, p. 77).

The concept of social exclusion widens the terms of reference for ABE from purely economic issues (putting people to work) to involvement in the whole of society. In England, long years of isolation and conflict with its European partners have prevented this concept from penetrating the consciousness of the citizenry as much as it might. But as central power shifts, concerns about the effects of social exclusion are increasing, as highlighted in a series of important reports (Tomlinson, 1996; Fryer, 1997). This increased concern is also reflected in the government's cross-departmental Social Exclusion Unit and new lifelong learning policy statement (Department for Education and Employment, 1998). Approaching education for the purpose of social inclusion provides a path forward that is perhaps not entirely emancipatory—the debate is not about rights—but is much broader than approaching it for the sole purpose of being competitive in the global economy.

Potential and Opportunities

This is a moment of potential for ABE in England, and a moment in which there is opportunity for the field to build on its history and carve out some new and exciting possibilities for the future. There are strong foundations on which to build: the history of participatory approaches to adult learning, the strength of the tradition of voluntary associations, and the flowering of research in the new literacy studies, which has enormous potential for shaping an entirely new approach to practice. The 1997 change of government from Conservative to Labor signaled a public readiness for change and a recognition of the social costs of Thatcherism.

To realize this potential, the field must become truly accountable—accountable, that is, to ABE students and their communities. What is needed is what Merrifield (1998) has called elsewhere a system of "mutual accountability." Practitioner and learner networks, enhanced teacher training, and a sense of professionalism and integration with the larger field of ABE theory and practice are crucial components. The field needs opportunities to reflect and connect. Reflection requires processes that enable experience to be analyzed and learned from in the context of theory. Connection requires networks within ABE and wider national and international links for basic education. We need pathways for a diversity of voices and perspectives to shape social policy. Especially in times of radical change and realignment in social policy, a strong practitioner-oriented research tradition can be a powerful tool for maintaining the visibility and agenda of ABE. The aim should be to develop a learning democracy that incorporates ways of consulting, allowing diverse voices to interrupt the dominant discourse.

Mechanisms of reflection and connection would create the conditions for a more responsive policy, which could reposition ABE in the United Kingdom and regain some of the ground lost over recent years. They would also strengthen communications among countries, allowing us to learn more readily from one another about how to deal with the common issues we face.

Appendix: Resources for More Information

A variety of resources in the United Kingdom can be contacted for further information on the programs and issues discussed in this chapter.

Resource Centers

Adult Basic Skills Resource Centre: c/o Young Help Trust, 23–31 Waring Street, Belfast BT1 2DX. Phone: 01232 560120; fax: 01232530016; e-mail: [adultbasic@unite.co.uk]

Basic Skills Agency Resource Centre: Institute of Education Library and Media Services, 20 Bedford Way, London WC1H OAL, U.K. Access to all BSA publications and many other sources referred to in this chapter is provided by the agency's Web site: [http://www.ioe.ac.uk/library/bsa.html].

Journals

Adults Learning. Published by the National Institute for Adult Continuing Education. Available from the NIACE, 21 De Montfort Street, Leicester LE1 7GE.

Basic Skills Agency Newsletter. Free from the Basic Skills Agency, ADMAIL 524, London WC1A 1BR, U.K.

Language Issues. National Association for Teaching English and Other Community Languages to Adults (NATECLA). Write for subscription rates to NATECLA National Center, South Birmingham College, 520–524 Stratford Road, Birmingham B11 4AJ, U.K.

Literacy Today. £14 per year from National Literacy Trust, 59 Buckingham Gate, London SW1E 6AJ, U.K.

Research and Practice in Adult Literacy (RaPAL) Bulletin. Membership costs £20 per year, available from Margaret Herrington, Membership Secretary, The Old School, Main Street, Tilton-on-the-Hill, Leicester LE2 9LF, U.K.

Studies in the Education of Adults. Available from the National Institute for Adult Continuing Education (NIACE), 21 De Montfort Street, Leicester LE1 7GE, U.K.

Useful Contacts

For information on England and Wales: Basic Skills Agency (BSA), Commonwealth House, 1–19 New Oxford Street, London WC1A 1NU, U.K. (Note the different address to order publications, listed under *Basic Skills Agency Newsletter* above.)

For information on Northern Ireland: Adult Literacy and Basic Education Committee (Northern Ireland). Contact Hilary Sloan, 344 Stranmills Road, Belfast BT9 5ED, Ireland. Phone: 0213 268 2379.

For information on Scotland: Scottish Community Education Association (SCEC), Rosebury House, 9 Haymarket Terrace, Edinburgh, Scotland EH12 5EZ. Phone: 0131 313 2488; fax: 0131 313 6800.

Department for Education and Employment. Web site: [http://www.dfee.gov.uk]. For access to policy information and downloadable publications.

Department for Education and Employment, Lifelong Learning Web site: [http://www.lifelonglearning.co.uk].

Federation of Worker Writers and Community Publishers, P.O. Box 540, Stoke on Trent ST6 6DR, England. Web site: [http://www.fwwcp.mcmail.com]. For links with writers' groups and community publishing projects around the country.

Further Education Development Agency, Dunbarton House, 68 Oxford Street, London W1N 0DA, U.K. Web site: [http://www.feda.ac.uk]. For access to policy information and downloadable publications.

Gatehouse Books, Hulme Adult Education Centre, Stretford Road, Manchester M15 5FQ, U.K. Phone: 0161 226 7152.

Lancaster Literacy Research Group, c/o Department of English and Modern Languages, Lancaster University, Lancaster LA1 4YL, U.K. Web site: [http://www.literacy.lancaster.ac.uk].

London Language and Literacy Unit, Southwark College, Southampton Way, London SE5 7EW, U.K. For publications on ESOL and family literacy.

National Institute for Adult Continuing Education (NIACE), 21 De Montfort Street, Leicester LE1 7GE, U.K. Web site: [http://www.niace.org.uk].

National Literacy Trust, 59 Buckingham Gate, London SW1E 6AJ, U.K. Web site database and information service: [http://www.literacytrust.org.uk]. E-mail: [contact@literacytrust.org.uk].

Research and Practice in Adult Literacy (RaPAL), Old School, Main Street, Tilton-on-the-Hill, Leicester LE2 9LF, U.K. Web site: [http://www.literacy.lancaster.ac.uk.rapal/rapal/htm].

UNISON Centre, 137 High Holborn, London WC1 IV6PL, U.K. For information on trades union education.

Workplace Basic Skills Network, c/o Fiona Frank, CSET, Lancaster University, Lancaster LA1 4YL.

Write First Time. Archive 1975–1985. Student-published newspaper. Contact the Librarian, Ruskin College, Oxford University, Walton Street, Oxford OX1 2HE, U.K. Web site: [http://www.ruskin.ac.uk].

Notes

1. We have used the term *United Kingdom* as the generic name for the union of England, Scotland, Wales, and Northern Ireland. Each of these countries is currently moving toward greater autonomy, and there are distinctive differences among them in the organization of educational provision. In many places in the chapter we refer only to England, or to the other countries by name where appropriate.

2. Because the system of ABE in the United Kingdom is complex, we can only sketch here the broad outlines of the scene. The lists of references and resources at the end of the chapter are designed to direct readers to more detailed information. Three recent publications are particularly useful for up-to-date statistics and information on policy and provision: the Moser report (Moser, 1999), a government policy review of ABE in England; the Further Education Funding Council's *Basic Skills Curriculum Area Survey Report* (FEFC, 1998); and the *Basic Skills Agency Annual Report 1997–98.*

3. In the United Kingdom the term most commonly used is *tutor,* which includes both paid and volunteer staff. However, to avoid confusion for an American audience, which commonly uses *tutor* to mean volunteer, we use the term *teacher* throughout to include paid and volunteer staff.

4. School leavers are young adults who have finished their compulsory education, usually at age sixteen, but not gone on to any further education.

5. This chapter is based on a review of the literature; approximately thirty-five interviews carried out in 1996–1997 with a variety of people who work for U.K. national institutions and local literacy programs; a roundtable discussion with an additional fifteen practitioners at the 1997 Research and Practice in Adult Literacy conference; and discussions that took place in an international action research group on ABE in institutional environments, sponsored by the United Nations Educational, Scientific, and Cultural Organization, which brought together more than forty representatives of countries from Eastern and Western Europe and North and Central America in 1995–1996 (Hamilton, 1997).

The chapter also represents the experience and knowledge that both authors bring to the subject. Mary Hamilton has been active in research and practice in adult literacy in England since the original adult literacy campaign in 1974. Juliet Merrifield, an educator and researcher who was born and now resides in England but lived in the United States from 1976 to 1996, is in a good position to identify the parallels of and differences in the systems of adult basic education in the two countries.

6. LEAs were set up through the 1902 Education Act. They are part of the local government structure, which raises its own taxes and administers funds allocated by the central government. England and Wales are divided into counties and boroughs administered by a local elected council. Each has an education committee made up of elected councilors and co-opted members. This committee controls the education budget and decision making over primary, secondary, and further education in the area.

Since the 1980s, some of this local control has been taken away; for example, the secretary of state for education took control of teachers' pay and conditions in 1987, and the 1988 Education Reform Act introduced local management of schools and centrally controlled, grant-maintained schools. The effect of taking power away from democratically elected local government and pushing it down to the level of individual schools was to weaken local control because there is no organization linking individual schools to provide a counterweight to the power of the central government. This arrangement thus provides the illusion of local control while actually increasing the powers of central government, which holds all the purse strings. Further education colleges, which were originally under LEA control, became independent in 1992.

7. General further education colleges (229 in England and 20 in Wales) offer a broad range of vocational and academic courses for students of

all ages from sixteen years upward. They do not offer higher-level or degree courses; these are provided by the university sector, except in a few cases where colleges provide both further and higher education, the latter in association with a university. Further education colleges provide annually for around 1.7 million students, 60 percent of whom are over the age of nineteen, the majority part time. After passage of the 1992 Further and Higher Education Act, further education colleges became state-supported corporations, financed largely through two funding councils, one for England and one for Wales, which are directly responsible to the secretaries of state for education in England and Wales (see Cantor & Roberts, 1995, p. 2).

8. Open College Networks are systems of regional accreditation, created to offer alternative routes for learners who wish to prepare for higher education but do not have the traditional qualifications. Institutions can apply to have a specific course accredited, declaring how they will verify competence of skills and knowledge within the OCN standards framework (see Cantor & Roberts, 1995, pp. 82–83; Martin, 1998; National Open College Network, 1996).

9. The University for Industry will be launched nationally in 2000. It aims to bring together the public and private sectors (educational institutions and employers) and will act as a broker to match learners with existing courses. It will have a significant marketing function through the Learning Direct hot line, will analyze needs and commission new content when there is a gap, and will be responsible for quality control. Individual learning accounts will be designed to encourage people to save to learn and will be linked to "smart cards" to help record their learning, with a £150 million investment in the first 1 million accounts. Among the aims of the program is to more than double the help available for basic literacy and numeracy skills among adults to involve more than 500,000 adults annually by 2002 (Department for Education and Employment, 1998).

10. In 1995, the Basic Skills Agency adopted its current name along with a broader mandate supporting basic skills in secondary schools as well as in further and adult education, so it no longer has a special focus on adult learners.

11. The controversial notion of functional literacy also served as the underpinning of the U.S. Adult Education Act and has been very influential in the United States. While the original meaning of the term simply involved the linkage of literacy with the practical needs of adult life, it has come to be identified with a narrow, vocational view of literacy that

serves the needs of business and employers, to the neglect of the personal and social development goals of individuals and local communities.

12. Briefly, they approached literacy education as a means of empowerment, viewed mainstream schooling as part of society's attempt to maintain social control and reproduce conformity with social norms, and saw their work as critical and participatory.

13. The absence of a central agency for ABE in both Scotland and Northern Ireland means that ABE statistics are not readily available there, as they are in England and Wales. Some figures and a recent context are given for Scotland in Macrae (1999).

14. The New Commonwealth countries are those that were once part of the British Empire but are now fully independent of the United Kingdom and members of a voluntary association based on (weakening) economic and cultural ties. The immigrant groups referred to here are mainly from African countries and the Indian subcontinent.

15. The figures on the kind of help people were receiving in 1995–1996 in England are from the BSA and FEFC. There are some minor discrepancies in the figures provided by the two agencies.

16. The City and Guilds is one of a number of agencies accrediting awards for which educational institutions then offer courses, in the same way that the GED is offered in the United States.

References

Adult Literacy and Basic Skills Unit (ALBSU). (1985). *Adult literacy: The first decade.* London: Author.

Adult Literacy and Basic Skills Unit. (1987). *Annual report.* London: Author.

Adult Literacy and Basic Skills Unit. (1989). *ESOL: A nation's neglect: Research into the need for English amongst speakers of other languages.* London: Author.

Adult Literacy and Basic Skills Unit. (1992). ESOL: Time to start afresh? *ALBSU Newsletter, 45,* 2–3.

Adult Literacy and Basic Skills Unit. (1993). *Open Learning Centers in England and Wales, 1988–92.* London: Authors.

Adult Literacy and Basic Skills Unit and Institute of Manpower Studies. (1993). *Basic skills and jobs.* London: Authors.

Advisory Council on Adult and Continuing Education. (1979). *A strategy for the basic education of adults: A report commissioned by the Secretary of State for Education and Science.* Leicester: Author.

Atkinson, J., & Spilsbury, M. (1993). *Basic skills and jobs.* London: Basic Skills Agency.

Ball, S. (1994). *Educational reform: A critical and post-structuralist account.* Buckingham: Open University Press.

Barton, D. (1994.) *Literacy: An introduction to the ecology of written language.* Oxford: Blackwell.

Barton, D., & Hamilton, M. (1998). *Local literacies: A study of reading and writing in one community.* London: Routledge.

Basic Skills Agency (BSA). (1994). *Basic skills in prisons: Assessing the need.* London: Author.

Basic Skills Agency. (1996). *Lost opportunities: The language skills of linguistic minorities in England and Wales.* London: Author.

Basic Skills Agency. (1997a). *Annual report 1996/7.* London: Author.

Basic Skills Agency. (1997b). *International Numeracy Survey: A comparison of the basic numeracy skills of adults 16–60 in seven countries.* London: Author.

Basic Skills Agency. (1997c). *Literacy and numeracy skills in Wales: A survey of the reading, writing, and numeracy skills of people between the ages of 16 and 64.* London: Author.

Basic Skills Agency. (1998). *Annual report 1997/8.* London: Author.

Basic Skills Agency. (n.d.). Promotional brochure. London: Author.

Beattie, A. (1997). *Working people and lifelong learning: A study of the impact of an employee development scheme.* Leicester: National Institute for Adult Continuing Education.

Bergin, S., & Hamilton, M. (1994). Who's at the center? The experience of open learning in adult basic education. In M. Thorpe & D. Gudgeon (Eds.), *Open learning in the mainstream.* Harlow: Longmans, 1994.

Bonnerjea, L. (1987). *Workbase trades union education and skills project.* London: Adult Literacy and Basic Skills Unit.

Bonnerjea, L., & Freud, B. (1988). *Workbase: A basic skills and education pack for manual workers.* London: Adult Literacy and Basic Skills Unit.

British Association of Settlements. (1974). *A right to read: Action for a literate Britain.* London: Author.

Brooks, G., Gorman, T., Harman, J., Hutchison, D., & Wilkin, A. (1996). *Family literacy works: The NFER evaluation of the Basic Skills Agency's demonstration programs.* London: National Foundation for Educational Research and the Basic Skills Agency.

Brown, Gordon. (1997, August 2). Why Labour is still loyal to the poor. *Guardian,* p. 19.

Bynner, J., & Parsons, S. (1997). *It doesn't get any better: The impact of poor basic skills on the lives of thirty-seven year olds.* London: Basic Skills Agency.

Bynner, J., & Steedman, J. (1995). *Difficulties with basic skills.* London: Basic Skills Agency.

Cantor, L. M., & Roberts, I. F. (1995). *Further education today: A critical review* (3rd ed.). London: Routledge and Kegan Paul.

Craven, J., & Jackson, F. (1986). *Whose language? A teaching approach for Caribbean heritage students.* Manchester: Central Manchester Caribbean English Project, Manchester Education Committee.

Davie, P., & Parry, G. (1993). *Recognizing access: The formation and implementation of the National Framework for the Recognition of Access Courses.* Leicester: National Institute for Adult Continuing Education.

Dearing, R. (1997). *Higher education in the learning society: Report of the National Committee of Inquiry into Higher Education.* London: Government Stationery Office.

Deigan, M., & McArthur, T. (1997, April). Teaching basic skills and ESOL in non-traditional venues. *Adults Learning, 8*(8), 210–211.

Department for Education, Secretaries of State for Education and Science, Employment, and Wales by Command of Her Majesty. (1991). *Education and training for the twenty-first century: Vol. 2, The challenge to colleges.* London: HMSO.

Department for Education and Employment. (1998). *The learning age* (Consultation paper on lifelong learning).

Derrick, J. (1996, March). *Adult learners in colleges and the FEFC.* Paper presented at the National Institute for Adult Continuing Education Annual Conference, Warwick University.

Elsdon, K., with Reynolds, J., & Stewart, S. (1995). *Voluntary organizations: Citizenship, learning, and change.* Leicester: National Institute for Adult Continuing Education.

European Bureau of Adult Education. (1983). Adult basic education. *EBAE Newsletter No. 1* (Further Education Funding Council).

Fieldhouse, R. (Ed.). (1996). *A modern history of adult education.* Leicester: National Institute for Adult Continuing Education.

Finch, J. (1984). *Education as social policy.* London: Longman.

Finegold, D., McFarland, L., & Richardson, W. (Eds.). (1993). *Something borrowed, something blue? A study of the Thatcher government's appropriation of American education and training policy.* Oxfordshire: Triangle Books.

Frank, F., & Hamilton, M. (1993). *Not just a number: The role of adult basic education in the changing workplace.* Final Report to Leverhulme Trust. Working Paper No. 37, Lancaster University Centre for the Study of Education and Training.

Frankel, A., Millman, L., & Reeves, F. (Eds.). (1998). *Basic skills and further education: Communities confront linguistic elitism and social exclusion.* Derby: Bilston College Publications and Education Now.

Freire, P. (1972). *The pedagogy of the oppressed.* Harmondsworth: Penguin.

Freire, P. (1985). *The politics of education, culture, power, and liberation.* New York: Bergin and Garvey.

Fryer, R. (1997). *Learning for the twenty-first century: First report of the National Advisory Group for Continuing Education and Lifelong Learning* (NAGCELL1. PP62/3111634/1297/33). London: Government Stationery Office.

Fullan, M. (1991). *The new meaning of educational change.* London: Cassell.

Further Education Funding Council (FEFC). (1998). *Basic skills curriculum area survey report.* London: Government Stationery Office.

Gardener, S. (1985). *Conversations with strangers: Ideas about writing for adult students.* London: Adult Literacy and Basic Skills Unit.

Gatehouse Books. (1985). *Where do we go from here? Adult lives without literacy.* Manchester: Gatehouse Publishing.

Gatehouse Books (1992). *Telling tales: A collection of short stories, poetry, and drama.* Manchester: Gatehouse Publishing.

Gee, J., Hull, G., & Lankshear, C. (1996). *The new work order: Behind the language of the new capitalism.* Sydney and Boulder, CO: Allen and Unwin and Westview Press.

Graff, H. (1996). The persisting power and costs of the literacy myth. *Literacy Across the Curriculum, 12*(2), 4–5.

Gurnah, A. (Ed.). (1992). Literacy for a change: A special issue on the black literacy campaign in Sheffield. *Adults Learning, 3*(8).

Gurnah, A. (1997). A new funding framework for adult education. *Research and Practice in Adult Literacy Bulletin, 34.*

Hamilton, M. (1989). The development of adult basic education in Britain. In N. Entwhistle (Ed.), *Handbook of educational ideas and practice.* London: Croom Helm.

Hamilton, M. (1992). The development of adult basic education in the U.K.: A cautionary tale. In *International Yearbook of Adult Education 19/20.* Cologne, FRG: Bohlau Verlag.

Hamilton, M. (1994). *Early days: Results of a survey of the effects of incorporation on ABE provision in England and Wales.* Lancaster: Lancaster University, Center for the Study of Education and Training.

Hamilton, M. (1996). Adult literacy and basic education. In R. Fieldhouse (Ed.), *A modern history of adult education.* Leicester: National Institute for Adult Continuing Education.

Hamilton, M. (1997). Keeping alive alternative visions. In J. P. Hautecoeur (Ed.), *ALPHA 97: Basic education and institutional environments.* Hamburg, FRG: UNESCO Institute for Education, and Toronto, Canada: Culture Concepts.

Hamilton, M., & Barton, D. (forthcoming). *The International Literacy Survey:* What does it measure? *International Journal of Education.*

Hamilton, M., Machell, J., & McHugh, G. (1997). *Access to L.I.N.C. motivational programs in Knowsley.* Final report to Knowsley LEA.

Hargreaves, D. (1980). *Adult literacy and broadcasting: The BBC's experience.* London: Pinter.

Hartley, T. (1992). *The tip of the iceberg: State funding and English language provision for bilingual adults in the U.K.: A critical review.* Unpublished master's thesis, Lancaster University.

Hautecoeur, J. P. (Ed.). *ALPHA 97: Basic education and institutional environments.* Hamburg, FRG: UNESCO Institute for Education, and Toronto, Canada: Culture Concepts.

Haviland, R. M. (1974). Provision for adult literacy in England. In A. H. Charnley (Ed.), *Research in adult education in the British Isles.* Leicester: National Institute for Adult Continuing Education.

Howarth, C., Kenqay, P., Palmer, G., & Street, C. (1998). *Monitoring poverty and social exclusion: Labor's inheritance.* York: Joseph Rowntree Foundation.

Hulin, Pat. (n.d.). *Using your Wordpower: An audio-cassette pack to support training courses in the teaching, assessment, and accreditation of Basic Communication Skills.* BBC Education and the Adult Literacy and Basic Skills Unit.

Hull, G. (Ed.) (1997). *Changing work, changing workers: Critical perspectives on language, literacy, and skills.* Albany: State University of New York Press.

Illich, I. (1973). *Deschooling Society.* Harmondsworth: Penguin Education.

Jones, A., & Charnley, A. (1978). *The adult literacy campaign: A study of its impact.* Leicester: National Institute for Adult Continuing Education.

Kambouri, M., & Francis, H. (1994). *Time to leave? Progression and drop out in basic skills programs.* London: Basic Skills Agency.

Kambouri, M., Toutounji, I., & Francis, H. (1996). *Where next? Drop out and progression from ESOL.* London: Basic Skills Agency.

Keddie, N. (1980). Adult education: An ideology of individualism. In J. Thompson (Ed.), *Adult education for a change.* London: Hutchison.

Kelly, T. (1992). *A history of adult education in Great Britain.* Liverpool: Liverpool University Press.

Kennedy, H. (1997). *Learning works: Widening participation in further education.* Coventry: Further Education Funding Council.

Limage, L. (1986). Adult literacy policy in industrialized countries. *Comparative Education, 30,* 50–72.

Limage, L. (1990). Adult literacy and basic education in Europe and North America: From recognition to provision. *Comparative Education, 26*(1), 125–140.

Lister, I. (1974). *Deschooling: A reader.* London: Cambridge University Press.

Lo Bianco, J., & Freebody, P. (1997). *Australian literacies: Informing national policy on literacy education.* Melbourne: National Languages and Literacy Institute of Australia.

Mace, J. (1979). *Working with words: Literacy beyond school.* London: Writers and Readers Publishing Cooperative.

Mace, J. (1993). *Talking about literacy.* London: Routledge.

Mace, J. (Ed.). (1995). *Literacy, language, and community publishing: Essays in adult education.* Clevedon: Multilingual Matters.

Mace, J., & Yarnit, M. (Eds.). (1987). *Time off to learn: Paid educational leave and low paid workers.* London: Methuen.

Macrae, C. (1999). *Literacy and community education.* Adult Literacies in Scotland. Project Paper 1. Edinburgh: Scottish Office.

Martin, P. (1998). Open College Networks: Success against the odds? *Journal of Further and Higher Education, 22*(2), 183–192.

McConnell, C. (Ed.) (1996). *Community education: The making of an empowering profession.* Leicester: National Institute for Adult Continuing Education.

McDuffus, R., Sharp, I., & Nolan, N. (1997, Spring). Student research, learning, and action. *Research and Practice in Adult Literacy Bulletin, 32,* 3–6.

Merrifield, J. (1998). *Contested ground: Performance accountability in adult basic education.* Boston: National Center for the Study of Adult Learning and Literacy. NCSALL Report No. 1.

Morris, C., & Nwenmely, H. (1994). The Kweyol language and literacy project. In M. Hamilton, D. Barton, & R. Ivanic (Eds.), *Worlds of literacy.* Clevedon: Multilingual Matters.

Moser, C. (1999). *A fresh start: Improving literacy and numeracy.* Sheffield: Department for Education and Employment.

National Open College Network. (1996). *Annual report.* Derby: Author.

Office for National Statistics. (1998). *Social trends (28).* London: Author.

Oppenheim, C., & Harker, L. (1996). *Poverty: The facts* (3rd ed.). London: Child Poverty Action Group.

Organization for Economic Cooperation and Development. (1997). *Literacy skills for the knowledge society.* Paris: Author.

O'Rourke, R., & Mace, J. (1992). *Versions and variety: A report on student writing and publishing in adult literacy education.* Stevenage: Avanti Books.

Pecket Well College. (1994). Forging a common language, sharing the power. In M. Hamilton, D. Barton, & R. Ivanic (Eds.), *Worlds of literacy.* Clevedon: Multilingual Matters.

Pecket Well College. (1995). *Changing lives: Annual report 1994/5.* Halifax, UK: Author.

RaPAL Bulletin. (1994, Autumn). *Special issue on bilingual literacy, 25.*

RaPAL Bulletin. (1996, Summer). *Special issue on staff development and training in adult basic education, 30.*

Reeves, F., et al. (1993). *Community need and further education: The practice of community-centered education at Bilston Community College.* Wolverhampton: Education Now Books in partnership with Bilston Community College.

Robinson, J. (1983). Broadcasting and adult learning in the U.K., 1922–1982. In M. Tight (Ed.), *Education for adults.* Buckingham: Open University Press.

Sargent, N., & Tuckett, A. (1997). *Pandora's box: Companion papers on motivation, access, and the media.* Leicester: National Institute for Adult Continuing Education.

Schwab, I., & Stone, J. (1987). *Language, writing, and publishing.* London: Afro-Caribbean Language and Literacy Project, Inner London Education Authority.

Street, B. (1995). *Social literacies: Critical approaches to literacy in development, ethnography, and education.* London: Longman.

Street, B. (1996). Literacy, economy, and society. *Literacy across the curriculum, 12*(3), 8–15.

Street, B. (1997). *Adult literacy in the U.K.: A history of research and practice.* National Center for Adult Literacy Policy Paper Series, University of Pennsylvania, Philadelphia; and published as RaPAL Occasional Paper/Issue 33.

Tomlinson, S. (1996). *Inclusive learning: Report of the Learning Difficulties and/or Disabilities Committee.* London: Government Stationery Office.

Tuckett, A. (1991). Counting the cost: Managerialism, the market and the education of adults in the 1980s and beyond. In S. Westwood & J. E. Thomas (Eds.), *Radical agendas? The politics of adult education.* Leicester: National Institute for Adult Continuing Education.

Tuckett, A. (1997). *Lifelong learning in England and Wales: An overview and guide to issues arising from the European year of lifelong learning.* Leicester: National Institute for Adult Continuing Education.

UNISON. (1993). *Skills training for the millennium: Vol. 1, Findings.* London: Author.

UNISON. (1994). *Open College: Pathways and opportunities: A guide to courses from UNISON Open College 1994/5.* London: Author.

Wells, A. (1996, September). ESOL—About time for a new start? *Adults Learning, 8*(1), 8–9.

Withnall, A. (1994, September). Literacy on the agenda: The origins of the adult literacy campaign in the United Kingdom. *Studies in the Education of Adults, 26*(1), 67–85.

CHAPTER EIGHT

Using Electronic Technology in Adult Literacy Education

David J. Rosen

~∿~

Students in adult literacy education, including basic and secondary education and English for speakers of other languages (ESOL), are increasingly using computers to write, find information, publish their writings, communicate by e-mail, learn basic skills, and for other purposes.

RANGE OF TECHNOLOGIES

Computer hardware and software can be found to varying degrees in almost all adult literacy programs, and to some extent literacy programs also have access to the Internet, especially e-mail, electronic lists, and the World Wide Web. Nevertheless, only about a third of adult literacy programs would describe themselves as engaged in significant use of computers for any purposes, and fewer than half use computers often or daily for instruction preparation activities (Sabatini, 1997).

Most programs have videocassette recorders and televisions (Turner, 1998), although, as Roberts (1993) points out, these are often underused. Some programs also have video cameras. Most programs, and many students, have audiocassette recorders. Newer kinds of technology, such as digital cameras, scanners, and CD-ROM recorders, are found less frequently. A few programs, especially those in community colleges and public schools, use two-way, interactive video broadcast equipment for instruction and sometimes teacher training. Some students use pocket calculators, spell checkers, and other personal data assistants.

In this chapter the focus is on computers, the Internet (including the World Wide Web), and, to a lesser extent, broadcast and recorded video technologies. Once separate electronic media, computers, the Internet, television, radio, and audio and video recordings are becoming an integrated, digital multimedium delivered now through the computer and soon by digital television broadcast. By some estimates, nearly all U.S. homes will be wired to the Internet early in the twenty-first century (Kaku, 1997). The capacity for an integrated and interactive electronic learning medium of hypertext, still and moving images, and sound to be delivered at high speed to home, work, or learning center anytime, almost anywhere, in real and asynchronous time, opens a new era of learning and teaching possibilities for adult literacy education.

USING TECHNOLOGY FOR LEARNING AND TEACHING

Although technology is used in adult literacy education for many purposes—information management, e-mail and electronic list communication, curriculum development, assessment, evaluation, and research, among others—one of its most important uses is to enable and strengthen teaching and learning.

Technology used in support of learning and teaching can be divided into two broad categories: instructivist and constructivist. The instructivist approach is widely found in adult literacy education technology laboratories and classrooms where learners use computer-assisted instruction to acquire knowledge and skills. Education programs may take one or both of two paths to computer-assisted instruction: by using large, comprehensive, often costly computer-based curricula, usually referred to as integrated learning systems, and by integrating specific single pieces of software, Web pages, or on-line documents into existing (or new) curricula. For those choosing the second path, a major issue is software integration. Challenges include how to identify good software that can meet defined purposes for different types of learners and how to find the time to review software and test it out with students before purchase.

Although an instructivist approach emphasizes computer-assisted teaching of skills or knowledge, most teachers also show their students how to use computers as tools, especially for word processing. Some teachers introduce students to spreadsheet, database, communications, graphics, desktop publishing, and presentation software, especially for job-related basic skills learning.

Constructivism is a theory of cognitive growth in which learning is believed to be an active process in which a person constructs new ideas or concepts while transforming his or her existing knowledge. Meaning is believed to be made from one's experiences and from a cognitive structure based on those experiences. A learner constructs knowledge by actively connecting and assimilating new information or experience into his or her existing knowledge structure. The new knowledge or ideas become useful and integrated as the learner sees relationships among existing concepts and knowledge and the new ideas. The learner selects and interprets information, constructs hypotheses, and makes decisions by relying on a cognitive structure of schema, or mental models. The roots of constructivism go back at least as far as the eighteenth century, to German philosopher Immanuel Kant, and more recently have grown from research conducted by Swiss psychologist Jean Piaget (1973). Other theorists and adherents include Bruner (1986, 1990), Papert (1993), Resnick (1989), and Vygotsky (1978).

The constructivist approach as applied in the classroom is referred to as project-based, student-centered, participatory, engaged, cooperative, or inquiry learning. It begins with a question, problem, topic, or product of high interest to students. The subject decided on is then organized into a project with specific goals and products through which basic skills can be acquired. Technology plays many important roles in constructivist learning: students use CD-ROM encyclopedias, dictionaries, and other research tools, as well as the Internet, to search for answers to their questions; they use computers to do word processing and publish the results of their projects; and they use presentation software to show their projects in class and in the community. Depending on the project, they may also make tables, charts, graphs, spreadsheets, and databases. To improve practice in reading and writing, many programs provide students with "key pals" (electronic penpals) or encourage them to participate in real-time conversations in on-line electronic forums or chats.

Both instructivist and constructivist approaches have value, and teachers often use a combination if their goal is to enable learners to acquire a specific body of content and skills and also to engage in learning in meaningful and motivating contexts.

Examples of Technology Products for Instruction

Public television has created several major products for adult literacy and ESOL instruction. Kentucky Educational Television has a series of videotapes (the KET/GED Video Series) for GED (General Education Development) and pre-GED students that it broadcasts on *GED on TV.* Intelecom's *Crossroads Café* and Boston's WGBH *Connect with English* are now widely broadcast throughout the country on public television stations. The broadcasts, accompanied by print materials, can be purchased on videotape, and students can record them for home use free of charge. A new and promising project being piloted in four cities is produced by the Adult Literacy Media Alliance. Described by some as the *Sesame Street* for adults who want to improve their basic skills, it will be available in broadcast and videocassette formats for use at home, school, work, and other places in the community.

There are numerous software products for adults available on computer disk and more recently on CD-ROM. One worth special mention is the English New Reading Disc, which offers instruction for basic-level literacy students in a constructivist context in which they learn to read by writing articles, letters, and responses to debates.

The Internet holds great potential for adult literacy instruction. Although student access is still limited, as costs come down and the Internet becomes integrated with television, it will be more widely available in students' homes, at work, as well as in classes. One of the first organizations to develop adult literacy Web-based learning was California's Outreach and Technical Assistance Network (OTAN). The California Distance Learning Project (CDLP) now includes several good examples of interactive, on-line reading materials. (Addresses for CDLP and other Web sites mentioned here are listed at the end of the chapter.) Among them is the San Francisco CNN Stories for New Readers. This site has full-text CNN stories with graphics. It also offers a simplified text edited for low-level readers, an outline of the story, and a variety of on-line interactive lessons with an immediate on-line answer-check feature. All text has a RealAudio option so learners can hear it read aloud. In January 1999 the site had sixty-five stories. Other CDLP features include the Voter Involvement Project, the E-mail Projects page, and nearly thirty family, community, and work-related on-line interactive lesson topics. LitLink, a new Web site sponsored by PBS and the National Center for Adult Literacy (NCAL), offers promise especially for adult secondary education learners. The site's PeerLit section includes reviews of Web sites offering adult instruction on-line. Finally, integrated learning systems such as Invest/Destinations and PLATO (comprehensive computer-assisted and computer-managed instruction software) are planning conversions to Internet-based delivery systems of computer-assisted instruction.

Many Web sites offer adult ESOL (or ESL) lessons on-line. Among those with the most content is Dave's ESL Café, which includes an ESL Idiom page and a Quiz Center. Another site rich in content and especially suited to advanced ESOL students is the HUT Internet Writing Project. Many of these ESOL sites can be found through the ESL Loop, a chain of Web sites focusing on ESOL content. A list of Web sites (and other useful on-line resources) for ESOL and ABE can be found on the Literacy List, a set of Web page links for adult basic and secondary education and ESOL teachers.

Constructivist Applications

One of the most interesting applications of technology in adult literacy involves the use of Web sites and computer tools for constructivist learning. Susan Gaer, an ESOL teacher at Santa Ana College in southern California, pioneered this work in adult ESOL learning with an international adult learner cookbook that is published on-line annually. Her projects and others, which are linked on the E-mail Projects Web site, include a range of student writings. Examples include strategies for dealing with stress, home remedies, home buying, cost-of-living comparisons in various parts of the country, and intergenerational writings. Each project involves English-language learning and student writings published on-line. In some projects students from two or more sites work together, using the Internet to communicate. Some of the Web pages are interactive, allowing readers to add their own comments. Another proponent of constructivist approaches, particularly project-based learning in the natural sciences, is Susan Cowles, literacy leader fellow at the National Institute for Literacy (Cowles, 1997).

A growing area of constructivist Internet use in adult literacy education is variously called student inquiry, information searching, or simply research. Although there are only a few examples of adult inquiry or research projects on the Web pages,[1] students in many programs are using CD-ROM encyclopedias and other CD-ROM references, and they are increasingly searching the Web for information.

CHALLENGES FOR POLICYMAKERS AND PRACTITIONERS: ACCESS, PLANNING, STAFF DEVELOPMENT, AND POLICY

Four challenges must be met before these new technologies are well integrated and used systematically and effectively in adult literacy education. First is access for teachers and students to hardware and software. Although there are many barriers to access, including limitations on physical space and the availability of telephone or fiber-optic cable, inadequate funding is the primary barrier. In most public elementary and secondary schools, where several thousand dollars are spent per student annually, there is still inadequate student and teacher access to technology. And in most states, adult literacy education is a poor cousin to elementary and secondary education; nationally, the total expenditure per adult student is still well under $300 annually. Thus the problem of access to technology in adult literacy education is many times as great as it is in K–12 public schools. In his study of computer use in midwestern states in 1997, Sabatini reported that in more than half of the adult literacy programs, nearly all teachers have access to computers, but only a third of the programs responding said that teachers use computers for instructional preparation activities, such as planning, assessing student work, and preparing course materials. Only a fourth of the programs reported the use of computers for instruction. This suggests that although adult literacy programs now have some access to computers, the access they have is not adequate for teachers' daily, practical use.

The best news for adult literacy programs—and teachers and students—is that the price of computers and some peripherals has dropped. This means that as resources for technology increase, the programs will get more value for their money. In many areas of the country, businesses and other organizations offer used (and in some cases refurbished) computers to nonprofit organizations at even lower costs. Because most students and many teachers cannot afford a computer at home yet, these essential tools need to be provided elsewhere: in programs, in libraries, and at other public places where access is free or available at low cost. This can be accomplished only with significant additional funding for hardware and software. One promising development is community computing centers, which are located in adult literacy programs, libraries, housing developments, community centers, and even in stores in shopping centers. Free or low-cost technology centers enable adult learners and other community members access to computers and the Internet, and the centers often provide free or low-cost training as well. One national organization, the Community Technology Centers Network (CTCNet), encourages the use of computers and provides technical assistance for nearly three hundred member programs across the country.

Another problem, teacher access to video- and audiocassettes, is being addressed in some communities. In the Los Angeles Adult Schools, for example, where thousands of adult learners are on waiting lists, there is a major effort to distribute instructional videotapes to those not able to enroll in classes. In Sacramento, California, in Boston, and elsewhere, cable TV broadcasts are used to deliver instruction.[2]

The second challenge is planning. Technology planning is a process that takes place at the local program, school, or agency level or at the state level, which produces a set of goals, objectives, activities, and projected resources for using technology for a variety of educational purposes. It is important at all levels because it engages a variety of stakeholders in envisioning not only what technology will be purchased but for what purposes it will be used and how it will be maintained. Those who have done this planning often find that they are able to get the public or private sector resources they need to carry out their plans.

Many states now have statewide technology plans for elementary and secondary education. Few of these K–12 plans include adult literacy education, however, and those that do include it do so as an afterthought. To date, only four states (Massachusetts, Texas, Arkansas, and California) are known to have begun statewide adult literacy technology planning processes, and only Massachusetts has implemented and funded a statewide literacy technology plan. At the program level, however, technology planning takes place in several states, including Pennsylvania, California, New York, and Massachusetts. This planning has sometimes brought in increased funds from the private sector, but so far it has not often resulted in additional funds for adult literacy technology from the state or federal government.

The National Center for Adult Literacy at the University of Pennsylvania pioneered program technology planning in adult literacy programs, and it has developed several good documents related to technology planning (Hopey, 1998). Several years ago NCAL brought technology planning to programs in Pennsylvania and New York. The Brooklyn Public Library Adult Literacy Program, with NCAL, became one of the first to publish its plan in 1995, and since then it has been a model for other programs. Drawing on this experience, Massachusetts now requires technology plans from all adult literacy programs funded by its Department of Education and provides funding for technology to adult literacy programs with approved plans. The Massachusetts Adult Literacy Technology Team has produced a statewide, three-year technology plan that the Department of Education has funded with nearly $4 million. Texas and Arkansas also have statewide plans under way.

The third challenge is staff development for teachers and other practitioners. To use technology well, teachers need to be properly introduced to the use of computers, and they need paid professional time to learn and practice their new skills. Some teachers may also need special attention to overcome their anxiety about using computers. Initial and ongoing training and technical support are necessary, but they are usually the exception rather than the rule in adult literacy practice.

In 1995 the National Institute for Literacy launched its Literacy Information and Communications System (LINCS) with a national Web page and four regional centers of technology activity covering the entire country and its territories. These centers (EasternLINCS, SouthernLINCS, WesternLINCS, and MidwestLINCS) have provided Internet technology training for representatives of organizations in their member states. MidwestLINCS, for example, has for several years offered training, including special initiatives at the program level. And EasternLINCS, in collaboration with the Literacy Assistance Center of New York City, has offered regional training for programs in New England and New York in Web use and Web page design.

Other organizations offer staff development, including NCAL, the Outreach and Technical Assistance Network, and state literacy resource centers such as the Massachusetts SABES, the Ohio Literacy

Resource Center, and the Illinois Resource Development Center. These have largely relied on state or special federal funding.

Two-way, interactive broadcast and Internet technologies have been used for staff development. NCAL and PBS, for example, have offered several national adult literacy training teleconferences. The Massachusetts Corporation for Educational Telecommunications, with the Massachusetts System for Adult Basic Education Support, has offered regular interactive broadcasts across the state for staff development, many of which were also interactive instruction supplements for students. Recently staff development courses in adult literacy and ESOL have become available from universities on the Internet.

One of the most exciting trends in staff development has been the use of electronic lists. These free e-mail lists enable members to send a single message that reaches all subscribers. Through them, adult literacy practitioners and other adult literacy experts raise and answer questions in daily public forums only an e-mail message away. The National Institute for Literacy now sponsors specialized electronic lists, focusing, for example, on literacy in the workplace, adult learning disabilities, literacy for the homeless, and family literacy.[3]

The fourth great challenge is public policy, especially federal technology policy, which excludes some kinds of adult education programs from funding. One example is federal policies that do not allow certain adult literacy programs—those in community-based organizations, churches, corrections institutions, colleges, and venues other than public schools and libraries—to benefit from the E-rate (a rate supported by federal policy that provides deep discounts in Internet connectivity costs for public schools and libraries). Another example is the federal literacy challenge grants, which are directed almost entirely toward K–12 education.

CONCLUSION

Almost no research exists on the effectiveness of technology in adult literacy education. We do not have answers to questions like these: Does the use of technology enhance learning, and, if so, what kinds of learning, and how? Does it increase learners' persistence in their studies? Does it help them become more employable? Can students use technology effectively to learn at home or at work, and, if so, under what conditions? Will the use of technology enable us to serve more students?

Researchers and policymakers alike want to know the answers to these questions, but there are almost no resources now devoted to this kind of research. In addition, policymakers who are concerned about access and good use of these technologies must address the issue of resources, in terms of both widening the reach of the public resources that now cover only K–12 and creating new national and state adult literacy technology funding initiatives. The goal for policymakers must be to have computers as readily available to adult literacy learners as they are to college students.

Finally, practitioners who use technology need staff development to become comfortable with and adept at using it. Such an effort needs to go beyond training in the use of hardware and software to focus on integration of technology in support of curriculum and instruction. It must also enable creative, constructivist uses of technologies in support of student inquiry and student project-based learning, and it must enable teachers to see beyond the classroom, to create new models for learning in a digital multimedia learning environment.

Notes

1. One kind of Web-based inquiry project is the student-made inquiry map, a short research project, based on learners' own questions, that uses a variety of sources, including the Internet. Web-based examples of inquiry maps can be found at [http://www2.wgbh.org/mbcweis/ltc/alri/I.M.html].
2. The Los Angeles and Sacramento examples were provided by OTAN director John Fleischman. The Mayor's Office of the City of Boston sponsors *Speak Easy,* an ESOL cable broadcast program.
3. For adult literacy electronic list addresses, see [http://www2.wgbh.org/mbcweis/ltc/alri/LiteracyList.html].

Resources

Resources on the Web

California Distance Learning Project (CDLP):
   [http://www.otan.dni.us/cdlp/cdlp.html]
Community Technology Centers Network CTC-Net:
   [http://www.ctcnet.org/]

Dave's ESL Café: [http://www.eslcafe.com/]
E-mail Projects: [http://www.otan.dni.us/webfarm/emailproject/email.htm]
ESL Loop: [http://www.linguistic-funland.com/esloop/]
Helsinki University of Technology (HUT) Internet Writing Project:
    [http://www.hut.fi/~rvilmi/Project/]
Literacy Information and Communications System (LINCS), National
    Institute for Literacy: [http://novel.nifl.gov]
Literacy List: [http://www2.wgbh.org/mbcweis/ltc/alri/LiteracyList.html]
LitLink: [http://www.pbs.org/learn/literacy/]
Massachusetts Adult Literacy Technology Team (MALTT) statewide
    adult literacy and technology plan:
    [http://www2.wgbh.org/mbcweis/ltc/alri/malttplan.html]
National Center for Adult Literacy (NCAL):
    [http://litserver.literacy.upenn.edu/]
San Francisco CNN Stories for New Readers:
    [http://www.cnnsf.com/education/education.html]
Teaching and Learning with Internet-Based Resources, a set of lesson plans
    and activities: [http://novel.nifl.gov/susanc/inthome.htm]
Texas Statewide Adult Literacy and Technology Plan
    [http://www.ideal.swt.edu/interalt/]

Television and Video Resources

Connect with English: Annenberg/CPB Collection, P.O. Box 2345, South
    Burlington, VT 05407–2345; (800) LEARNER (532–7637); go to
    [http://www.learner.org]; or visit Learner On-line.
Crossroads Café: For print materials contact Heinle & Heinle Publishers,
    Boston, Mass., or call (800) 553–6454. For information regarding video
    licensing or purchases, contact INTELECOM at (800) LRN-BY-TV.
GED on TV: Call Kentucky Educational Television at (800) 354–9067 or
    write Enterprise Division, 560 Cooper Drive, Lexington, KY 40502.

References

Bruner, J. (1986). *Actual minds, possible worlds.* Cambridge, MA: Harvard
    University Press.
Bruner, J. (1990). *Acts of meaning.* Cambridge, MA: Harvard University Press.
Cowles, S. K. (1997, September). Technology melts classroom walls. *Focus
    on Basics,* 11–13.
Hopey, C. E. (1998). Planning and funding for technology. In *Technology,
    basic skills, and adult education: getting ready and moving forward.*

Columbus, OH: ERIC Clearinghouse on Adult, Career, and Vocational Education.

Kaku, M. (1997). *Visions: How science will revolutionize the 21st century.* New York: Doubleday, Anchor Books.

Papert, S. (1993). *The children's machine: Rethinking school in the age of the computer.* New York: Basic Books.

Piaget, J. (1973). *To understand is to invent.* New York: Grossman.

Resnick, L. B. (1989). Developing mathematical knowledge. *American Psychologist, 44,* 162–169.

Roberts, L. (1993). *Adult literacy and new technologies.* Washington, DC: Office of Technology Assessment, U.S. Congress.

Sabatini, J. (1997). *Instructional technology utilization survey of midwestern adult literacy programs.* Philadelphia: National Center on Adult Literacy, Graduate School of Education, University of Pennsylvania. See also an NCAL Brief at *Literacy On-line:* [http://www.literacyonline.org/NCRTECSVY/ncrel1.html].

Turner, T. (1998). Technology in adult education. In *Technology, basic skills, and adult education: getting ready and moving forward.* Columbus, OH: ERIC Clearinghouse on Adult, Career, and Vocational Education.

Vygotsky, L. S. (1978). *Mind in society: The development of higher psychological processes.* Cambridge, MA: Harvard University Press.

Resources on the Use of Electronic Technology in Adult Literacy Education

Jeff Carter
Lou Wollrab

T he following selections are intended to provide readers with a general understanding of some of the key issues and practices that bear on the implementation of educational technologies in adult literacy programs. The sources listed are not exhaustive but cover two dozen major reports, articles, and Web sites produced by the federal agencies and literacy organizations that have been most engaged with this topic recently.

BOOKS, GUIDEBOOKS, HANDBOOKS, AND REPORTS

Cantrell, C. (Ed.). (1996). *Software buyer's guide, 1996 edition* (63 pages). Seattle, WA: Northwest Regional Literacy Resource Center.

Availability: Northwest Regional Literacy Resource Center, 2121 South Jackson Street, Seattle, WA 98144; (206) 587-4988.
Recommended audience: Teachers

Underwritten by the Northwest Regional Literacy Resource Center, these software reviews were provided by approximately thirty teachers who used the listed software in classes for at least two weeks. The 180-plus software programs listed are divided into six subject categories: science and social studies content areas, mathematics, language, life skills, reading, and support. Each program is rated on a four-point scale in a tabular report, and thirty of the programs are featured with brief descriptive and evaluative sections. (The selection criteria for the featured subset are not made clear.) One caution is that close to half of the listed programs were written for now-dated DOS or Apple II computers, but the (slight) majority of titles are available for Windows and/or Macintosh operating systems.

Intended as background on the incorporation of software into adult literacy programs, three short articles follow the reviews: "Planning for Technology," "Characteristics of Effective Instructional Technology," and "Integrating Software into the Curriculum." The 1997 edition of this guide is available in print and on-line: [http://www.literacynet.org/nwrlc/buyersguide/home.html].

Cowles, S. K. (1997). *Teaching and learning with Internet-based resources* (Literacy Leader Fellowship Program Reports, Vol. 3, No. 2, 133 pages). Washington, DC: National Institute for Literacy.

Availability: Copies can be obtained by calling the National Institute for Literacy hot line at (800) 228-8813; also available in full text on the NIFL Web site at [http://novel.nifl.gov/susanc/inthome.htm].
Recommended audience: Teachers

This extensive set of curricular materials for adult literacy practitioners and students using Web sites, e-mail, and other Internet technologies in instruction was created as part of a 1996–1997 National Institute for Literacy fellowship. Designed in response to a needs assessment conducted with 245 adult learners and 123 adult education instructors in Oregon, these materials were then tested with instructors and learners around the country.

Although the lessons themselves are designed to help teachers introduce learners to the Internet, the accompanying narrative also introduces teachers themselves to basic Internet concepts. Teachers who are new to using the Internet (but are somewhat familiar with basic computer functionality and basic Internet concepts) can thus use this resource to orient themselves and their students simultaneously. The last chapter includes guidelines for project implementation and staff development.

Elmore, J. (1998). *Adult literacy, technology, and public policy: An analysis of the southeastern United States region* (10 pages). Philadelphia: National Center on Adult Literacy.

Availability: National Center on Adult Literacy, 3910 Chestnut Street, Philadelphia, PA 19104-3111; (215) 898-2100; Web address: [http://literacyonline.org/seirtec/Seirtec1.htm].

Recommended audience: Policymakers, program directors

In a concise, coherent manner, this policy brief, drawn from interviews with staff members of several adult literacy programs, provides a glimpse of current puzzles and solutions pertaining to technology planning, staff development, and cross-program collaboration, along with a short set of concrete recommendations.

Hopey, C. E. (Ed.). (1998). *Technology, basic skills, and adult education: Getting ready and moving forward.* Columbus, OH: ERIC Clearinghouse on Adult, Career, and Vocational Education, Center on Education and Training for Employment.

Availability: Center on Education and Training for Employment, Center Publications, 1900 Kenny Road, Columbus, OH 43210-1090; also available in full text on the ERIC/ACVE Web site: [http://ericacve.org/].

Recommended audience: Program directors, teachers, policymakers

A collection of writings by leaders in the field of technology and adult education, this book is organized into two sections. Section I, "Getting Ready," designed to help teachers and program directors plan for and integrate technology into adult education, discusses the technology planning process, offers guidelines for software and hardware selection, and suggests a number of approaches for integrating technology with instruction. Section II, "Moving Forward," addresses the interconnections between adult learning theory and educational technology, distance learning, policy issues, and other topics. Many chapters were explicitly written for teachers and program directors in the field, but the depth of topics included makes this a useful source for those interested in adult education technology policy in general. A list of national adult education agencies, with Web addresses, is included.

Mansoor, I. (1993). *The use of technology in adult ESL programs: Current practice—future promise* (51 pages). Washington, DC: Southport Institute.

Availability: Southport Institute for Policy Analysis, Suite 460, 820 First Street, N.E., Washington, DC 20002; (202) 682-4100.

Recommended audience: Policymakers, academic researchers, program directors

This report provides a solid overview of the possible uses and key issues pertaining to the incorporation of educational technologies in the adult ESOL (English for speakers of other languages) classroom and offers two overarching recommendations for adult literacy policymakers and practitioners: a sustained commitment of resources and a significant research base on ESOL instruction. Mansoor encourages efforts that seek a broader understanding of both the programmatic supports and the educational factors that have bearing on the successful implementation of technology by adult ESOL populations. Her summary of such supports and factors offers a starting point for further research and debate.

Along with several engaging anecdotes related by ESOL practitioners, the report provides a summary of a few of the early 1990s studies on technology use in adult literacy programs and highlights the policy issues relating to purchasing decisions, educational practice, technical assistance, and product development. Mansoor's overview of the policy implications and the general challenges facing administrators and practitioners who are seeking to implement technology poses questions and observations as relevant in 1999 as in 1993.

Miller-Parker, D. (1993). *Instructional technology resource guide for staff Development* (46 pages). Washington, DC: U.S. Department of Education, Division of Adult Education and Literacy.

Availability: ED Pubs, P.O. Box 1398, Jessup, MD 20794-1398; (877) 4-ED-PUBS; fax: (301) 470-1244.

Recommended audience: Teachers, program directors, policymakers

This guidebook provides examples and guidelines for creating staff development programs for the effective use of technology in adult basic education programs. It includes an overview of the existing literature on staff development for technology integration (up to 1993), a synthesis and discussion of these authors' findings, and a proposal for the integration of technology into adult education programs. Because it was published in 1993, some of the information presented about organizations, on-line services, and certain hardware and software products (and their costs) is now well out of date; nonetheless, the general suggestions on how to create effective staff development programs will still be relevant to policymakers, program directors, and others.

Rosen, D. J. (1998). *Driver education for the information superhighway* (Literacy Leader Fellowship Program Reports, Vol. 2, No. 2, 88 pages). Washington, DC: National Institute for Literacy.

   Availability: National Institute for Literacy hot line at (800) 228-8813. An updated version of two chapters is available on the Web: "The Literacy List" is at [http://www2.wgbh.org/mbcweis/ltc/alri/websites.html], and "The Adult Education Teacher's Annotated Webliography" is at [http://www2.wgbh.org/mbcweis/ltc/alri/webliography.html].
   Recommended audience: Researchers, program directors, teachers

   The first half of this book is a look at how teachers are using the Internet, based on responses to questionnaires and focus groups conducted in 1995–1996. It is useful for teachers seeking information on how other practitioners have accessed the Internet and used it as a teaching tool. The information collected on the barriers teachers face in trying to use the Internet (training time, access, purchase of hardware and software) should also be useful for staff development and strategic planning around the uses of technology. A staff development model is included. The second half of the book includes a comprehensive list of World Wide Web pages, directories, and search tools related to adult literacy program development, policy, and teaching and a collection of Web site reviews, "The Adult Education Teacher's Annotated Webliography," written by adult literacy, basic education, and ESOL educators in the Boston area in spring 1996. The book assumes some familiarity with computer and Internet concepts but is presented in a style that is friendly to teachers relatively inexperienced in this area.

Stites, R. (1998). *Assessing lifelong learning technology (ALL-Tech): A guide for choosing and using technology for adult learning: Practice guide* (21 pages). Philadelphia: National Center on Adult Literacy.

   Availability: National Center on Adult Literacy, 3910 Chestnut Street, Philadelphia, PA 19104-3111; (215) 898-2100; Web address: [http://literacyonline.org/products/ncal/pdf/PG9801.pdf].
   Recommended audience: Policymakers, program directors, teachers

Amplifying a 1995 publication, *Plugging in: Choosing and using education technology,* this report provides an overview of some of the opportunities and barriers inherent in implementing educational technologies in adult literacy programs. The document includes detailed operational indicators (defining aspects of assessment, learning contexts, instructional models, teacher-learner roles, and so on) and worksheets for engaged learning as that endeavor might be accomplished through the use of classroom technologies.

Turner, T. C. (1993). *Literacy and machines: An overview of the use of technology in adult literacy programs* (72 pages). Philadelphia: National Center on Adult Literacy.

Availability: NCAL/ILI, University of Pennsylvania, 3910 Chestnut Street, Philadelphia, PA 19104-3111; (215) 898-2100; fax: (215) 898-9804; e-mail: [smith@literacy.upenn.edu]; on-line version available on the Literacy Online Web site at [http://www.literacyonline.org/products/ncal/pdf/TR9303.pdf].
Recommended audience: Researchers, policymakers

This report provides a framework for obtaining technology and incorporating it into the adult literacy curriculum, offers a brief look at the history of technology use in adult literacy programs, and attempts to identify the value that the use of technology can have for learners in the larger cultural context in which literacy instruction resides. A summary of the applications of technology in programs at the time this document was written is included. Also included are future projections for the technology development. Because many technology applications available today were not available in 1993, this is not a good source for those looking for the most up-to-date summary of the types of technologies currently being used in the field. On the other hand, the issues raised concerning the proper role of technology in the field remain highly relevant.

U.S. Congress, Office of Technology Assessment. (1993). *Adult literacy and new technologies: Tools for a lifetime* (OTA Publication No. OTA-SET-550, 275 pages). Washington, DC: U.S. Government Printing Office.

Availability: Superintendent of Documents, U.S. Government Printing Office, P.O. Box 371954, Pittsburgh, PA 15250-7954; (202)

512-1800. Also available from the National Technical Information Service, (703) 487-4650, and from the OTA Legacy Web site at [http://www.wws.princeton.edu:80/~ota/ns20/alpha_f.html].

Recommended audience: Researchers, policymakers

This remains the most comprehensive report to date on the use of technology in adult literacy. Although it is somewhat dated (published in 1993, it has no discussion of the Internet or the World Wide Web), the wealth and detail of the information it presents on the types of technology being used in adult literacy programs and especially on the issues surrounding implementation of technology make this volume useful reading for policymakers, program directors, and practitioners. It also serves (although again, some of this information is dated) as a primer on adult learners, the adult literacy instructional delivery system in the United States, the role of the federal government in adult literacy education, and the ways in which technology might be used to improve the system. A reader with relatively little background in this area would find the overview discussions both useful and understandable.

U.S. Congress, Office of Technology Assessment. (1995). *Teachers and technology: Making the connection* (OTA Publication No. OTA-EHR-616) (292 pages). Washington, DC: U.S. Government Printing Office.

Availability: New Orders, Superintendent of Documents, P.O. Box 371954, Pittsburgh, PA 15250-7954; (202) 512-1800.

Recommended audience: Policymakers, program directors, teachers

This lengthy report devotes considerable space to reviewing current and possible future uses of educational technology, but the larger, more significant sections examine critical factors relating to teacher education, training, and professional development. Throughout the report, numerous boxes, figures, and tables provide succinct, highly useful supplementary information: potential practices, current barriers, past and current federal technology initiatives, statewide technology planning examples, and so forth. Although the content of the report is drawn from and directed toward the experiences of K–12 school system staff, the analysis of the multifarious struggles that teachers and administrators face as they wrestle with new technologies is applicable to adult literacy practitioners as well.

U.S. Department of Education, Office of Educational Research and Improvement. (1993). *Using technology to support education reform*

(OERI Publication No. OR-93-3231) (110 pages). Washington, DC: U.S. Government Printing Office.

Availability: New Orders, Superintendent of Documents, P.O. Box 371954, Pittsburgh, PA 15250-7954; (202) 512-1800.
Recommended audience: Policymakers, academic researchers

This report ties the core features of education reform to respective "potentially supportive technology," drawing supportive data and illustrative examples from nearly two hundred studies and articles published between 1978 and 1992. There are chapters devoted to the necessary support mechanisms for students and teachers, the impact on student achievement, and implementation issues. Although published in 1993, the report's review of effective teacher professional development practices and guidelines, along with a gloss on the possible consequences of education reform efforts, is quite applicable to contemporary federal- and state-level education debates and decisions.

Wright, B. A. W., et al. (1994). *ESL technology user's guide, 1994 edition* (48 pages). Seattle, WA: Northwest Regional Literacy Resource Center.

Availability: Northwest Regional Literacy Resource Center, 2121 South Jackson Street, Seattle, WA 98144; (206) 587-4988.
Recommended audience: Program directors, teachers

Although a bit dated, this guide provides ESOL practitioners with a decent introduction to a mix of educational technologies: computer software and videotapes (primarily), along with a few on-line services and hand-held tools (such as electronic transcribers). A table rates more than one hundred products, with forty of those products also described in fuller reviews listing the specific strengths and weaknesses of each. One drawback is that the software listings and reviews do not indicate the required computer operating systems (Windows, Macintosh, DOS).

JOURNAL ARTICLES

Bixler, B., & Askov, E. N. (1994). Characteristics of effective instructional software. *Mosaic: Research Notes on Literacy,* 4(2), 1, 7.

Recommended audience: Program directors, teachers

This article looks at the characteristics of technology (such as feedback, learner control, and organization) that the authors contend is successful in empowering learners and helping them take responsibility for their own learning. It is useful to program directors and teachers who are planning for and integrating computer technology into their programs, especially around issues of hardware and software selection.

Hopey, C. E., Rethemeyer, R. K., & Harvey-Morgan, J. (1994, September). Voices from the field: The use of computer technology in adult literacy. *NCAL Connections.*

Recommended audience: Policymakers, program directors

This survey of computer technology in adult literacy was designed to identify the extent and scope of computer technology use, achieve a better understanding of the experiences and attitudes of adult literacy programs in implementing technology, and inventory the computer technology currently in use. The results, based on the responses from six states (Pennsylvania, New York, Delaware, North Carolina, Illinois, and California) surveyed in spring 1994, will likely be of use to policymakers trying to identify the issues facing technology integration throughout the field. Program directors engaged in technology planning will likely find the findings useful as well. Both audiences should find the issues raised to be relevant, despite the likelihood that some of the statistical information is probably out of date, especially with regard to access to technology.

Merrifield, J., & Bell, B. (1994). Don't give us the Grand Canyon to cross: Participatory literacy and the information society. *Adult Learning, 6*(2), 23–24, 30.

Recommended audience: Teachers, program directors

Based on a pilot project providing twenty Tennessee adult literacy programs with Internet access, this article succinctly clarifies the need and the rationale for giving teachers and learners frequent, practice-based, real-world opportunities to master new technologies. With a mixture of optimism and frustration, the authors anticipate uses of on-line resources that could embrace reflective practice and critical thinking, uses that a few years later are beginning to become an integral piece of adult literacy programs' planning and practice.

Rachal, J. R. (1995). Adult reading achievement comparing computer-assisted and traditional approaches: A comprehensive review of the experimental literature. *Reading Research and Instruction, 34*(3), 239–258.

Recommended audience: Researchers, policymakers

This study presents a comprehensive review of experimental investigations comparing computer-assisted instruction with traditional approaches to adult reading instruction. A formal research paper summarizing existing data, this is not a hands-on guide for practitioners; the more obvious audience seems to be policymakers and other researchers.

WEB SITES

Dave's ESL Café: http://www.eslcafe.com

More of an on-line message center than an electronic library, this site gives teachers and learners opportunities to exchange questions, ideas, and experiences. Sifting through the hundreds of accumulated postings (many from teenagers) is a bit exhausting, but two features quickly draw one's eye: the ESL Idiom Page (good for classroom use and discussion) and the ESL Café Bookstore (short subject lists of recommended titles for teachers).

Educational Resources Information Center (ERIC): http://www.accesseric.org:81

The Educational Resources Information Center is a national database of education-related literature. Supported by the Office of Educational Research and Improvement (a division of the U.S. Department of Education) and the National Library of Education, this searchable database contains more than 950,000 abstracts of documents and journal articles on education research and practice. In addition, most of the several dozen digests produced to date by the ERIC Clearinghouses are available on-line, including titles from the two adult literacy–focused outposts: the Clearinghouse on Adult, Career, and Vocational Education and the National Clearinghouse on ESL Literacy Education. Both collections contain several full-text documents on issues pertaining to technology.

ESL Home Page: http://www.lang.uiuc.edu/r-li5/esl

Maintained by a graduate assistant at the University of Illinois, this site, intended primarily for intermediate and advanced ESOL learners, serves as an index to a large number of Web sites, organized by broad skill area: listening and speaking, reading and understanding, and grammar and writing. Although little more than an expansive bookmark list, the site does provide a gateway to the Web for on-line novices.

Literacy Information and Communication System (LINCS)

Eastern LINCS: [http://easternlincs.worlded.org]
Midwestern LINCS: [http://archon.educ.kent.edu/Midwest]
Southern LINCS: [http://hub2.coe.utk.edu]
Western/Pacific LINCS: [http://www.literacynet.org]

Funded by the National Institute for Literacy, the four regional LINCS projects provide training, technical assistance, and resources for their member-state literacy resource centers and, by extension, adult literacy programs and practitioners. In addition to providing links to education- and technology-related Web sites, the LINCS sites provide varying degrees of original content, including lesson plans, program technology plans, curricula, learner-generated materials, and training guides.

Literacy Online: http://www.literacyonline.org

As the on-line home for the National Center on Adult Literacy and the International Literacy Initiative, this site provides a wealth of online, full-text reports on adapting new technologies to adult literacy learning and instruction.

National Adult Literacy Database (NALD): http://www.nald.ca

Based in Canada, the Resources Database available at this site is a good source for information on technology and adult education in the United States and the rest of the world. Access to the resources varies from full-text, on-line documents to abstract and ordering information only. (Those looking for complete documents can browse all of them on the full-text documents page.) The site also serves as a host for adult literacy agencies and organizations from across Canada, offering on-line issues of numerous national and provincial newsletters.

National Institute for Literacy (NIFL): http://novel.nifl.gov

Established by the National Literacy Act of 1991, the National Institute for Literacy primarily crafts policy initiatives and funds research projects related to adult literacy. The NIFL's Web site is intended to serve as a one-stop electronic resource center for practitioners, administrators, and policymakers, offering grant information, policy updates, a national calendar of events, a directory of state literacy contacts, and a search engine that connects users to resource collections maintained by ERIC, the Library of Congress, and the four LINCS Web sites. Visitors to this site have access to the archives of several literacy-related listservs, as well as the reports of the Literacy Leadership fellows: [http://novel.nifl.gov/nifl/fellowpubs.htm].

PBS LiteracyLink: http://www.pbs.org/literacy

LiteracyLink is an integrated instructional system of video and on-line computer technology (including this Web site) designed to help adult students advance their GED (General Educational Development) and workplace skills. The project also seeks to improve the quality of instruction for adult students by offering professional development resources and training, and it provides the public with general information about literacy. Until product development is completed in 2001, only portions of LiteracyLink are available.

Rural Clearinghouse for Lifelong Learning and Distance Education: http://www-personal.ksu.edu/~rcled

This site is an extremely rich source of on-line, full-text articles on the topics of rural literacy, distance education, multicultural reform in rural schools, and leadership and community development. Many of the articles have at least a moderate level of applicability to circumstances found in adult literacy programs.

⟵⟋⟍⟶ Name Index

Subject Index

A

ABE. *See* Adult basic education, U.K.; Adult basic education, U.S.; Learners, adult

ABLE. *See* Adult Basic Learning Examination

Access issues: electronic technology, 309–310, 312, 313; federal funding assistance, 312; lower admission standards, 117, 119

Access to adult education: AEFLA's direct and equitable, 6; open, 106, 117, 119, 282; postsecondary, 112, 117, 118, 119, 142–143; youth, 105–106

Access to postsecondary education, expanding, 117–118

Accountability of adult education: common framework for, 231; comprehensive national learning system needed for, 231, 233, 235, 237; performance measures for, 203–205; policy recommendations, 233–235; reflection and connection and, 290–291; statewide systems for, 231–232

Accreditation of learners: in developmental or remedial education, 147; in the U.K., 250, 268–273, 276, 277, 287, 288. *See also* GED (General Educational Development credential), U.S.

Accreditation of teachers: in the U.K., 272, 276–277; in the U.S., 66–67

Admission rates, hospital, 172, 174

Admissions standards, higher education, 117, 119, 135

Adult basic education (ABE), U.K.: changing culture of, 281–286; eco-nomic and social climates affecting, 244–249, 282–283; and the economy, 244–245; and ESOL, 253–254; formalization and statutory status of, 243–244, 275, 281–286, 287, 288; health-related initiatives in, 184; history of, 249–255, 282–283, 293n.2; learner ages and genders, 257; mainstreaming, effects of, 285–286; need for, 255–258; potential and opportunities, 290–291; statistics, 256–258, 260; summary and assessment, 286–291; total funding of, 258–259; types of organizations providing, 259, 260; underlying issues, 289–290. *See also* U.K. system for adult basic education (ABE)

Adult basic education (ABE), U.S.: case histories of reading profiles, 43–61; and childhood reading difficulties, 40–43; comparison to community colleges, 145; coordination by providers lacking in, 119–120; coordination with postsecondary education, 144–148; first-level learners, 38–39; goal change to college preparation, 112, 144; and health literacy, 168–170, 176, 184; high school credit programs, 99; linkages with postsecondary education, 143–144; national system needed for, 231, 233, 235, 237; population, 38–43; postsecondary, 142–148; *PRD* relevance to, 38–39, 66; reading and learning disabilities, 39–43; reading comprehension levels, 38–39; socioeconomic

307, 308–309; instructivist, 305–306; reviews, 317–318, 324. *See also* Electronic technology

Software programs: integration of, 305–306; readability assessment by word processing, 163, 170, 181; spell checker, 61

South Dakota, 87, 108n.1

Spanish speakers: and patient literacy, 168; TOFHLA health literacy test for, 166, 167–168

Special education. *See* Remedial education, basic skills

Special learning needs. *See* Groups, special learner

Spelling, 61, 209

SPI (Sample Progress Indicator), 224

SPL test. *See* Student Performance Level (SPL)

Staff development. *See* Teacher training; Workplace training

Stakeholders: adult ESOL program, 201, 237; controversies among U.K., 268; remedial education, 118–119. *See also* Advocacy organizations

Stamp commemorating adult literacy, 18

Standardized assessment tools: ABLE, 179, 207, 208–210, 237; for achievement versus placement, 211–212; A-LAS, 207, 210–213, 238; in Australia, 226–227; BEST, 207, 208, 215–217, 238; in Canada, 228; CASAS Life Skills, 205, 207, 208, 213–215, 238; DAR reading, 68; GED2000 test changes, 19–20; general observations on, 149–150, 218–219; and learner success issues, 150, 205; NYS Place Test, 207, 208, 217–218, 238; oral instruments, 216, 217–218; ordering information, 237–238; program-based alternatives to, 219–222; REALM, 166–167, 176, 181; relevant to ESOL applications, 207–208; Rosner Test of Auditory Awareness Skills, 67–68, 69n.6; TABE, 207, 210, 211, 238; TOFHLA, 166, 167–168; using item response theory (IRT), 210; WRATR, 166, 177. *See also*

Assessment tools for adult ESOL; Performance measures in adult education

Standards, literacy: NALS literacy scales, 120, 127, 130–131, 151nn.3, 9, 11; NALS proficiency levels, 124–129; national (U.K.), 268–269

Star Schools projects, 15

State basic skills certification systems, 11

State directors of adult education, 78, 237; accountability and NRS reporting, 204; and student leadership, 18; survey interviews, 108n.1

State leadership activities: adult learner conferences and, 17; AEFLA, 6–7; literacy resource centers, 311–312; in youth literacy programs, 96–97, 108n.1. *See also specific state names*

State Workforce Investment Boards, 4

Statewide education plans, 314; AEFLA-mandated, 4; California adult basic education, 213–215; and compulsory school attendance, 85, 86–88; coordination with federal policy and initiatives, 147–148; and ESOL assessment, 213, 217–218; for literacy, lack of, 310; NRS outcome measures for, 204–205; and reform efforts, 84–85; and technology, 310; and youth literacy programs, 77–78, 104

Statistics, adult education: international comparisons, 256; remedial education, 133–137; staff, 250; U.K., 250, 256–258, 260, 296nn.13,15; on youth in literacy programs, 77–79, 82, 109n.2. *See also* Demographics; Dropout data

Statistics on youth education. *See PRD* report findings on children's literacy; Youth in literacy education

Student organizations, adult, 261

Student Performance Level (SPL), 216; descriptors, 204–205, 227, 233; revisions needed, 234. *See also* Proficiency levels; Standardized assessment tools